THE
ENVIRONMENT
SINCE 1945

ISSUES &
CONTROVERSIES
— IN —
AMERICAN HISTORY

THE
ENVIRONMENT
SINCE 1945

MARCOS LUNA, PH.D.
BALLARD C. CAMPBELL, PH.D., SERIES EDITOR

An Infobase Learning Company

Issues and Controversies in American History: The Environment since 1945

Copyright © 2012 by Infobase Learning

Facts On File, Inc.
An imprint of Infobase Learning
132 West 31st Street
New York NY 10001

Library of Congress Cataloging-in-Publication Data
Luna, Marcos.
   The environment since 1945 / Marcos Luna.
       p. cm.—(Issues and controversies in American history)
   Includes bibliographical references and index.
   ISBN 978-0-8160-7884-4 (acid-free paper) 1. United States—Environmental conditions. 2. Environmental policy—United States. 3. Environmental disasters—United States. 4. Environmental policy. 5. Environmental disasters. I. Title.
   GE180.L86 2011
   304.20973—dc22   2011007697

Text design by Kerry Casey
Composition by Annie O'Donnell
Cover printed by Yurchak Printing, Landisville, Pa.
Book printed and bound by Yurchak Printing, Landisville, Pa.
Date printed: September 2012
Printed in the United States of America

This book is printed on acid-free paper.

CONTENTS

⸿LIST OF DOCUMENTS⸿

※ABOUT THE AUTHOR※

Marcos Luna, Ph.D., is an associate professor in the Geography Department at Salem State University in Salem, Massachusetts. He researches and teaches environmental policy and science issues, including climate change, environmental and public health, urban sustainability, natural resource management, toxic materials management, energy production and use, and environmental justice, and works with community organizations in identifying and understanding local environmental problems. He has published numerous articles in both scholarly and popular venues and contributed four articles on environmental disasters and public health to Facts On File's *Disasters, Accidents, and Crises in American History: A Reference Guide to the Nation's Most Catastrophic Events*.

PREFACE

From a distance, we tend to see history as a continuous narrative that flows from one period to another. When the largest building blocks of history are considered, such as the American Revolution, slavery, the Civil War, industrialization, the role of women, and the degradation of the environment, history indeed can be viewed as a nearly seamless web of events, with only an occasional sharp shift in direction. On closer inspection, however, we see that historical development entailed numerous conflicts, controversies, and choices. And at virtually every crossroad in American history the future hung in the balance until the key issues were confronted and resolved. It was at these times that individuals debated the central issues at stake. History didn't just happen. Individuals made it happen.

The Issues and Controversies in American History series focuses on these critical disputes. The authors believe that historical understanding is furthered by studying the choices that contemporaries debated, how they envisioned these options, and how their decisions influenced the way history unfolded. This approach to history helps us to see the contingency in historical causation—that the directions that individuals, groups, and society took depended in large measure on the outcome of debates at critical junctures in the nation's history. When studied closely, history reveals a landscape of controversies. Some of these issues remained subjects of dispute decades after their initial resolution. Yet every major debate shaped the future course of the nation's history.

The Issues and Controversies series is constructed to illuminate the great debates in American history and to illustrate the contingencies by which they unfolded. Each volume focuses on an important topic in American history and is composed of chapters, usually arranged chronologically, that address major controversies about the subject. Every chapter opens with a summary of the issue and the debate about it and then lays out the historical background of the chapter's subject. Two short essays in each chapter provide fuller glimpses of selected subjects. The heart of each chapter contains a summary of the debate on the controversy. These discourses are illustrated by primary sources, which present the opposing arguments. These documents also offer a sampling of the tone, flavor, and logic of the participants. The conclusion of each chapter examines the impact of the debate and offers thoughts on how different decisions could have produced different outcomes. These "What If?" sections are intended to illustrate contingency and dependency in history— that history isn't inevitable but shaped by the decisions people make. A list of discussion questions in each chapter is designed to provoke reflection about the issues that contemporaries faced. The bibliography and list of Web sites for each chapter will help students locate additional resources about each controversy.

Environmental policy in the United States has been the product of constant controversy and negotiation throughout U.S. history. The roots of American environmental policy run deep, but the period after World War II represents a particularly remarkable period in the development of attitudes and approaches to the environment. Modern environmental policy encompasses a broad range of issues, from public health and pollution control to management of natural resources and protection of wildlife. Moreover, debates over the management of the environment have touched nearly every aspect of governance—property rights, land use, the role of the courts, liability, the public's right to know, federalism, and relationships among different social groups. Luna's volume vividly demonstrates how American environmental policy expanded its scope and reach in the years since World War II, often in response to crises provoked by rapidly expanding industrial activity, growing scientific understanding of the consequences of environmental modification, and changing public attitudes about our relationship to the environment and to each other. Luna's volume leads the reader through these and other controversies with background, analysis, primary source documents, maps, and images, which together illustrate landmark debates and decisions that have shaped environmental policy, from 1948 to the first decade of the 21st century. As his book demonstrates, debate over environmental policy is a perennial negotiation over competing goals and values, and it is by no means over. As the reach of human activity on the Earth expands, so does the need to manage the impacts of that expanding influence, both now and into the future.

Ballard C. Campbell
Series Editor

⸜⸜⸜⸜⸜INTRODUCTION⸝⸝⸝⸝⸝

American environmental policy has a long history, but the modern form came into being in the period after World War II. Before World War II ended in 1945, environmental policy was largely local, fragmented, and almost entirely secondary to economic interests. Indeed, one could say that "the environment" hardly existed as a definable concept during this earlier time. After World War II, Americans increasingly found it necessary to resolve competing claims and conflicts over the health and ecological impacts of economic activity, unchecked natural resource use, and environmental modification. These environmental conflicts arose because of material changes in the way people lived, the growing size and complexity of economic activity, growth in scientific understanding, and evolving social values and priorities.

During the course of the 20th century, America more than tripled its population size. The country became much more urban and predominantly suburban. The automobile became the major mode of transportation. Energy use grew faster than the population, and reliance on fossil fuels became central to the economy. America went from being an economy based on agriculture and heavy industry to a service-based economy. The federal government and large commercial institutions have played ever larger roles in shaping the experiences and opportunities of life. Americans also changed their attitude toward the natural environment, from one based on the need to dominate nature to one of increasing tolerance and appreciation. Thanks to the environmental movement, and despite growing economic activity, the air and water in many places actually became cleaner by the end of the 20th century with stricter regulation of pollution resource extraction, and environmental modification. However, increasing scientific understanding also revealed new impacts and threats that could barely have been conceived of previously, while some threats have merely been displaced or relocated. Few places on Earth remain untouched by human hands. Globalization has accelerated—tying the world's inhabitants and places ever more closely together by the spread of communication and transportation technologies, by expanding economic interests, by new trade dependencies, and by a complex web of cultural and political relationships.

The evolution of American environmental policy has been shaped by these larger social forces and by the perennial need to resolve competing claims and negotiate conflicts in a changing world. Environmental policy since World War II has become more important, more institutionalized, more widespread, and more complex. Environmental policy involves the statements and actions of government that affect the environment. It includes the protection of private property, public health, and ecological systems from adverse impact by human activity, the management of natural resources for human use, and the protection of the nation's natural and cultural heritage. This volume presents a sample of key debates that occurred during the evolution of modern American environmental policy, highlighting the crises and the choices made by individuals in the face of constrained options and limited knowledge, but which set the path for future possibilities. The chapters in this volume represent environmental debates since World War II that tie into the evolving environmental experience of the nation and illustrate important turning points in the development of environmental politics and policy.

In response to the pressures of World War II, the United States accelerated the process of industrialization and dramatically increased the country's capacity for resource extraction and development. For the United States, World War II was proof of the power of superior science and technology and of command over energy and materials and even nature itself. This productive capacity had economic benefits as well, lifting the country firmly out of prewar depression and stimulating unparalleled and sustained economic growth for the next generation. The period immediately following the war was a dynamic time for the institutions of science, technology, and industry. America's fascination with and faith in the promise of science and technology were fulfilled in part by access to a bewildering array of new products and services. The industrial capacity for material and energy production developed during the war continued into the postwar years, and was matched by rising affluence and mass consumption. American society after 1945 was very energy and resource intensive, increasingly dependent on fossil fuels—petroleum, natural gas, and coal—for manufacturing, transportation, heating, cooling, and seemingly every kind of technology. However, this growing energy and material dependence came at the cost of worsening air and water pollution, as well as the introduction of new chemical hazards, many of which would take decades to discover and understand.

An early warning to the nation about worsening air quality and the very real threats to health it posed can be found in the case of Donora, Pennsylvania, a small industrial town struck by a deadly smog event in 1948 (chapter 1). Although air pollution was already an old problem, new sources of emissions exacerbated and complicated the issue, especially when it came to determining causes and responsibility. The controversy over responsibility for the deadly smog was further heightened by the very real economic threat to the town's largest employer. The debate over Donora's smog illustrates the perennial tension between economic activity and environmental quality and the problem of scientific uncertainty and disagreement—themes common to most environmental debates. At the time, there was no specific government authority or capacity to handle air pollution problems, either at the local or national level. The Donora disaster seemed an exceptional case, but it was soon followed by similar air pollution crises in major cities across the country. These air pollution crises were blamed for thousands of deaths and significant economic damage. These crises forced the issue of air pollution onto the federal policy agenda. By the mid-1960s, the U.S. government began to require states to meet minimum air-quality standards in order to safeguard public health and welfare. These federal laws usurped the ad hoc role played by local and state authorities and ushered in a trend of greater federal influence. Notably, federal leadership on air (and water) pollution control through the mid-1960s occurred largely in the absence of pressure from major environmental or citizen organizations. This would soon change.

While the U.S. government began to assume leadership in limiting environmental degradation, it was increasingly perceived as part of the problem. This was particularly the case with respect to large federal agencies whose resource development missions came into conflict with changing attitudes about the environment. The first two decades after World War II were an especially active period for water resource development, consistent with the country's economic and industrial expansion. The U.S. Bureau of Reclamation was erecting dams throughout the West to tame and harness the nation's rivers. In the 1950s, Reclamation proposed a series of high dams throughout the Upper Colorado River Basin for the purposes of flood control, water storage, electricity generation, and regional economic development. A number of these dams intruded into areas managed by the National Park Service, specifically Dinosaur National Monument. One large dam in particular would inundate Echo Park, a scenic and remote canyon on the Colorado-Utah border. The debate that erupted over the Echo Park Dam (chapter 2) generated unprecedented opposition from a growing segment of Americans who no longer looked at nature simply for its economic potential—what could be extracted or produced from natural resources or how it could be "improved" or "reclaimed." A sizable segment of postwar America valued natural environments for their leisure and aesthetic qualities—unspoiled, wild, and undisturbed. The triumph of these preservationists was testament to a new political savvy on the part of environmental organizations and to widespread and growing public interest in protection of nature and wilderness. It was all the more remarkable because these citizen organizations had few legal resources at the time. Battles with federal agencies over water and power development (chapters 3 and 5) would happen again, but later environmentalists would have access to more powerful legal tools.

By the 1960s, the faith and optimism of the immediate postwar years gave way increasingly to criticism and doubt. The 1960s were a tumultuous period for American society. The Civil Rights movement forced the country to look critically at itself and its values, while the movement against the Vietnam War engendered a new boldness to question institutional authority and priorities. America's identity and its faith in economic and technological progress were under assault. It was during this period that the modern American environmental movement gained the most ground in the public consciousness and in law. The 1960s and 1970s witnessed an explosion of public interest in environmental issues, from pollution prevention to wildlife preservation. Congress responded to this outpouring of environmental sentiment with a raft of new environmental laws. Environmental protection became a priority, but it had implications that were not always immediately apparent. Indeed, the real test for the nation's professed commitment to environmental values emerged in the heat of debate over the meaning of these laws and how strictly they were to be enforced.

Chapter 3 follows the development and early conflict over the National Environmental Policy Act of 1969—the Magna Carta of American environmental policy. While the legislation's developers focused on the law's declaration of environmental principles, its most powerful aspect turned out to be a little-noticed provision enabling private citizens to sue the government for failure to consider environmental impacts and alternatives *before* a project was initiated or completed. This provision has become a cornerstone of modern environmental policy, but the law's meaning and its survival were not so clear at the time. A similar debate erupted over the Endangered Species Act (ESA) of 1973 and its unlikely application to preserving the existence of a species of fish with no apparent aesthetic or economic value (chapter 5). These controversies not only helped to define the new legislation but established enduring precedents in the use of the courts for enforcing environmental law and resolving environmental conflicts.

Few issues are more illustrative of the dramatic change in attitudes in the postwar period than the case of DDT (chapter 4). When it was first introduced in the late 1940s, this pesticide was hailed as a miracle of technology in the battle against agricultural and disease-carrying pests. Less than two decades later, the same chemical was vilified for its impacts on wildlife and its potential hazard to humans. Indeed, the revelation of the hazards presented by DDT was at the very heart of the new environmental consciousness that erupted in the 1960s. The debate over DDT was also an important catalyst in changing public understanding about ecological systems and the complicated interrelatedness between environmental systems and human health and welfare. The far-reaching and often unpredictable implications of damage to ecosystems generated a sense of uncertainty and caution. As in the case of the ESA, however, government action was only spurred after citizen environmental organizations filed lawsuits. The ultimate decision over this chemical was put before the U.S. Environmental Protection Agency, providing this newly created agency with the opportunity to make its mark by taking a tough stance against environmental threats.

The debate over DDT was only the beginning of growing anxieties over the proliferation of synthetic and toxic chemicals and the threats posed by both past and ongoing industrial activity. In the late 1970s and early 1980s, a series of toxic crises brought the threat of contamination even closer to home. In the late 1970s, residents of a quiet suburb near Niagara Falls, New York, discovered toxic chemicals leaking from Love Canal, an old industrial waste pit buried years before (chapter 6). The controversy over Love Canal highlighted a nationwide problem concerning the disposal of enormous quantities of hazardous waste generated by modern industrial processes and raised the question of liability for disposal and cleanup. In response, Congress created the Superfund (a name commonly used for the Comprehensive Environmental Response, Compensation, and Liability Act of 1980), the most expensive environmental cleanup program in the nation's history, codifying the principle that the "polluter pays" when it comes to hazardous waste. It was shortly after the Love Canal crisis that the world's worst industrial disaster occurred in Bhopal, India—an uncontrolled release of deadly pesticide chemicals in a dense urban area in 1984 (chapter 7). It was an unthinkable disaster that killed thousands and injured hundreds of thousands. While the catastrophe occurred in India, one of America's largest and most well-known chemical companies—Union Carbide Corporation—was directly implicated. The debate over Bhopal raised critical questions about potential threats in the United States and the level of trust that could be granted to corporations to act responsibly on their own. As a result, Congress passed community right-to-know legislation in 1986, compelling companies to divulge information about the chemicals they handle and release. This forced transparency had a profound impact on industrial behavior and provided new leverage to residents and environmental organizations in assessing threats and holding companies accountable.

No human activity has had a greater impact on the environment than energy production and consumption. Since the late 19th century, U.S. energy policy has focused on promoting the extraction and development of important sources of energy: coal, petroleum, natural gas, uranium. Moreover, government support for energy development has been premised on the idea that economic success and national security are dependent on cheap and abundant energy. The environmental consequences of this policy and energy dependence were apparent early on through worsening air quality and, by the 1960s, a series of spectacular oil spills. In response, Congress imposed new regulations on oil production. However, pressures for environmental controls competed with concerns about energy security. Indeed, the growing appetite for energy in the United States had made the country ever more dependent on the importation of petroleum. In the early 1970s, a series of energy supply crises resulting from conflict in oil-rich states of the Middle East spurred U.S. leaders to push for greater domestic production of energy, especially oil. Greater development of oil resources and oil infrastructure increased the potential for environmental damage. In 1989, the *Exxon Valdez* oil tanker struck a reef in Prince William Sound, Alaska, creating one of the largest oil spills in U.S. history (chapter 8). Despite decades of repeated promises of safety, the event exceeded the capacity of either industry or government to respond. Public outrage at Exxon raised difficult questions about ultimate culpability, fair compensation, and punishment.

Although U.S. environmental policy increasingly became a national issue during the latter half of the 20th century, not everyone is concerned about the same things. There are segments of society who have not shared in the growing material wealth of the nation or else found their cultural priorities to be at odds with the interests of the majority population. In the late 1990s, the Makah, a Native American tribe on Washington's Olympic Peninsula, announced their decision to resume whaling (chapter 10). The Makah decision put them directly at odds with prevailing sensibilities about whales and decades of effort to save these unique creatures. For the Makah, however, the conflict was about much more than whales and connected directly to centuries of oppression.

The legacy of historical social and political inequality in America has had other environmental manifestations. Shortly after World War II, new federal policies to address a housing crisis for returning veterans sparked an unprecedented movement of Americans to the suburbs, with their bucolic allure of clean and healthy living away from the gritty urban congestion and dirty industry, yet with convenient access to urban amenities. The suburban transition that began in the 1950s was enabled by rapid growth in automobile ownership, cheap fuel, and federal and state investments in the interstate highway system, a complex network of concrete and steel tying the country together like never before. But these changes in residential patterns were not open to everyone. And while the suburbs expanded, many older urban centers languished, while continuing to serve as convenient locations for unwanted or noxious land uses. These practices continued for decades, contributing to a persistent pattern of uneven development. In the late

1990s, residents of Camden, New Jersey, drew attention to the very unequal concentration of noxious industry and environmental burdens in their poor, nonwhite community, and they attracted national attention when they sued their state environmental agency for environmental discrimination (chapter 11). The case was part of a larger movement for environmental justice across the country that highlighted the unequal environmental experiences of marginalized communities. For these communities, strict adherence to environmental laws has failed to address the threat of cumulative risks and the legacy of institutionalized discrimination that has perpetually favored some neighborhoods, while concentrating environmental risks among others.

For most of its history, U.S. environmental policy has been focused on domestic issues. However, the natural environment does not follow political boundaries—many species of fish, birds, and mammals migrate across national boundaries and even across the planet. Pollutants also do not respect arbitrary boundaries and are taken wherever wind and water will carry them. The need for international cooperation on environmental issue has long been recognized. By the early 20th century, the United States and other countries had begun to negotiate international agreements to protect bird migration routes and to limit harvesting of whales. The need for international cooperation has only grown as the world economy has become more integrated and as human influence on the environment has expanded. By the late 20th century, a number of global environmental crises highlighted the fragility of Earth's environment: acid precipitation in the 1970s, destroying forests in northeastern North America and Europe, the Chernobyl nuclear plant meltdown in 1986, contaminating a large area of western Russia and much of Europe, and the discovery of a thinning ozone layer in the mid-1980s, exposing the Earth to increased levels of dangerous ultraviolet radiation. However, few human impacts loom larger than that of climate change—arguably the largest environmental threat faced by humanity. Concerns over human alteration of the atmosphere have existed for decades, but consensus on the problem, let alone action, has been complicated by its global scope and its economic implications.

The principal culprits in the alteration of Earth's atmosphere— fossil fuels—are the lifeblood of modern society. In 1997, the nations of the world debated the Kyoto Protocol—the first concerted effort at a global treaty to control the emissions of gases believed to be causing climate change (chapter 9). For some, climate change has been a dark confirmation of the profound and unwise changes to the environment. A vocal minority continue to dispute that so large a thing as the world's atmosphere could be irrevocably changed by humans. The sheer scale and complexity of the problem have generated one of the largest cooperative scientific efforts in history, although action has been slow in the face of substantial uncertainty, not just about the nature of the problem but about the effect of proposed solutions.

U.S. environmental policy has been continually informed and challenged by social and ecological complexity and the growing appreciation for their interrelationships. Indeed, the traditional separation between man and nature has become harder to maintain in a world so dramatically altered by human activity. This complicated perspective is illustrated by the debate that followed the catastrophic flooding of New Orleans in 2005 (chapter 12). While the flooding was ostensibly attributed to the assault by Hurricane Katrina, many investigators have rejected the idea that the flooding was simply a natural disaster. In a landscape so thoroughly modified by human activity, it is difficult to maintain a meaningful distinction between human-made and natural events. Every proposed solution involves conscious, human decisions about the fate of the landscape and the human relationships to that environment.

While many may wish to roll back the clock and restore what has been changed by human hands, most environmental policies call instead for orderly management of competing human priorities in the face of environmental constraints. The success of these policies will depend on the degree to which they influence human behavior. As another chronicler of environmental policy history has observed, in order to manage the environment, we must manage ourselves.

THE DONORA SMOG:
What Was Responsible for the Deadly Donora Smog of 1948?

—∽—

THE CONTROVERSY

The Issue

A few days before Halloween 1948, the town of Donora, Pennsylvania, and nearby communities were blanketed in a dense and choking smog that led to the deaths of 20 people and sickened nearly 6,000 others. The tragedy generated national media coverage and prompted a months-long investigation by the U.S. Public Health Service (PHS), elevating the issue of air pollution from a nuisance to a public health threat. Donora joined places like Los Angeles as emblems of a national crisis in air pollution. The government investigation found no single explanation for the lethal smog, but local residents and some outside experts blamed the local zinc smelter, accusing it of releasing toxic gases that led to the widespread sickness and death. Who or what was responsible for the deadly Donora smog of 1948?

- ♦ *Arguments that U.S. Steel's Donora Zinc Works was responsible:* Many local residents and some outside experts argued that the local zinc smelting mill was to blame for the deadly 1948 smog episode. Since its establishment in 1915, the works had been the subject of repeated complaints and lawsuits by local residents for the nuisance and damage caused by its noxious air emissions. Some experts argued that the health symptoms experienced during the smog were consistent with excessive exposure to gases emitted by the works.

- ♦ *Arguments that the smog was a freak confluence of events:* Donora Zinc Works managers asserted that it was operating normally when the smog episode developed and that they responded responsibly by shutting down operations when it was apparent that the smog episode had become a crisis. A five-month study by the PHS concluded that the deadly smog was likely due to unusual weather conditions that caused the air in the narrow river valley to become stagnant. They reasoned that normal pollutants emitted by cars, ships, trucks,

1

trains, and industry in the area became trapped, reaching abnormally toxic levels that caused sickness and death.

—⚍—

INTRODUCTION

On Saturday night, October 30, 1948, a national radio broadcaster reported to the nation that residents of Donora, Pennsylvania, were suffering from a killer smog. For some Donora residents, it was only through this national radio broadcast that they realized the deadly seriousness of their own situation. The town had been engulfed in a dense and choking smog since Tuesday, and by Saturday afternoon more than a dozen people were dead from apparent asphyxiation. Thousands more were sick and gasping for breath. Local hospitals were inundated, and emergency personnel groped their way blindly through smoke-darkened streets in order to bring aid to those most in need. The smog finally dissipated the next morning with the arrival of rain, but the confusion and controversy had only just begun.

Most area residents suspected that the local zinc smelter was responsible, but company managers, town officials, and steel union representatives were reluctant to assign blame so quickly or to act against the works based solely on these assumptions. The Donora Zinc Works was a major employer for the town, and so the economic stakes were high. State health officials and company-hired scientists suggested that the deadly smog was due to unusual atmospheric conditions that concentrated the area's normal pollutants and not the result of a single source of deadly emissions. Suspicious critics, however, questioned the credibility of these experts. While environmental disputes were historically handled at the local level, the community found itself at an impasse. After repeated requests, the PHS agreed to investigate the issue. Direct federal involvement in local environmental issues was unusual, but both critics and defenders of the Donora Zinc Works hoped that an objective, scientific investigation by an outside federal agency would settle the issue once and for all.

The Donora smog was an important event in modern environmental history. It was the first recognized air pollution disaster in the United States. Donora confirmed that air pollution was more than a nuisance—it was a health threat. The name *Donora* became infamous shorthand for air pollution disaster. (See "'Death in Donora,' a Ballad by Donora Resident John P. Clark, 1949," on page 30 in the Primary Sources section.) However, the nature of air pollution was changing and so was the nation's response. For centuries, air quality problems were synonymous with excessive smoke and ash—the visible effluent of inefficient combustion or low-grade fuel. From the mid-19th century onward, rapidly expanding industrial activity and growing reliance on fossil fuels—especially coal—resulted in dramatic increases in smoke and other air quality problems. By the late 19th century, civic-minded citizens and industries were banding together in anti-smoke groups to combat the problem in cities and towns throughout the country, usually to control the most egregious offenders. Despite the ubiquity of the problem, air quality problems were still considered local nuisance issues and were thus handled on a local, ad hoc, and largely voluntary basis.

By World War II, both the extent and nature of air pollution were changing nationwide. The U.S. population was growing and becoming more urban. Motorized, petroleum-fueled transport for both goods and people had become the norm—whether by train, plane, boat, or increasingly, automobile. Factories produced ever more sophisticated products using new synthetic chemicals, which meant that the composition of their air emissions kept changing. As a result of these and other changes, air pollution investigators in large metropolitan areas—places like Los Angeles, New York City, and Denver—faced air quality problems that went beyond simple smoke. Their highly publicized efforts to identify the sources and evolving nature of air quality problems complicated the nation's understanding of air pollution. (See the sidebar "Smog Town, USA" on page 6.) When the Donora smog event occurred, this complication and uncertainty played an important part in the debate.

Almost as soon as the Donora smog had cleared, the community was embroiled in a heated debate over what to do and who to blame. Decades of conflict between the Donora Zinc Works and its immediate neighbors, as well as the day-to-day experience of smoke and dust that belched forth from its smokestacks, led most community members to suspect that the works was at fault. Indeed, such suspicions were consistent with the antismoke efforts of the last century. Some of the more staunch critics called for the work's closure, and many assumed that lawsuits would soon follow. The works's managers denied any culpability. Municipal and union leaders were more cautious, believing that the zinc smelter was implicated but hesitant to threaten one of

The smog is so thick that streetlights are on at midday in downtown Donora, Pennsylvania, on Sunday, October 31, 1948. (Associated Press)

the community's largest employers. Scientific investigation promised to settle the question of culpability, and both critics and defenders believed that such analysis would inevitably support their positions. However, investigations of the causes of the smog produced ambiguous conclusions, findings that reflected both the limited scientific knowledge and the conservative approach of federal public health officials. The Donora smog dispelled any doubts that air pollution could harm health, but it did not settle the question of how to deal with air pollution or how to apportion responsibility.

BACKGROUND

Air pollution is an old problem. Nearly 2,000 years ago, Roman chroniclers complained about air pollution. In fact, wherever humans have congregated in dense settlements and burned fuel for cooking, heating, and industry, there have been problems with air quality. Air pollution became a particularly serious problem for medieval London, the largest and most densely populated city of early modern Europe. Starting sometime in the 1200s, energy-intensive industries in London began to use coal in place of wood for fuel. From the beginning, many Londoners found coal to be unnatural and offensive. As London expanded, however, wood for fuel became increasingly scarce and expensive. By the mid-1600s, virtually everyone in London was reliant on coal for fuel. Unfortunately, the coal used in London was bituminous, or soft coal—a form with a high concentration of impurities. When burned, soft coal creates large quantities of smoke as well as acrid and acidic fumes that are not only offensive but can damage property and harm health. As early as the 14th century, London officials were already desperately seeking ways to ban or at least reduce the growing nuisance of smoke and noxious fumes that plagued the region. For all its shortcomings, however, coal became the fuel that powered the machines of the Industrial Revolution and helped to propel the British economy to world leadership. As a result, London faced severe air quality problems that extended well into the 20th century. (See the sidebar "The Killer Fog of '52" on page 18.)

Similar air pollution problems developed in the United States, albeit somewhat later. As in London, these air quality problems could often be traced to growing urban populations, increasing industrialization, the depletion of native wood sources for fuel, and the increasing use of coal. However, the problem was not the same everywhere. While the Northeast was one of the earliest regions of the country to deplete its forests (as much as 80 percent of land was cleared by the late 19th century), it had access to anthracite, or hard coal—a form with fewer impurities that burns more efficiently with less smoke or other fumes. As a result, the Northeast escaped the worst air pollution problems until the mid-20th century. Similarly the Southwest, where natural gas and oil were abundant locally, also delayed its encounters with serious air quality problems. In contrast, industrial cities in the Midwest and Southeast relied on soft coal, which was abundant locally. As early as 1815, Cincinnati, Ohio, was regularly suffering from excessive smoke. St. Louis, Missouri, had similar problems in the 1820s. Pittsburgh, Pennsylvania, which had emerged as the nation's capital for iron and steelmaking in

(continues on page 8)

SMOG TOWN, USA

Since the arrival of the Spanish explorers in the 1500s, chroniclers had noted the propensity of the Los Angeles basin to concentrate smoke and other atmospheric particulates. By the 1860s, severe air quality problems were common despite a population of only 5,000. In the late 19th century, discoveries of oil and natural gas allowed California to move away from imported coal, which spared the region much of the smoke and soot problems so common in other industrialized regions. Nevertheless, as the population grew, air quality problems persisted. Los Angeles began to issue smoke control laws in 1905 and hired its first smoke control inspectors in 1907 to respond to complaints. In the late 1930s, meteorologists began to document a steady deterioration of visibility as the region's air quality worsened. By the early 1940s, atmospheric scientists concluded that the region's air quality problems were due in part to frequent temperature inversions and high mountains that surrounded the basin and helped to trap pollutants.

In summer 1940, people in downtown Los Angeles were beset by stinging eyes and sore throats. The irritation lasted through the fall and then disappeared when rains arrived in the winter. The following summer and fall, the mysterious affliction returned. By summer 1943, officials recognized that this was a recurring phenomenon and suspected that air emissions from offending industries in the area were to blame. A local newspaper observed, "Everywhere the smog went that day, it left behind a group of irate citizens, each of whom demanded relief." Los Angeles mayor Fletcher Brown formed a committee to study the problem and predicted that the smog would be eliminated within four months. Late summer 1944 was the worst yet. Smog covered the Los Angeles basin in a thick reddish-brown haze that rose so high into the atmosphere that it interfered with the work of astronomers at the 5,700-foot-high Mount Wilson Observatory. Residents of Los Angeles and surrounding communities, especially those at the foot of the San Gabriel Mountains that surround the basin, suffered debilitating stinging of eyes and throats. The most vulnerable were afflicted by coughing fits, nausea, and vomiting. Individuals with asthma and other pulmonary conditions were particularly hard hit. Truck farms in and around Los Angeles County experienced severe damage to their leafy crops. Desperate residents and business owners demanded action from city and county officials. Like most people at the time, they assumed that one or a few industries were to blame, with suspicions falling hardest on a few local industrial plants with visible smoke emissions. As residents of Southern California were to learn, however, their air pollution problems were much more complicated.

Beginning in 1946, and over the course of the following decade, state and county officials launched an unprecedented attack on the problem of air pollution. Using a combination of scientific investigation and aggressive enforcement, officials systematically brought area emissions sources under control—iron foundries, steel mills, and even backyard incinerators. In the early 1950s, scientists determined that the Los Angeles basin's air pollution was due to a photochemical reaction between nitrogen oxides, volatile organic compounds (such as hydrocarbons of oil or gasoline), and sunlight. This photochemical process created the characteristic reddish-brown haze of airborne particles and ground-level ozone, which was corrosive to materials and damaging to the health of both plants and animals. By the late 1950s, the last remaining uncontrolled source of unburned hydrocarbons—precursors to photochemical smog—was the automobile.

Despite the overwhelming weight of evidence, efforts to control auto emissions met with heavy resistance. Southern California, and especially Los Angeles, was uniquely dependent on—if not in love with—the automobile. Indeed, by the mid-1950s, the Los Angeles basin had the greatest concentration of automobiles in the world—over 2.3 million in 1954. This was more cars than were owned in any country outside the United States except for the United Kingdom, Canada, and France. Officials and anti-smog activists faced formidable obstacles in succeeding decades to control auto emissions and to rid Los Angeles of its infamous reputation as Smog Town, USA. Despite these obstacles, or because of them, California would move to the legal and scientific forefront in regulation of vehicle emissions and would eventually set the standard for the nation.

(continued from page 5)

the late 18th century, had earned a reputation as "the Smoky City" by the 1860s. Chicago, Illinois, was reportedly under a continuous pall of smoke by the 1880s. Though ever more common, these conditions were increasingly perceived by municipal officials and urban elites as intolerable.

Organized campaigns to combat air pollution began to take form in the most affected cities during the late 19th and early 20th centuries. These early efforts were led by urban reformers in antismoke campaigns, which were often composed of political elites and middle class reformers as well as a growing class of professionals. In 1881, Chicago passed the nation's first serious smoke control ordinance, declaring "dense smoke" from places other than private residences a public nuisance. The law authorized the city's commissioner of health and the superintendent of police to levy fines against offenders. St. Louis and Pittsburgh passed similar ordinances in the 1890s. However, much of the antismoke campaign was not led by government, but rather by citizen activists who sought to educate industry and government and promote voluntary activity to reduce smoke. These early antismoke campaigns were motivated both by the desire to eliminate the nuisance and to conserve resources and reduce the wastefulness that smoke represented. These efforts were not accepted without resistance, especially by industries that stood to lose money due to restrictions on smoke emissions. In an 1892 speech before the Union League Club of Chicago, the coal dealer William P. Rend declared, "Smoke is the incense burning on the altars of industry. It is beautiful to me." Indeed, the association between smoke and economic activity was strong. It was said that clear skies over a city was a bad omen because it meant a labor strike or closed factories. The implication that antismoke efforts threatened economic progress was serious. Equally problematic, opponents of antismoke campaigns questioned assertions that smoke caused harm to either health or property. Opponents of antismoke campaigns repeatedly called for more research and scientific evidence, knowing that the onus of proof rested on those who claimed harm, especially with regard to health.

During the first decade of the 20th century, numerous investigations throughout the country were launched to document and understand air quality problems. Most notable were studies undertaken by the University of Pittsburgh between 1912 and 1914 that were sponsored by the wealthy industrialist and philanthropist Richard B. Mellon. These investigations resulted in the publication of numerous volumes documenting the effects of smoke on health, vegetation, weather, building materials, mental health, and the economy. Similar studies in places like St. Louis, Cleveland, Cincinnati, and Chicago documented millions of dollars in smoke-related damages. However, many cities were not content to wait for conclusive scientific evidence of harm but instead responded to citizen complaints and political pressure for action. By 1912, 23 of 28 American cities with populations greater than 200,000 had created municipal smoke abatement bureaus to address the problem of smoke. By 1916, 75 cities had passed antismoke ordinances of one sort or another. The battle against air pollution would continue to have to be fought repeatedly in communities throughout the country for decades to come.

One catastrophic incident would, however, change the nation's conception of air pollution. During World War I, a shortage of metal prompted the American Steel & Wire Company, a subsidiary of the massive U.S. Steel Corporation, to construct a zinc smelting plant in Donora, Pennsylvania. Donora was a small farming and mining community situated in a horseshoe bend of the Monongahela River, 30 miles south of Pittsburgh. The location was important because it offered easy access to river and rail transportation, as well as fuel and raw materials. Equally important, nearby Pittsburgh was the single largest consumer of zinc in the nation. The Donora Zinc Works was constructed in 1915 on 40 acres of land along the Monongahela River, adjacent to the American Steel & Wire Company. Together, the zinc smelter and steel and wire plant would form an unbroken complex of smelting and processing facilities that extended for three miles along the Monongahela's western shore. Directly across the river, and connected by a bridge to Donora, was the community of Webster.

At the time of construction, the Donora Zinc Works was the largest zinc smelter of its kind. It produced solid zinc metal, sulfuric acid, and a variety of by-products that were used by the galvanizing and metallurgical industries. In 1918, U.S. Steel opened a by-product coking works in a nearby town, which provided a ready customer for the sulfuric acid produced by the Donora Zinc Works. The coking works turned bituminous coal into coke, a processed fuel very similar to coal that produces less smoke and burns hotter. The coking process used sulfuric acid to capture ammonia gas, which was released during the coking process, transforming it into ammonium sulfate. The ammonium sulfate could then be sold as a fertilizer. The Donora Zinc Works thus became an integral part of a regional metal and coal industry in the Monongahela Valley. These industries formed the backbone of the region's economy.

Despite its economic importance, it was not long before neighbors of the Donora Zinc Works began to complain about smoke and other noxious emissions. The first civil suit against the mill was filed in 1919 by Frank and Mamie Burkehardt, who lived next door. They sought $10,000 in compensation for damages to their property and health. The Burkehardts claimed that corrosive fumes from the zinc smelter had destroyed the shrubs and fence surrounding their home, as well as the paint on the house itself. In addition, they sought damages to pay for Mamie's illness and medical treatment. Mamie had been suffering from mysterious ailments, and she had noticed that her symptoms diminished only when she left home to visit her sister in New York. In court, witnesses for the plaintiffs described foul odors emanating from the smelter—"like emptying an old toilet" according to one person—as well as striking environmental changes in the nearby landscape. Witnesses described withered vegetation and severe erosion of the surrounding hillsides and even more dramatic impacts in the community of Webster, which was across the river but directly downwind of the zinc works.

Representatives of the Donora Zinc Works contested these claims, arguing that it was impossible to separate the contributions of the zinc works from all the other sources of air pollutants in the area. They pointed to the smoky, steam-powered trains that regularly ran up the Pennsylvania Railroad within 100 feet of the Burkehardts' property. More fundamental, the defendants challenged the very basis of the plaintiffs' evidence, arguing that proof of noxious emissions and damage from the zinc works could only come from the scientific instruments and methods of trained chemists. The court found differently, however, and awarded the Burkehardts $500 in compensation. In 1935, 189 residents filed a joint lawsuit charging the zinc works and nearby Clairton Works for regional air pollution and seeking $1.5 million toward a trust fund for reparations. A second joint claim by 659 plaintiffs in the same area sought a $4.5 million trust fund. These latter claims were eventually abandoned in 1942. Nevertheless, in response to repeated lawsuits, zinc works managers devoted more resources to rebut these claims. They hired more and better experts to testify on their behalf in court and invested in high-profile agricultural demonstrations to discredit complaints that farming had become more difficult because of the zinc works's emissions.

Up through World War II, air pollution problems continued to worsen throughout the country, especially in cities and communities with heavy industry and high population growth. Efforts to address this problem met with rare success, but understanding of the different factors that could contribute to air pollution grew. In particular, the role of local atmospheric and topographic factors drew greater attention. Beginning in the early 1940s, investigators in Los Angeles came to understand how that area's growing smog problem could be traced in part to the very stable atmospheric conditions of the area. The same atmospheric conditions that produced consistently clear and sunny skies also prevented the dispersion of pollutants. These conditions were exacerbated by the high mountains that surrounded the area, creating a virtual bowl and further hindering atmospheric dispersion. In subsequent years, the conditions for smog in Los Angeles were frequently invoked for comparison in other communities, though often incorrectly.

One of the biggest shifts in the understanding of air pollution came from identifying the sources of air pollutants. Since at least the early 19th century, large industry had borne the brunt of blame for air pollution problems. Indeed, heavy industry was often the worst offender. However, industry leaders and others increasingly pointed to the small but cumulatively large contributions of private homes that used low-grade coal for heating or cooking, commercial establishments, and other less noticed sources. In nearby Pittsburgh, the role of nonindustrial contributions to air pollution became especially clear in the late 1940s. In 1947, after years of failed attempts to control local smoke emissions and worsening air quality, municipal officials implemented an ordinance requiring residential consumers, as well as industry and transportation, to change their fuel or their combustion equipment. Officials hoped that the new policy would force consumers to switch to higher-grade smokeless coal to reduce smoke and meet new air quality standards. At the time, there were approximately 100,000 homes with hand-fired coal-burning stoves and furnaces in Pittsburgh. Rather than trying to enforce the new ordinance on each individual home, officials focused instead on regulating distributors of coal. That winter of 1947–48, the air over the city was dramatically less smoky—50 percent less so according to reports. The *Pittsburgh Press* declared "PITTSBURGH IS CLEANER," and the city's lead antismoke organization boasted that Pittsburgh was shedding its reputation as "the Smoky City."

Indeed, over the next few years, heavy smoke would almost completely disappear from Pittsburgh's skies, aided in part by a rapid transition from coal to natural gas as the latter became cheaper. Because of the new policy's visible success, public approval of antismoke efforts grew substantially. Pittsburgh's success in bringing its legendary smoke problem under control drew national attention. Ironically, at almost the same moment that Pittsburgh had achieved its most impressive gains in air quality, Donora was headed into its worst period. During the last week of October 1948, a dense and suffocating smog descended on Donora. Smoky fogs were common in the fall, but this one was different. On Tuesday, October 26, the usual morning haze refused to dissipate. Over the next two days, it thickened considerably. By Thursday, traffic on and along the Monongahela River was paralyzed. Stranded motorists scrambled to find places to stay. By Friday morning, visibility beyond 100 feet was nearly impossible and was even poor at 30 feet. One local physician recalled looking out his window to see nothing but rooftops peeking out like islands in a sea of fog. He noticed a freight train moving slowly along the riverbank just south of town and was stunned by the sight. "It was the smoke," he said. "They were firing up for the grade and the smoke was belching out, but it didn't rise. I mean it didn't go up at all. It just spilled out over the lip of the stack like a black liquid, like ink or oil, and rolled down to the ground and lay there. My God, it just lay there! I thought, well, God damn— and they talk about needing smoke control up in Pittsburgh." No less ominously, local hospitals were inundated by people complaining of cramping, headaches, and breathing problems. Pharmacists dispensed all kinds of prescription and over-the-counter remedies to desperate sufferers—hypodermics of adrenalin, Benadryl, and morphine. Local volunteer firefighters were dispatched on emergency calls with canisters of oxygen to aid those who could not breathe, though they found it nearly impossible to navigate through the thick, bluish haze that had enveloped the town. That afternoon, an 84-year-old man became the smog's first victim. The annual Donora Halloween parade took place as usual later that Friday, October 29, although it was an uncomfortable affair. Attendees stood around coughing with handkerchiefs covering their noses and mouths, and onlookers found it difficult to see the children passing before them, "like shadows marching by," according to one witness. By 10 A.M. the next morning, the town undertaker had retrieved nine corpses, and funeral homes were overwhelmed. The Red Cross and American Legion set up an emergency shelter and command center in Donora's municipal building. Physicians advised those who were suffering the worst symptoms to leave the area immediately, but it was nearly impossible to drive through the thick pall that enveloped the valley. Amazingly, the annual "smog bowl" football game between Monongahela and Donora High Schools continued as usual, although players ran the ball because they could not see it when it was in the air. Donora High School suffered an unusual loss.

Donora Zinc Works managers were aware of the worsening situation but later reported nothing unusual in the plant's operations or emissions. Nevertheless, in the early hours of Sunday, October 31, officials from the U.S. Steel headquarters in Delaware ordered the zinc works to halt production as a precaution. Company-contracted chemists from the University of Pittsburgh and the Mellon Institute's Industrial Hygiene Foundation, along with industrial hygienists from the Pennsylvania Department of Public Health, arrived in Donora shortly after 6 A.M. to make atmospheric measurements of sulfur compounds associated with the burning of soft coal like that used in smelting. Dr. Joseph Shilen, a Pennsylvania Department of Public Health official, told a reporter at the time that he did not expect to "find anything worthwhile." A light rain had developed overnight and continued through the morning, and by noon the smog had largely dissipated.

THE DEBATE

In the immediate aftermath of the devastating smog, area residents faced at least two urgent questions: 1) Would the smog return, and 2) who or what was responsible for the deadly event? For most local residents, immediate suspicion fell hardest on local industry, specifically, the Donora Zinc Works. Suspicion was not enough, however, to guide action. Not everyone was convinced that the zinc works was responsible. However, even some who did suspect the zinc smelter were reluctant to take strong action against one of the area's most important economic actors. Without some clear resolution, the issue would likely result in expensive litigation, with no assurance that another deadly smog would not return.

Hours after the smog had finally cleared on Sunday, October 31, Donora community leaders held a series of emergency meetings to take stock of the crisis and to decide on a course of action. The first meeting was called by the local board of health president, Charles Stacey. At that first closed-door meeting, Stacey reported to municipal and state officials, as well as mill managers who were in attendance, that 600 people had been made ill by the smog, with 45 still in area hospitals and 19 dead (shortly to increase to 20). Donora's burgess (an elected town leader), August Chambon, asked the zinc smelter to remain closed until Pennsylvania's secretary of health determined that it was safe to restart the plant.

The next evening, borough council president John Duda, Jr., called a closed-door session of Donora's borough council and invited the area's business, industrial, labor, civil, and medical officials to decide whether to reopen the zinc works and how to cope with the aftermath of the smog. At that meeting, and in subsequent days, critics and defenders of the zinc works put forth their arguments in an effort to resolve the question of blame and to lay out a course of action.

The Case Against the Donora Zinc Works

The zinc works had no lack of critics, both official and unofficial. During the emergency borough council meetings, Board of Health officials made it clear that they thought the zinc smelter should remain closed permanently. One physician speculated that if the smog had lasted one more day, there would have been 1,000 dead rather than 20. He asserted that the zinc smelter's effluent had been poisoning area residents for years. Abe Celapino, a business owner from Webster, blamed Donora's borough council for willfully ignoring the warning signs of environmental deterioration in the surrounding landscape. Celapino recounted a conversation he had had with borough council president

When the Donora Zinc Works restarted operations for a test conducted by the U.S. Public Health Service, smoke blew across the river toward the community of Webster, Pennsylvania. One Webster resident, Evangeline Lach, holds a handkerchief to her face to keep out fumes as she goes to pump water on the afternoon of April 19, 1949. (Associated Press)

Duda months earlier in which the latter allegedly said, "I've got a darn good job and I'm going to keep it. I don't care what it [the plant] kills." In fact, six out of the seven borough council members were employees of American Steel & Wire, which owned the zinc works, as well as being United Steelworkers union leaders.

The case against the zinc works was supported by historical tensions, daily experience, and circumstantial evidence. Donora was an especially smoky town, and the sight of dense, white clouds of smoke billowing from the smokestacks of the local mills was a common one. Longtime residents were also quite aware of the complaints and lawsuits against the zinc works, but the deadliness of this smog event raised the problem to a whole new level. The afternoon after the smog cleared, Pittsburgh smoke control officials toured Donora and speculated that sulfur compounds emitted by zinc smelting likely combined with water to create sulfur trioxide, a poisonous gas. Dr. I. Hope Alexander, a Pittsburgh Department of Health official and one of the leaders of the successful antismoke efforts in that city, noted that, "The smoke from the Zinc Works at Donora is of a very toxic variety." Philip Sadtler, an independent chemist, also suspected a toxic agent in the works's emissions. Sadtler had been sent by a group of farmers in Florida fighting industrial fluorine air pollution. He offered his services to investigate the possibility that a similar problem was behind Donora's deadly smog. The editor of the *Monessen Daily Independent,* a local newspaper serving Webster, wrote a series of editorials calling for the mill to be renovated or else moved to some remote region where it would not threaten residents. (See "A Valley Problem, November 3, 1948," on page 30 in the Primary Sources section.) The *Independent* and other Pittsburgh area papers devoted considerable coverage to the Donora smog, often accompanied by images of dramatic soil erosion at the Gilmore Cemetery, directly across the street from the zinc works.

Critics of the zinc smelter called for either its closure or modernization. (See the letters from local residents Helen Dzyban and Gerald Gillingham to the governor of Pennsylvania on pages 31–32 in the Primary Sources section.) The zinc works's smoky production process was in fact quite obsolete and had been almost from the day it opened. While the zinc smelter had been constructed as a coal-dependent process, other smelters built around the same time were already being designed to use electricity, which was not only less smoky but more cost-effective. Management of the zinc works had also failed to take advantage of well-established pollution control methods. In response to repeated litigation and tightening legal standards, smelting plants in other parts of the country had adopted the practice of constructing much taller chimneys—often 400 to 600 feet in height—in order to better disperse or dilute their effluent. By contrast, the zinc works's smokestacks were about 150 feet in height, which was far below the 400-foot mountain ridges that hemmed in the narrow river valley in which the mill and surrounding communities sat. The zinc works management had considered the possibility of changing the smelter's production process. In fact, one month before the deadly Donora smog, the company had hired an engineering firm to develop plans for a less smoky process. However, the plans were never implemented because they were regarded as too expensive.

The Case in Defense of the Donora Zinc Works

Those who disputed or downplayed the zinc smelter's culpability did so for a variety of reasons. M. M. Neale, superintendant at the zinc works, staunchly defended the company. He asserted that engineers had monitored the plant's emissions carefully and that nothing unusual had occurred at the plant before or during the smog event. He argued that the plant had operated without incident since 1915. In response to questions about the timing of the plant's emergency shutdown, Neale insisted that this had been entirely a precautionary measure and not an admission of guilt. Both he and town leader August Chambon suggested that the deadly smog might have been due to an accumulation of emissions from a number of different sources in the industrialized valley and not just the smelter.

Federal and state officials who arrived in Donora shortly after the smog speculated from the start that unusual weather circumstances had a role. The day after the smog cleared, officials from the United States Bureau of Mines (USBM) Central Experimental Station in Pittsburgh arrived in Donora to study the problem. Based on their experience working with air-quality officials in Los Angeles, USBM staff assumed that Donora, like Los Angeles, was a victim of industrial emissions that had been trapped by unusually stagnant atmospheric conditions. However, they were unable to investigate this possibility as long as the smelter was shut down. Pennsylvania Department of Health officials offered a similar explanation upon their arrival and went so far as to assure the community that a reoccurrence was unlikely given the unique circumstances necessary to create the problem in the first place. Moreover, early air sampling did not indicate the presence of dangerous levels of sulfur compounds as would be expected if the coal-fired smelter's emissions were to blame. Nevertheless, they announced that they would investigate the issue more thoroughly.

Both USBM and Pennsylvania health officials were stymied in their investigations as long as the smelter remained closed. Local residents were still fearful, however, that the deadly smog might return when the smelter was restarted. With the encouragement of an official from the PHS, Pennsylvania health officials went before the borough council and argued that it was not in the community's long-term economic interest to keep the smelter closed. Moreover, without knowing for sure what caused the deadly smog, they might create a false sense of security. The council agreed, and on the morning of Monday, November 8—one week after the smog disaster had ended—the zinc smelter was restarted

---

THE KILLER FOG OF '52

The British Isles have always been a place of mists and fog. As London and surrounding communities grew and industrialized, their smoky emissions mixed with these fogs to produce what came to be known as pea soupers— exceptionally dense, smoky fogs that shrouded cities and surrounding lands in misty twilight. Beginning in the early 1800s, these fogs took on a dirty, yellowish hue as they became increasingly laden with the sulfurous emissions from coal-fired industry and home heating. In his 1852 novel *Bleak House*, Charles Dickens described the regular fogs this way:

> Fog everywhere. Fog up the river, where it flows among green aits and meadows; fog down the river, where it rolls defiled among the tiers of shipping and the waterside pollutions of a great (and dirty) city. Fog on the Essex marshes, fog on the Kentish heights. Fog creeping into the cabooses of collier-brigs; fog lying out on the yards, and hovering in the rigging of great ships. . . . Fog in the eyes and throats of ancient Greenwich pensioners, wheezing by the firesides of their wards; fog in the stem and bowl of the afternoon pipe of the wrathful skipper, down in his close cabin; fog cruelly pinching the toes and fingers of his shivering little 'prentice boy on deck.

Indeed, London's fogs were legendary and figured prominently in the art and romance of this old city, from Robert Louis Stevenson, to Sir Arthur Conan Doyle's Sherlock Holmes mysteries, to the visual art of Claude Monet and James Abbot McNeil Whistler. However, the reality of these thick fogs was not so romantic. By the late 19th century, city life was disrupted repeatedly by episodes of exceptionally thick and smoky fogs that made travel treacherous, begrimed clothing and buildings with black soot and ash, and made breathing difficult. In 1905, Dr. H. A. Des Voeux of the Coal Smoke Abatement Society coined the word *smog* to describe the combination of smoke and fog that had become so common in London. The word became a

at half-capacity. One hundred state air monitors, arranged in concentric circles, ringed the smelter, and officials took detailed notes of atmospheric conditions. At a borough council meeting the next day, state health officials reported no positive findings of any likely airborne toxin.

generic reference for air pollution, even in places where the causes (such as Los Angeles's photochemical air pollution) were quite different.

During the first half of the 20th century, London's smoky fogs became less intense and less frequent, and many believed that they were disappearing altogether. However, during a particularly cold week in December 1952, the pea souper returned with a vengeance. Between Friday, December 5, and Tuesday, December 9, London was brought to an almost complete standstill. A choking yellowish-brown fog reduced visibility in some places to less than a few yards. Planes were grounded and rail and bus services were halted, often because employees simply could not find their way to work. In at least one case, a suburban train nosing its way through the fog ran over a gang of railway workers, killing at least two and trapping others beneath the engine and coaches. Motorists who were caught out unexpectedly or were foolish enough to venture out were in no less danger. Some nevertheless attempted to continue with passengers walking out in front to guide their way. Many simply abandoned their cars and walked home. One London resident recalled how a frustrated bus driver finally stopped and forced passengers off for fear of killing them all. The passengers then formed a human chain in order to make their way on foot without losing sight of anyone.

After four days, the fog finally retreated, revealing streets littered with abandoned cars and buildings covered in a slimy film of black soot. As Londoners took stock of the episode, the magnitude of the crisis became increasingly clear. Officials reported that approximately 4,000 people had died as a result of the smoky fog, many of them elderly or with preexisting respiratory or pulmonary conditions. Later analyses raised the death toll to 12,000, making it one of the worst environmental disasters ever. In the wake of the disaster, British authorities passed new legislation in 1956 that forced industry and residents to shift from coal to smokeless fuels. However, because of expense and other obstacles, the transition happened slowly. In 1962, London was struck again, though this time fewer than 1,000 deaths were the result.

However, officials cautioned that, "pollution could not be checked fully until a heavy fog holds the discharge from the industrial plants near the earth." In essence, the deadly smog event would have to happen again in order to know for sure.

Borough council and Steelworkers Union representatives defended the zinc works against calls for closure or even new, stricter regulation, though they did not necessarily doubt that the zinc works was at least partly responsible. Instead, they sought out opportunities to preserve the works and to address long-standing community concerns about pollution. The zinc works accounted for almost 1,000 of the 5,000 factory jobs in the community, so its economic welfare was vital to the community's welfare. Chambon argued that blame was irrelevant and instead advocated for a cooperative approach to promote the town's long-term interests. "These deaths were a blessing in disguise," he said. "They brought this matter to a head. Let's all pull together and eliminate this trouble."

Outside Scientific Investigation as the Answer

During and immediately after the air pollution crisis, there were numerous calls for scientific investigation. Though many people held strong opinions and suspicions about who or what was to blame, virtually everyone appreciated that the issue had to be settled in some kind of authoritative way. All sides argued that assumption or suspicion was poor ground on which to compel expensive changes or base important decisions. Defenders of the smelter feared that uninformed hysteria and popular suspicion threatened the town's economic livelihood, while critics worried that the zinc works would simply deny responsibility and leave residents with little recourse. Looming over everything was the very real possibility of expensive and divisive litigation. While most agreed that investigation was necessary, there was less agreement on who should do the investigation or in what manner.

There were numerous competing proposals for investigation. Early in the controversy the Pennsylvania Department of Health had asserted its prerogative to conduct an investigation, but many local residents expressed strong doubt that state officials would be competent or unbiased. The state had a history of inaction on local complaints, and there was suspicion that Pennsylvania's industry-friendly governor would not act against the zinc works. The United Steelworkers union offered $10,000 to sponsor an independent investigation. The borough council accepted this offer and appointed a special investigating committee—including members of the local board of health and borough council—to survey the health impact of the smog and to begin drafting a local smoke control ordinance. At the same time, the United Steelworkers union launched its own internal study of the smog through its workmen's compensation commission. Phil Sadtler, the independent chemist from Florida, announced the preliminary results of his own study and argued that the deadly smog had been caused by the release of toxic fluorine gas. His analysis was publicly rejected by state and local officials. On November 16—two weeks after the smog crisis—American Steel & Wire, owner of the Donora Zinc Works, formally denied responsibility for the smog crisis, arguing that it was caused by "an unprecedent[ed] ly heavy fog." (See "American Steel & Wire Rejects Blame for the Smog, November 17, 1948," on page 32 in the Primary Sources section.) In addition, the company announced that it had contracted with the University of Cincinnati's Kettering Laboratory of Applied Physiology to do an internal study of plant hazards. Thus, within the first two weeks following the deadly Donora smog, at least five independent studies were either planned or under way by various groups trying to build support for their own claims or to counter the claims of others.

From the height of the crisis, borough council officials had repeatedly called on the PHS for assistance, but these early requests were either refused or ignored. The PHS did not normally perform services directly for communities but rather assisted state and local health departments through training, grants, or dissemination of research. The PHS had a reputation for rigorous health research and, equally important, for avoiding political bias or even confrontation. Indeed, the PHS regularly worked with both industry and government but only cooperatively and only by invitation. A few days after the smog disaster, the borough council, with the support of the United Steelworkers, passed a resolution formally requesting an investigation by the PHS. This request was opposed initially by state officials, though they later changed their position. However, it was only after American Steel & Wire extended an invitation that officials in the PHS's Division of Industrial Hygiene announced they would conduct a comprehensive survey of air pollution in Donora. For everyone involved, the prospect of a PHS analysis offered hope that the issue would be settled conclusively and without bias. Zinc works officials expected the analysis to absolve the company of blame; Donora officials and union members expected a technical solution to the problem of smog; and critics of the zinc works expected that it would be found guilty.

OUTCOME AND IMPACT

In 1948, no federal agency was authorized to coordinate the issue of air pollution. While the PHS had conducted national surveys of the issue in previous years, the USBM was just as active. Since 1947, USBM officials had been working with state and local officials in California to deal with the growing smog problem in the Los Angeles area, principally through the control of emissions from industrial sources. While the PHS assumed federal leadership in investigating the Donora smog, Dr. Helmuth H. Schrenk from the USBM's central experimental station in Pittsburgh was named as principal investigator of the PHS effort because of his superior experience with the measuring and control of air pollution from industrial sources. Nevertheless, the PHS approach reflected its goal of understanding the health significance of the smog event.

Beginning in January 1949, the PHS launched a five-month investigation of Donora and surrounding communities. The study included a household survey, air-quality sampling for fumes and particulates, surveys of domestic animals, sanitation, and housing, and meteorological investigations from the U.S. Weather Bureau and aerial photographs from the Coast Guard. From January to March 1949, a team of public health nurses canvassed the residents of Donora and neighboring Webster and Carroll Township with detailed surveys of residents' experiences and self-reported health. The nurses managed to reach 1,308 out of the 1,451 households targeted. Sanitary engineers assessed housing and living conditions, while veterinarians interviewed pet owners and farmers. Physicians interviewed people identified as seriously affected by the smog, the relatives and friends of those who had died, and reviewed hospital records and autopsy results. They also conducted chest X-rays of smelter workers to determine whether preexisting respiratory conditions influenced reactions to the smog. With the help of USBM personnel, air-monitoring equipment was set up throughout the area to measure the composition and concentration of various pollutants. The air-sampling scheme did not attempt to determine the zinc smelter's contribution to local air pollution but rather sought to determine the overall quality of the air and, more specifically, to identify those elements that were injurious to health. Locals participated enthusiastically under the assumption that the PHS investigation would settle the question of responsibility for the smog, one way or the other.

In mid-October 1949, nearly a year after the deadly Donora smog event, the PHS released its findings. (See "The Surgeon General on Air Pollution in Donora, 1949," on page 33 in the Primary Sources section.) The final tally of illnesses from the smog showed that nearly half of the area's residents were affected by the smog—6,000 people in all. This was nearly 10 times what the local board of health had initially thought. Surveys revealed that those most affected were elderly with preexisting cardiorespiratory problems. Investigators concluded that the smog likely consisted of water droplets, sulfur dioxide, and other atmospheric pollutants from a variety of sources. The pollutants reached deadly concentrations when the smog became trapped within the narrow valley due to an atmospheric temperature inversion. A layer of warm air developed above the cooler air near the surface, creating a lid over the valley that prevented the air near the ground—and the pollutants in it—from diluting or dispersing. This was the same explanation that had been offered by the Pennsylvania Department of Health in the immediate aftermath of the smog event. The PHS report recommended that local industries reduce their emissions and that a weather-monitoring system be put in place to anticipate similar atmospheric conditions in the future. The report failed to satisfy critics who sought to place blame on the steel and zinc works. Shortly thereafter, dozens of area residents filed suit against American Steel & Wire, owner of the zinc works, for the impacts of the smog and property damage. For its part, American Steel & Wire claimed that the disaster was essentially an "act of God" due to the role of unusual weather circumstances. Nevertheless, in 1951, American Steel & Wire made an out-of-court settlement of $235,000 with plaintiffs seeking $4,643,000 for deaths due to the Donora smog.

In the year following the release of the Donora study, the PHS division of hygiene received nearly two dozen requests from industrial communities across the country for similar investigations in order to prevent a Donora-type disaster. After the report was released, U.S. surgeon general Leonard Scheele and industrial hygiene division chief James G. Townsend repeatedly cited the survey's inconclusive results to argue for federally sponsored research into newly outlined uncertainties about air pollution and its health effects. Pennsylvania representatives worked with the PHS to submit bills for a supplemental appropriation of $750,000 to continue fieldwork near Donora. Numerous bills for increased funding for research by the PHS were submitted to Congress, but none made it out of committee.

Federal policy proposals to deal with air pollution did not really proliferate in Congress until after 1950. During the 81st and 82nd Congress (1949—52), seven bills were proposed to expand the federal government's role in dealing with air pollution. All authorized the Secretary of the Interior and the Surgeon General to conduct research and disseminate information on the prevention and health effects of air pollution. None emerged from the House Committee on Interstate and Foreign Commerce before 1952. While the name *Donora* remained an infamous and oft-repeated reference in both the media and Congress, the Donora smog was soon joined by air-quality crises in major cities throughout the country and abroad. In December 1952, thick smog smothered London for five days and led to thousands of deaths. In 1953, a temperature inversion over New York City lasting 10 days was blamed for 200 deaths. However, no city sustained media attention on the issue of air pollution like Los Angeles, which helped to explain why California representatives were on the front lines of proposals for federal legislation.

The push for some sort of federal role in addressing air pollution intensified between 1952 and 1955, as a growing number of representatives and senators expressed alarm over worsening air-quality conditions in cities across the United States. Proposals ranged from research by the USBM and the PHS to tax deductions for industrial air-filtration equipment. The first successful proposal for federal involvement was drafted by an ad hoc Interdepartmental Committee on Community Air Pollution organized by the secretary of the newly established U.S. Department of Health, Education and Welfare (HEW) in 1954. In April

1955, Senator Thomas Kuchel of California introduced a bill, jointly sponsored by Senators William Knowland of California and Edward Martin and James Duff of Pennsylvania, which amended the Federal Water Pollution Control Act in order to provide for the study and control of air pollution. On July 14, 1955, President Dwight D. Eisenhower signed Public Law 84-159 into law. The first federal law to address air pollution codified the policy that state and local governments had principal responsibility for dealing with air pollution problems. The federal government was given no power of regulation or enforcement. However, similarly to the 1948 federal water pollution legislation that had preceded it, the air pollution legislation authorized a federal program of technical assistance and research on air pollution, overseen by the secretary of HEW and the PHS. While this first federal law on air pollution prescribed a very modest federal role, it nevertheless marked the beginning of increasing federal involvement. The 1955 law also reaffirmed PHS leadership of the federal government's approach to issues of pollution, though this leadership would only last for another decade.

WHAT IF?

What if PHS investigators had concluded that the zinc works was responsible?

If the PHS had concluded that the zinc works was principally responsible for the deadly Donora smog event, debilitating lawsuits would likely have forced the closure of the smelting plant. While such an outcome would certainly have satisfied the smelter's worst critics, this outcome would also have diminished the political significance of the Donora smog. Donora's experience would likely have been classified as an isolated industrial disaster and reinforced assumptions about the role of industry as principal offender. Donora might not have become the infamous example of uncontrolled air pollution and thus would not have contributed to the national debates about air pollution, particularly those surrounding health.

Donora served as a constant touchstone for those concerned with the problems of air pollution and an unequivocal confirmation that under the right (or wrong) circumstances, air pollution could kill. The health questions surrounding air pollution were important concerns. Ironically, the uncertainty of the PHS investigation of Donora—the inability to find a single cause—was an important driver of PHS interest in pushing for governmental support of more research into the causes and consequences of air pollution on human health. The PHS was not the most obvious agency to lead on the issue of air pollution, but its principal role in Donora and in other communities provided support to the PHS's bid for leadership on these issues. Had PHS proclaimed that the answer to Donora's experience was a release of some deadly industrial gas, there would have been little left to investigate.

CHRONOLOGY

1915   Zinc works established in Donora.

1919   First lawsuit brought against zinc works by next-door neighbor for damage to property and health. Plaintiffs awarded $500.

1922   Group of residents from nearby Webster file $100,000 lawsuit against zinc works for destruction of gardens, farms, and houses. All suits are dismissed in 1930.

1931   Residents downwind of zinc works file lawsuit for damages to farm soil, livestock, crops, and vegetable gardens. All plaintiffs awarded sizable cash compensation.

1935   One hundred eighty-nine residents file joint lawsuit charging the zinc works and nearby Clairton Works for regional air pollution and seeking $1.5 million toward a trust fund for reparations. A second joint claim by 659 plaintiffs in the same area sought a $4.5 million trust fund. All claims abandoned in 1942.

1947   Pittsburgh implements its antismoke policy with dramatic success.

1948   *October 26:* Thick smog settles over Monongahela River Valley. *October 28–31:* Monongahela River Valley is paralyzed by persistent, thick smog. Thousands are made ill and 20 die.

November 1: Donora's borough council holds a special closed-door meeting to decide whether the zinc works should be reopened and how to deal with the smog's aftermath.

November 2: Donora's borough council passes a resolution to request investigation by the U.S. Public Health Service (PHS) despite opposition by state health officials.

November 3: Pennsylvania Department of Health official Dr. Joseph Shilen submits preliminary report on Donora smog to Pennsylvania's secretary of health. Shilen announces that the

Commonwealth will conduct its own survey of air pollution in the Monongahela River Valley.

Mid-November: PHS official Dr. James G. Townsend announces that the PHS division of industrial hygiene has chosen Donora for its first comprehensive survey of air pollution.

November 29: Independent investigator Phil Sadtler submits his report to the borough council and blames toxic smog on fluorine emissions from American Steel & Wire's plants.

December 25: Independent investigator Clarence Mills publishes his analysis of the smog, laying blame on toxic emissions from the zinc works.

1949   *January:* PHS investigators begin their analysis and surveys of Donora.

October: PHS releases its preliminary findings on the Donora smog event.

1951   *April:* Plaintiffs seeking $4,643,000 from American Steel & Wire for deaths due to the Donora smog accept an out-of-court settlement of $235,000.

1955   Air Pollution Control Act passed as amendment to the 1948 Federal Water Pollution Control Act.

DISCUSSION QUESTIONS

1. Was the Donora Zinc Works to blame for the deadly Donora smog? Consider the evidence for and against your conclusion.

2. Should the PHS have become involved in the investigation of the Donora smog or should it have remained a local issue? Why?

3. In its report on the Donora smog, the PHS recommended that the plants do a better job of reducing emissions and that a weather-monitoring system be set up in order to predict conditions that might lead to another dangerous smog event. Were these recommendations an adequate response? Why or why not?

4. In the debates over air pollution, both in Donora and elsewhere, commentators often argued that no action should be taken until complete and thorough scientific investigation was completed. Do you agree? Why or why not?

5. The PHS study concluded that air pollutants accumulated in the valley because of unusually stable atmospheric conditions, which prevented dispersion or dilution of local air emissions. Did this atmospheric condition exonerate the zinc works? Why or why not?

6. How did the Donora smog crisis contribute to greater awareness and federal oversight of air pollution?

WEB SITES

California Environmental Protection Agency. Air Resources Board. *Clearing California Skies* (video). Available online. URL: http://www. arb.ca.gov/videos/clskies.htm. Accessed March 11, 2011.

"Days of Toxic Darkness." BBC News (Dec. 5, 2002). Available online. URL: http://news.bbc.co.uk/1/hi/uk/2542315.stm. Accessed March 18, 2011.

"Deadly Smog." NOW with Bill Moyers (Jan. 17, 2003). Available online. URL: http://www.pbs.org/now/science/smog.html. Accessed March 18, 2011.

Donora Fluoride Fog: A Secret History of America's Worst Air Pollution Disaster. Available online. URL: http://www.actionpa.org/fluoride/ donora-fog.html. Accessed March 18, 2011.

Donora Smog Disaster October 30–31, 1948. Letter of Mrs. Lois Bainbridge of Webster, Pa., to the Governor. Pennsylvania State Archives. Available online. URL: http://www.docheritage.state.pa.us/ documents/donora.asp. Accessed March 18, 2011.

"Donora Smog Kills 20 October, 1948." Pennsylvania Department of Environmental Protection. Available online. URL: http://www. depweb.state.pa.us/heritage/cwp/view.asp?a=3&Q=533403&PM=1. Accessed March 18, 2011.

EPA—Center for Innovation in Engineering and Science Education. *Air Quality: Learning Science with Models, EPA's Internet Geographic Exposure Modeling System*—The Donora Disaster. Available online. URL: http://www.ciese.org/curriculum/downwind/ airmodel/activities/donora/donora_page1.html. Accessed March 11, 2011.

Fifty Years of Progress Toward Clean Air: A Photographic Retrospective. Available online. URL: http://www.aqmd.gov/news1/Archives/History/50th_photos.htm. Accessed March 11, 2011.

"Great Smog of 1952" Met Office. Available online. URL: http://www.metoffice.gov.uk/education/secondary/students/smog.html Accessed March 18, 2011.

Killer Fog of '52: Thousands Died as Poisonous Air Smothered London. Available online. URL: http://www.npr.org/templates/story/story.php?storyId=873954. Accessed March 18, 2011.

Pennsylvania Historical Markers—1948 Donora Smog. Available online. URL: http://www.waymarking.com/waymarks/WM1QAN_The_1948_Donora_Smog. Accessed March 11, 2011.

Scorecard: Pollution Locator—Smog and Particulates. Available online. URL: http://www.scorecard.org/env-releases/cap. Accessed March 18, 2011.

BIBLIOGRAPHY

Brimblecombe, Peter. *The Big Smoke: A History of Air Pollution in London Since Medieval Times.* New York: Routledge, 1987.

Davies, J. Clarence, and Barbara S. Davies. *The Politics of Pollution.* 2d ed. Indianapolis, Ind.: Bobbs-Merrill, 1975.

Dewey, Scott Hamilton. *Don't Breathe the Air: Air Pollution and U.S. Environmental Politics, 1945–1970.* College Station: Texas A & M University Press, 2000.

Kiester, Edwin, Jr. "A Darkness in Donora." *Smithsonian Magazine* (November 1999).

Schrenk, H. H., Harry Heimann, George D. Clayton, W. M. Gafafer, and Harry Wexler. "Air Pollution in Donora, Pa.: Epidemiology of the Unusual Smog Episode of October 1948—Preliminary Report." Public Health Bulletin No. 306. Federal Security Agency, 1949.

Snyder, Lynne Page. "'The Death-Dealing Smog Over Donora, Pennsylvania': Industrial Air Pollution, Public Health Policy, and the Politics of Expertise." *Environmental History Review* 18, no. 1 (1994): 117–139.

Tarr, Joel A. "Changing Fuel Use Behavior and Energy Transitions: The Pittsburgh Smoke Control Movement, 1940–1950." *Journal of Social History* 14, no. 4 (1981): 561–588.

PRIMARY SOURCES

Document 1: "Death in Donora," a Ballad by Donora Resident John P. Clark, 1949

The deadly smog that affected Donora and Webster, Pennsylvania, left a lasting impression on many people. In 1949, folklorist Dan Hoffman collected poems from across the country from individuals who reflected on the Donora smog. This ballad by Donora resident John P. Clark is one of the more commonly remembered pieces, evoking the eeriness and gloom of that tragedy.

> Death in Donora
> I have felt the fog in my throat—
> The misty hand of Death caress my face;
> I have wrestled with a frightful foe
> Who strangled me with wisps of gray fog-lace.
> Now in my eyes since I have died,
> The bleak, bare hills rise in stupid might
> With scars of its slavery imbedded deep;
> And the people still live—still live—in the poisonous night.

Source: John P. Clark. "Death in Donora." Quoted in Dan G. Hoffman. "Three Ballads of the Donora Smog." *New York Folklore Quarterly* 5 (Spring 1949): 51–59.

—ɷ—

Document 2: "A Valley Problem," November 3, 1948

Many commentators attempted to draw lessons from the deadly smog that afflicted Donora and Webster, Pennsylvania, in 1948. In this editorial, which appeared in a local newspaper only a few days after the event, the author argued that smog was part of a more general problem of air pollution, which could and should be addressed by both government and industry.

> The lesson of the terrible smog tragedy at Donora will not have been learned completely, in our judgment, if all the communities of this valley do not make an attack upon the whole problem of air pollution. . . .
> The problem is, of course, what we are going to do about it. If we are going to make steel here, we are going to have to burn coal and other fuels. That inevitably means smoke and dirt and air pollution.

However, many communities are discovering that this pollution can be markedly reduced. They are proving that it can be done.

Our plea now is that the Monongahela Valley, through its municipal and industrial officials, keep abreast of these developments and that they be adopted as rapidly as they seem to be feasible in our situation.

The people of Pennsylvania are spending millions and millions of dollars to free their streams of pollution. That program is going to cost the people of Monessen alone well over a million dollars.

The air we breathe is no less important to our well being than the water we drink and fish in.

Source: "A Valley Problem," *Monessen Daily Independent,* November 3, 1948.

—∽—

Document 3: Letter from Webster Resident Helen Dzyban to Pennsylvania Governor James H. Duff, October 31, 1948

The smog episode that affected the communities of Donora and Webster, Pennsylvania, in late October 1948 revived long-standing complaints from residents about the environmental damage and nuisance of life near the industrial plants. In this letter to the governor of Pennsylvania on the day of the worst smog episode, Webster resident Helen Dzyban describes the damaged landscape and recounts her own efforts to bring about change.

Dear Sir . . . Our town looks like a desert, once a beautiful town before the Zinc Works of Donora took over. It killed all vegetation. Not even a blade of grass will grow here. It eats the paints off the houses. Takes the nails and draws them out of houses and fences and has caused asthmatic conditions in the towns of Donora and Webster. The high officials of Donora Zinc Works have moved out in the country and they can say that the acid from the mill doesn't bother them. Already half of the people of Webster and Donora are dying, or being murdered from the zinc sulphuric acid and fumes. . . . For fifteen years we have been fighting the Zinc Works, so that they would do something about that terrible acid, but all the lawyers were bought off by the mill officials. I am sure that this Company with all its millions can afford to do something about the smoke and acid or else move it to a place where it won't kill humans. It's really a shame that poor people have to suffer for the millions of the industrialists. To watch the victims die is pathetic, gasping for breath.

The town is still and like a morgue. Nineteen people died in one night. A few more foggy nights and there will be many more deaths.

Source: Letter from Helen Dzyban to Pennsylvania governor James H. Duff, October 31, 1948.

———

Document 4: Petition Letter Sent by Gerald Gillingham to Pennsylvania Governor James H. Duff, November 3, 1948

A few days after a deadly smog descended on the communities of Donora and Webster, Pennsylvania, resident Gerald Gillingham sent a letter to the governor blaming the environmental degradation of the area on Donora Zinc Works and appealing for the governor's help.

To the Governor of the Commonwealth of Pennsylvania:
     We believe that if you see for yourself the damage wrought here, you will join us in this fight. Before the Donora mills began operations, Webster was a thriving community with grass and trees. Now it is completely shorn of vegetation. The hillsides surrounding the community are torn with erosion. Deep ditches have ruined once productive farm land. When health of the public, in addition to property, is in jeopardy, positive action is called for."

Source: Petition letter sent by Gerald Gillingham to Pennsylvania governor James H. Duff, November 3, 1948.

———

Document 5: American Steel & Wire Rejects Blame for the Smog, November 17, 1948

After the smog event in late October 1948, many critics laid blame squarely on the Donora steel and zinc plant. This facility had been the subject of complaints for smoke and odors for decades. Two weeks after the event, American Steel & Wire, the company that owned the plant, issued a public denial of these charges, blaming the event on unprecedented fog.

CLEVELAND, Nov. 16 (UP)—The American Steel and Wire Company said today it was "certain" its zinc works at Donora, Pa., was not responsible for the smog linked to twenty deaths there last month.

The company, in a statement released here and carried as an advertisement in the *Donora Herald American,* declared that "our conviction from the start has been that the zinc works was not the cause of the disaster

"We are certain," it added, "that the principal offender in the tragedy was the unprecedentedly heavy fog which blanketed the borough for five consecutive days—a phenomenon which no resident could recall ever happening before."

The smog enveloped the town Oct. 27 and by Oct. 31 nineteen elderly persons suffering from heart and asthmatic conditions had died. Another person died a week later. Ill effects were felt by almost 600 residents.

Source: "Denies Smog Zinc Blame: Owners of Donora Plant Issue Statement Stressing Fog." *New York Times,* November 17, 1948.

—∞—

Document 6: The Surgeon General on Air Pollution in Donora, 1949

A year after the Donora smog, the Public Health Service (PHS) released its analysis of the event. The long-anticipated report was cautious in its assessment of the effects of the smog and its contributory factors. While many hoped that the analysis would provide a basis for assigning (or refuting) blame, the report emphasized questions rather than answers, and advocated for more research. Below is the foreword to the report by PHS surgeon general Leonard Scheele.

This study is the opening move in what may develop into a major field of operation in improving the Nation's health. We have realized during our growing impatience with the annoyance of smoke, that pollution from gases, fumes, and microscopic particles was also a factor to be reckoned with. But it was not until the tragic impact of Donora that the Nation as a whole became aware that there might be a serious danger to health from air contaminants. . . .

The Donora report has completely confirmed two beliefs we held at the outset of the investigation. It has shown with great clarity how little fundamental knowledge exists regarding the possible effects of atmospheric pollution on health. Secondly, Donora has emphasized how

long-range and complex is this job of overcoming the problem of air pollution—after we get the basic knowledge of its effects. . . .

Our first step now, of course, is immediate basic research. We need
to investigate for instance, what long-range effect continued low concentrations of polluted air has on the health of individuals—not only
healthy individuals, but those with chronic diseases and the aged and
children. We know nothing about the indirect effect of air pollution on
persons with diseases other than those of the respiratory tract. We also
need immediate research into another indisputable effect of air pollution; its ability to shut out some of the healthful rays of the sun. When
we find the answers to all of these unknowns, we can proceed to the
problem of eliminating the causes. As a proof that air pollution is a
health matter, as a model for future studies in air pollution, and as an
important phase of our increasing efforts in the field of environmental
health, this study will be invaluable."

Source: Foreword by USPHS surgeon general Leonard Scheele to *Air Pollution
in Donora, Pa.: Epidemiology of the Unusual Smog Episode of October 1948—
Preliminary Report,* released in 1949.

2

ECHO PARK:
Should Dams Be Allowed within a National Monument?

—ɯ—

THE CONTROVERSY

The Issue

In the early 1950s, proponents of water resource development battled with conservationists and wilderness preservation advocates over plans to dam the Green River and flood Echo Park, a scenic valley within Dinosaur National Monument on the Colorado-Utah border. Developers argued that the Echo Park Dam was an important component of a larger regional plan to harness the water resources of the upper Colorado River basin. This development, they argued, would provide for water storage, irrigation, regulation of the river, and hydroelectric power production, which would spur economic development in underdeveloped parts of the American West. A coalition of conservation-minded critics and others assailed plans to dam Echo Park, arguing that erecting a dam within a national monument would undermine the integrity of the national park system and destroy an important wilderness area. The Echo Park controversy brought attention to the unique landscape and politics of the American West, and it engaged the nation in a debate over the benefits of natural resource development, conservation, and wilderness preservation. The question that faced Congress and the nation was: Should dams be allowed within a national monument?

♦ **Arguments for damming Echo Park:** Supporters of an Echo Park Dam argued that it was an integral part of the larger Colorado River Storage Project (CRSP), an ambitious public works program to meet the growing water needs of the West, allowing arid and semiarid lands to be used for agriculture, regulation of the flow of the Colorado River, water storage, hydroelectric power generation, economic development, and new and more accessible recreational opportunities. Representatives of states in the upper Colorado River basin were particularly concerned with getting their fair share of Colorado River water as well as meeting their obligations to water users downstream. They argued that the

35

Echo Park site was specifically important because of its ideal location and physical properties. Dam supporters argued that water and power development were not inconsistent with the area's designation as a national monument and that a reservoir would actually enhance the area's appeal for recreation.

♦ **Arguments against damming Echo Park:** Opposition to the damming of Echo Park came from different groups for different reasons. Conservationists and wilderness advocates argued that damming Echo Park would represent an unacceptable intrusion into a national monument, undermine the integrity of the national park system, and set a dangerous precedent for future incursions into other national parks or monuments. They argued that the dam would destroy an incomparable and unique natural treasure. They asserted that the government had failed to adequately consider alternatives that could spare the national monuments and meet the needs of CRSP. Other critics questioned the entire premise of CRSP. Representatives from states in the lower Colorado River basin, especially California, feared that dams in the upper Colorado basin would compromise the quality and quantity of Colorado River water that arrived downstream. Other critics of CRSP argued that the program was a waste of money—subsidizing irrigation of land that could never be very productive.

—ᴍ—

INTRODUCTION

Echo Park is a picturesque canyon river valley at the confluence of the Green and Yampa Rivers in western Colorado, near the Utah border. Since 1938, Echo Park has been a part of Dinosaur National Monument—an area managed by the National Park Service (NPS), encompassing 220,000 acres of rivers, canyons, and benchlands straddling the Colorado-Utah border. In the late 1940s, the U.S. Bureau of Reclamation (Reclamation) proposed building a large dam on the Green River in a high-walled canyon just downriver of Echo Park. If constructed, the water impounded by the dam would have inundated Echo Park and miles of upstream canyons within Dinosaur National Monument under hundreds of feet of water. When Reclamation's plans became public, conservation organizations and wilderness advocates mobilized their members and an increasingly sympathetic public to oppose the dam.

Between 1950 and 1956, the conflict over Echo Park became a national debate and a defining moment in the historical balance of power between conservationists and developers in the American West. The

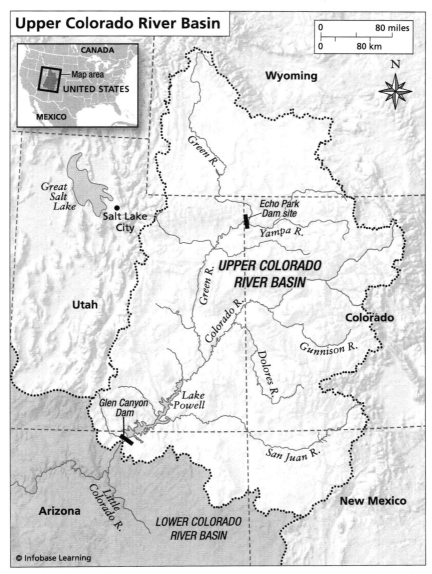

The upper Colorado River basin encompasses more than 17,000 square miles and crosses five states: Wyoming, Utah, Colorado, Arizona, and New Mexico. Rivers within the basin ultimately drain into the Colorado River. (Map by Dale Williams)

conflict's resolution marked an important milestone in the development of conservation, wilderness, and resource development politics.

The proposed Echo Park Dam was only a piece of the much larger CRSP. CRSP was a regional plan that called for the construction of dams, canals, hydroelectric power plants, and irrigation projects throughout the upper Colorado River basin—an area encompassing portions of Wyoming, Utah, Colorado, Arizona, and New Mexico (see map). CRSP promised to enable the upper basin states to finally take control of their legal share of the water in the Colorado River, a river that runs for 1,400 miles through some of the driest and remotest parts of the continental United States. In the American West, water is everything. Western Congress members and their constituents saw CRSP as an opportunity to spur economic growth through the development of abundant and cheap water and power. Growth and economic development of the West have been highly dependent on the development of water resources. In 1902, the federal government created Reclamation with a mission to "make the desert bloom" by "reclaiming" or subjugating desert lands for human use. Reclamation would be accomplished by harnessing water resources in order to make irrigated farming possible where it was otherwise not.

At the time, western communities and states were developing a complex and contentious legal framework to manage competing claims over limited water resources, such as the Colorado River. Reclamation's water development plans were an integral part of this evolving legal and political framework around water resources. In the 1930s, the federal government began an ambitious and unprecedented program of dam building, constructing the world's largest structures (at the time) to capture and control some of the nation's largest rivers. These dams and their associated works were materially and symbolically important for the country, enabling further economic growth in the West and demonstrating the power and promise of American ambition and ingenuity. Economic and industrial expansion during World War II and after put added pressure on the country to develop its natural resources, both for national defense and economic prosperity. CRSP fit squarely within this national agenda.

The post–World War II period was also a time of growing interest in the protection and preservation of the country's unique and scenic natural landscapes, whether for recreation or aesthetic enjoyment.

While the country had been setting aside and protecting national parks since the late 19th century, it was after World War II that many more Americans started to take an interest in and visit such places. However, pressure for continued economic and industrial expansion threatened national parks and other undeveloped spaces. Development interests sought access to public lands in order to exploit untapped mineral, timber, and water resources. When Reclamation released plans to dam and inundate portions of an obscure national monument in a remote part of the West, national park advocates and conservation organizations saw this proposal as an ominous and significant threat to the entire national park system. In response, they organized unprecedented political opposition and were supported by a surprisingly large and sympathetic public.

The battle over Echo Park and Dinosaur National Monument was a historically significant confrontation between those interested in the efficient economic development of natural resources and those who believed that some of these places should be left unimpaired and wild. Between 1950 and 1956, the debate over Echo Park moved from internal government deliberations to the public arena as Congress took up the question: Should dams be allowed within a national monument? Dam proponents included Reclamation, most western members of Congress, as well as civic and commercial representatives from throughout the states of the upper Colorado River basin. These supporters argued that Echo Park was an ideal location for a dam and would be an integral part of CRSP. Moreover, they asserted that CRSP was absolutely necessary for the economic future of the upper Colorado basin. They assured opponents that a reservoir in Echo Park would only enhance the area by increasing its overall utility; harnessing the economic potential of an underutilized resource and, at the same time, making it more accessible to more people.

Dam opponents included conservation and wilderness recreation organizations, members of Congress from the lower Colorado River basin and other regions of the country, and a vocal proportion of the public. Opponents argued that damming Echo Park would destroy a unique, primeval landscape, violate the purpose of national parks and monuments, and rob future generations of enjoyment of this piece of American natural heritage. Worse, construction of a dam within a national monument would set a dangerous precedent by undermining the sanctity of the national park system, thereby putting other national parks and monuments under pressure for development and, thus, at further risk.

To the surprise of many in Congress, the public response was overwhelmingly against the dam. However, public sympathy was not enough. In the 1950s, conservation organizations and other advocates of wilderness had very few legal resources at their disposal. As a result, they forged political alliances with other CRSP opponents and sought out alternatives that dam proponents could support. Dam supporters were faced with increasingly threatening opposition, not just to the Echo Park Dam, but to the entire CRSP. The question of whether to allow dams within a national monument would have to be decided through political compromise.

BACKGROUND

The American West begins at approximately the 100th meridian. This is a line of longitude that runs north-south through North and South Dakota, Nebraska, Kansas, Oklahoma, and Texas. West of this invisible line, precipitation drops below 20 inches per year—the critical amount needed to support forests and rain-fed agriculture. In some places, such as the extreme Southwest, it drops below five inches annually—creating true deserts. Early Spanish settlers and later American explorers found these arid environments to be remarkable but largely inhospitable. In 1816, Major Stephen Long set out to explore the lands west of the Mississippi River and east of the Rocky Mountains. He later described this area as the "Great American Desert"—a label that stuck for many years after, although this vast area included everything from mountain scrubland to prairie grasslands. Nevertheless, early would-be settlers were challenged by these landscapes that are so unlike the more humid, flat, and forested lands in the eastern half of the continent.

In May 1869, Major John Wesley Powell and nine companions set out to explore the Colorado River and the Grand Canyon by boat, beginning at the headwaters on the Green River in Wyoming. With funding from the Illinois Natural History Society and Chicago Academy of Sciences, the one-armed Civil War veteran embarked on a soon-to-be famous expedition and scientific investigation. Throughout their harrowing three-month journey, the explorers encountered many spectacular sights. On June 18, 1869, after surviving turbulent rapids, Powell and his crew found quiet waters and made camp on a beach at the confluence of the Green and Yampa Rivers. Across from their camp stood a perfectly vertical 800-foot sandstone wall. The explorers were impressed by the site, even more so when they discovered its unusual acoustic qualities. In his journal, Powell wrote, "Standing opposite the rock, our words are repeated with startling clearness, but in a soft, mellow tone, that transforms them into magical music." Powell named the place Echo Park—a name that was later adopted on official government maps. Echo Rock, however, was renamed Steamboat Rock because it resembled a steamboat's prow. Powell made two trips down the Green and Colorado Rivers, first in 1869 and then again in 1871. His published accounts made him a national hero, and he became one of the country's most honored scientists.

Powell was fascinated by the West and spent much of his career studying its issues, especially in regard to its potential for development. In 1876, he published *A Report on the Lands of the Arid Regions of the United States, with a More Detailed Account of the Lands of Utah*. In his report, and in later testimony to Congress, Powell argued that two-fifths of the continental United States had a climate that could not support farming without irrigation. And while irrigated farmland in the West could be quite productive, he warned that limited water supplies meant that only a small fraction of the land could actually be reclaimed through irrigation. He wrote, "When all the waters running in the streams found in this region are conducted on the land, there will be but a small portion of the country redeemed, varying in the different territories from one to three percent." However, members of Congress from the western regions in question and their constituents would not accept such low estimates, nor would they be thwarted in their efforts to reclaim and develop the West.

The scarcity of water resources and the sheer expense of irrigation infrastructure required federal assistance and interstate cooperation. In June 1902, President Theodore Roosevelt signed the Reclamation Act into law. This legislation established a revolving fund to pay for irrigation projects, at first with revenue from the sale of public lands and later from the sale of irrigation water to farmers. The program was administered by the Reclamation Service (later renamed the Bureau of

Reclamation), and it was neither successful nor popular during the first two decades of its existence. This would change. In 1917, farmers in southern California's Imperial Valley petitioned the federal government for help in building a canal to channel water from the Colorado River to their farmlands. Reclamation responded to their call and suggested that what they really needed was a sizable dam to control the Colorado River and provide a steady source of water. Other interests in California, especially the rapidly growing and water-starved City of Los Angeles, threw their support behind this idea. However, the Colorado River basin is shared by seven states—Arizona, California, Colorado, Nevada, New Mexico, Utah, and Wyoming—all of which laid claim to its waters. Reclamation and California could not dam the Colorado River without the agreement of the other states.

Clarifying claims on the Colorado River was a matter of major importance. According to western water law, and specifically the tradition known as prior appropriation, the first entity to put water to beneficial use gained ownership rights to that water. Indeed, the Supreme Court ruled in June 1922 that prior appropriation could be applied to the states. States in the upper Colorado River basin worried that California would lay claim to the entire flow of the Colorado River unless an agreement over appropriate shares was worked out first. Over the course of 11 months in 1922, Secretary of Commerce Herbert Hoover worked with representatives from all seven states to negotiate the Colorado River Compact (Compact)—the first major agreement governing use of the Colorado River. The Compact divided the Colorado River basin into two units—an upper basin and a lower basin. The upper basin consisted of Colorado, New Mexico, Utah, and Wyoming, while the lower basin consisted of Arizona, California, and Nevada. Based on spotty river gauge data, Reclamation estimated the Colorado River's average annual flow at 16.4 million acre-feet (amount of water that would cover an acre of land under one foot of water—325,851 gallons), a significant overestimate. Under the Compact, the upper basin was entitled to 7.5 million acre-feet from the Colorado River annually, as long as it ensured that the lower basin received the same amount. The remaining 1.4 million acre-feet would be allowed to flow to Mexico. The states within each basin were responsible for divvying up their basin's share among themselves. Every state but one ratified the Compact. Arizona refused because it did not want to have to compete with California. In

1928, Congress bypassed Arizona's objection and authorized construction of a dam at Black Canyon on the lower Colorado River, on the border between Arizona and Nevada and 30 miles southeast of Las Vegas. Begun in 1931 and finished in 1935, Hoover Dam (initially named Boulder Dam) was completed ahead of schedule and within budget. At 726 feet in height, it was by far the largest dam in the world and the world's largest electricity-generating station as well. Hoover Dam was a nationally celebrated accomplishment and an important symbol of President Franklin D. Roosevelt's New Deal program, coming as it did during the nation's worst economic crisis. Hoover Dam was only the beginning. Even before this mammoth project was completed, Reclamation had begun construction of even larger dams in the Pacific Northwest. More important, Reclamation's reputation was secure, and the era of dam building had begun. With the blessing of Congress, Reclamation sought out new locations for dams and irrigation projects throughout the West.

The Great Depression had taken its toll, and upper basin states were eager to get their share of federal largesse and to develop their resources. By the late 1930s, they were clamoring for their own reclamation projects. In 1939, Reclamation began to scout the upper Colorado River and its tributaries in search of potential dam sites. It found a number of good locations on the Green River, a major tributary of the Colorado, as well as on the main stem of the Colorado River itself. One ideal location was Whirlpool Canyon (named by Powell), a narrow canyon immediately downriver of Echo Park. At this site, sheer cliffs of solid quartzite narrow to within a few hundred feet of each other, hemming in the swift waters of the Green River. A dam at this location would require a relatively small structure to block the river and yet would capture the waters of both the Green and Yampa Rivers just below their confluence at Echo Park. It would create a large reservoir for water storage and hydroelectric power generation. Moreover, the narrowness and depth of the canyon reservoir would minimize the exposed water surface area and thus reduce water loss from evaporation—a major concern for Reclamation engineers. The only complication was that the Echo Park dam site was within the recently expanded Dinosaur National Monument.

Dinosaur National Monument was created by President Woodrow Wilson in 1915. When first created, the national monument encompassed 80 acres surrounding a dinosaur fossil quarry in northeastern

Utah. When the NPS was created in 1916, it took over jurisdiction of the monument. However, by the mid-1920s, nearly all of the dinosaur fossils had been excavated and removed, leaving the tiny national monument with little to show. In the 1930s, there was a resurgence of interest in the area, although this time it was not for dinosaur fossils but for the scenery of the surrounding rivers and canyons. A new set of

THE PLACE NO ONE KNEW

On April 11, 1956, the Colorado River Storage Project (CRSP) became law—a program of water resource capture and development in the upper Colorado River basin that included the construction of dams, canals, hydroelectric generators, and irrigation programs. One of the projects was the Glen Canyon Dam, a massive water storage and hydroelectric dam on the Colorado River in Page, Arizona. In contrast to the controversy over plans to dam Echo Park, the proposal to dam Glen Canyon encountered relatively little opposition before 1956. In an effort to save Echo Park and preserve the integrity of national parks and monuments, conservation organizations offered an alternative: eliminate the proposed Echo Park Dam and increase the size of the Glen Canyon Dam. Although few members of the leading conservation organizations knew anything about Glen Canyon at the time, they knew that it was not within a national park or monument.

After CRSP and the enlarged Glen Canyon Dam were approved, however, many came to regret this compromise. David Brower, executive director of the Sierra Club, had been on the front lines in the battle to save Echo Park, and he, like the members of the other conservation organizations, had advocated for a larger Glen Canyon Dam. He first toured Glen Canyon in the summer of 1957 and, much to his dismay, found that it was just as beautiful as some had warned—even more beautiful than Echo Park. Previous visitors had described Glen Canyon as the living heart of the Colorado River—quiet and colorful, riddled with small side canyons leading to fern-draped grottoes, caves, and even amphitheaters. Construction on the Glen Canyon Dam began soon after its approval, and many people came to visit Glen Canyon one last time before it was inundated under hundreds of feet of water. Like Brower, many of these visitors expressed a deep sense of regret and resentment for the impending loss of Glen Canyon. Mourning recreation and wilderness enthusiasts brought attention to the scenic and recreational qualities of the area.

The 1930s were also a period of expansion for the NPS. As a result of all the publicity, Roger Toll, superintendent of Yellowstone National Park, was sent to inspect the nearby Lodore and Yampa canyons for their potential as national monuments or parks. Toll reported that

over the damming of Glen Canyon was compounded by the realization that the reservoir behind the enlarged dam would back up water into Rainbow Bridge National Monument, a 160-acre preserve surrounding the country's largest natural stone arch—about 40 miles upriver from Glen Canyon Dam. Although the CRSP legislation had included a proviso stating that, "As part of the construction, operation, and maintenance of the Glen Canyon unit the Secretary of the Interior shall take adequate protective measures to preclude impairment of the Rainbow Bridge National Monument," it was apparent by 1960 that neither the Interior secretary nor Congress intended to take any action to prevent reservoir water from entering the monument. Once again, conservationists were mobilized into action by a threat to the inviolability of national parks and monuments, as well as fears that water flowing beneath the arch might weaken the rock and lead to its collapse.

The campaign to save Glen Canyon was vigorous but in the end unsuccessful. On January 21, 1963, the final diversion tunnel that allowed the Colorado River to bypass Glen Canyon Dam was closed, stopping the Colorado River behind the dam and initiating the filling of the reservoir that would become Lake Powell. Brower, who felt uniquely responsible for failing to save Glen Canyon, collaborated with photographer Eliot Porter to produce a public eulogy in the form of an exhibit-format book entitled *The Place No One Knew: Glen Canyon on the Colorado*, published in March 1963. The book contained spectacular photographs of the canyon and its unique scenery, juxtaposed with poetry and prose from a variety of historical figures and noted contemporary authors, such as the famed Western historian Wallace Stegner. In the foreword to the book Brower lamented, "Glen Canyon died in 1963 and I was partly responsible for its death. So were you. Neither you nor I, nor anyone else, knew it well enough to insist that at all costs it should endure."

there was much to recommend. The exposed canyon walls provided a unique glimpse into the geologic past. The area featured a diverse array of interesting wildlife and vegetation, as well as evidence of long human habitation. The Fremont people had inhabited the area from 500 A.D. to 1200 A.D., leaving behind tantalizing remnants such as petroglyphs and pictographs on canyon walls, as well as pit houses and pottery. In the more recent frontier past, the area had been visited by early Mormon pioneers, historically popular explorers like Powell, as well as miners and outlaws. Toll also commented on the uniquely attractive and serene qualities of Echo Park. In his 1933 report of his inspection, he wrote:

> [Echo Park] is one of the most beautiful and impressive places in the area. Here on the bank of the Green River, where the Yampa joins it, one can easily visualize the parties of early explorers on their way down the river. The same scene that they saw is there today, unchanged. On the outer side of the loop that the Green River makes is a park-like meadow, with large cottonwoods and box elders, golden in their autumn foliage, at the time of our visit. Across the river stands Steamboat Rock, a great sentinel, with a smooth cliff that suggests a small El Capitan, in color, or perhaps the mystery of the Enchanted Mesa. It is a beautiful place to camp, and the Indians doubtless found it so for there are pictographs nearby. Steamboat Rock throws back an exceptionally perfect echo, and repeats some six or seven words, spoken rapidly. No wonder Major Powell called it Echo Park. Its equal is hard to find.

In July 1938, President Roosevelt issued a proclamation to expand Dinosaur National Monument to encompass portions of the Green and Yampa Rivers, spanning northern Utah and northwestern Colorado. Almost overnight, Dinosaur National Monument became one of the largest areas in the national park system—more than 360 square miles. The expansion was welcomed by local residents of nearby Vernal, Utah, as well as the business community, which looked forward to an increase in economic activity from tourism. However, with little funding, the NPS was unable to develop the monument, and it remained virtually unknown and unvisited for more than a decade—until the controversy unfolded.

During World War II and immediately after, the upper basin states saw rapid economic change and expansion, due in large part to federal investments for the war effort—military bases, hospitals, research laboratories, defense-related industry, and manufacturing. In addition, there was a significant increase in oil refining and the mining and processing of minerals such as manganese, copper, zinc, iron, and uranium. Utah alone saw 50,000 jobs created during the war, drawing more than 100,000 new residents. Other states in the upper Colorado River basin saw similar growth of both industry and population. All of this growth increased the pressure to find new sources of water as well as low-cost electricity to power existing industries and attract others. In 1946, Reclamation issued a report on potential reclamation projects throughout the Colorado River basin, entitled, "The Colorado River: A Comprehensive Report on the Development of Water Resources—A Natural Menace Becomes a Natural Resource." The report listed 134 potential projects throughout the upper and lower basins, though Reclamation warned that only a subset of the projects could be pursued since there was nowhere near enough water in the Colorado River for all of them. The report represented a truly ambitious plan. (See "'Wealth from Water,' 1946," on page 65 in the Primary Sources section.) In the foreword to the report, Reclamation wrote:

> Tomorrow the Colorado River will be utilized to the very last drop. Its water will convert thousands of additional acres of sagebrush desert to flourishing farms and beautiful homes for servicemen, industrial workers, and native farmers who seek to build permanently in the West. Its terrifying energy will be harnessed completely to do an even bigger job in building bulwarks for peace. Here is a job so great in its possibilities that only a nation of free people have the vision to know that it can be done and that it must be done.

Reclamation's upper basin plan was CRSP. The upper basin states were ecstatic about the possibilities and made every effort to promote CRSP's realization. In 1948, the four upper basin states ratified the Upper Colorado River Basin Compact, which settled the question of how to allocate their basin's share of Colorado River water: 51.75 percent to Colorado, 23 percent to Utah, 14 percent to Wyoming, and 11.25 percent to New Mexico. This interstate agreement cleared the way for federal water development projects. Colorado agreed to allow 500,000 acre-feet of water from the Yampa River to flow to Utah annually. This agreement would allow Utah to pursue its own Central Utah Project (CUP)—a major water development plan to divert water from the Uinta basin in northeastern Utah over 100 miles west to Utah Lake and the Salt Lake City region. In order to replace the diverted water for farmers in the Uinta basin, Utah needed access to water from the Yampa River. The proposed dam at Echo Park would capture and store that needed water. The CUP was a participating project in CRSP, which of course made the Echo Park Dam essential. As a result, when Reclamation began to choose among the various potential dam sites, Echo Park was firmly among the finalists.

Ever since Reclamation's first surveys of dam sites in Dinosaur National Monument in 1939, officials of NPS had expressed discomfort with the possibility of water and power development within a national monument. However, there was relatively little that they could do. Reclamation and NPS were both agencies within the Department of the Interior (DOI). As sister agencies, it was not appropriate for one to publicly criticize the plans or activities of the other. Moreover, Reclamation was considerably more powerful than NPS, both in terms of resources and political clout. Nevertheless, as Reclamation's plans to develop Echo Park gained traction, NPS director Newton Drury and his staff increasingly voiced their opposition to the commissioner of Reclamation and to their mutual boss, Secretary of the Interior Oscar Chapman. As internal arguments between the two agencies escalated, both pushed the secretary to resolve the dispute. In response, Secretary Chapman called for a public hearing on the question: Should the Bureau of Reclamation be allowed to build a dam within Dinosaur National Monument?

THE DEBATE

The debate over the Echo Park Dam would not end with Secretary Chapman. Indeed, it was only the beginning of a debate that would last for another six years as it made its way through Congress. However, Chapman had to approve Reclamation's report before Congress could introduce legislation for CRSP. Chapman withheld such approval until all of the interested parties—upper basin states and federal agencies with jurisdiction over the Colorado River—had a chance to submit comments. Despite complaints from representatives of the upper basin states for quicker action, Chapman convened a hearing on April 3, 1950, to allow both Reclamation and NPS and their respective supporters to air their views. During this hearing, the two sides articulated many of the core arguments that would be repeated in subsequent hearings before Congress, as well as other public venues.

The Case for Echo Park Dam

Dam proponents who appeared at Chapman's hearing included a number of western senators and members of Congress (including Utah's entire congressional delegation), a variety of delegates representing business and municipal interests of the upper basin states, and a cadre of bureau engineers. They argued that an Echo Park dam was crucial to

Echo Park's Steamboat Rock in Dinosaur National Monument marks the confluence of the Yampa and Green Rivers. This formation, noted for its spectacle and its historical importance as a landing site for Major John Wesley Powell in 1869, was threatened with inundation by the proposed Echo Park Dam. (© Tom Till/Alamy)

CRSP and pointed out that the upper basin had a much more erratic water supply than the lower basin. In order to meet its obligation to the lower basin under the 1922 Compact, the upper basin needed to have adequate water storage capacity to regulate the river's flow. This would ensure consistent supply to the lower basin while allowing the upper basin to use its share of water. A Reclamation spokesman also revealed the alarming discovery that the Compact had been based on a significant overestimate of the Colorado River's annual flow. While the previous studies on which the Compact had been based estimated the river's annual average flow to vary between 16 and 18 million acre-feet, more recent studies had shown that in some years the river's flow dropped to as low as 5.5 million acre-feet. Thus, there was an even more pressing reason to develop adequate storage capacity and river regulation.

Reclamation engineers explained that the Echo Park site was ideally suited to their purposes. A narrow and deep canyon just below the confluence of two rivers would permit maximum water capture and storage, minimize water loss to evaporation, and enable adequate hydroelectric power production. They argued that Echo Park Dam would be "one of the very few sites which can accomplish such control in the upper reaches of the basin to any large degree. . . . Any group of reservoirs which does not include Echo Park and Split Mountain cannot meet the objectives heretofore outlined only at the cost of increased evaporation loss, less annual revenue, and higher unit power costs." (The proposal called for two dams within Dinosaur National Monument: one dam immediately downriver of Echo Park and another lower dam farther downriver at Split Mountain. The Split Mountain Dam would be considerably smaller than Echo Park, and more important, would only come after Echo Park was constructed. The controversy focused almost exclusively on Echo Park Dam.) According to Reclamation plans, Echo Park Dam would host a power plant capable of producing 200,000 kilowatts of electricity. As with many Reclamation projects, the sale of hydroelectric power was an important source of revenue to replenish the reclamation fund, helping to offset the cost of dam construction and other irrigation projects. In this case, Reclamation stated that power sales would provide funds toward the completion of the Central Utah Project. Upper basin officials welcomed the prospect of increased power supplies for the region. Ralph Goodrich, a former dean of the engineering college at the University of Wyoming and a member of the

Upper Colorado River Commission, predicted that "if Echo Park was started at once and completed in five years, its output could be entirely absorbed by the rapidly expanding power market of what is coming to be an industrial empire of the West."

Dam supporters also complained that opposition by the NPS was inconsistent with previous agreements and governmental intent. They pointed to Roosevelt's 1938 proclamation expanding Dinosaur National Monument, which explicitly recognized prior claims by Reclamation for specific dam sites within the monument (one of which was far to the north of Echo Park), as well as the authority of the Federal Power Commission (FPC) to develop power sites. In addition, the commissioner of Reclamation pointed to a series of previously unreleased memos and agreements from the early 1940s between Reclamation and NPS director Drury that stated that the NPS would not object to dams within the monument, including Echo Park. The latter were not revealed publicly at the time but discreetly shown to the secretary during the hearing.

In anticipation of conservationists' arguments, dam proponents argued that Dinosaur National Monument would not be seriously diminished or ruined by a dam or reservoir. They argued that it would actually be enhanced. Reclamation noted that "Present visits to the monument . . . are limited essentially to the museum and quarries located at the original site. Views of the canyon sections of the monument have been appreciated by a mere handful of hardy river runners who on infrequent occasions have made the hazardous boat trip through the rapids." As the dam filled the canyon with still water, it would become safer and more accessible for the general public to enjoy—precisely the purpose for which the area had been protected in the first place. Indeed, only two members of the dam opponents present at the hearing had ever visited the monument. Dam supporters asked, what was the use of a national monument that almost no one could visit and appreciate?

The Case Against Echo Park Dam

Opponents of an Echo Park Dam included the NPS and their advisory board and members of a number of outdoor recreation and conservation organizations, including Izaak Walton League, Sierra Club, Wildlife Management Institute, National Audubon Society, National Parks Association, Wilderness Society, and others, such as the American

Planning and Civic Association. Dam opponents argued that it was imperative to safeguard Dinosaur National Monument from encroachment by development interests in order to uphold the principles upon which the national park system had been founded—namely the conservation of places of scenic beauty or historical importance *unimpaired* for the enjoyment of future generations. Anything less would undermine the system and open it up to future intrusions and degradation. They argued that a dam in or around Echo Park would cause irreparable harm to a unique, primeval wilderness. Ira Gabrielson, president of the Wildlife Management Institute, disputed arguments that a reservoir would enhance the monument. He said, "Flowing water is an essential part of an exhibit of the Colorado River. . . . Conservationists do not subscribe, and probably never will subscribe, to this specious argument that the stinking debris left by a fluctuating reservoir adds to the beauty of any natural scenery." Frederick Law Olmstead, Jr. (son of the famous landscape designer), one of the few present who had actually visited the monument to conduct a recreational survey for the NPS and Reclamation in 1943, argued that the monument was worth protecting and would be "greatly damaged and reduced" by a dam and its reservoir.

Conservationists and wilderness advocates asserted repeatedly that the values of protected parks and wilderness were important and demanded by the public. Indeed, visitation to national parks had grown nationwide by more than 40 percent since 1940. Conservationists argued that untrammeled wilderness was vital for emotional and spiritual renewal and well-being, especially in the face of modern, rapid-paced industrial life. The president of the American Planning and Civic Association said, "Our industrial civilization is creating an ever greater need for the average man, woman, and child to re-establish contact with nature, to be inspired by and appreciate the wonders of nature, and to be diverted from the whirling wheels of machinery and chance." Kenneth Morrison of the National Audubon Society made a similar point: "Even a few days in places where canyons rise sharply overhead, swift waters tumble at their feet, and bird songs blend with wind through trees, sends wilderness travelers back home with renewed mental and physical vigor." (See the sidebar "Flooding the Sistine Chapel" on page 54.)

While dam opponents extolled the values and importance of preserving wilderness, they were in fact most concerned with the principle of the matter—preserving the integrity of the national park system. They argued that the principle of park inviolability had to be protected, both to satisfy the purposes for which the national park system had been created and, just as important, to avoid setting a dangerous precedent. General Ulysses S. Grant III (grandson of the former president), a 40-year veteran of the Army Corps of Engineers (Corps), declared, "Such a precedent, if allowed, will naturally and necessarily be emulated over and over again, whenever anyone finds some possible profit in the similar desecration and injury to other National Parks and Monuments." Although he was not present, Harold Ickes, former secretary of the interior under President Roosevelt, made a similar point in his submitted statement. "Once a national park has been created, they should be held inviolable. To violate one monument is to invite violation of others. We must mean what we say when we declare that any area is to be dedicated to future generations." Defenders of the national park system had cause to worry. Since World War II, numerous national parks had been pressured to open up to mining and extraction of natural resources. The pressure continued, even in some of the nation's most celebrated parks. Dam proposals were currently pending in places like Glacier, Mammoth Cave, and Kings Canyon national parks, as well as Grand Canyon National Monument.

Most of the groups who opposed damming Echo Park were by no means radical opponents of economic development or natural resource use. In fact, they stressed that their opposition was quite specific to Dinosaur National Monument, and they were eager to appear reasonable. Joe Penfold of the Izaak Walton League said, "We recognize thoroughly the importance of water. No one in his right mind can be opposed to the sound and logical development of that prime resource." A representative of the Sierra Club said, "I am in thorough accord with the basic conception that our rivers must be developed for power and water, so far as is economically feasible and not inconsistent with more important national policies." Horace Albright, past NPS director under Presidents Hoover and Roosevelt, stated, "It would be . . . silly . . . for us to claim that all of the scenic areas in the United States . . . should be preserved without encroachment. We do not take that stand."

(continues on page 56)

FLOODING THE SISTINE CHAPEL

On January 21, 1963, the same day that the Glen Canyon Dam finally began to fill its reservoir, Secretary of Interior Stewart Udall and Reclamation commissioner Floyd Dominy stood before a crowd of reporters in Washington, D.C., to announce plans for a Pacific Southwest Water Plan (Plan). In addition to other reclamation projects, the Plan envisioned two new dams on the Colorado River, one in Marble Gorge and the other in Bridge Canyon— at opposite ends of Grand Canyon National Park. Marble Gorge Dam, 12 miles from the park's northern border, would create a 40-mile-long reservoir upriver from Grand Canyon National Park. Bridge Canyon Dam, downriver of the park, would back water up the Colorado River for 93 miles, flooding about 40 miles of the lower portions of the greater Grand Canyon and 13 miles of Grand Canyon National Park itself. The purpose of these dams was to provide hydroelectric power to pump water from existing reservoirs on the Colorado River, up over 1,200-foot mountain ranges and into the Phoenix-Tucson corridor in southern Arizona.

The Sierra Club's David Brower was at the press conference when the secretary and the commissioner made their announcement. Brower had just flown in to make one last plea to delay the filling of Glen Canyon's reservoir. However, the new plan to erect dams within the Grand Canyon quickly took center stage. This was an affront to the national park system like no other. With lessons learned from the recent battles over Echo Park and Rainbow Bridge, conservationists geared up to fight once again. This time, conservationists sought out technical experts from the start in order to critique the proposed dams on technical grounds. They argued against the need for the two dams and emphasized the high costs of construction—nearly $1 billion for the pair—as well as operation. They pointed out that it would be much cheaper to obtain the needed electricity from modern coal-fired power plants. Indeed, coal deposits were abundant in the area. A number of witnesses who appeared before Congress to oppose the dams voiced confidence that nuclear power would be a cheaper alternative as well. Moreover, they argued that there was not nearly enough water in the Colorado River to support two more reservoirs that would simply lose water to evaporation and seepage. This was all the more unacceptable because the reservoirs would not be used to supply water, but simply to produce power.

However, it was the publicity campaign that seemed to have the biggest political influence. By spring 1966, national periodicals were publishing articles critical of the dams. Dan Dreyfus, an official with Reclamation at the time, recalled the magnitude of the response. "Right after the *Reader's Digest* article, *Life* ran a big, goddamned diatribe. Then we got plastered by *My Weekly Reader* [a children's newspaper]. You're in deep shit when you catch it from them. Mailbags were coming in by the hundreds stuffed with letters from school kids." Beginning in June 1966, David Brower worked with a San Francisco advertising agency to publish newspaper ads attacking the dams. The first was a two-page ad declaring in bold lettering: "NOW ONLY YOU CAN SAVE GRAND CANYON FROM BEING FLOODED . . . FOR PROFIT." The text below read, "This time it's the Grand Canyon they want to flood. *The Grand Canyon*." The day after the ad ran, the Sierra Club was visited by a messenger from the Internal Revenue Service (IRS) with a letter warning that its tax-exempt status was in jeopardy because of its efforts to influence legislation—something nonprofits are prohibited from doing. Whether or not the IRS action was politically motivated, its swift and conspicuous enforcement generated even more publicity and sympathy for the Sierra Club. More important, conservationists were not deterred. In response to repeated government arguments that the reservoirs would make the Grand Canyon's sights even more accessible to the public, the Sierra Club ran another ad in August 1966 that rhetorically asked, "SHOULD WE ALSO FLOOD THE SISTINE CHAPEL SO TOURISTS CAN GET NEARER THE CEILING?"

The aggressive publicity campaign had a dramatic impact, spawning unprecedented volumes of letters to the House and Senate. Dreyfus said, "I never saw anything like it. Letters were arriving in dump trucks. Ninety-five percent of them said we'd better keep our mitts off the Grand Canyon and a lot of them quoted the Sierra Club ads." The weight of political pressure was too much. In February 1967, Interior Secretary Udall finally withdrew support for the Bridge Canyon Dam (Marble Gorge had already been withdrawn months before) and Congress authorized the larger project a year later without the dams. In place of the hydroelectric power to pump water to Arizona, Reclamation purchased power from coal-fired power plants. One of these was the Navajo Generating Station, constructed on the south shore of Lake Powell and fueled by strip-mined coal from Black Mesa on the Navajo and Hopi reservations. This generating station was later blamed for creating smog in the Grand Canyon.

(continued from page 53)
Widening the Debate

In June 1950, two months after the hearing, Interior Secretary Chapman announced his decision in favor of Echo Park Dam. He explained that he had been impressed by the low evaporation rates as well as the fact that the possibility of dams within the monument had been openly contemplated since its enlargement in 1938. Conservationists and their allies were stunned, while dam proponents were gleeful. However, the battle had only just begun. A month after the secretary's announcement, Bernard DeVoto, a popular columnist, published a scathing critique of the Echo Park Dam proposal in the *Saturday Evening Post,* a widely read periodical. His article, entitled "Shall We Let Them Ruin Our National Parks?" drew national attention to the controversy, especially after it was reprinted a few months later in *Reader's Digest.*

DeVoto's article galvanized conservation-minded Americans and others who were sympathetic to the national parks and generated a flood of angry letters to DOI, although not everyone was in agreement with DeVoto's position. (See "'Shall We Let Them Ruin Our National Parks?' 1950," and "'There's Plenty of Scenery for Us Western Natives,' 1950," on pages 66 and 67 in the Primary Sources section.)

The controversy grew when NPS director Newton Drury suddenly resigned in April 1951. However, the most influential critique came not from bad publicity but rather from mounting evidence of inconsistencies in Reclamation's calculations of revenue to be generated from Echo Park's power production. These inconsistencies were revealed as critics sought alternatives that did not require dams within the monument in order to meet the stated water storage and power needs of CRSP. By late 1951, the weight of such critiques had begun to change Chapman's mind. In December 1952, he issued his final report on CRSP and reversed his earlier approval of the Echo Park Dam. All was not lost for dam proponents, however. In January 1953, Dwight Eisenhower assumed the presidency and appointed Douglas McKay as his new secretary of the interior. In December 1953, Secretary McKay announced his acceptance of CRSP and of the Echo Park Dam, clearing the way for the issue to be taken up by Congress.

The controversy over Echo Park hit its high point between 1954 and 1956, during which time Congress held four separate hearings on

CRSP and Echo Park. (See "'The Dam at Dinosaur,' 1954" on page 68 in the Primary Sources section.) The CRSP bill that came before Congress in January 1954 proposed six large dams and 12 participating irrigation projects throughout the upper basin with an up-front price tag of $1.3 billion. In the years leading up to the legislative debates, however, conservation organizations had become more sophisticated in creating publicity around the controversy and in mobilizing political opposition. Since 1950, thousands had trekked or boated through Dinosaur National Monument and Echo Park, discovering its charm and communicating their enthusiasm to friends and family. In 1954, 71,000 people visited the national monument—three times the number of people who came the year before. Conservation organizations collaborated to produce a flood of publicity through news and opinion articles in major publications, pamphlets, books, and even independently produced films. By the spring and summer of 1954, letters to Congress were tallied at 80 to 1 against the Echo Park Dam.

The campaign against Echo Park Dam was aided significantly by political opponents of the entire CRSP bill. California representatives opposed the projects for fear that they would affect the quality and quantity of water downriver in the lower basin. Members of Congress from the East and Midwest were increasingly critical of the merits and costs of large reclamation projects in the West, and CRSP proponents struggled to maintain political support in the face of growing hostility from so many quarters. Conservationists undermined some of Reclamation's credibility and created delay when they exposed a basic (and embarrassing) mathematical error in Reclamation's calculation of evaporation rates from different dam alternatives—a central premise in Secretary McKay's approval of Echo Park Dam. While most conservationists had been quick to assert that their opposition was strictly concerned with preserving the integrity of Dinosaur National Monument, their efforts to undermine the bureau's rationale for Echo Park Dam naturally allied them with critics of CRSP as a whole.

By summer and fall 1955, CRSP supporters in Congress were losing political support and made tentative offers to consider alternatives to Echo Park in order to mollify conservationists and lessen opposition to the CRSP bill as a whole. However, Secretary McKay continued to express support for the version of CRSP that included Echo Park Dam. On November 1, 1955, senators from upper basin states convened a special meeting in Denver to consider their options with regard to Echo Park and the CRSP bill. In anticipation of the special meeting, conservationists took out a full-page advertisement in the *Denver Post* on October 31, declaring their opposition to the entire CRSP so long as any version of the bill "needs, encompasses, anticipates, or secretly hopes for a dam or reservoir in a National Park or Monument."

OUTCOME AND IMPACT

CRSP supporters finally acquiesced to conservationist demands. They agreed to remove Echo Park Dam from the bill. On November 29, 1955, Secretary McKay announced the deletion of the dam from CRSP. California members of Congress tried to convince the conservationists to continue their fight against the entire CRSP, warning them that they would be fooled and lose in the long run. Some conservationists, such as the Sierra Club's executive director, David Brower, wanted to continue opposition to CRSP, having come to believe that the alternatives to an Echo Park Dam were no better and possibly even worse.

Conservationists had lobbied Reclamation to offset the water and power lost from Echo Park by raising the height and water storage capacity of Glen Canyon Dam, another CRSP dam slated for construction on the Colorado River near Lee's Ferry, Arizona. While Glen Canyon was not within a national park or monument, Brower had come to believe that the loss of this scenic area would be no less tragic. In addition, the added capacity at Glen Canyon Dam would mean that the reservoir water could intrude into Rainbow Bridge National Monument, a natural stone arch in a side canyon farther upriver. However, the majority of conservation organizations accepted the higher Glen Canyon alternative —with provisos to protect Rainbow Bridge—because it would protect Dinosaur National Monument (the key issue of their campaign). In addition, they wanted to honor their promise to CRSP supporters to withdraw opposition if the Echo Park Dam was removed.

As part of the agreement, two provisos were added to the CRSP bill. The first proviso stated, "It is the intention of Congress that no dam or reservoir constructed under the authorization of this Act shall be within any national park or monument." The second proviso stated that,

"As part of the construction, operation, and maintenance of the Glen Canyon unit the Secretary of the Interior shall take adequate protective measures to preclude impairment of the Rainbow Bridge National Monument." In late January 1956, conservation groups signed an open letter declaring the withdrawal of their opposition to CRSP. With the removal of conservationist opposition, the bill was now able to move forward.

The final CRSP legislation was approved by Congress in late March 1956 and signed into law by President Eisenhower on April 11, 1956. The final legislation authorized $750 million for the construction of four main storage dams—Curecanti Dam on the Gunnison River in Colorado, Flaming Gorge Dam on the Green River in Wyoming, Navajo Dam on the San Juan River in New Mexico, and Glen Canyon Dam on the Colorado River in Arizona—as well as 11 irrigation projects. Conservationists hailed the defeat of Echo Park Dam as a significant victory for the national parks and for wilderness preservation, although it would later be regarded as a bittersweet victory as more people came to lament the loss of Glen Canyon and the unfulfilled promise to protect Rainbow Bridge National Monument. (See the sidebar "The Place No One Knew" on page 44 and *"Lake Powell: Jewel of the Colorado, 1965,"* on page 69 in the Primary Sources section.)

The Echo Park controversy was a major milestone in the development of the wilderness movement and conservation more generally, because it marked the first time that wilderness advocates wielded sufficient political power to thwart large-scale economic development in the West. Conservation and wilderness preservation advocates established their cause as a legitimate public concern and a political force to be reckoned with. Finally, the conflict helped bring attention by conservation groups and the general public to the long-neglected American West.

WHAT IF?

What if conservationists had opposed the entire CRSP and not just the proposal to dam Echo Park? Could they have saved more than just Dinosaur National Monument?

If conservationists had decided to oppose the entire CRSP it is likely that the entire bill would have been delayed indefinitely as a result of the combined political opposition of conservationists, the California delegation, and members of Congress from the East and Midwest. CRSP proponents were struggling to maintain political support and had already delayed a full vote on the bill several times in order to shore up support and avoid an official defeat. Most CRSP proponents were convinced that California represented the largest threat, and many openly suspected that conservationists were simply acting on California's behalf in order to secure a monopoly on the Colorado River. At the same time, conservationists were the only opponents of significance who were offering to strike a bargain. The same political leverage that allowed conservationists to bargain was also the only viable option for CRSP supporters to win passage.

While defeat of CRSP in the late 1950s would have spared more canyons from dams, it may only have created a delay, rather than a permanent fix. Like most political struggles, no decision is ever permanent. As before, CRSP supporters could simply bide their time and revive their proposals in the future when political conditions were better. More significant, no compromise on the CRSP legislation would also have meant that there was no proviso in the final legislation precluding the construction of dams within national parks and monuments. Without this legislation, conservationists would have to revisit the battle over the integrity of the national park system every time a development project was proposed.

There would have been political costs to an aggressive stance against the entire CRSP as well. Howard Zahniser, executive secretary of the Wilderness Society, was one of the key individuals who brokered the delicate deal with CRSP proponents on the rewording of the final legislation to preclude dams from national parks and monuments. Since 1947, the Wilderness Society had pursued the idea of creating a national wilderness system to protect undisturbed and remote areas of high scenic value. Soon after CRSP was signed into law, Zahniser resumed work on a national wilderness system, which would eventually come to fruition with the 1964 Wilderness Act—a landmark law preserving millions of acres of wilderness throughout the country. In the meantime, Zahniser needed to cultivate political support and avoid creating too many political enemies. Wholesale opposition to CRSP, and its defeat, would have clearly created more enemies, making future passage of the Wilderness Act less certain and possibly costing the wilderness movement more in the long run. Indeed, after passage of CRSP and its compromise provisos, resentful delegates from the upper Colorado River basin steadfastly blocked proposals to expand Dinosaur National Monument or to convert it to a national park.

CHRONOLOGY

1869 *May–August:* John Wesley Powell, an American Civil War veteran, takes a three-month journey exploring the Colorado River via boat; names Echo Park, Glen Canyon, and various other features. His exploits are popularized in print. He becomes head of U.S. Geological Survey in 1879.

1902 Reclamation Act passed, creating Reclamation Service (later Bureau of Reclamation).

1915 President Woodrow Wilson creates 80-acre Dinosaur National Monument on Utah-Colorado border to protect dinosaur fossils.

1922 *June:* Supreme Court rules that law of prior appropriation applies regardless of state lines.
December 22: Colorado River Compact is signed by six states: Colorado, Utah, Wyoming, New Mexico, Nevada, and California. Arizona refuses.

1928 Colorado River Compact is approved by Congress and signed into law by outgoing president Calvin Coolidge. Hoover Dam is approved by Congress, along with need for only six states to sign on.

1935 Hoover Dam is completed.

1946 Bureau of Reclamation releases "The Colorado River: A Comprehensive Report on the Development of Water Resources: A Natural Menace Becomes a Natural Resource."

1950 *April 3:* Interior Secretary Oscar Chapman convenes a public hearing to resolve dispute between the National Park Service and Reclamation over damming of Echo Park within Dinosaur National Monument.
June 27: Interior Secretary Chapman rules in favor of Reclamation proposal.
July 22: Bernard DeVoto's article "Shall We Let Them Ruin Our National Parks?" appears in *Saturday Evening Post* criticizing proposal to inundate Dinosaur National Monument.
Conservation organizations begin to mobilize against flooding of Dinosaur National Monument.

1952 *December:* Interior Secretary Chapman reverses decision favoring Echo Park Dam.

1953 *Summer:* David Brower organizes trips on the Green River through Dinosaur National Monument. Many tourists visit Green and Yampa Rivers and Dinosaur National Monument in response to articles in *Saturday Evening Post* and *Reader's Digest.* *December:* Interior Secretary Douglas McKay issues report favoring the Colorado River Storage Project (CRSP) with Echo Park Dam.

1954 *January 18:* House Subcommittee on Irrigation and Reclamation begins hearings on CRSP with particular attention to Echo Park Dam in Dinosaur National Monument.
June: Senate Subcommittee on Irrigation and Reclamation holds hearings; largely a repeat of testimony in House. Brower advocates higher Glen Canyon Dam so long as effort is made to protect Rainbow Bridge National Monument.

1955 *January:* Sierra Club publishes *This Is Dinosaur.* Copies are mailed to every member of Congress.
March: Reclamation testifies to Senate on CRSP hearings that Glen Canyon Dam is a favorable dam site. On March 30, Senate Interior Committee favorably reports CRSP bill.
April 2: Senate bill S. 500 passes by 53 to 28—authorizes construction of six dams and storage reservoirs, including Glen Canyon and Echo Park.
July 8: House Interior Committee favorably reports CRSP bill without Echo Park.
August 2: House goes into recess without taking action on CRSP to avoid close vote and to deal with conservationist opposition.
October: Meeting of upper basin officials takes place in Denver. Howard Zahniser flies to Denver and takes out full-page ad in *Denver Post* on Oct. 31 threatening total opposition to CRSP by conservationists if Echo Park Dam is not completely deleted.
November: Interior Secretary Douglas McKay announces decision to drop plans for Echo Park Dam in Dinosaur National Monument.

1956 *January 23:* Brower, Zahniser, and other conservationists draft a letter to Colorado representative Wayne Aspinall withdrawing opposition to CRSP.
March 28: House-Senate conference report on CRSP is approved.

April 11: President Eisenhower signs CRSP bill into law.

October 15: Construction of Glen Canyon Dam officially begins.

1960 *May:* House Committee on Appropriations deletes $3.5 million from Reclamation budget in public works appropriation bill specifically earmarked for Rainbow Bridge protection. Committee states that it sees "no purpose in undertaking an additional expenditure in the vicinity of $20 million in order to complete the complicated structures."

1962 *December 12:* National Park Association files suit in U.S. District Court in Washington, D.C., for preliminary injunction to prevent Interior Secretary Udall from closing water diversion gates at Glen Canyon.

1963 *January 21:* Brower flies out to Washington, D.C., to make last plea with Interior Secretary Stewart Udall to save Glen Canyon. Udall and Reclamation commissioner Floyd Dominy announce the Pacific Southwest Water Plan.

High-pressure gates in right diversion tunnel are closed, initiating filling of Glen Canyon's reservoir.

March: Sierra Club publishes *The Place No One Knew.*

1964 *September 3:* Wilderness Act is signed into law by President Lyndon B. Johnson. It creates the legal definition of wilderness in the United States and protects some 9 million acres of federal land.

1965 Reclamation issues *Lake Powell: Jewel of the Colorado* book and film.

1966 *June 9:* Sierra Club runs national ad campaign to criticize Grand Canyon dams.

September 22: Glen Canyon Dam is dedicated by Lady Bird Johnson.

1967 *January:* Interior Secretary Udall cancels both Grand Canyon dams.

DISCUSSION QUESTIONS

1. Was Echo Park an appropriate location for a dam and reservoir? Why or why not?

2. How was the debate over a dam at Echo Park influenced by the original 1922 Colorado River Compact?
3. Why were conservationists so opposed to a dam within Dinosaur National Monument?
4. Dam proponents complained that most of those who opposed Echo Park Dam, including most conservationists, were not residents of the upper Colorado River basin. Was this a legitimate criticism? Why or why not?
5. In the debates over the damming of Echo Park and other canyons, proponents argued that reservoirs would allow many more people to see the sights of the canyons. Indeed, many of these places were almost unknown to the general public and somewhat inaccessible. Was this a legitimate argument? Why or why not?
6. In order to save Echo Park, conservationists struck a deal with dam proponents to support a higher Glen Canyon Dam. Was this a good compromise? Why or why not?

WEB SITES

Dinosaur National Monument. National Park Service. Available online. URL: http://www.nps.gov/dino. Accessed March 21, 2011.

Reclamation History Web site. U.S. Bureau of Reclamation. Available online. URL: http://www.usbr.gov/history/index.html. Accessed March 21, 2011.

Survey of the Recreational Resources of the Colorado River Basin: Dinosaur National Monument. National Park Service online book. Available online. URL: http://www.nps.gov/history/history/online_books/colorado/chap9.htm. Accessed March 21, 2011.

BIBLIOGRAPHY

Cosco, Jon M. *Echo Park: Struggle for Preservation.* Boulder, Colo.: Johnson Books, 1995.

Farmer, Jared. *Glen Canyon Dammed: Inventing Lake Powell and the Canyon Country.* Tucson: University of Arizona Press, 1999.

Harvey, Mark T. *A Symbol of Wilderness: Echo Park and the American Conservation Movement.* Albuquerque: University of New Mexico Press, 1994.

Martin, Russell. *A Story That Stands Like a Dam: Glen Canyon and the Struggle for the Soul of the West.* New York: Henry Holt, 1989.

Nash, Roderick. *Wilderness and the American Mind.* Rev. ed. New Haven, Conn.: Yale University Press, 1979.

Porter, Eliot. *The Place No One Knew: Glen Canyon on the Colorado.* San Francisco, Calif.: Sierra Club, 1963.

Powell, James Lawrence. *Dead Pool: Lake Powell, Global Warming, and the Future of Water in the West.* Berkeley: University of California Press, 2008.

Reisner, Marc. *Cadillac Desert: The American West and Its Disappearing Water.* New York: Viking Penguin, 1986.

Richardson, Elmo. *Dams, Parks & Politics: Resource Development & Preservation in the Truman-Eisenhower Era.* Lexington: University Press of Kentucky, 1973.

Stegner, Wallace, ed. *This Is Dinosaur: Echo Park Country and Its Magic Rivers.* New York: Alfred A. Knopf, 1955.

Worster, Donald. *Rivers of Empire: Water, Aridity & The Growth of The American West.* New York: Pantheon, 1985.

PRIMARY SOURCES

Document 1: "Wealth from Water," 1946

In 1946, the U.S. Bureau of Reclamation issued a report that described numerous possible irrigation and hydroelectric projects throughout the Colorado River basin. The report provided technical details about the logistics and potential benefits of these projects, but it also served as a promotional tool for resource development in the West. This is an excerpt from one chapter of that report.

Thousands of acres of desert land in the Colorado River Basin produce nothing more than sagebrush or cacti. Millions of acre-feet of water waste annually into the Pacific Ocean. Billions of tons of copper, coal, and other minerals lie buried in mountains. In their present state this land, this water, and these minerals are not wealth because they are not being utilized economically. They can, however, become wealth or produce wealth. Man's ingenious nature has assured him of this. Water can be brought to this land to produce crops; these minerals can be mined and processed with an abundance of low-cost hydroelectric energy made available; trade can be established; and in general, the wealth produced can be converted into more and better opportunities for the American people. . . .

The Colorado River Basin is in the heart of the arid west where water, because of scarcity, is especially precious. The basin has vast resources in land, fuels, oils, fertilizers, timber, metals, and recreational attractions, all dependent on water in one way or another for their development. Only by irrigation can this parched land become productive. Water is required to preserve and enhance the excellent fishing and recreational allurements. Water and the electric energy that can be generated by falling water are necessary to bring forth and process the basin's great mineral wealth. Water, so important, and yet so limited in this area, is the resource that above all others will determine the extent to which the bounties of the Colorado River Basin can be pressed into the service of the Nation. . . .

Any water unused today is lost forever to useful purpose. Each year that development is delayed diminishes the potential cumulative value of the water to mankind. Delay means waste, loss of potential wealth. Said Herbert Hoover, 'Every drop of water that runs to the sea without rendering a commercial return is a public waste.' . . . The welfare of the Nation demands that the most be made of this 'National resource,' the waters of the Colorado River.

Source: Bureau of Reclamation. U.S. Department of the Interior. "Wealth from Water." Chapter VII of *The Colorado River—"A Natural Menace Becomes A National Resource":* A Comprehensive Report on the Development of the Water Resources of the Colorado River Basin for Irrigation, Power Production, and Other Beneficial Uses in Arizona, California, Colorado, Nevada, New Mexico, Utah, and Wyoming. Washington, D.C.: Bureau of Reclamation, 1946.

—∞—

Document 2: "Shall We Let Them Ruin Our National Parks?" 1950

In June 1950, Secretary of the Interior Oscar Chapman announced preliminary approval of the proposal to construct the Echo Park Dam. While conservation organizations were quite aware and concerned about this decision, the general public was not. Bernard DeVoto, an established journalist and longtime critic of the U.S. Bureau of Reclamation and other western development interests, decided to change that. A month after the secretary's announcement, DeVoto published a scathing critique of the decision in the Saturday Evening Post. *His article not only attacked the merits of the project but drew widespread attention from the general public and, just as important, from people outside the region.*

No Western state should receive any benefit from the construction of these dams inside the monument that could not be insured by alternative construction outside it. What about the people of the United States as a whole whose property the monument is? On behalf of sectional and even local interests, the general public will have to pay the non-recoverable cost, always a large fraction of the total cost, of a $207,000,000 project. In return it will suffer the permanent ruin of an area of great natural beauty.

For it will be permanently ruined. If you cut down a forest, Nature will probably grow another one in the course of a few centuries, but if you change a river, a mountain or a canyon, you can never change it back again. The downriver dam in Dinosaur Monument [Split Mountain] would defile the mountain-park country along and below it and substitute a placid reservoir for the turbulent river above it. The other one, Echo Park Dam, would back water so far that throughout the whole extent of Lodore Canyon the Green River, the tempestuous, pulse-stirring river of John Wesley Powell, would become a mere millpond. The same would happen to Yampa Canyon. Throughout both canyons the deep artificial lakes would engulf magnificent scenery, would reduce by from a fifth to a third the height of the precipitous walls, and would fearfully degrade the great vistas. Echo Park and its magnificent rock formations would be submerged. Dinosaur National Monument as a scenic spectacle would cease to exist.

Source: Bernard DeVoto. "Shall We Let Them Ruin Our National Parks?" *Saturday Evening Post* (July 22, 1950) p. 17. © SEPS licensed by Curtis Licensing.

—⚜—

Document 3: "There's Plenty of Scenery for Us Western Natives," 1950

DeVoto's widely read critique of the Echo Park Dam drew a strong reaction from editorialists in local newspapers, such as the Salt Lake Tribune *and the* Denver Post. *They resented the intrusion of "outside" interests into what they regarded as essentially a local issue of economic development. Some accused DeVoto of secretly working in concert with the National Park Service to undermine long-promised development projects.*

Mr. DeVoto complains that local, western communities have lined up behind the reclamation bureau in support of the Dinosaur monument dam projects. Is that any worse than for Mr. DeVoto to play the game of another government agency—the national park service which is opposed to the dams and apparently has inspired Mr. DeVoto's switch from concern about the welfare of people to concern about scenery.

One thing Mr. DeVoto forgets: There's plenty of scenery left in our west for us natives. We see no reason to encourage those who want to maintain the west as a colony so that nature-lovers from east of the Alleghenys can come out every five to ten years to sniff the clean air. Despite the 'desecration' of Dinosaur monument, there's still plenty of scenery left for all America.

Source: "There's Plenty of Scenery for Us Western Natives." *Denver Post* (July 22, 1950).

—∞—

Document 4: "The Dam at Dinosaur," 1954

Criticism of the Echo Park Dam proposal came from throughout the country. The letter to the editor below expresses common arguments by dam critics who asserted a legitimate stake in the issue. Moreover, these critics called for due consideration of "intangible" values of wilderness preservation.

This is a matter in which all the people of the country have a direct interest. It is a fair question whether a national monument should be invaded and virtually destroyed even if the proposed location for the dam were the only practicable one. There are intangible values that even in this materialistic age are still considered of prime importance. But the suggested site is not the only one, nor is it, according to some experts, the cheapest or most efficient. Congress should not be high-pressured into this proposal.

Source: "The Dam at Dinosaur." *New York Times* (March 9, 1954): p. 26.

—∞—

Document 5: *Lake Powell: Jewel of the Colorado,* 1965

Floyd Dominy, commissioner of the U.S. Bureau of Reclamation from 1959 to 1969, was a controversial figure who oversaw the completion of the Glen Canyon Dam and many others. In order to counter the aggressive publicity campaign by conservation organizations against the dam and its reservoir, Dominy produced a booklet extolling the virtues of Glen Canyon's Lake Powell reservoir. He wrote much of the text himself. Thousands of copies were printed and distributed to every member of Congress and other important government officials.

Sired by the muddy Colorado in magnificent canyon country, a great blue lake has been born in the West. It is called Lake Powell. When full, it will be 186 miles long. Its shoreline will total 1,860 miles. It formed behind Glen Canyon Dam, which is at the town of Page, Ariz. The lake begins in the northern part of that State. Most of it is in Utah.

Lake Powell holds working water—water for many purposes. And one of those purposes is to provide the people of this country with the finest scenic and recreational area in the country. . . . All you need is a boat—or there are excursion boats for hire if you prefer. Where you go and what you do in this water wonderland is for your personal choice. You are rich with opportunity before you begin.

I'd like to invite you to visit Lake Powell and especially to see that natural marvel Rainbow Bridge. Before Lake Powell, Rainbow Bridge National Monument could be visited only by the rugged few who 'packed' in. Now all of you can see it—easily. Your boat will moor to floating docks at the entrance to Rainbow Bridge Canyon. Then you take a walk on a trail along the canyon's side. You'll find the bridge undamaged by Lake Powell's waters—for even when the lake is at maximum elevation its waters can never reach the ledge upon which the bridge rests. And you can marvel at its arched and graceful beauty in the peace and quiet of its natural setting. How can I describe the sculpture and colors along Lake Powell's shores? Every time I go back, I search again for a new set of words. And they always seem inadequate.

Over eons of time, wind and rain have carved the sandstone into shapes to please ten thousand eyes. The graceful, the dramatic, the grand, the fantastic. Evolution into convolution and involution. Sharp edges, round edges, blunt edges, soaring edges. Spires, cliffs, and castles in the sky.

Colors like a symphony of Nature's music. Bright orange, brick red, ocher, pink, deep brown, vivid purple, granite black, mustard yellow—and a soft, pale green so delicate no artist could ever capture it with paint.

If I sound partisan toward Lake Powell, you are correct. I am proud of this aquatic wonder and want to share it with you.

Do you like to fish? Lake Powell has been stocked with millions of trout and bass. They'll be good fighting size this summer and good eating, too.

Feel like exploring? Hundreds of side canyons—where few ever trod before the lake formed—are yours. They have names like Cathedral and Twilight—the list is long and many are still nameless.

Fun sports? Yes. This is sun country. Water skiing, swimming, scuba diving—all in clean, blue water that looks like deep blue sky.

And if you feel lazy and just want to soak up sun and beauty, this is your place. Don't hike—amble. Lie in the sun. Putter along the shore. You'll never run out of places and space.

Source: Bureau of Reclamation. United States Department of the Interior. *Lake Powell: Jewel of the Colorado.* Washington, D.C.: Government Printing Office, 1965.

3

NATIONAL ENVIRONMENTAL POLICY ACT (NEPA) OF 1969:
Does NEPA Create New and Enforceable Duties on the Government to Treat the Environment Differently?

—ᵐ—

THE CONTROVERSY

The Issue

The National Environmental Policy Act of 1969 (NEPA) was an important development in the evolution of the nation's approach to the environment. The law declared an ambitious set of environmental goals and values for the nation. It charged federal agencies with the task of evaluating and publicizing the environmental impacts of future actions significantly affecting the environment, and it created a Council on Environmental Quality (CEQ) to help implement the law and oversee the nation's environmental progress. When it was first passed, however, the law's newness and vague language created uncertainty as to how it should be implemented. In 1971, a group of environmental organizations opposing the construction of a nuclear power plant on the shore of Chesapeake Bay decided to test NEPA's potential by suing the U.S. Atomic Energy Commission (AEC) for not complying with NEPA. The lawsuit forced the court to address a fundamental question about the law: Did NEPA create new and enforceable duties on the government with respect to the environment? If so, what were these duties? The court's ruling would not only define the interpretation of NEPA, it would radically change the landscape of environmental politics.

♦ *Arguments that NEPA created new and enforceable obligations on the federal government to change its behavior and take environmental values seriously:* The framers of NEPA and the environmental group suing the AEC argued that the law was intended to force the federal government to take environmental impacts more seriously by incorporating environmental considerations and perspectives into the thinking and decision making of every federal activity. They argued that NEPA effectively expanded the responsibilities of all federal agencies to examine, document, and consider the full range of environmental impacts of their actions and to faithfully and meaningfully incorporate these considerations into their decision-making processes.

♦ **Arguments that NEPA was a general statement of policy goals and did not create new or specific obligations:** The AEC, like many other federal agencies, argued that NEPA was a flexible statement of environmental goals that left the specifics of implementation to the discretion of the agencies themselves. They argued that NEPA did not change their core missions, nor was it their responsibility to evaluate environmental impacts that were outside of their normal expertise. They argued that independent environmental analyses were unnecessary for issues that were already addressed by existing pollution control laws. Finally, the AEC argued that issues such as energy development were too important to be delayed by environmental reviews.

—❦—

INTRODUCTION

NEPA has been described as "the environmental Magna Carta"—the cornerstone of modern environmental law in the United States. NEPA established the concept of the environmental impact statement (EIS)—the requirement to assess the potential environmental impacts of any federally funded project that might significantly affect the environment *before* the project was started or completed. NEPA opened up government decision making to the public and enabled private citizens to sue in court if NEPA's requirements were not met—a powerful legal and political tool that threatened endless delay and could force even the largest entities to seek compromise with their opponents. NEPA was part of a flurry of environmental legislation in the late 1960s and early 1970s. President Richard Nixon signed the bill into law on January 1, 1970, at his West Coast home in San Clemente, California. The law's enactment made the front page of the *New York Times* the next day, though the headline—"Nixon Promises an Urgent Fight to End Pollution"—demonstrated some misunderstanding about the new legislation. The article focused heavily on the role of the CEQ, with barely any mention of the law's other provisions. However, the meaning and implications of NEPA were far from settled. It would take a court battle

President Richard Nixon is seen here on January 1, 1970, shortly after signing the National Environmental Policy Act of 1969 in his home office in San Clemente, California. (Richard M. Nixon Library and Birthplace, File/Associated Press)

to determine the potential and future of NEPA and environmental law more generally.

In spring 1971, the Calvert Cliffs' Coordinating Committee—an umbrella organization representing a number of environmental organizations—filed suit in federal court against the U.S. AEC for not complying with NEPA. The plaintiffs argued that the AEC failed to adequately assess the environmental impacts of nuclear power plants in its licensing processes, as required by NEPA. Moreover, they argued that the AEC inappropriately exempted numerous plants from the law's review requirements. The AEC contended that NEPA gave federal agencies the freedom to implement NEPA in ways that the agency deemed to be appropriate. More fundamentally, the AEC argued that it was not appropriate for it to perform independent analyses of environmental issues that were either outside of the agency's mission and expertise or else addressed by other state and federal laws. While the *Calvert Cliffs'* lawsuit was based on a dispute over a specific nuclear power plant in Maryland, it took on much wider significance because it essentially asked the court to rule on the meaning of NEPA: What duties, if any, did NEPA impose on federal agencies? How could compliance with the law be measured? The *Calvert Cliffs'* case was not the first lawsuit involving NEPA, but it was the one that would have the largest impact on the future interpretation of the law.

BACKGROUND

The 1960s saw a sea change in both the intensity and scope of environmental concerns. By the late 1960s and through the early 1970s, the environment became a widely popular and politically important issue for the nation. A growing sense of crisis over environmental degradation spurred lawmakers to action. Indeed, by the late 1960s, 120 members of Congress authored or cosponsored at least 30 separate environmental bills, which made their way through 19 separate congressional committees. The pressure for the government to do something about the environment had been building since the publication of Rachel Carson's *Silent Spring* in 1962. *Silent Spring* was an alarming wake-up call about the complex and unintended ecological consequences of the widespread use of pesticides and other synthetic chemicals. The chemical industry, along with more conservative scientists, attacked Carson's claims and her credibility, but her book resonated strongly with more critical scientists, the public, and many in the government. Fears of chemical exposure combined with growing concerns over pollution and exposure to radiation fallout from nuclear weapons testing, all of which seemed to point to a bleak future of environmental devastation. Concerns about the relationship between human activities and environmental quality, health, and safety greatly expanded the idea of what environmental conservation was about. In February 1965, President Lyndon Johnson described this new view of conservation in a "Special Message to the Congress on Conservation and Restoration of Natural Beauty." He said, "Our conservation must be not just the classic conservation of protection and development, but a creative conservation of restoration and innovation. Its concern is not with nature alone, but with the total relation between man and the world around him. Its object is not just man's welfare but the dignity of man's spirit."

Lawmakers responded to the growing sense of crisis by passing a variety of new environmental legislation: the Clean Water Act of 1960, Partial Nuclear Test Ban Treaty of 1963, Wilderness Act of 1964, Water Quality Act of 1965, and Solid Waste Disposal Act of 1965, to name a few. Despite the proliferation of environmental laws, there was still considerable frustration among lawmakers and the growing environmental community over this piecemeal and uncoordinated approach to environmental problems. These early environmental laws focused on one problem at a time, without addressing their interrelated aspects. For example, laws to prevent dumping of waste into bodies of water meant that the waste had to be diverted elsewhere, often to landfills. As space for landfills was scarce, many communities and industries incinerated their waste to reduce its volume, but waste incineration simply created or exacerbated air pollution problems. Equally problematic, the federal government itself seemed to occupy a contradictory role. Some agencies acted as protective stewards, while others were rapacious exploiters of the nation's natural resources. While the government tried to bring pollution and environmental degradation under control, agencies like the Bureau of Reclamation (Reclamation) or the Army Corps of Engineers (Corps) continued to follow their narrow agency missions of resource development, often without regard to the environmental impacts. Other agencies, such as the AEC, served incompatible roles: promoter of industry development and protector of public welfare from that industry. The government seemed to be in dire need of more coordinated and rational organization.

The effort to develop a more comprehensive and coordinated response received a significant boost with a House-Senate Joint Colloquium to Discuss a National Policy for the Environment. The colloquium, held on July 17, 1968, at the Capitol, was a special meeting between the Senate's Committee on Interior and Insular Affairs and the House of Representative's Committee on Science and Astronautics. The colloquium was cochaired by Senator Henry Jackson of Washington, chair of the Senate committee, and Representative George Miller of California, chair of the House committee. The purpose of the meeting was to discuss environmental management, committee jurisdictions, the need for better environmental information, and future directions for environmental policy. The event was attended by members of Congress, members of academia, and environmental groups. A specific item on the colloquium's agenda was a report issued by the Senate's Committee on Interior and Insular Affairs entitled *A National Policy for the Environment.* The report was written for the Senate committee by Lynton Caldwell, a professor of political science at Indiana University and a member of the Conservation Foundation. Professor Caldwell was one of the first professionals to write about the environment as a comprehensive policy issue that deserved attention from lawmakers in its own right. His report to the Senate provided an outline for a coordinated and unified approach to federal environmental policy.

During the colloquium, various speakers urged Congress to take action. They focused on the need for a uniform, empowering set of environmental goals and guidelines for the federal government that took into account the new environmental realities. Laurance S. Rockefeller, philanthropist and prominent conservationist, convened the 1968 colloquium with remarks about the need for institutional change. He said, "Our federal government structure is still designed for the problems of an earlier day. The basic allocation of responsibilities among departments reflects a nation which was predominantly rural, which had to dispose of its vast public lands and tame its rivers and forests. It is not designed for the complex, highly urban society in which we are now living, or the changed circumstances in our rural areas." A number of proposals for change came out of the colloquium: the need for uniform federal environmental goals and policy, the need for new legislation with new environmental ethics and administrative ideas, and strengthened congressional oversight. The ideas and proposals discussed at the colloquium were expanded and published in an influential congressional white paper. The paper argued for new environmental values and ethics and, notably, the importance of ecological analysis as a tool for planning.

> Alteration and use of the environment must be planned and controlled rather than left to arbitrary decision. Alternatives must be actively generated and widely discussed. Technological development, introduction of new factors affecting the environment, and modifications of the landscape must be planned to maintain the diversity of plants and animals. Furthermore, such activities should proceed only after an ecological analysis and projection of probable effects. Irreversible or difficult reversible challenges should be accepted only after the most thorough study.

The late 1960s saw an increasing number of proposals for government reorganization to better respond to environmental crises. While most of these proposals were never enacted, one set of ideas was successful. In 1969, Senator Jackson and Representative John Dingell of Michigan introduced separate bills in the Senate and House to create a council on environmental quality to oversee and coordinate the government's environmental programs and policies and to monitor and report on the state of the environment. These bills would eventually be joined to form NEPA. However the initial versions of these bills were still a far cry from what they would become through the process of hearings, compromises, and amendments. Senator Jackson introduced his bill, S.1075, on February 18, 1969. Jackson's bill directed the Secretary of the Interior to conduct ecological research on the state of the environment, and it established the CEQ to advise the president and to prepare an annual environmental report. Senator Jackson conducted hearings on his bill before the Committee on Interior and Insular Affairs on April 16, 1969. Much of the testimony from witnesses during the hearing supported the idea of creating a centralized source of ecological advice that could also provide oversight for the myriad agencies and departments that affected the environment. Some witnesses went so far as to suggest that the CEQ be given stop-order authority to halt, at least temporarily, environmentally destructive activities conducted by federal agencies. However, few committee members favored giving so much power to appointed officials.

The most influential advice and testimony came from Lynton Caldwell. Caldwell argued that an effective environmental policy needed to include a strong statement of the nation's environmental goals and benchmarks against which the nation's progress could be measured. At the same time, he cautioned that such a statement of environmental goals would be meaningless unless there was some way to force federal agencies to implement the policy.

> We ought to think of a statement which is so written that it is capable of implementation; that it is not merely a statement of desirable goals or objectives; but that is a statement which will compel or reinforce or assist all of these things, the executive agencies in particular, but going beyond this, the Nation as a whole, to take the kind of action which will protect and

reinforce what I have called the life support system of this country.

He proposed an action-forcing mechanism in the form of a requirement that agencies evaluate the effects of their proposed activities on the environment. He argued that all federally proposed activities be scrutinized for their environmental impacts. In addition, he suggested that the licensing procedures of regulatory agencies include requirements for the evaluation of environmental impacts.

After the committee hearings had concluded, Senator Jackson amended his bill in large part following Caldwell's suggestions. He deleted references to the secretary of the interior, added a more elaborate statement of national environmental goals and aspirations, and included a statement that "each person has a fundamental and inalienable right to a healthful environment." He added a section that expanded the authority of federal agencies to incorporate the goals articulated in this statute and included Section 102 of Title I, which provided the action-forcing mechanism that Caldwell had suggested. The latter directed federal agencies to develop environmental impact findings for all project proposals. The language describing the environmental impact findings was written by aides to the Senate committee who sought to make environmental considerations a key part of decision documents that accompanied all project proposals. In addition to documenting environmental consequences, the findings were to include alternative options for decision makers. The framers argued that once the environmental consequences of their projects were exposed, agencies would choose the least environmentally harmful course of action in order to fulfill the national environmental goals declared in Title I of the law. According to Caldwell, "Fewer environmentally controversial decisions would be made because ecologically injurious projects would be denied serious consideration in these early stages." Indeed, this idea spoke to the very heart of the bill's purpose: to infuse ecological consciousness and values into the federal government so that better environmental decisions would be made.

Both the House and the Senate must pass identical legislation before anything can be sent to the president for approval. Bills may originate in either chamber, but it is sometimes more efficient for senators and representatives to introduce similar bills simultaneously and then to reconcile the differences after the bills have passed their respective chambers. Congressman Dingell had introduced a proposal to create a council on environmental quality as early as 1967, but that bill made little headway. Dingell's reintroduced bill, H.R. 6750, was almost identical to Senator Jackson's bill—a brief statement of environmental policy, establishment of a CEQ, and the preparation of an annual environmental report to be submitted to the president and Congress. Dingell's subcommittee convened hearings on H.R. 6750 in May and June 1969, after those of Senator Jackson.

Both the House and Senate bills made their way relatively quickly through Congress. By summer 1969, the bills had been referred out of their respective subcommittees. Through savvy administrative maneuvering, Jackson's bill was approved by the full Senate on July 11 without debate or amendment. On the House side, Dingell's bill took a little longer because of resistance from Representative Wayne Aspinall of Colorado. Aspinall was concerned about the vagueness of the bill's language. He thought the use of the word "environment" was too broad and could cause jurisdictional problems between congressional committees. As a strong advocate of economic development of natural resources, Aspinall was also wary of providing conservationists with new tools to stop or delay economic development. The price of Aspinall's approval was the addition of a no change clause in the bill that stated: "Nothing in this Act shall increase, decrease, or change any responsibility or authority of any Federal official or agency created by other provisions of law." In addition, Aspinall would be given a seat at the House-Senate conference committee where the House and Senate versions would be melded. Before the two bills could be reconciled, however, Senator Jackson had to settle his own conflict with Senator Edmund Muskie of Maine. Senator Muskie chaired the Air and Water Pollution Subcommittee of the Senate Public Works Committee—the principal committee through which the nation's most important environmental legislation passed. As a distinguished champion of antipollution legislation, Muskie was certainly sympathetic to the intentions of Senator Jackson's bill. However, he was concerned that the proposed legislation would dilute or even cancel out already existing environmental laws and antipollution programs. More specifically, Muskie wanted to make sure that compliance with Jackson's NEPA would not replace or substitute compliance with other environmental laws or programs.

Muskie and Jackson differed on the basic philosophy of governance that underpinned the bill. Jackson wanted to improve the federal government's environmental behavior by forcing agencies to take responsibility for making better decisions. Muskie did not trust federal agencies that had previously been neglectful of the environment to either police themselves or to come to the right decision. Muskie warned that even when agencies were fully informed about the environmental consequences of their actions, they were still left with the final decision about whether to proceed with their proposals. He preferred some kind of external review with the possibility of sanctions or enforcement, whether through outside agencies, public opinion, judicial review, or criticism from other agencies. Following lengthy negotiations, Senators Muskie and Jackson agreed to several revisions to the bill. Environmental impact statements would be opened up to review by federal, state, and local agencies, the president, Congress, and the public. In order to answer Muskie's concerns about protecting existing environmental laws, a new section was added to the bill that stated that the preparation of an environmental impact statement would not change the obligation of federal agencies to comply with preexisting environmental laws or regulations.

In December 1969, the House-Senate conference managed to resolve the differences between the two bills, most of which tilted in favor of the Senate version. Among the more notable changes, Aspinall's no change provision was deleted and replaced with language granting "authority to every federal agency to implement the environmental policy act as part of its established responsibilities." In exchange, Jackson's provision that every citizen has a "right to a healthful environment" was deleted for fear that it would give new constitutional powers to environmentalists to go to court. Other more subtle changes in language were made as well. The conference report on the merged bill was approved by the Senate on December 20, 1969, with little debate. Most of the discussion consisted of statements by Senators Jackson and Muskie on the implication of NEPA for existing environmental laws and programs. House debate on the conference report took place on December 22, 1969, and it too was brief. Representative William Harsha of Ohio was the lone dissenting voice on the bill as a whole. He warned about the potentially large impact of NEPA. "I must warn the Members that they should be on guard against the ramifications of a measure that is so loose and ambiguous as this . . . this is a major revision of the administrative functions of the U.S. Government . . . The impact of S. 1075, if it becomes law, I am convinced, would be so wide sweeping as to involve every branch of the Government, every committee of Congress, every agency, and every program of the Nation." Harsha urged the House to delay a vote until January to allow for more debate, but with only three days before Christmas the House was eager to finish its business and adjourn. The bill passed without delay.

The final bill that arrived on President Nixon's desk was a remarkably brief document with what appeared to be straightforward, if vague, language. (See "National Environmental Policy Act of 1969," on page 100 in the Primary Sources section.) NEPA contains two titles. Title I declares a national environmental policy. The declaration of policy is followed by a list of six enumerated policy goals. Section 102 of Title I mandates that federal agencies follow NEPA's policies and use a "systematic, interdisciplinary approach" to prepare a "detailed statement" of environmental impacts, as well as alternatives. Title II directs the president to submit an annual environmental quality report, and it establishes a CEQ in the Executive Office to advise the president, gather information on the state and trends of the environment, and report these to the president, review the environmental performance of federal activities and programs, and develop and recommend policies to the president.

Despite the law's brevity, the press showed little understanding. The law received remarkably little attention from the environmental community either. President Nixon was lukewarm to the bill, but he signed it anyway, recognizing that there was more to be gained by embracing new environmental legislation than opposing it. (See "Statement by President Richard Nixon, January 1, 1970," on page 104 in the Primary Sources section.) In fact, President Nixon went one step further and created the Environmental Protection Agency at the end of 1970. (See the sidebar "Environmental Protection Agency" on page 82 and "William D. Ruckelshaus on the EPA, 1970," on page 105 in the Primary Sources section.) Public support for tougher environmental initiatives was at an all-time high. Indeed, the previous year had been an eventful one for environmental concern. In January 1969, a massive oil spill off the coast of Santa Barbara, California, had flooded the nation with images of oil-stained beaches and dying fish and birds. Six months later,

(continues on page 84)

ENVIRONMENTAL PROTECTION AGENCY

In 1970, the United States entered a new era of environmental policy that was characterized by a greatly expanded federal role. While the federal government had decades of experience in managing the nation's natural resources, it had relatively little experience in managing environmental quality, particularly with regard to pollution. Until this time, pollution control was treated as a local nuisance or a sanitation issue and considered the responsibility of state and local public health agencies. However, the increasing concern over pollution in the 1960s and the growing dissatisfaction with inadequate state and local environmental protection led to calls for greater federal involvement. In response, Congress passed more than a dozen new laws to protect public health and the environment from pollution, and it was the Environmental Protection Agency (EPA) that it charged with the task of enforcing these new mandates.

As with the flurry of new environmental laws, the EPA was born during a period of heightened environmental concerns. In 1969, President Richard Nixon created a task force to investigate institutional strategies to address the nation's environmental problems. Though he had little history of concern or involvement with environmental matters before this time, the president recognized the growing political importance of the environmental issue. He was eager to take some kind of visible action to burnish his environmental credentials with the public. Initially, the task force suggested the establishment of a new Department of Environment and Natural Resources (DENR). DENR would replace the Department of the Interior and absorb federal agencies concerned with resource development and environmental regulation: the Forest Service, Soil Conservation Service, Army Corps of Engineers, certain pesticide programs from the Department of Agriculture, and the newly created Air Pollution Control Program. The idea of a DENR-like agency had been floating around since at least the 1950s as part of a long-standing desire to create a single agency responsible for issues related to natural resources and conservation. However, critics had repeatedly argued that such an agency would only create problems by combining the conflicting goals of resource development and conservation. Conservationists were especially concerned that such an agency would be "captured" by the interests of powerful economic forces, as was often alleged of the Department of the Interior. When the task force presented its idea for DENR to the president and his cabinet in spring 1970, the same criticisms were raised once again. This time, however, they were joined by howls of protest from departments that stood to lose functions or personnel to the proposed agency. Worse, the president's advisers warned that such a drastic reorganization would anger key members of Congress because of the havoc it would cause with congressional committees that conducted oversight of those agencies. President Nixon was impressed by this opposition, and so the idea was dropped.

After the DENR idea was rejected, the president's task force proposed an alternative idea: Consolidate just the federal pollution control programs in a new, independent agency that would answer directly to the president. This alternative had the advantage of being highly visible to the public, but it was also a compromise between those who advocated radical reorganization and those who wanted no change at all. In July 1970, the president sent a reorganization plan to Congress to create an Environmental Protection Agency. The president declared: "Our national government today is not structured to make a coordinated attack on the pollutants which debase the air we breathe, the water we drink, and the land that grows our food. . . . Despite its complexity, for pollution control purposes the environment must be perceived as a single, interrelated system." The administration argued that the EPA would take a holistic approach to pollution and transcend the narrow mission bias of existing federal agencies.

With no formal opposition by Congress, the reorganization plan went into effect on September 9, 1970. The reorganization plan transferred pollution-related programs from across the government to the new agency: the Federal Water Quality Administration and the Office of Research on Effects of Pesticides on Wildlife and Fish from the Department of the Interior; the Bureau of Water Hygiene, Bureau of Solid Waste Management, the National Air Pollution Control Administration, the Bureau of Radiological Health, and the Office of Pesticide Research from the Department of Health, Education and Welfare; the Pesticides Regulation Division from the Department of Agriculture; the Division of Radiation Standards from the AEC; and the entire Interagency Federal Radiation Council. Almost overnight, a completely new agency with a budget of $1.4 billion and some 6,000 people came into existence to combat pollution.

(continued from page 81)
debris and oil on the heavily polluted Cuyahoga River in Cleveland, Ohio, caught fire. Such fires had happened many times before, but the image of a burning river caught the imagination of the press and the public as a symbol of the times and served to reinforce the idea that something was terribly wrong. A few months after Nixon signed NEPA into law, he appointed Russell Train, under secretary of the Department of the Interior and former president of the Conservation Foundation, as the first CEQ chairman.

The first year of NEPA's enactment was plagued by uncertainty about how to implement the law. Congressman Dingell played a constant watchdog role over the law's implementation and was commonly in disagreement with the CEQ and federal agencies about the proper interpretation of the law. While Dingell, the CEQ, and numerous federal agencies struggled to fill in the details on the meaning and reach of the law, it was the courts that would play a deciding role. One court case in particular, concerning the construction of a nuclear power plant, would emerge as the most influential interpretation of NEPA's meaning and the duties it did, and did not, impose on federal agencies.

The Case of Calvert Cliffs Nuclear Power Plant

The use of nuclear energy to generate electricity grew out of the development of the atomic bomb in World War II. Immediately after the war in 1946, Congress passed the Atomic Energy Act, which created the AEC to promote the development of atomic energy for national security and to regulate it to protect public health and safety. In 1954, the Atomic Energy Act was amended to authorize and encourage the development of nuclear power by private industry, especially for electrical power generation. Lewis Strauss, then chairman of the AEC, famously declared at a 1954 science writers' convention: "It is not too much to expect that our children will enjoy in their homes electrical energy too cheap to meter." However, utility companies were initially hesitant to adopt this new technology because of its complexity, cost, and uncertainty. In order to demonstrate the potential of this technology and encourage its adoption, the federal government used a naval nuclear reactor to build the nation's first nuclear power plant in Shippingport, Pennsylvania, in 1957. Two years later, the first private nuclear reactor went online in

Dresden, Illinois. By the late 1960s, electrical utilities across the country were either planning or constructing nuclear power plants.

In June 1966, the *Washington Post* reported that the Baltimore Gas and Electric Company (BG&E) was seeking 985 acres in Calvert County, Maryland, on which to build a nuclear power–generating plant. A year later, in May 1967, BG&E officially announced plans to erect a nuclear power plant in Calvert Cliffs, Maryland. The site was in a relatively rural area on the western shore of Chesapeake Bay in southern Maryland, 60 miles south of Baltimore and 45 miles south of Washington, D.C. News of this announcement received little reaction. Before the plant could be brought online, however, BG&E had to obtain a construction license and then an operating license from the AEC. The AEC licensing process was designed to ensure that a nuclear power plant would be constructed and operated safely and was the only real opportunity for outside interests—the public or local government officials—to participate.

The AEC licensing process was also very limited and specific in its scope; only issues relating directly to the safety of the construction process itself or issues relating to radiation would be considered by the AEC license hearing board. AEC rules dictated that it could not withhold a license if the applicant addressed these specific issues satisfactorily. The first public hearing on the proposed Calvert Cliffs nuclear power plant was convened by the Atomic Safety and Licensing Board on May 12, 1969. The purpose of this hearing was to consider the utility's application for a construction license. At the outset of the meeting, the chairman explained to those assembled that comments on zoning, transmission lines, power costs, and thermal effects would not be relevant; the hearing would only be concerned with construction safety or radiological issues. Attendees nevertheless proceeded to express both opposition and support for the nuclear plant and to air a variety of concerns and complaints. The Chesapeake Environmental Protection Association, a local conservation organization, was particularly concerned about the path of power lines, though it addressed a variety of environmental issues. One environmental concern that was drawing a lot of attention was that of thermal pollution to nearby bodies of water.

Nuclear power plants work by producing enormous quantities of heat from the splitting of uranium atoms. This heat is then used to boil water, creating steam, which then spins turbines to create electricity. Nuclear power plants use large volumes of water both to create steam to produce electricity and to cool the system—sometimes more than 1 million gallons a second. The need for such enormous volumes of water meant that nuclear power plants were inevitably located near large bodies of water—lakes, rivers, or the ocean. By the mid-1960s, scientists were cautioning that the release of large volumes of heated water back into these bodies of water threatened to seriously disturb aquatic ecosystems. However, thermal pollution was neither a radiological nor a safety issue, and the AEC refused to take it into consideration during licensing. Conservation groups were very concerned about the impacts of thermal pollution on Chesapeake Bay, a body of water renowned for its fishing and blue crabs. Shortly after the BG&E applied for a license with the AEC in January 1968, the Chesapeake Bay Foundation organized a committee of scientists from nearby Johns Hopkins University to study the plant's potential environmental impacts on the bay. The scientists declared that the nuclear power plant could cause considerable environmental disruption, which prompted Maryland governor Spiro Agnew (later vice president to President Richard Nixon) and Senator Millard Tydings to call for a hold on the plant's construction until a comprehensive and objective analysis of its environmental impacts was completed. At the time, there was little that state officials could do because the process was almost entirely controlled by the federal AEC. In July 1968, a new state law went into effect giving Maryland's Public Service Commission (PSC) power to issue licenses for power plants, but it was not clear at the time whether the PSC could intervene in the Calvert Cliffs plant. In January 1969, the AEC's division of reactor licensing granted a temporary exemption to BG&E to allow the utility to begin certain construction activities (i.e., grading of the site) before the actual construction permit was issued. Officials had little doubt that licensing would be granted.

THE DEBATE

Critics of the proposed Calvert Cliffs plant charged that the licensing process was unfairly stacked in favor of the power plant and that the hearings provided no real opportunity to actually change the outcome. Days before the first hearing in May 1969, the *Washington Post* interviewed residents who complained that BG&E had already spent millions of dollars on land, equipment, and plans, "thereby making the ultimate creation of the plant virtually a foregone conclusion." The same could be said for the licensing process as a whole, since an operating license would only be granted by the AEC *after* the plant had been fully constructed. It seemed highly unlikely that the AEC could withhold an operating license after the utility had spent over $300 million constructing the plant. In many ways, the hearing for the construction license was the only real opportunity for intervention, albeit a narrow one. However, not everyone was opposed to the plant. During the hearing for the construction license, expressions of support for the plant proposal came from the county commissioners of Calvert County, members of the Maryland House of Delegates, the Calvert County Board of Trade, the local economic development agency, local bankers, and a real estate developer. Opposition was voiced mainly by conservation organizations, including the Chesapeake Environmental Protection Association, Chesapeake Bay Foundation, Potomac River Association, St. Mary's County Waterman's Association, as well as local civic groups. Since no issues relating to radiation or construction safety were raised, the AEC granted BG&E a construction license on June 30, 1969. The possibilities for intervention were further diminished in August when the PSC ruled that it did not have jurisdiction over the Calvert Cliffs nuclear power plant because construction (i.e., grading of the site) had begun before the state law went into effect.

Despite the setbacks, conservation organizations continued to seek opportunities to halt the construction of the Calvert Cliffs plant. NEPA seemed to offer a potential point of leverage. After NEPA's enactment in January 1970, every federal agency was charged with the task of creating official regulations that would govern the specifics of how an agency would implement the law. The AEC released a draft of proposed regulations on how it would implement NEPA in June 1970, and conservationists contended that the AEC's proposed regulations fell far short of the new law's requirements. Shortly after the draft regulations were released, the National Wildlife Federation, the Sierra Club, and a new umbrella organization representing numerous local and national conservation organizations—the Calvert Cliffs' Coordinating Committee—petitioned the AEC to halt construction of the plant until a study of its effects on the ecology of Chesapeake Bay was completed. The AEC countered that it had already changed its rules to require an environmental statement to be prepared for the plant before the final operating license would be issued. Conservationists pointed out that the operating license would not even be considered until *after* the plant was already constructed, which would make it almost impossible for the AEC to withhold the license, regardless of its environmental impacts. Nevertheless, the AEC refused to halt construction. In October, following a lawsuit by the Chesapeake Environmental Protection Association, the court of appeals ruled that the Maryland PSC did have jurisdiction over the Calvert Cliffs nuclear power plant. However, the ruling did little for conservationists because the PSC issued the necessary state permit in January 1971 to allow the power plant to move forward.

In December 1970, almost a year after NEPA became law, the AEC issued Appendix D to its nuclear power plant licensing regulations. Appendix D directed the applicant for a nuclear power plant construction license to prepare an environmental report, presenting its assessment of the environmental impact of the planned facility and possible alternatives that would alter the impact. When construction was completed and the applicant applied for a license to operate the new facility, it would again submit an environmental report, noting any factors that had changed since the original report. At each stage, the AEC's regulatory staff was to take the applicant's report and prepare its own detailed statement of environmental costs, benefits, and alternatives. The statement would then be circulated to other interested and responsible agencies and made available to the public. After comments were received from those sources, the staff would prepare a final detailed statement and make a final recommendation on the application for a construction permit or operating license.

Although the AEC staff was to file its environmental statement with all of the other licensing application materials, the license hearing board would not use the environmental statement or report for its decision making unless nonradiological environmental issues were brought up or challenged by the AEC staff or some intervening party. In addition, the AEC would not consider environmental questions on issues for which it had already received certification from other government agencies, such as for water pollution. Finally, these rules were not retroactive. The AEC's rules prohibited any consideration of nonradiological environmental issues by its hearing boards for projects that began before March 4, 1971, in order to allow for an orderly implementation

of the new rules and not to create undue disruption to power development. For conservationists, the AEC's new rules fell far short of NEPA's
requirements. Ironically, this failure offered conservation organizations
an important opportunity: a test of NEPA's enforceability in the courts.
With all administrative channels now exhausted, the Calvert Cliffs'
Coordinating Committee filed suit in the Washington, D.C., court of
appeals against the AEC for failing to comply with NEPA.

The Argument for a Strict Interpretation of NEPA

The case of *Calvert Cliffs' Coordinating Committee, Inc. v. U.S. Atomic
Energy Commission* was heard by the U.S. Court of Appeals, District
of Columbia, on April 16, 1971. Lawyers for Calvert Cliffs' Coordinating Committee argued that the AEC's regulations failed to comply with
NEPA. Specifically, the plaintiffs argued that NEPA required early and
independent analysis of all environmental impacts of every nuclear power
plant. They argued that the Appendix D rules inappropriately allowed
the license hearing board to ignore nonradiological environmental issues
unless these issues were raised by the staff or outside parties. Similarly,
they argued that NEPA required the AEC to independently evaluate and
balance environmental factors even when "other responsible parties" had
certified that environmental standards were met (e.g., by state agencies
or federal laws on water pollution). They drew particular attention to
the AEC's refusal to analyze the impacts of thermal pollution. Finally,
they criticized the AEC's decision to exempt power plants already under
construction or permitted before March 4, 1971, which they argued was
unsupportable since NEPA had been law for more than a year already.

The Argument for a Flexible Interpretation of NEPA

The AEC contended that NEPA was flexible and that its Appendix D
regulations were sufficient to comply with the law. AEC had grounds
for support. During oversight hearings before Congressman Dingell's
subcommittee in December 1970, the CEQ had praised the AEC for
its efforts to comply with NEPA. While the AEC accepted that NEPA
expanded the agency's environmental responsibilities to nonradiological issues, it argued that NEPA permitted, if not required, the agency
to defer to state and federal water quality agencies. The defendants

asserted that this policy interpretation was actually preferable because the AEC did not possess the legal or technical competency in all environmental areas. More important, there was evidence from the legislative history that AEC's interpretation was consistent with the framers' intentions. Senators Jackson and Muskie had specifically discussed the relationship between NEPA and existing federal pollution laws and agreed before Congress, albeit unofficially, that NEPA was not to conflict with or override existing federal laws on pollution.

OUTCOME AND IMPACT

On July 23, 1971, the court of appeals ruled that the AEC's Appendix D regulations did not comply with NEPA. (See "Ruling by Judge J. Skelly Wright, 1971," on page 106 in the Primary Sources section.) Judge Skelly Wright, writing for the three-judge panel, scolded the AEC for "making a mockery" of NEPA with its "crabbed interpretation" of the law. The court came to several important conclusions regarding the AEC's rules and, more important, the meaning of NEPA and how it was supposed to be applied:

1) NEPA declared that environmental protection was now part of the basic mission of every federal agency, including the AEC. Judge Wright wrote, "[The AEC's] responsibility is not simply to sit back, like an umpire, and resolve adversary contentions at the hearing stage. Rather, it must itself take the initiative of considering environmental values at every distinctive and comprehensive stage of the process beyond the staff's evaluation and recommendation." The AEC's rule that the hearing board need not consider environmental factors unless raised by the staff or outside parties was not proper under NEPA because it left the problem of addressing environmental issues to others.

2) The AEC's extraordinary delay in implementing NEPA requirements until after March 4, 1971, was "shocking" and not justified. While the court sympathized with the AEC's desire to prevent disruption of the nation's power system through orderly transition, the judge wrote that "the obvious sense of urgency on the part of Congress should make clear that a transition,

however orderly, must proceed at a pace faster than a funeral procession."

3) NEPA required a case-by-case analysis of every federal project in order to consider its particular economic and technical benefits and costs to the environment. Because this balancing required an entirely different kind of judgment than that used by other agencies or laws, the hearing board could not simply rely on other agencies' certification of environmental standards—the AEC had to conduct its own independent evaluation. This included water quality issues such as thermal pollution.

4) The hearing board had to consider environmental factors in issuing operating permits, even if a construction permit had been issued prior to NEPA's enactment.

The court's ruling was a stinging rebuke to the AEC and it invalidated its Appendix D rules. The AEC not only had to issue new rules consistent with the court's ruling, it now also had to revisit the licenses it had already issued. In September 1971, the head of the AEC announced its decision to review the operating permits of all nuclear power plants and ordered the submission of environmental statements retroactively for all licenses issued since the date of NEPA's enactment. As a result, construction on all nuclear power plants throughout the country was stopped for 18 months while the AEC rewrote its regulations and prepared new environmental impact statements, this time with the close supervision of the CEQ. Congress was astounded by the magnitude of NEPA's impact, and many members scrambled to find some way of either amending or bypassing NEPA, lest the country be brought to a standstill for lack of enough energy production. (See the sidebar "Alyeska and the Trans-Alaska Pipeline" on page 92.) In the end, NEPA was left unaltered, but the new regulations for licensing and environmental impact analysis were a blow to the nuclear power industry. The heightened level of scrutiny contributed to an overall slowdown in the industry's growth due to a combination of increasing costs and regulatory complexity, as well as to growing public anxieties about the safety of nuclear energy.

The *Calvert Cliffs'* decision had a dramatic impact on environmental law and policy. The ruling by the court of appeals was the first and most

(continues on page 94)

ALYESKA AND THE TRANS-ALASKA PIPELINE

In 1968, oil was discovered beneath Prudhoe Bay on Alaska's North Slope, along the Arctic Ocean coast. A few months later, seven major oil companies formed a consortium named the Alyeska Pipeline Service Company to build a pipeline to transport the oil 800 miles south across Alaska from Prudhoe Bay to the port of Valdez. From there, the oil could be loaded onto tanker ships and carried to major markets in the lower 48 states. Because the pipeline would cross federal land, Alyeska had to apply to the Department of the Interior for permits. Before Interior could grant permits, however, it had to file an environmental impact statement (EIS) for this major activity, which would have a significant impact on the environment. On March 20, 1970, only three months after Congress passed the National Environmental Policy Act (NEPA), the Interior Department issued its first EIS for the Trans-Alaska Pipeline project. It was only eight pages long. Not surprisingly, environmental organizations challenged the EIS in court, and on April 23, 1970, a federal district court ruled that the EIS did not comply with NEPA. No permits could be issued nor construction begun until an adequate EIS was produced. Interior officials would have to try again.

After months of work and with the help of numerous federal agencies, Interior released a substantially revised and much longer draft EIS on January 15, 1971. After its release, Interior held hearings and solicited comments on the draft EIS from both federal agencies and the public. More than 2,700 individuals and groups submitted comments or testified at the public hearings held in Washington, D.C., and Anchorage, Alaska, producing a 37-volume record more than 10,000 pages long. Most of these comments, both from the public and sister agencies, were critical. Much of this criticism focused on the inadequate consideration of oil spills that would inevitably result from transporting so much oil by tanker. In addition, critics pointed to the lack of consideration for alternative pipeline routes to minimize or even eliminate the need for transport by ship. Although there were numerous other potential environmental impacts of concern, the issue of oil spills was particularly sensitive. Since 1968, there had been a number of spectacular oil spills, both from tankers and offshore oil wells, which had captured the public's attention and galvanized the environmental community.

In March 1972, Interior released its final EIS. This document filled six volumes and included three supplemental volumes. The final EIS refined the environmental impact analyses, as well as discussions of alternatives, and even attempted to answer many of the comments submitted. The EIS concluded that alternative pipeline routes would minimize environmental impacts, but both Interior and Alyeska nevertheless chose the original plan without significant alteration. In May 1972, the Center for Law and Social Policy filed suit on behalf of three environmental organizations to prevent the issuance of a construction permit, arguing that the EIS was still inadequate. Once again, the EIS began to make its way through the courts.

On October 17, 1973, the Arab member nations of the Organization of the Petroleum Exporting Countries (OPEC) announced an oil embargo against the United States and other countries in retaliation for providing support to Israel during the Yom Kippur War. Because the United States imported nearly one-third of its oil from abroad, the effects of the embargo were immediate and dramatic. The abrupt fuel scarcity led to massive increases in the price of oil and gasoline and fuel shortages across the country. The sudden energy crisis changed the balance of political sentiment. In response to pressure from the public and the president, Congress hastily drafted and then passed the Trans-Alaska Pipeline Authorization Act. The law directed the secretary of the interior to authorize construction of the pipeline and banned the courts from considering environmental lawsuits against the project. President Nixon signed the bill into law on November 16, 1973. Construction on the pipeline began in 1974, and oil began to flow in 1977. Alyeska originally estimated the cost of construction at $900 million, although it would eventually cost $8 billion. Prudhoe Bay emerged as the largest oil field in the United States, and the oil transported through the Trans-Alaska pipeline accounted for one-quarter of all U.S. domestic oil production.

On March 24, 1989, after being loaded with oil at the port of Valdez, the oil tanker *Exxon Valdez* ran aground on Bligh Reef in Alaska's Prince William Sound. Within six hours, 10.9 million gallons spilled into the sound. The oil slick covered 11,000 square miles of ocean and killed tens of thousands of birds, fish, mammals, and other sea life. The 1972 EIS predicted a worst-case spill scenario of 140,000 gallons of oil. It remained the largest oil spill in U.S. waters until the 2010 *Deepwater Horizon* spill in the Gulf of Mexico.

(continued from page 91)
influential interpretation of NEPA's meaning and proper application. The ruling institutionalized the principle that government-sponsored projects should be rigorously assessed for their environmental impacts and alternatives considered before those projects were initiated. The ruling established a precedent that enabled private citizens and non-governmental organizations to challenge a federal agency's decision if an EIS was either not prepared or prepared inadequately. Because of the serious consequences of noncompliance, agencies went to great lengths to open up their decision-making processes to public scrutiny and participation, as well as document those processes, simply to prevent costly and time-consuming litigation. Nevertheless, even after *Calvert Cliffs*, there were a number of other high-profile lawsuits against government agencies for failure to comply with NEPA, and these lawsuits generated significant publicity. Only a small fraction of agency projects were actually challenged in the courts for NEPA noncompliance, but the perception by many people, especially hostile lawmakers, was that NEPA and the courts had spawned a legal monster. Despite the hostility and misgivings, NEPA's environmental impact statement process became one of the most widely copied environmental legal provisions in the world. More than 80 countries and most of the states adopted a similar kind of environmental impact analysis process in succeeding years, and it has become a cornerstone of modern environmental law.

Calvert Cliffs' was not only remarkable for what it did, but also for what it did not do. The ruling helped to establish a strict procedural requirement for environmental impact analysis, but it did not dictate any particular decision or outcome, nor did it give the courts the power to overturn a particular decision because of the decision itself. Judge Wright wrote, "The reviewing courts probably cannot reverse a substantive decision on its merits, under Section 101, unless it be shown that the actual balance of costs and benefits that was struck was arbitrary or clearly gave insufficient weight to environmental values." So long as an agency could show that it followed the proper procedures—analyzing all environmental impacts, evaluating alternatives, demonstrating a good-faith effort of "consideration"—then it was in compliance. The transformative vision of NEPA's policy statement that charged government agencies to think "environmentally" could not be enforced by the courts—this was something only the agencies themselves could do.

A view of the Calvert Cliffs Nuclear Power Plant in Lusby, Maryland, on June 21, 1995. The plant began operation in 1975. In March 2000, it became the first nuclear power plant in the United States to be granted 20-year extensions of its operating licenses from the U.S. Nuclear Regulatory Commission. (Carlos Osorio/Associated Press)

NEPA had a monumental impact on environmental law and the nuclear industry, but ironically, it had very little impact on Calvert Cliffs itself. After the AEC issued its revised regulations, BG&E prepared a full environmental impact statement and went ahead with the licensing and eventual construction of the plant. The first of its two 850-megawatt nuclear power generators came online in 1975. When it was completed, Calvert Cliffs was supplying one-third of Maryland's power needs. The power plant's original operating license was set to expire in 2014, but in 2000, Calvert Cliffs became the first nuclear power plant in the country to receive an extension of its operating license for another two decades.

WHAT IF?

What if Senator Jackson's original statement that "each person has a fundamental and inalienable right to a healthful environment" had remained in NEPA?

If NEPA had guaranteed every individual "a fundamental and inalienable right to a healthful environment" it is likely that the courts would have been flooded with lawsuits by individuals and organizations before the president's signature had even dried on the paper. Aside from the simply unimaginable deluge of litigation, both the courts and the administration would have been confronted by a question that is both politically and scientifically difficult to answer, let alone achieve: What constitutes a "healthful environment"? In many ways, the goal of a "healthful environment" was implicit in much of the groundbreaking environmental legislation that Congress passed from the late 1960s through the 1970s. Indeed, these new laws set a variety of new legal standards in an effort to reach a better environment: maximum pollutant emissions, minimum levels of pollution-abatement technology, minimum air- and water-quality standards. However, the granting of a legal right would have been something wholly different.

As it was, Congress was surprised by the volume and power of litigation that rose around NEPA. Many members of Congress and the public felt that the law's purpose had been twisted and that the courts had gotten out of hand in their power to influence government functions and policy. In the first few years after NEPA's passage and after a number of high-profile lawsuits, some lawmakers called for NEPA to be amended or even repealed. (See "'Acting to Save NEPA's Integrity,' 1972," and "'Public Works Planners Assail Ecology Review,' 1972," on pages 108 and 109 in the Primary Sources section.) Although Congress did in fact bypass NEPA in the case of the Trans-Alaska Pipeline, the law itself remained in place and largely untouched. Had NEPA been endowed with the guarantee to a "healthful environment," it is likely that Congress would have acted more aggressively to either amend or repeal the law.

CHRONOLOGY

1959 Senator James E. Murray (Montana) introduces the Resources and Conservation Act of 1960. Though the bill does not pass, many elements are later incorporated into the National Environmental Policy Act (NEPA): declaration of policy, advisory council in the Executive Office of the President, an annual report, and a structure similar to that of the Council of Economic Advisers. Similar bills will be introduced and considered in 1960, 1961, and 1963.

1962 Rachel Carson publishes *Silent Spring*.

1965   White House convenes Conference on Natural Beauty.

1966   *June:* Baltimore Gas and Electric Company (BG&E) requests rezoning of 985 acres on Chesapeake Bay in Calvert County, Maryland, as the possible site of a nuclear power plant.

1967   *May 30:* BG&E announces plans to build a nuclear power plant at Calvert Cliffs, Maryland.

1968   *February:* Scientists from Johns Hopkins University raise concerns about thermal pollution effects on Chesapeake Bay.

March 28: Maryland governor Spiro T. Agnew and Senator Millard Tydings declare that no further construction should be done on the Calvert Cliffs plant until a comprehensive study of its potential environmental impacts is conducted.

July 1: Maryland law giving the Public Service Commission (PSC) jurisdiction over nuclear power plants permits goes into effect.

July 17: Joint House-Senate colloquium discusses a national policy for the environment.

September: Jess Malcolm establishes Calvert Cliffs' Coordinating Committee.

1969   *January:* Chesapeake Environmental Protection Association forms to oppose Calvert Cliffs nuclear power plant.

January 10: The Atomic Energy Commission's division of reactor licensing grants an exemption to BG&E to begin certain construction activities before actual construction permit is issued.

January 31: Santa Barbara offshore oil well blows out, releasing 235,000 gallons of oil and covering 30 miles of beach with tar. Well is capped February 8.

April 16: Only Senate hearing is held on S1075, the bill that will eventually become the National Environmental Policy Act of 1969 (NEPA). Testimony introduces concept of environmental impact statement (EIS).

May 12: Atomic Energy Commission (AEC) licensing board conducts public hearing for construction permit for Calvert Cliffs plant.

May 29: President Nixon issues Executive Order 11472 establishing the Cabinet Committee on the Environment and the Citizens' Advisory Committee on Environmental Quality.

June 22: Cuyahoga River bursts into flames.

June 30: AEC grants construction permit for Calvert Cliffs nuclear power plant.

August: Maryland PSC rules that it does not have jurisdiction over the Calvert Cliffs nuclear power plant because construction (i.e., grading of site) began before the PSC was created.

December 22: Congress passes NEPA.

1970 *January 1:* President Nixon signs NEPA into law (Pub.L. 91–190).

January 29: President Nixon appoints Council on Environmental Quality (CEQ) members Russell Train, chairman, Robert Cahn, and Gordon T. F. MacDonald.

April 22: First nationwide Earth Day celebration is held.

April 30: CEQ issues interim guidelines to federal agencies for preparing environmental statements.

June 30: National Wildlife Federation, Sierra Club, and Calvert Cliffs' Coordinating Committee petition AEC to halt building Calvert Cliffs plant near Lusby, Maryland, pending study of effects on ecology of Chesapeake Bay.

July 9: Executive Office of the President submits reorganization plans to Congress to create the Environmental Protection Agency (EPA).

October: Court of appeals overturns Maryland PSC ruling that it has no jurisdiction over Calvert Cliffs nuclear power plant after appeal by Chesapeake Environmental Protection Association.

December 2: Senate confirms William Ruckelshaus as first administrator of the EPA.

December 4: AEC issues Appendix D to its licensing rules, requiring applicants for a construction permit to submit an environmental report.

1971 *January 19:* Maryland PSC approves construction permit for Calvert Cliffs nuclear power plant.

April 16: Court of appeals for District of Columbia hears arguments in *Calvert Cliffs' Coordinating Committee, Inc. v. U.S. Atomic Energy Commission.*

July 23: U.S. Court of Appeals for Washington, D.C. issues ruling on *Calvert Cliffs' Coordinating Committee, Inc. v. U.S. Atomic Energy Commission.*

September 3: AEC announces decision to review operating permits of all nuclear power plants in conformance with environmental impact statement requirements of NEPA.

1973   *October 10:* Arab member nations of the Organization of Petroleum Exporting Countries impose petroleum embargo on United States, creating fuel shortages.

November 16: President Nixon signs Trans-Alaska Pipeline Authorization Act into law, ordering the pipeline to be built and exempting it from NEPA lawsuits.

DISCUSSION QUESTIONS

1. Supporters of NEPA argued that the way to get the federal government to improve its environmental behavior was to collect better environmental information and to include that information in the decision-making process. Do you think this was a good strategy? Why or why not?

2. Should citizens or nongovernmental organizations be able to sue the government? Why or why not?

3. When NEPA was being developed, Congress spent a lot of time discussing the role of the CEQ. Should Congress have given the CEQ power to approve or reject agency decisions affecting the environment? Why or why not?

4. In *Calvert Cliffs,* the court ruled that NEPA imposed strict procedural obligations but not substantive ones. What is the difference between *procedural* and *substantive* obligations? Why is this distinction important?

5. Should Congress have required federal agencies to always choose the least environmentally harmful option? Why or why not?

6. Should certain government activities or programs be exempted from NEPA? What criteria, if any, should be used to exempt a program or project from NEPA?

WEB SITES

Council on Environmental Quality. Available online. URL: http://www. whitehouse.gov/administration/eop/ceq. Accessed March 22, 2011.

Council on Environmental Quality. "A Citizen's Guide to the NEPA: Having Your Voice Heard." Available online. URL: http://nepa.gov/ nepa/Citizens_Guide_Dec07.pdf. Accessed March 22, 2011.

Environmental Protection Agency. "The Origins of EPA." Available online. URL: http://www.epa.gov/history/origins.htm. Accessed March 22, 2011.

National Environmental Policy Act of 1969, as amended. Available online. URL: http://nepa.gov/nepa/regs/nepa/nepaeqia.htm. Accessed March 22, 2011.

BIBLIOGRAPHY

Caldwell, Lynton Keith. *The National Environmental Policy Act: An Agenda for the Future.* Bloomington: Indiana University Press, 1998.

Clark, Ray, and Larry Canter, eds. *Environmental Policy and NEPA: Past, Present, and Future.* Boca Raton, Fla.: St. Lucie Press, 1997.

Davies, J. Clarence, and Barbara S. Davies. *The Politics of Pollution.* 2d ed. Indianapolis, Ind.: Bobbs-Merrill Company, 1975.

Gottlieb, Robert. *Forcing the Spring: The Transformation of the American Environmental Movement.* Washington, D.C.: Island Press, 1993.

Landy, Marc K., Marc J. Roberts, and Stephen R. Thomas. *The Environmental Protection Agency: Asking the Wrong Questions from Nixon to Clinton.* New York: Oxford University Press, 1994.

Lindstrom, Matthew J., and Zachary A. Smith. *The National Environmental Policy Act: Judicial Misconstruction, Legislative Indifference & Executive Neglect.* College Station: Texas A&M University Press, 2001.

Liroff, Richard A. *A National Policy for the Environment: NEPA and Its Aftermath.* Bloomington: Indiana University Press, 1976.

Tarlock, A. Dan. "The Story of Calvert Cliffs: A Court Construes the National Environmental Policy Act to Create a Powerful Cause of Action." In *Environmental Law Stories.* Richard J. Lazarus and Oliver A. Houck, eds. New York: Foundation Press, 2005.

PRIMARY SOURCES

Document 1: National Environmental Policy Act of 1969

The National Environmental Policy Act of 1969 was passed by Congress in late December 1969 and signed into law by President Nixon on January 1, 1970. It contains two titles. Title I declares and describes a national environmental policy and directs the federal government to prepare a detailed statement of environmental impacts for federal actions that "significantly" affect the environment. Title II establishes and describes the duties of a Council on Environmental Quality. Below are excerpts of major sections from the National Environmental Policy Act of 1969.

An Act to establish a national policy for the environment, to provide for the establishment of a Council on Environmental Quality, and for other purposes.

Be it enacted by the Senate and House of Representatives of the United States of America in Congress assembled, That this Act may be cited as the "National Environmental Policy Act of 1969."

PURPOSE

Sec. 2. The purposes of this Act are: To declare a national policy which will encourage productive and enjoyable harmony between man and his environment; to promote efforts which will prevent or eliminate damage to the environment and biosphere and stimulate the health and welfare of man; to enrich the understanding of the ecological systems and natural resources important to the Nation; and to establish a Council on Environmental Quality.

TITLE I

Declaration of National Environmental Policy

Sec. 101. (a) The Congress, recognizing the profound impact of man's activity on the interrelations of all components of the natural environment, particularly the profound influences of population growth, high-density urbanization, industrial expansion, resource exploitation, and new and expanding technological advances and recognizing further the critical importance of restoring and maintaining environmental quality to the overall welfare and development of man, declares that it is the continuing policy of the Federal Government, in cooperation with State and local governments, and other concerned public and private organizations, to use all practicable means and measures, including financial and technical assistance, in a manner calculated to foster and promote the general welfare, to create and maintain conditions under which man and nature can exist in productive harmony, and fulfill the social, economic, and other requirements of present and future generations of Americans.

(b) In order to carry out the policy set forth in this Act, it is the continuing responsibility of the Federal Government to use all practicable means, consistent with other essential considerations of national policy, to improve and coordinate Federal plans, functions, programs, and resources to the end that the Nation may—fulfill the responsibilities of each generation as trustee of the environment for succeeding generations; assure for all Americans safe, healthful, productive, and aesthetically and culturally pleasing surroundings; attain the widest range of beneficial uses of the environment without degradation, risk to health or safety, or other undesirable and unintended consequences; preserve important historic, cultural, and natural aspects of our national heritage, and maintain, wherever possible, an environment which supports diversity, and variety of individual choice; achieve a balance between population and resource use which will permit high standards of living and a wide sharing of life's amenities; and enhance the quality of renewable resources and approach the maximum attainable recycling of depletable resources. (c) The Congress recognizes that each person should enjoy a healthful environment and that each person has a responsibility to contribute to the preservation and enhancement of the environment. Sec. 102. The Congress authorizes and directs that, to the fullest extent possible: (1) the policies, regulations, and public laws of the United States shall be interpreted and administered in accordance with the policies set forth in this Act, and (2) all agencies of the Federal Government shall—

(A) utilize a systematic, interdisciplinary approach which will insure the integrated use of the natural and social sciences and the environmental design arts in planning and in decision making which may have an impact on man's environment;

(B) identify and develop methods and procedures, in consultation with the Council on Environmental Quality established by Title II of this Act, which will insure that presently unquantified environmental amenities and values may be given appropriate consideration in decision making along with economic and technical considerations;

(C) include in every recommendation or report on proposals for legislation and other major Federal actions significantly affecting the quality of the human environment, a detailed statement by the responsible official on—

(i) the environmental impact of the proposed action,
(ii) any adverse environmental effects which cannot be avoided should the proposal be implemented,
(iii) alternatives to the proposed action,
(iv) the relationship between local short-term uses of man's environment and the maintenance and enhancement of long-term productivity, and
(v) any irreversible and irretrievable commitments of resources which would be involved in the proposed action should it be implemented. . . .

Sec. 104. Nothing in section 102 or 103 shall in any way affect the specific statutory obligations of any Federal agency (1) to comply with criteria or standards of environmental quality, (2) to coordinate or consult with any other Federal or State agency, or (3) to act, or refrain from acting contingent upon the recommendations or certification of any other Federal or State agency. . . .

TITLE II

Council on Environmental Quality

Sec. 201. The President shall transmit to the Congress annually beginning July 1, 1970, an Environmental Quality Report . . . which shall set forth (1) the status and condition of the major natural, manmade, or altered environmental classes of the Nation. . . .

Sec. 202. There is created in the Executive Office of the President a Council on Environmental Quality. . . . The Council shall be composed of three members who shall be appointed by the President to serve at his pleasure . . .

Sec. 204. It shall be the duty and function of the Council—to assist and advise the President in the preparation of the Environmental Quality Report . . . to gather timely and authoritative information concerning the conditions and trends in the quality of the environment . . . to review and appraise the various programs and activities of the Federal Government in the light of the policy set forth in Title I of this Act . . . to develop and recommend to the President national policies to foster and promote the improvement of environmental quality . . . to conduct investigations, studies, surveys, research, and analyses relating to ecological systems and environmental quality; to document and define changes in the natural environment . . . to report at least once each year to the President on the state and condition of the environment; and to make and furnish such studies, reports thereon, and recommendations with respect to matters of policy and legislation as the President may request. . . .

Source: Richard A. Liroff. *A National Policy for the Environment: NEPA and Its Aftermath.* Bloomington: Indiana University Press, 1976.

—ᴍ—

Document 2: Statement by President Richard Nixon, January 1, 1970

On January 1, 1970, President Richard Nixon signed the National Environmental Policy Act of 1969 into law at his home in San Clemente, California, often referred to as the Western White House. At the signing, President Nixon drew attention to the nation's heightened attention to environmental problems, predicting that the 1970s would be the decade when the nation embarked on an ambitious path to change its ways and repair damage to the environment. He famously declared, "It is literally now or never."

It is particularly fitting that my first official act in this new decade is to approve the National Environmental Policy Act.

The past year has seen the creation of a President's Cabinet Committee on Environmental Quality, and we have devoted many hours to the pressing problems of pollution control, airport location, highway construction and population trends.

By my participation in these efforts I have become further convinced that the nineteen-seventies absolutely must be the years when America pays its debt to the past by reclaiming the purity of its air, its waters and our living environment. It is literally now or never.

I, therefore, commend the Congress and particularly the sponsors of this bill, Senator Stevens and Jackson and Representative Dingell, for this clear legislative policy declaration. Under the provisions of this law a three-member Council of Environmental Advisers will be appointed.

I anticipate that they will occupy the same close advisory relation to the President that the Council of Economic Advisers does in fiscal and monetary matters. The environmental advisers will be assisted by a compact staff in keeping me thoroughly posted on current problems and advising me on how the Federal Government can act to solve them. . . . We are most interested in results. The act I have signed gives us an adequate organization and a good statement of direction. We are determined that the decade of the seventies will be known as the time when this country regained a productive harmony between man and nature.

Source: Text of Nixon Statement. *New York Times,* January 2, 1970.

—⁓—

Document 3: William D. Ruckelshaus on the EPA, 1970

On December 2, 1970, the U.S. Senate confirmed William Ruckelshaus as the first administrator of the newly created Environmental Protection Agency (EPA), marking the true beginning of the nation's top environmental agency. Ruckelshaus moved quickly to establish the new agency's reputation as an aggressive enforcer of environmental law. Two weeks after his confirmation, Administrator Ruckelshaus held a press conference during which he described the new agency's broad environmental duties and stressed the EPA's independence from other federal agencies that were traditionally associated with economic development and natural resource exploitation.

The Environmental Protection Agency became law only two weeks ago today, but several of the most important principles to which we will adhere are already evident.

EPA is an independent agency. It has no obligation to promote agriculture or commerce; only the critical obligation to protect and enhance the environment. It does not have a narrow charter to deal with only one aspect of a deteriorating environment; rather it has a broad responsibility for research, standard-setting, monitoring and enforcement with regard to five environmental hazards; air and water pollution, solid waste disposal, radiation, and pesticides. EPA represents a coordinated approach to each of these problems, guaranteeing that as we deal with one difficulty we do not aggravate others.

As we work toward pollution abatement, we shall also strive to provide information and leadership; to enhance the environmental awareness of all the people and all of the institutions of this society. A clean and healthy environment is up to all of us. So we shall be an advocate for the environment with individuals, with industry, and within government.

The job that must be done now to restore and preserve the quality of our air, water, and soil can only be accomplished if this new Federal agency works closely with industry and with other levels of government. The technology which has bulldozed its way across the environment must now be employed to remove impurities from the air, to restore vitality to our rivers and streams, to recycle the waste that is the ugly by-product of our prosperity. And municipal and state governments must do more than curb pollution where it occurs now; they must plan for healthy and balanced and pollution-free growth in the future. . . .

Our hopes for this agency are high. We know all environmental problems will not be solved this year or next. But if we remain flexible in approach and firm in our commitment, we believe we will live up to the President's challenge that "the 1970s absolutely must be the years when America pays its debt to the past by reclaiming the purity of its air, its water, and its living environment."

Source: William D. Ruckelshaus. "First Administrator on Establishment of EPA." EPA Press Release. December 16, 1970. Available online. URL: http://www.epa.gov/history/org/origins/first.htm. Accessed March 22, 2011.

—⚹—

Document 4: Ruling by Judge J. Skelly Wright, 1971

On July 23, 1971, the court of appeals for the D.C. circuit issued its ruling on the Calvert Cliffs' *case, finding that the Atomic Energy Commission's rules for reviewing nuclear power plant proposals violated the National Environmental Policy Act (NEPA). The ruling of the three-judge panel was written by Judge J. Skelly Wright, who scolded the Atomic Energy Commission for making a "mockery" of the law. This ruling set an important precedent for future interpretations of the law, with an emphasis on NEPA's procedural requirements. Below are excerpts from* Calvert Cliffs' Coordinating Committee, Inc. v. U.S. Atomic Energy Commission *(449 F2d 1109).*

CALVERT CLIFFS' COORDINATING COMMITTEE, INC., et al., Petitioners, v. UNITED STATES ATOMIC ENERGY COMMISSION and United States of America, Respondents, Baltimore Gas and Electric Company, Intervenor. CALVERT CLIFFS' COORDINATING

COMMITTEE, INC., et al., Petitioners, v. UNITED STATES ATOMIC
ENERGY COMMISSION and United States of America, Respondents

UNITED STATES COURT OF APPEALS FOR THE DISTRICT OF COLUMBIA CIRCUIT 449 F.2D 1109

J. SKELLY WRIGHT, Circuit Judge:

These cases are only the beginning of what promises to become a flood
of new litigation—litigation seeking judicial assistance in protecting our natural environment. Several recently enacted statutes attest
to the commitment of the Government to control, at long last, the
destructive engine of material "progress." But it remains to be seen
whether the promise of this legislation will become a reality. Therein
lies the judicial role. In these cases, we must for the first time interpret
the broadest and perhaps most important of the recent statutes: the
National Environmental Policy Act of 1969 (NEPA). We must assess
claims that one of the agencies charged with its administration has
failed to live up to the congressional mandate. Our duty, in short, is to
see that important legislative purposes, heralded in the halls of Congress, are not lost or misdirected in the vast hallways of the federal
bureaucracy. . . .

[T]he general substantive policy of the Act is a flexible one. It leaves
room for a responsible exercise of discretion and may not require particular substantive results in particular problematic instances. However, the
Act also contains very important "procedural" provisions—provisions
which are designed to see that all federal agencies do in fact exercise the
substantive discretion given them. These provisions are not highly flexible. Indeed, they establish a strict standard of compliance. NEPA, first
of all, makes environmental protection a part of the mandate of every
federal agency and department. The Atomic Energy Commission, for
example, had continually asserted, prior to NEPA, that it had no statutory authority to concern itself with the adverse environmental effects of
its actions. Now, however, its hands are no longer tied. It is not only permitted, but compelled, to take environmental values into account. Perhaps the greatest importance of NEPA is to require the Atomic Energy
Commission and other agencies to consider environmental issues just as
they consider other matters within their mandates. . . .

We hold that . . . the Commission must revise its rules governing consideration of environmental issues. We do not impose a harsh

burden on the Commission. For we require only an exercise of substantive discretion which will protect the environment "to the fullest extent possible." No less is required if the grand congressional purposes underlying NEPA are to become a reality. . . .

Source: *Calvert Cliffs' Coordinating Committee, Inc., et al., Petitioners v. United States Atomic Energy Commission and United States of America, Respondents, Baltimore Gas and Electric Company, Intervenor,* 449 F.2d 1109 (D.C. Cir. 1971). Available online. URL: http://openjurist.org/449/f2d/1109/calvert-cliffs-coordinating-committee-inc-v-united-states-atomic-energy-commission. Accessed June 3, 2011.

—⚇—

Document 5: "Acting to Save NEPA's Integrity," 1972

As conservation and environmental organizations discovered the power of National Environmental Policy Act (NEPA) and the courts to delay or stop large government actions with significant environmental impacts, some members of Congress called for action to either amend or even repeal NEPA because of its unforeseen consequences. In this op-ed from the Washington Post, *Peter Harnik, an outspoken advocate for the conservation of urban green space and bicycling, argues that NEPA is an important new tool worth preserving. Harnik later became a leader of the rails-to-trails movement. In 1986, he cofounded the Rails-to-Trails Conservancy and has since published extensively on related issues of community and environmental sustainability.*

When the National Environmental Policy Act was signed into law by President Nixon on Jan. 1, 1970, many of our elected representatives in Capitol Hill smiled, winked and wrote home to their constituents, "We've done our part to save the environment; the rest is up to you. After all, people cause pollution."

Many of Washington's high-powered industrial lobbyists also smiled and winked and dreamed harmonious thoughts of green pastures dotted with profitable, politically unassailable factories. While they were smiling and winking, a handful of environmental and public interest lawyers were studying the new law to see what was so funny. Since then, they have used NEPA to halt construction of the Cross-Florida Barge Canal; to stop the building of the Gilham Dam across the Cosatot River in Arkansas; to delay numerous highway projects . . . to revamp the Atomic

Energy Commission's licensing procedure; to re-evaluate the stream channelization program carried out by the Soil Conservation Service; to delay the trans-Alaska pipe line for over two years; to halt the work on the mammoth Tennessee-Tombigbee Waterway in the Deep South; and to delay the leasing of oil and gas tracts in the Gulf of Mexico.

NEPA, passed as a token measure to appease "ecology nuts," provided the environmental movement with the very teeth it was never supposed to develop. Defying its creators, it turned into a force which has done more to preserve and protect the environment than all the previous environmental protection measures combined.

And now NEPA is in serious trouble. . . . At present there are eight bills in the House and one in the Senate which could weaken NEPA in one way or another. . . . In response to this, environmentalists have launched the "Save NEPA" campaign, pressuring representatives to maintain NEPA's integrity from any onslaught, no matter what form it takes.

There is no question that it will be an uphill struggle. But if NEPA is emasculated, the environment movement will find itself worse off than it was before Earth Day, 1970.

Source: Peter Harnik. "Acting to Save NEPA's Integrity." *Washington Post,* April 17, 1972: A23.

—⁂—

Document 6: "Public Works Planners Assail Ecology Review," 1972

Many in Congress were surprised and disturbed by environmentalists' successful use of National Environmental Policy Act (NEPA) and the courts to disrupt government programs. While there was considerable complaint about the use of litigation for these purposes, critics of NEPA were aware that environmental protection was very popular with the public, and they were concerned about appearing antienvironmental. In May 1972, members of the House of Representatives Public Works Committee were embarrassed by the leak of transcripts describing their hostile sentiments toward NEPA.

Key members of the House Public Works Committee are exploring ways to exempt major public works projects and federal highways from the nation's environmental protection law. Their strong opinions that there should be no environmental review after the committee approves a dam or a highway are revealed in the transcript of a secret meeting the committee held in February.

In one instance, the law is described as "a menace." In another, federal judges who have halted projects for environmental reasons are called "ignoramuses." . . . "I want to find something that will shortstop all of these little pestiferous suits that are hamstringing the programs," said Rep. Jim Wright (D-Tex.) during the closed session. Commenting on the transcript, Wright said that he did not know that a stenographic record was being made.

"I could have expressed myself better. You can't win on that kind of statement. You lose the Baptists when you say 'hell,' and you lose the Catholics when you say 'the hell with fish.'" The transcript, he said, accurately reflected his view that citizen suits should be limited to residents of the area affected by a project. He remarked that he supported NEPA in the 1969 House vote that created it.

At another point Wright said, "Well, the hell with the fish . . . I like wildlife and fishlife and animal life, but mainly the environment exists for human life, and we are improving the environment for human life."

Wright and the acting committee chairman, Rep. Robert E. Jones (D-Ala.), proposed specifying that projects authorized by the committee be "presumed to have on balance a favorable environmental impact."

"It seems to me that after a project has been analyzed and considered in the democratic, legislative process, that should have some finality," Jones contended. The lawsuits, he protested, "are being maliciously used to halt the projects that Congress has worked for years and years to accomplish." . . .

Source: "Public Works Planners Assail Ecology Review." *Washington Post,* May 2, 1972: A2.

4

DDT:

Should the Environmental Protection Agency Have Banned DDT?

—∿—

THE CONTROVERSY

The Issue

In the early 1970s, the newly created Environmental Protection Agency (EPA) was faced with the decision of whether or not to ban DDT, a pesticide that had been used heavily since World War II to combat insect pests in agriculture and to protect public health. Since the late 1950s, wildlife scientists, conservationists, and a growing number of the public complained that DDT was having devastating effects on wildlife, especially birds. Critics argued that DDT's properties made it inherently unsafe to use and that it posed an unacceptable risk to human health. Defenders of DDT, which included pesticide manufacturers, many farmers, and others involved in the agriculture industry and in public health, asserted that DDT was essential to agricultural productivity and to public health. They argued that the benefits of DDT strongly outweighed its costs, and they asserted that DDT was safe if used responsibly. They warned that banning DDT would result in increased costs for agriculture and increase the incidence of preventable diseases. The debate over DDT was one of the most visible environmental controversies of the period and it was significant because it forced the public to consider the consequences, both intentional and unintentional, of attempts to control nature. At the same time, the debate revealed the limitations of science to resolve questions or provide conclusive answers. Nevertheless, after more than a year of hearings on the issue from both sides, the EPA administrator had to answer the question: Should DDT be banned?

- ◆ ***Arguments to ban DDT:*** Critics of DDT argued that the pesticide should be banned because it posed a serious threat to the ecosystem and to human health. They pointed to DDT's unusual mobility through the environment, its persistence, its bioaccumulative qualities, and evidence that it was deadly to many forms of wildlife. Moreover, they argued that it posed an unacceptable risk to human health. They asserted that DDT could not be used safely.

♦ **Arguments against banning DDT:** Defenders of DDT argued that the pesticide was essential to agriculture and to the protection of public health from disease-carrying pests. They argued that DDT had proven its worth and its safety over the years and that there was no evidence that DDT was unsafe for humans despite widespread use and exposure. Finally, they disputed the significance and veracity of claims of widespread contamination and damage to wildlife and warned that banning DDT would have unacceptable consequences.

—◊◊◊—

INTRODUCTION

DDT is the common name of the chemical dichlorodiphenyltrichloroethane, which was used as an insecticide beginning in the early 1940s. DDT became one of the most commonly used pesticides in the country following its dramatic success in combating disease-carrying insects during World War II. After 1945, DDT was used extensively to control insect pests that carry disease or damage crops, especially cotton. In the immediate postwar period, there was considerable optimism for the promises of scientific and technological progress, and few people questioned the benefits of newly developed chemical products. However, doubts about DDT began to emerge in the late 1950s as the government embarked on its most aggressive pesticide campaigns to eradicate a range of insect pests across the country. Wildlife scientists and many others complained about heavy losses of songbirds and fish, as well as beneficial insects, in areas where the pesticides were applied. However, it was the publication of a book by Rachel Carson entitled *Silent Spring* in 1962 that aroused public alarm about the widespread environmental effects of pesticides and other chemicals. Until the publication of *Silent Spring,* few people had considered the possibility that pesticides could pose a serious threat to both the ecosystem and human health.

The debate over DDT reached its pinnacle in the late 1960s and early 1970s just as the environmental movement was at its height. Indeed, the debate over DDT was a defining issue of the new environmental consciousness; it embodied critical questions about the role of science and technology in society, the meaning of progress, and the relative priorities of economic activity, public health, and environmental stewardship. The debate over DDT was also remarkable because it reflected the dramatic transformation in public attitudes that had occurred. When it was first introduced, DDT was hailed as another miracle of modern technology, but two decades later it was now feared to be another unforeseen failure of technology. DDT was repeatedly analyzed and debated by scientists, the popular media, and the government. However, the most influential debates took place through a series of agency and court hearings between 1968 and 1972, during which the critics and defenders of DDT presented their arguments before government officials with the power to control its use.

Critics of DDT argued that the pesticide was inherently unsafe both for the ecosystem and human health. Numerous wildlife scientists and other experts pointed to a growing body of scientific evidence that showed that DDT was a dangerously persistent chemical in the environment. More specifically, they argued that DDT had a tendency to build up in the bodies of a wide variety of organisms and became more concentrated as one organism was eaten by another organism—a process called bioaccumulation. The end result was toxic levels of DDT in creatures that were higher up the food chain, such as fish and especially birds. They argued that entire species were at risk and that there was no way to control this problem so long as the pesticide remained in use. Finally, critics pointed to laboratory evidence that showed that DDT could cause cancer and other problems in laboratory rats, leading some scientists to warn that DDT was also a threat to humans. They demanded that DDT be banned.

The defenders of DDT brought forth their own scientists and experts who challenged both the significance and the veracity of claims made by environmentalists and other critics of DDT. They were especially critical of claims surrounding DDT's potential threat to human health. Defenders argued that there was no direct evidence that DDT was a threat to human health despite decades of use and studies. More important, however, supporters of DDT argued that critics failed to appreciate the importance of the benefits of DDT for agriculture and for protecting public health from disease. The criticisms of DDT, they argued, were exaggerated and shortsighted. They warned that banning DDT would result in economic hardship for farmers and threaten public health. Substitutes for DDT would be more expensive and would likely be even more toxic.

By spring 1972, formal hearings on DDT had concluded. It was now the responsibility of officials in the recently created Environmental Protection Agency to issue a judgment based on the arguments and evidence presented. Could DDT be used safely? Should DDT be banned?

BACKGROUND

Insect-borne disease has always been an unwelcome companion to war and other social disasters. Indeed, for much of history, disease during war has been a bigger source of death and disability than combat itself. During the American Revolution in 1776, one-third of the Continental army was infected and debilitated by louse-borne typhus during the Long Island campaign. When Napoleon's army invaded Russia in 1812, typhus and other diseases played a significant part in his defeat. During World War I, millions of soldiers and refugees in eastern Europe were infected by typhus and malaria, leading to large numbers of deaths. In Russia alone, more than 3 million died from typhus. During a British campaign into Salonika, Greece, for every one British soldier killed or injured in combat, six were debilitated due to malaria.

At the outset of World War II, Allied military leaders were quite aware of the threat from insect-borne diseases, especially typhus and malaria. However, little progress had been made since the previous war. Researchers knew that the key was to control the insects that transmitted these diseases. For typhus, this was the human body louse, and for malaria, the mosquito. The urgency of insect control became apparent early in the war. Less than a year after the United States had entered the war, the entire 1st Marine Division had to be withdrawn from the Pacific theater because more than half of the troops had contracted malaria. The U.S. Office of Scientific Research and Development worked closely with the U.S. Department of Agriculture's (USDA) Bureau of Entomology to find an effective way to combat insects on the battlefield. The solution arrived in the form of a synthetic pesticide in the winter of 1942. J. R. Geigy, a Swiss chemical dye company, had developed the pesticide, which they named Gesarol, in 1939, and applied it to a number of crop pests in Europe with great success. The pesticide displayed a profound toxicity for insects, while appearing to have almost no toxic effects on mammals, including humans. Moreover, unlike traditional pesticides, it was extremely long lasting, requiring infrequent reapplication. U.S. researchers identified the active ingredient as dichlorodiphenyltrichloroethane—or DDT for short.

U.S. researchers analyzed DDT for its effectiveness and safety, but the real test came in the field when it was called on to control an incipient outbreak of typhus. In October 1943, the American army captured the city of Naples, Italy, and found that public health and hygiene conditions had deteriorated badly during the war. By some estimates, nearly 90 percent of the city's residents suffered from body lice. By December, there were reports of typhus outbreaks, which marked the beginning of an epidemic. Nearly a quarter of those infected died. The army instituted an emergency delousing campaign using DDT. By the end of January 1944, more than 1 million residents of Naples and surrounding communities had been treated with an insecticidal bath of DDT powder. The number of new cases of typhus dropped dramatically, and by March the epidemic was over. This was the first time that a typhus epidemic had been stopped through human intervention. DDT thereafter became an integral part of the war effort in both Europe and the Pacific. By the end of 1944, American production of DDT had grown to more than 2 million pounds per month, almost entirely for the war effort.

U.S. authorities released DDT for civilian use in August 1945, and like many wartime inventions—from radar to nuclear energy—it was received enthusiastically as another modern marvel of technology. (See "'How Magic Is DDT?' 1945," on page 141 in the Primary Sources section.) DDT was adopted for a wide variety of applications: agriculture, suppression of disease-carrying insects, and control of a wide variety of pests that were simply annoying. As both the Swiss and American researchers discovered, DDT had a number of unique properties that made it not only different but superior to previous forms of pest control, especially for agriculture. Prior to DDT, farmers relied on a limited set of chemical products to control pests, such as copper arsenate, calcium arsenate, and lead arsenate. These older forms of chemical pest control were problematic because they were expensive, short-lived, requiring frequent reapplication, and acutely toxic, not only to pests, but to humans as well. Many contained arsenic and lead, which posed a constant threat for both farmworkers and consumers if too much residue remained. By contrast, DDT was cheap to produce, required very little to be effective, lasted for a long time without reapplication, and, by most accounts, was only really toxic to insects. Except in massive doses, DDT was not acutely toxic to humans or other mammals. DDT thus became the pesticide of choice for commercial agriculture, especially for intensively farmed crops such as cotton. Indeed, DDT came to be used extensively throughout the world both for agriculture and public health.

Because of its low acute toxicity to humans, DDT was adopted for use in urban and suburban communities. By the late 1940s, the USDA recommended that DDT be used to control beetles that were spreading Dutch elm disease, a fungus that was destroying the stately elm trees that lined streets in communities throughout the East and Midwest. In addition, public health agencies widely adopted DDT to control mosquito populations. In the southern United States, malaria was virtually eliminated. Globally, the World Health Organization estimated that 5 million deaths from malaria had been prevented by 1950 as a result of DDT mosquito-eradication programs. The importance of DDT for public health was such that Paul Müller, the Swiss scientist who discovered DDT's insecticidal properties, was awarded the Nobel Prize in physiology or medicine "for his discovery of the high efficiency of DDT as a contact poison against several arthropods."

Enthusiasm for DDT was high in the immediate postwar years, but it was also apparent early on that DDT had its limitations. Despite heavy and repeated applications in certain regions, mosquitoes and other insect pests were never completely eradicated. In addition, some insects were already showing resistance to DDT as early as the late 1940s. There was also the problem of collateral damage to beneficial insects and other nontarget organisms, since DDT did not discriminate among insects. In some cases, when mosquitoes did return to an area previously treated, their numbers were even greater because natural predators had been eliminated.

The more important concern for some authorities was the potential harm to human health from the chemical itself. While DDT was largely judged safe, officials at the U.S. Food and Drug Administration (FDA) and some in the medical community warned that little was known about the long-term effects of chronic exposure to DDT. One particularly worrisome property of DDT was its tendency to become concentrated in the body fat of many different animals, including humans. In fact, the FDA early on issued recommendations that DDT not be used on or near dairy farms because it tended to show up in cows' milk, even without direct exposure. However, the only national law governing pesticides was the 1947 Federal Insecticide, Fungicide and Rodenticide Act (FIFRA), which was aimed principally at ensuring that pesticide manufacturers labeled their products accurately and did not make false promises to farmers about a product's effectiveness. There was no system in place to judge or regulate the overall safety of any chemical product before it was distributed or sold.

DDT reached its peak usage in the United States in the mid- to late 1950s, and it was during this time that wildlife scientists and many in the general public first became concerned about the chemical's impacts. The U.S. Fish and Wildlife Service (FWS) was one of the first agencies to systematically test the use of DDT around wildlife, and they recommended that DDT not be sprayed indiscriminately over large areas, especially not over bodies of water, because it resulted in high mortality of birds, fish, and other organisms besides insects. Despite these warnings, the USDA and leading members of Congress developed ambitious pest-eradication programs using DDT. The campaign to control Dutch elm disease was joined in 1957 by a massive DDT spray program to contain and then eliminate the gypsy moth, a pest that threatened forests in the Northeast. As DDT use increased, scientists and observant members of the public noticed high numbers of dead and dying birds, or else the near complete absence of birds, in areas that had been sprayed with DDT. (See "'Backfire in the War Against Insects,' 1959," on page 143 in the Primary Sources section.)

On Long Island, New York, a prominent ornithologist led a group of residents to file suit against the secretary of the USDA in an unsuccessful attempt to stop the spraying. Despite a growing public outcry, the USDA subsequently announced another campaign to eradicate the fire ant, an imported pest in the southern part of the United States. Poison bait containing dieldrin, a persistent pesticide similar to DDT, was spread liberally over large areas of the South. As some critics had predicted, the fire ant campaign caused enormous losses of birds and fish and was especially damaging to commercial fisheries. As a result, several southern states withdrew from the program or refused to participate. The outcry prompted Congress to allocate funds to investigate and monitor the distribution of insecticides and their effects—one of the first such programs to do so. Although many people were critical of the pesticide programs, most blamed the problems on the USDA's incompetence and indiscriminate or excessive use of the pesticides, rather than any inherent problem with the chemicals themselves. Moreover, general public attention to pesticide problems was short-lived and exceptional.

Scientific understanding about DDT's environmental effects built up slowly. Beginning in the mid-1950s, scientists sought to understand how and why applications of DDT resulted in such heavy mortality among birds, especially since the birds did not ingest the chemical directly. One explanation was that the DDT had eradicated their food sources, thus starving them to death, a phenomenon that had been observed among fish in streams or ponds that were sprayed. However, one scientist studying the effect of DDT on robins in Wisconsin hypothesized that the birds absorbed the pesticide when they ate worms, which in turn had absorbed the pesticide after eating the leaf litter beneath trees that had been sprayed. One of the more remarkable observations of this analysis was that the dead birds had toxic concentrations of DDT that were many times the concentration in the worms. This seemed to indicate that the birds were not ingesting toxic levels of the pesticide all at once, but rather were accumulating the chemical in their bodies one worm at a time, until it eventually reached toxic levels. The most startling analysis on this front came from a study in California released in 1960.

Between 1948 and 1957, park managers had witnessed waves of die-offs of Western grebes, a waterbird, in Clear Lake, California (100 miles north of San Francisco). Investigators discovered that the dead birds contained toxic levels of DDD (a chemical similar to DDT). DDD had been applied to Clear Lake in 1948, 1954, and 1957, in order to control the Clear Lake gnat, an insect nuisance for vacationing campers and other visitors. Although the pesticide had been applied to the lake in extremely minute quantities—one part in 70 million—the investigators reasoned that the grebes had been killed off through a process of bioaccumulation of the chemical. Samples of lake plankton contained 5.3 million parts per million (ppm) of DDD—265 times the concentration of the water itself. Fish that ate the plankton had concentrations twice that amount, while carnivorous fish and some of the birds that ate the fish had levels of DDD that were up to 85,000 times that

Former federal wildlife biologist and nature writer Rachel Carson at her home on September 24, 1962. Her book *Silent Spring* changed the world's attitude toward DDT and other synthetic chemicals in the environment. (Alfred Eisenstaedt/Time & Life Pictures/Getty Images)

of the lake water. Thus, the chemical became more concentrated as it moved up the food chain. This study and similar ones provided a better understanding of the mechanisms by which birds and other organisms were affected and the implications were disturbing. Pesticides like DDT and DDD were not degrading in the environment but rather were accumulating in the bodies of a variety of organisms. No matter how small or diluted the application, the evidence indicated that these chemicals persisted and could build up to toxic levels.

As understanding of bioaccumulation grew, ornithologists around the world were also confronted by alarming evidence of declining populations of raptors: bald eagles in Florida, ospreys in Long Island Sound, and peregrine falcons along the U.S. East Coast and in western Europe. Rather than large numbers of dead birds, researchers observed that these birds were failing to produce offspring. DDT was strongly suspected, but the evidence was still incomplete and the scientific community was very cautious about assigning blame without more conclusive evidence. Until the early 1960s, serious concerns and debate about DDT were largely confined to the scientific community and occasionally government officials. This would change.

The debate over pesticides became unexpectedly public in summer 1962 with the publication of Rachel Carson's *Silent Spring.* (See *"Silent Spring,* 1962," on page 146 in the Primary Sources section.) Carson was a former government biologist and renowned nature writer who had followed the scientific debate over persistent pesticides since the late 1950s. In *Silent Spring,* parts of which first appeared in the *New Yorker,* Carson did something that no one else had yet done or even considered—she drew public attention to the widespread damage caused by pesticides and the potential for human harm. In exceptionally lucid and accessible prose, she explained what was then known about the effects of pesticides on wildlife, the ecological implications of these impacts, and, more alarmingly, the risk to human health. She made a case for the use of nonchemical control of pests and argued that humanity would be better served by finding ways to work with nature, rather than seeking ways to conquer or dominate nature. *Silent Spring* sold hundreds of thousands of copies and generated a storm of controversy. Carson's message resonated with the growing public anxiety about the proliferation of synthetic chemicals in the environment. It was also a public relations nightmare for the agriculture and pesticide industries, many of whom accused Carson of exaggerating and generating unwarranted panic.

As the publicity around *Silent Spring* and its warning about the risks of pesticides grew, the pesticides and agribusiness industry representatives responded with a deluge of articles and expert statements in the popular media to calm fears and educate the public about the importance of pesticides and their safety. Other groups were not so restrained. Economic entomologists (those entomologists who study insects that are of benefit or cause harm to humans, domestic animals, or crops) and other scientists directly involved with pesticides and agriculture were particularly harsh in their criticisms of both *Silent Spring* and Carson herself. They responded as if Carson had impugned their discipline, scientific competence, and objectivity. Indeed, Carson had pointed out that many of the scientific authorities on pesticides, including those on the elite National Research Council of the National Academy of Sciences panel on pesticides, worked directly for or were funded by chemical companies. However, the most vehement criticism was in response to Carson's questioning of technological progress and her critique of society's attempt to exert control over nature. This argument threatened the very notion of modern progress. (See "'Silence, Miss Carson,' 1962," on page 148 in the Primary Sources section.)

The public had reason to question the idea of technology and science as a panacea and humanity's ability to control nature. Americans were at a critical juncture in their understanding and faith in science and technology. When *Silent Spring* was published, the country was in the midst of a heated political debate over proposals to ban aboveground testing of atomic bombs. Since the late 1950s, the public had learned how the fallout from the testing of atomic bombs in otherwise remote areas—the Nevada desert and atolls in the Pacific Ocean—was actually spreading around the globe, carried by fast-moving winds in the upper atmosphere. According to reports, strontium 90, a radioactive by-product of atomic explosions, was raining down on everyone, showing up in cows' milk, and threatening to unleash an epidemic of cancer. Other concerns were also at play. Only a year before the publication of *Silent Spring,* researchers in Australia and Europe traced an alarming increase in bizarre birth defects to prescription drugs containing the chemical thalidomide. Since the late 1950s, physicians had prescribed thalidomide as a gentle sleep and antinausea medication for pregnant women. Thousands of children were later born without arms or legs, some with hands attached directly to their shoulders. More than 8,000 children in 46 countries were affected, many born blind, deaf, or epileptic. When researchers made the connection between thalidomide and the birth defects, the drug had not yet been approved for use in the United States, though it might easily have been had the problem not been discovered. A month after the *New Yorker* ran Carson's articles, the *Washington Post* ran a front page story about a "heroic" FDA physician who had stubbornly resisted approving thalidomide for U.S. distribution despite pressure and lobbying efforts by its drug company. Thus, the timing of *Silent Spring* was significant, emerging at the height of public awareness and concern about the dangers of synthetic chemicals.

The public reaction to *Silent Spring* prompted greater government scrutiny of pesticides, particularly DDT. In August 1962, President John F. Kennedy ordered the President's Science Advisory Committee (PSAC) to study the issues raised by Carson. PSAC issued its report less than a year later in May 1963. (See "President's Science Advisory

Committee, 1963," on page 150 in the Primary Sources section.) The report acknowledged the many benefits to society from pesticides but concluded that decision making concerning pesticides was based more on pest control efficacy than on safety. It noted that "until publication of *Silent Spring* by Rachel Carson, people generally were unaware of the toxicity of pesticides." PSAC recommended tighter federal regulation of pesticides, better coordination between federal agencies that dealt with pesticides, and more research on the efforts of both chemical as well as nonchemical pest-control technologies. It also called for a federal monitoring program to track the production, sale, and use of chemical pesticides across the country. More significant, the PSAC report lent credibility to Carson's argument. It recommended that the federal government phase out all uses of persistent pesticides like DDT. President Kennedy publicly endorsed the PSAC report and directed executive agencies to implement its recommendations. The president's stance seemed to indicate a bold, new direction for national pesticide policy, but it was actually only the beginning of the debate. Between 1963 and 1964, Congress held almost a dozen separate committee and subcommittee hearings on pesticides. Six bills to reform pesticide policy were introduced in 1963 alone. Moreover, the PSAC report was only one of several major government studies in the 1960s on the issue of pesticides, and not all of them agreed on the alleged problem or the future direction of pesticide policy.

Despite considerable government deliberation, there was relatively little change in pesticide policy through most of the 1960s. Indeed, many controversial practices, such as the USDA's pesticide campaign against the fire ant, continued despite widespread complaints. But public concern about environmental issues grew dramatically toward the end of the decade, and environmental organizations adopted new tactics to force change. One environmental organization in particular—the Environmental Defense Fund (EDF)—led the charge against DDT. Instead of lobbying legislators or raising funds through membership drives, the EDF used the courts to pursue its agenda. (See the sidebar "'Sue the Bastards!'" on page 124.) More specifically, the EDF sought out opportunities to bring the scientific case against DDT before the public and into the legal record. These efforts eventually forced the government to hold a formal hearing on the case for and against DDT and to make a decision: Should DDT be banned?

THE DEBATE

By 1968, DDT and pesticide policy in general were the subject of growing criticism. In September, investigations by the U.S. General Accounting Office (GAO) revealed systematic failures by the USDA to enforce existing pesticide regulations under FIFRA, despite widespread violations. In November 1968, the Wisconsin Department of Agriculture and the University of Wisconsin announced that they would not recommend DDT for control of Dutch elm disease. In January 1969, Arizona began a moratorium on DDT in agriculture. It was followed in April by Michigan, which became the first state in the nation to ban DDT after the FDA seized 22,000 pounds of the state's Coho salmon because the fish contained excessively high concentrations of pesticides. Public alarm was especially roused after the National Cancer Institute (NCI) issued a report in June 1969 showing that mice exposed to low levels of DDT had an increased incidence of liver tumors. The mounting criticisms prompted the USDA and the U.S. Department of Health, Education and Welfare (HEW)—agencies with jurisdiction over federal pesticide policy—to initiate renewed investigations of the health and safety issues surrounding the use of DDT and other pesticides.

With growing public sentiment on their side, the EDF and other environmental organizations filed a formal petition requesting the USDA and HEW to immediately suspend all use of DDT and to initiate the process to cancel its status as a legally registered pesticide under FIFRA. In response to the petition, HEW secretary Robert Finch announced on November 12, 1969, that the federal government planned to phase out all but essential uses of DDT by the end of 1971. He specifically cited concerns raised by the NCI study. USDA secretary Clifford M. Hardin also announced a ban on residential uses of DDT to begin in 90 days. However, environmentalists were not satisfied with these concessions, nor did they trust the promises made. In December 1969, the EDF filed suit with the court of appeals in Washington, D.C., to force the agencies to take more aggressive action. In May 1970, the court of appeals sided with the EDF and ordered the USDA to suspend all DDT use within 30 days or justify its failure to do so. USDA secretary Hardin refused, arguing that DDT was not an imminent threat to human health or wildlife and that it was essential for certain agricultural products. A

(continues on page 126)

"SUE THE BASTARDS!"

During the 1960s, Carol Yannacone had become increasingly concerned about recurring fish kills in Yapshank Lake, her childhood home in Long Island, New York. In 1966, she learned that the fish kills were due to applications of DDT and that the Suffolk County Mosquito Control Commission was planning on adding another 60,000 gallons of the pesticide to the lake in order to kill mosquito larvae. She asked her husband, Victor Yannacone, a local lawyer and environmental activist, to do something. Victor Yannacone filed suit against the county to get an injunction on behalf of Carol Yannacone and "all others entitled to the full use and enjoyment" of the lake. For help in building the case, he turned to the Brookhaven Town Natural Resources Committee (BTNRC), a local environmental group that included scientists from the Brookhaven National Laboratory and the State University of New York at Stony Brook. When the case went before the state supreme court in November 1966, Yannacone and the BTNRC presented an argument based on scientific evidence of DDT's harm and on the novel argument that everyone in Suffolk County had a right to an undegraded environment. The judge was persuaded of DDT's harm and ordered a temporary injunction blocking the county's use of DDT. Although the judge did not have the authority to permanently ban the use of DDT, county officials decided to discontinue use of DDT for fear of more lawsuits. Yannacone and BTNRC scientists were surprised and thrilled by the outcome and looked for ways to build on their success.

In September 1967, Victor Yannacone was invited to address an annual convention of the National Audubon Society, where he attempted to convince the conservation organization to establish an environmental legal defense fund in order to address the pesticide issue. Although Audubon members were concerned about DDT, the organization's conservative leadership was uncomfortable with such adversarial tactics. Nevertheless, they agreed to provide partial financial support to Yannacone and his colleagues through Audubon's Rachel Carson Memorial Fund. Shortly thereafter, Yannacone and the BTNRC officially formed the Environmental Defense Fund (EDF). The new organization's mission was to use science and the courts to halt environmentally destructive activities and to build legal case law recognizing citizens' rights to a clean environment.

From the very beginning, the EDF adopted an aggressive strategy to seek out court opportunities where it could build the legal-scientific case against DDT and attract public attention. Victor Yannacone became known for his trademark phrase, "Sue the bastards!" which was fitting both for his approach and style: flamboyant, dramatic, quick-witted, and always aware that he was talking to the court and to the media. In the initial years, the EDF was rarely successful in its courtroom efforts, but it was almost always successful in the court of public opinion.

The EDF had to be creative in its legal maneuvers. Before 1970, few courts would give the EDF the opportunity to bring its cases to trial. However, in late 1968, the EDF found an opportunity in an unusual regulatory process under Wisconsin law that allowed citizens to request a hearing on environmental regulations. The EDF had finally found the opportunity to present its case against DDT, and it did so effectively and with maximum publicity. Indeed, the Wisconsin hearings allowed the EDF to develop most of the arguments and scientific testimony that would constitute much of the case that would eventually come before the Environmental Protection Agency. Although representatives of the pesticide industry and the U.S. Department of Agriculture appeared at the Wisconsin hearing as well, they were completely unprepared for such a vigorous and comprehensive trial. The event was a major public relations victory for the EDF and against DDT.

The EDF's dramatically successful use of the courts to influence environmental policy established a new precedent for environmental advocacy, and it was followed by a number of new and established organizations, including the Natural Resources Defense Council (1970) and the Sierra Club Legal Defense Fund (1971). At the same time, opportunities for environmental litigation increased in the 1970s as the courts liberalized the qualifications for legal standing to sue. Congress expanded the possibilities as well. In several pieces of environmental legislation, such as the Clean Water Act of 1972 and the Endangered Species Act of 1973, Congress incorporated citizen suit provisions, which specifically gave individuals the right to sue federal agencies in order to compel those agencies to follow the law, meet their statutory obligations, or prosecute violations of environmental law. Environmental litigation thus had become an integral part of environmental policy.

(continued from page 123)
few months later, the USDA announced cancellation of more than 50 uses of DDT, but exempted cotton, which accounted for more than 75 percent of all DDT use in the nation.

In December 1970, jurisdiction over pesticide registration and regulation was transferred from the USDA to the newly created Environmental Protection Agency (EPA). Environmentalists had high hopes for the new agency, which they regarded as a likely ally in their campaigns against environmentally destructive activities and industries. Nevertheless, the EDF wasted no time in filing suit against the EPA to force the new agency to review the USDA's decision not to suspend use of DDT or cancel the pesticide's registration. In January 1971, the court of appeals in Washington, D.C., ordered EPA administrator William Ruckelshaus to suspend all uses of DDT immediately and to begin cancellation proceedings. Administrator Ruckelshaus followed the court's

A plane dusts sheep against ticks using a pesticide containing 10 percent DDT powder on the Hoover ranch in Medford, Oregon, in 1948. Before concerns about its environmental impacts arose in the 1960s, the pesticide was applied with few constraints. (Associated Press)

orders but, after a 60-day review, lifted the suspension because the agency found that DDT was not an imminent hazard to human health. Nevertheless, the EPA had initiated the process for permanent cancellation of DDT's registration as a legal pesticide.

Pesticide manufacturers and the USDA protested the cancellation and requested a formal hearing, which was their right under FIFRA. In August 1971, the EPA convened a consolidated DDT hearing, which would provide the final forum for a direct confrontation between critics and defenders of DDT. The hearing was conducted like a trial, with each side given an opportunity to present its case, cross-examine witnesses, and rebut the other's arguments. The hearings would last until March 1972, bringing forth 125 expert witnesses and generating more than 9,000 pages of testimony—the most extensive public discussion on DDT ever held. The question before the contestants was straightforward: Could DDT be used safely?

The Case for DDT

Defenders of DDT included 33 companies, called group petitioners, as well as the USDA. Because the EPA had already initiated cancellation proceedings, the petitioners bore the burden of showing that DDT was safe when used as directed. They argued that three decades of experience had proven that the benefits of DDT to agriculture and public health outweighed any risks. More important, they argued that history and more recent studies had shown that DDT was not a hazard to humans. Their most impressive and reliable ally was Dr. Wayland Hayes, professor of toxicology at Vanderbilt University and former head of toxicology at the U.S. Public Health Service (PHS). Hayes had conducted studies of direct human exposure to DDT since the late 1950s involving men who worked in the manufacture of DDT and prisoners who voluntarily ingested DDT for over a year. He cited his own work and that of others to argue that there was no evidence that DDT led to any identifiable health problems in humans. Moreover, he and others criticized the use of laboratory results from animals as a basis for predicting human risk, including cancer. One petitioner argued, "We find it inconceivable that [the EPA] and [EDF] have, in effect, placed 72 mice ahead of a quarter century of DDT's usage unsurpassed in the history of man in terms of safety as a chemical pesticide."

The petitioners asserted that continued use of DDT was necessary and justified. For cotton crops, in particular, they argued that available alternatives were expensive, impractical, and, in some cases, more acutely toxic to humans than DDT. Ned Bayley, director of science and education for the USDA, acknowledged that DDT could be harmful to nontarget organisms, but he argued that the pesticide would eventually be replaced. Indeed, uses of DDT had already declined significantly. In the interim, however, the agricultural community needed more time. The petitioners disputed arguments that DDT was inherently dangerous to wildlife or that it was responsible for widespread harm to certain species of wildlife. They blamed such harm, as well as the chemical's widespread presence, on past abuse and misuse of the pesticide. Finally, the petitioners argued that DDT was still important for safeguarding human health from insect-borne diseases. They warned that banning DDT would have dire consequences in other countries that depended on DDT to combat malaria, which would inevitably follow the U.S. lead if the pesticide was judged unsafe.

The Case Against DDT

The case against DDT was led by a lawyer for the EPA, the agency whose decision it was to cancel registration. The EDF's lawyer assisted the EPA as an Intervenor representing several environmental organizations, including the Sierra Club, the National Audubon Society, and the West Michigan Environmental Action Council. The EPA lawyer and the intervenors argued that DDT was inherently unsafe and unnecessary. They asserted that DDT was responsible for widespread environmental contamination, threatened various species of birds, and posed an unacceptable risk to human health. The strongest body of evidence had to do with DDT's impacts on birds. Since the mid-1950s, wildlife scientists had amassed a considerable body of evidence indicating that DDT was most likely the cause of widespread population declines in raptors, including the symbolically important bald eagle. In addition to the bioaccumulation of toxins, scientists had concluded that DDT interfered with egg formation, resulting in the production of eggs with excessively thin shells that could not support the weight of the nesting birds. As a result, the eggs were literally crushed by their parents. The most affected species of bird seemed to be the peregrine falcon, whose global population decline was so conspicuous and dramatic that it had prompted emergency conferences of the world's top wildlife scientists. The critics of DDT argued that the direct danger of the pesticide to wildlife was compounded by its mobility. Studies revealed the presence of DDT in Antarctic penguins and in whales at sea, creatures that were far from the places where DDT had been directly applied. Thus, they argued, there was no way to control or limit the pesticide's spread and impact.

The EPA and the intervenors argued that the benefits of DDT did not justify the damage done to the ecosystem or the risks posed to humans. In direct contrast to the petitioners, the EPA and the EDF argued that laboratory tests on animals were legitimate measures of the potential threats to human health. Expert witnesses acknowledged that there was no direct evidence of pathological effects in humans, but there was evidence that the presence of DDT led to biochemical changes in the body, whose long-term impacts could not be adequately judged. Moreover, scientists had for years documented the ubiquitous and increasing presence of DDT in the bodies of most Americans, whether or not they had ever been directly exposed. These facts alone, they argued, warranted extreme caution. Finally, the EPA and the intervenors disputed the necessity of DDT. The U.S. surgeon general testified that DDT had not been used in the United States for public health applications in years. While critics acknowledged that DDT had in the past been beneficial for cotton production, they argued that this was no longer the case because of increasing pest resistance, as well as the availability of other forms of pest management that did not appreciably increase costs.

OUTCOME AND IMPACT

A month after the DDT hearings concluded, the hearing examiner Edmund Sweeney delivered his opinion in favor of the petitioners. He argued that the issue was essentially about a balance of risks and benefits. The benefits of DDT to public health and agriculture were well known and well documented, while the risks to human health and the ecosystem were inconclusive and even weak. He concluded

(continues on page 132)

FARMWORKERS, PESTICIDES, AND ENVIRONMENTALISTS

No group of people was more directly affected by pesticides than farmworkers. Farmwork has always been a uniquely dangerous occupation; workers are routinely at risk of injury from animals, machinery, and chemicals. As pesticide use in agriculture increased during the 20th century, so did injuries and poisonings. In the late 1960s, the issue of pesticides became an important part of labor disputes for farmworkers in California and enabled a brief alliance between farmworker unions and environmentalists.

Before the mid-1960s, California agriculture had come to rely almost exclusively on DDT and similar chlorinated hydrocarbon chemicals to control pests. However, after the mid-1960s, DDT became less effective and thus less popular as insects developed immunity to these types of pesticides. In response, farm owners in California began to switch to organophosphates, a new class of pesticides. Unlike DDT, organophosphates were acutely toxic but short-lived, which was good for consumers and wildlife. However, their acute toxicity increased the risk of pesticide poisoning for farmworkers who came into contact with recently treated crops. Indeed, as farms increasingly switched to organophosphates, there was an upsurge in pesticide poisonings. In January 1969, the California Department of Health released a survey showing that 71 percent of farmworkers displayed one or more symptoms of pesticide poisoning. Based on these findings, the state director of public health estimated that official reports of pesticide incidents represented only 1 percent of the number of actual poisonings, which he calculated to be 100,000 nonfatal poisonings a year.

The United Farm Workers (UFW), an organization devoted to unionization of farmworkers in California, pointed to the new findings as further evidence of the persistent exploitation and neglect of farmworkers. The UFW had struggled to unionize California farmworkers since the early 1960s but faced severe obstacles in trying to organize largely impoverished migrant laborers, many of whom feared retribution by their employers or the authorities. Indeed, these unionization efforts were vehemently opposed by the powerful California agribusiness industry and many public officials. While the UFW was genuinely alarmed by the risk of pesticides, it also saw the issue as an opportunity to generate public support and to gain leverage in its efforts to negotiate union contracts with farm owners. From the spring of 1969 onward, the UFW emphasized the pesticide problem as an issue of workplace health and safety, social justice, and consumer safety from poisonous residues on food. Throughout 1969 and into 1970, the UFW launched an aggressive publicity campaign and boycott of California grapes, highlighting the threat of pesticides to both farmworkers and to consumers. Beginning in June 1969, the UFW allied with the Environmental Defense Fund (EDF) to petition both California officials and the U.S. Department of Agriculture (USDA) to cancel use of DDT. In fact, the EDF represented UFW members in court when it later sued the USDA to cancel registration of DDT.

However, this alliance between farmworkers and environmentalists only went so far. While the EDF and other environmental organizations were eager to ban DDT, they were less interested in joining the UFW in its unionization efforts or in the campaign against the acutely toxic substitutes for DDT, such as organophosphates. Although none of the environmental organizations favored a proliferation of chemical pesticides, they reasoned that the short-lived organophosphates were preferable to persistent pesticides such as DDT. In response to the general problem of pesticide exposure, which included both DDT and the more toxic substitutes to which farms were switching, the UFW made pesticides a central issue in union contract negotiations. Specifically, the UFW demanded that a union contract committee have control over the application and monitoring of pesticides, and it called for a complete ban of "dangerous" pesticides, including DDT and a variety of organophosphate pesticides. Although farm owners initially balked at these demands, the bad publicity and economic impact of the boycott forced them to negotiate. By June 1970, farm owners throughout California began to sign union contracts with the UFW, which included the UFW's stipulations about pesticides. While significant, the UFW's unionization success was short-lived. By the mid-1970s, new economic pressures in agriculture, a changing workforce, and a lack of public interest led to a decline in the number and proportion of unionized farmworkers, which has continued to date. Pesticide exposure remains a pernicious health and safety risk for farmworkers.

(continued from page 129)

that DDT was not a hazard to either humans or wildlife. However, the final decision rested not with Sweeney but with EPA administrator Ruckelshaus.

In June 1972, the EPA administrator overruled the hearing administrator and issued an order banning all remaining uses of DDT on crops within six months, but allowing continued use of DDT for quarantine, public health, and manufacture for export to other countries. (See "'DDT Ban Takes Effect,' 1972," on page 152 in the Primary Sources section.) The administrator argued that the long-range risk of DDT outweighed any benefits for crop use. He explained that the evidence had convinced him that "once dispersed, DDT is an uncontrollable, durable chemical that persists in the aquatic and terrestrial environments." He concluded that the evidence had shown that DDT was not necessary for adequate cotton production. He validated the arguments put forth by the EDF that DDT was persistent, bioaccumulative, toxic to many organisms, and that there was no way that DDT could be used in such a way to prevent its undesirable environmental impacts. With regard to arguments about evidence of the risks to human health, Ruckelshaus argued that the possibility of harm could not be ignored, nor should it if alternatives were available. He stated, "The possibility that DDT is a carcinogen is at present remote and unquantifiable; but if it is not a siren to panic, it is a semaphore which suggests that an identifiable public benefit is required to justify continued use of DDT." Since there were pest control options that offered the same benefits but did not pose the same risks, Ruckelshaus argued, continued use of DDT was unjustifiable. The EPA administrator ordered that all crop uses of DDT should end in six months.

The case against DDT was part of an array of attacks on persistent pesticides, including dieldrin, aldrin, and mirex, and the DDT decision marked a significant change in environmental policy. The cancellation of DDT was contested in the courts for another year before appeals were finally exhausted and the EPA's decision upheld. Although the cancellation of DDT represented a major victory for the campaign against persistent pesticides, it did not signify a complete end to the use of all persistent pesticides, or even DDT. In addition to the slow process of the court appeals, EPA cancellation orders allowed for exceptions and for emergency uses. Nevertheless, domestic DDT use declined dramatically after the EPA's decision. The results of the decline were mixed, confirming predictions of both advocates and critics. Raptors, such as the bald eagle and peregrine falcon, made dramatic recoveries

Children playing in the DDT fog left behind by a TIFA (Todd Insecticidal Fog Applicator) truck in New Jersey in 1948. DDT was considered completely safe for human exposure until the 1960s, and neighborhood spraying was a common practice to control mosquitoes and other nuisance insects. (George Silk/Time Life Pictures/Getty Images)

in their numbers as the amount of DDT in the environment declined. Farmworkers, however, experienced an increase in pesticide injuries as DDT and similar chemicals were replaced by shorter-lived but more acutely toxic organophosphates. (See the sidebar "Farmworkers, Pesticides, and Environmentalists" on page 130.)

While the EPA had banned most domestic uses of DDT, it allowed for continued manufacture and export of DDT. As predicted, other countries followed the lead of the United States. By the 1980s, countries throughout the world had reduced or eliminated their use of DDT. However, public health officials found few effective alternatives for controlling mosquitoes and malaria, a serious disease and leading cause of death and disability in tropical and subtropical regions of the world. The tension between public health needs to control insect-borne diseases and environmentalist efforts to control persistent chemical pollutants found some compromise by the mid-1990s. In 1996, the United Nations Environmental Programme coordinated an international treaty to control the use and spread of persistent organic pollutants, but allowed for limited use of DDT to protect public health. The reasoning was that control of malaria was a pressing public health need, with few alternatives. At the same time, public health use of DDT would constitute a very controlled and limited application (especially in comparison to past uses for agriculture). In 2006, the World Health Organization (WHO) announced support for indoor use of DDT to control malaria in regions where the disease was endemic and posed a significant public health threat. Notably, the EDF, Sierra Club, and other environmental organizations joined the WHO in endorsing the limited use of DDT to control malaria in order to protect public health.

WHAT IF?

What if the EPA had not banned DDT?

If EPA administrator William Ruckelshaus had decided not to ban DDT, the debate over the persistent pesticide would have been extended indefinitely. Without question, the EDF and other environmental organizations would have taken the EPA back to court over such a decision, resulting in years of litigation. Such a decision would also have put pressure back on Congress to amend the federal insecticide law in order to address the lack of explicit consideration for health and environmental risks, especially if it appeared that the EPA was incapable or unwilling to exert control over such an unpopular product like DDT. Even without a federal ban, however, DDT use would likely have declined. Indeed, it had declined significantly before the ban due to increasing insect resistance as well as a proliferation of alternative products, many of which were no less potent. Manufacturers and distributors also faced a complicated and costly patchwork of pesticide regulations as states and localities passed their own restrictive rules or bans on DDT in the absence of federal leadership.

It is less certain what would have happened to bird species that were most affected by DDT. A year after the EPA administrator made his decision, Congress amended and significantly strengthened the Endangered Species Act (ESA), providing government officials and environmental activists with powerful legal tools to protect threatened or endangered plant and animal species. Only after the EPA ban on DDT and the passage of the strengthened ESA did bird species on the brink of extinction, such as the bald eagle and peregrine falcon, make dramatic recoveries. Without the ban, it is not clear if these species would have recovered so quickly, if at all.

CHRONOLOGY

1874   DDT was first synthesized by Othman Zeidler, a German chemist, as part of work on the substitution products of aromatic hydrocarbon compounds.

1910   Federal Insecticide Act requires chemical makers to list product ingredients and to guarantee to farmers that the products do what label claims. First federal law regulating pesticides is passed in response to proliferation of chemical products and fraudulent claims of effectiveness.

1939   Swiss scientist Paul Hermann Müller discovers DDT's insecticidal properties while working in the laboratory of the J. R. Geigy Dye-Factory Company. DDT used successfully against Colorado potato beetle and moths.

1942   American representative of Swiss company J. R. Geigy Dye-Factory secretly ships samples of DDT to United States as possible aid for Allies who are having great difficulties with vector-borne diseases. American Research Council for Insectology in Orlando (Florida) conducts trials and determines DDT performs as promised. DDT produced on massive scale for war effort.

1943   *October:* Heavy outbreak of typhus occurs in Naples, Italy.

1944   *January:* Approximately 1.3 million people are treated with DDT, and epidemic is halted in three weeks; first large-scale use of DDT to control an epidemic. First time in history a typhus outbreak was brought under control in winter. DDT is hailed as a miracle insecticide and used extensively in the war effort.

1945   *August:* DDT is allowed for civilian use.

1946   U.S. Food and Drug Administration (FDA) sets provisional tolerance levels for residues of DDT on food products. Zero tolerance level set for milk because of importance to infant diets. Warning issued against use of DDT on food or forage crops. Economic entomologists warn about collateral damage to other organisms from use of DDT.

1947   Federal Insecticide, Fungicide, and Rodenticide Act requires Department of Agriculture to register all pesticides prior to their introduction in interstate commerce. Manufacturers must ensure that product is safe and effective as claimed.

1948   Swiss scientist Paul Hermann Müller is awarded the Nobel Prize in physiology or medicine "for his discovery of the high efficiency of DDT as a contact poison against several arthropods."

1950–1951   House Select Committee to Investigate the Use of Chemicals in Food Products, chaired by James J. Delaney of New York, holds first public debate on safety of DDT, as well as other food additives and chemicals. FDA calls for changes in the law to establish safety of pesticides before allowing registration and sale.

1956   U.S. Department of Agriculture (USDA) conducts broadcast DDT spray campaign to control Dutch elm disease and gypsy moths in the Northeast. Public concern over collateral damage to birds and fish elicits protests.

1957	*March:* Congress passes legislation enabling USDA to conduct pesticide campaign to eradicate fire ants in the South. Illinois Audubon Society charges DDT spraying with massive die-off of birds.

April: USDA conducts spray campaign against gypsy moths in the Northeast.

May: New York governor notes significant fish kills as a result of spray campaigns against gypsy moths.

1958   *January:* USDA initiates campaign to eradicate fire ants in nine southern states using quarantine and ground and aerial spraying of dieldrin and heptachlor. Protests by conservation organizations and public about collateral damage to wildlife.

June: Federal court rejects suit by group of residents on Long Island, New York, to halt spraying of DDT to control gypsy moths. Court cites lack of evidence of harm to humans and rules that federal and state governments have a legal right to spray DDT for compelling public interest.

November: Delaney amendment to the 1938 Federal Food, Drug, and Cosmetic Act declares that the FDA cannot approve any food additive found to induce cancer in a person or animal.

1959   *November:* U.S. secretary of Health, Education and Welfare (HEW) warns that some cranberries grown in Oregon and Washington may be contaminated by aminotriazole, a herbicide to control weeds that is known to cause cancer in rats. Widespread fear causes havoc for cranberry industry.

1960   Study of die-off of western grebes in Clear Lake, California, provides startling evidence of persistence and bioaccumulative qualities of pesticides.

1962   *April:* Media reports crippling deformities in thousands of babies born in Europe due to thalidomide in sleeping pill prescribed to pregnant women.

June: New Yorker runs first of three articles excerpted from Rachel Carson's forthcoming book, *Silent Spring,* drawing attention to unintended consequences of widespread and indiscriminant use of chemicals.

August: President Kennedy announces formation of the President's Science Advisory Committee (PSAC) to study pesticide issues and concerns raised by *Silent Spring.*
September: Silent Spring is published.

1963 *April:* CBS airs "The Silent Spring of Rachel Carson."
May: PSAC releases report on pesticides that recommends limited use of pesticides and stronger regulatory controls. Report is endorsed by the president.

1966 Group in Long Island files suit in Suffolk County court to halt spraying of DDT to control mosquitoes, citing widespread damage to wildlife. Court rules against plaintiffs, but county halts spraying in response to bad publicity. Long Island group forms the Environmental Defense Fund (EDF).

1968 U.S. General Accounting Office releases report critical of Federal Insecticide, Fungicide, and Rodenticide Act and its enforcement by USDA.
December: EDF and Citizens Natural Resources Association of Wisconsin petition the Wisconsin Department of Natural Resources for a declaratory ruling on whether or not DDT is a water pollutant. The department conducts five months of hearings on DDT question.

1969 *January:* Arizona institutes one-year ban on use of DDT and DDD.
March: FDA seizes 22,000 pounds of Coho salmon in Michigan due to high levels of pesticide.
Michigan Department of Agriculture cancels all DDT registrations, except to control rodents and human body lice.
April: Sweden bans DDT for two years. Michigan is first state in the nation to institute full, permanent ban on DDT.
November: EDF, Sierra Club, West Michigan Environmental Action Council, and Audubon Society petition USDA and HEW to suspend registration of DDT and initiate cancellation proceedings to permanently ban DDT and to set zero tolerance levels for the presence of DDT in human food. HEW secretary Robert Finch announces plans to

phase out all but essential uses of DDT by end of 1971. USDA secretary orders end of use of DDT on shade trees, tobacco plants, around homes, and on marshes (except for disease control) and announces that DDT use will be largely halted by 1971. Vermont Agriculture Department announces ban on DDT, except for specified uses.

December: EDF petitions for review with court of appeals in D.C., asking court to direct secretaries of HEW and USDA to take "swifter and more effective action."

1970   *January:* Wisconsin bans sale and use of DDT.

May: Three-judge panel of court of appeals in D.C. orders USDA to suspend all DDT use within 30 days or justify failure to do so. Another court panel orders the HEW secretary to publish a proposed zero tolerance policy on DDT residue on raw food in the *Federal Register.*

December: Responsibility for pesticide registration and regulation is transferred to newly created Environmental Protection Agency (EPA).

1971   *January:* Court of appeals orders EPA administrator Ruckelshaus to cancel all uses of DDT immediately. EPA complies but, after 60-day review, refuses to suspend registration because DDT is not an imminent health hazard. EPA nevertheless proceeds with permanent cancellation process.

August: Consolidated DDT hearings are convened in response to protests of cancellation by 33 petitioners, including formulators, manufacturers, and users of DDT. Hearings last until March 1972.

1972   *April:* Consolidated DDT hearing examiner Edmund Sweeney issues opinion upholding petitioners' case against cancellation of DDT.

June: EPA administrator overrules the hearing examiner and bans all uses of DDT on crops but allows use for quarantine and public health, as well as emergencies, and manufacture for export.

1973   *December:* Court of appeals rules against industry appeals against DDT cancellation.

1974   EPA bans manufacture of dieldrin and aldrin, persistent
        pesticides similar to DDT, and cancels most uses of hepta-
        chlor and chlordane.

DISCUSSION QUESTIONS

1. Should the EPA have banned DDT? Why or why not?
2. What were the main criticisms of DDT? How did supporters of DDT respond to these criticisms?
3. Was the problem with DDT due to its misuse or was it inherently unsafe?
4. How did *Silent Spring* affect the DDT debate?
5. Was DDT an unacceptable risk for human health? Why or why not? Consider the contrasting forms of evidence presented by critics and supporters of DDT.
6. When the EPA issued its ban on DDT, far more DDT was being produced for export to other countries than was being used domestically. Nevertheless, production of DDT for export was not banned. Should the ban on DDT only apply to domestic uses? Why or why not?

WEB SITES

Agency for Toxic Substances and Disease Registry (ATSDR). Frequently Asked Questions for DDT, DDE, and DDD. Available online. URL: http://www.atsdr.cdc.gov/tfacts35.html. Accessed March 23, 2011.

Nobelprize.org. Nobel Prize in physiology or medicine 1948. Presentation Speech. Available online. URL: http://nobelprize.org/nobel_prizes/medicine/laureates/1948/press.html. Accessed March 23, 2011.

PBS. *Bill Moyers Journal.* "Rachel Carson." Available online. URL: http://www.pbs.org/moyers/journal/09212007/profile.html. Accessed March 23, 2011.

U.S. Environmental Protection Agency. DDT. Available online. URL: http://www.epa.gov/history/topics/ddt. Accessed March 23, 2011.

World Health Organization. Malaria. Frequently Asked Questions (FAQs) on DDT Use for Disease Vector Control. Available online. URL:

http://www.who.int/malaria/publications/atoz/who_htm_rbm_2004
_54/en/index.html. Accessed March 23, 2011.

BIBLIOGRAPHY

Bosso, Christopher J. *Pesticides & Policies: The Life Cycle of a Public Issue*. Pittsburgh, Pa.: University of Pittsburgh Press, 1987.
Carson, Rachel. *Silent Spring*. Boston, Mass.: Houghton Mifflin, 1962.
Dunlap, Thomas R. *DDT: Scientists, Citizens, and Public Policy*. Princeton, N.J.: Princeton University Press, 1981.
————. *DDT, Silent Spring, and the Rise of Environmentalism*. Seattle: University of Washington Press, 1987.
Stapleton, Darwin H. "The Short-Lived Miracle of DDT." *Invention and Technology Magazine* 15, no. 3 (Winter 2000). Available online. URL: http://www.americanheritage.com/articles/magazine/it/2000/3/2000_3_34.shtml.
"WHO Gives Indoor Use of DDT a Clean Bill of Health for Controlling Malaria." World Health Organization News Release, September 15, 2006. Available online. URL: http://www.who.int/mediacentre/news/releases/2006/pr50/en.

PRIMARY SOURCES

Document 1: "How Magic Is DDT?" 1945

DDT first proved its worth to American officials during World War II, helping to control insect-borne diseases such as malaria and typhus that were deadly threats to both troops and civilians alike. DDT was initially held as a closely guarded secret, but, beginning in August 1945, this "miracle" pesticide was officially released for civilian use. In this January 1945 article, U.S. brigadier general James Stevens Simmons, Chief of Preventive Medicine for the army, provided the public with an early account of the chemical's history and the exciting possibilities.

The initials DDT are used as a convenient nickname for a jawbreaking chemical term, dichloro-diphenyl-trichloroethane. In everyday language, this high-sounding chemical compound is a stable, almost colorless and practically odorless crystalline solid.

It is not soluble in water, but can be dissolved in many organic solvents, including kerosene and various other oils. It is one of the most powerful insect poisons known, one which affects the nervous system of the insect and produces jittery, spasmodic movements, followed by paralysis and, later, by death.

It is effective when used in infinitely small amounts and can be used highly diluted either as a powder or in oily solutions. It can kill many of our innumerable insect enemies, not only the annoying household pests and many of the plant parasites that ravage our crops and food supplies but also lice, mosquitoes and other dangerous, blood-sucking insects which are responsible for the spread of typhus fever, malaria and other serious diseases.

DDT is of great importance to all of us, both in helping to win the war and in improving the country's health after the war is over. DDT itself is fairly old. It has been known for seventy years, and its ability to kill certain of the insect pests of plants was observed about four years ago in Switzerland. However, its value as a military weapon for the control of insect-borne diseases has been discovered and developed by scientists in this country only during the past two years. At first, the results of this experimental work were blanketed by military secrecy. Recently, however, this secrecy has been lifted; the story of the use of DDT to control typhus in Naples has been announced and statements have been released concerning its effective use against malaria in many theaters.

Such reports have fired the popular imagination, and the symbol of DDT is acquiring a mysterious, romantic aura. It is coming so rapidly into common use that it bids fair to join the ranks of such well-known war-born Army terms as "jeep," "radar" and "bazooka." . . .

During the last few years, many new agricultural uses of DDT have been discovered and its great military value for the control of typhus and malaria has been demonstrated. However, we have only scratched the surface of its potentialities. . . . To those of us who believe that, when a magic key can work only in a lock well lubricated with the magic oil of world health, these potentialities are interesting. Therefore, the increasing production of DDT continues at full speed and the program of experimentation is being intensified and expanded in order to obtain answers to the innumerable questions which arise concerning its future use. . . .

It is fully realized that such a powerful insecticide may be a double-edge sword, and that its unintelligent use might eliminate certain valuable insects essential to agriculture and horticulture. Even more important, it might conceivably disturb vital balances in the animal and plant kingdoms and thus upset various fundamental biological cycles. In order to investigate all phases of these broader problems as well as to give additional help to the armed forces during the present emergency, an important new board on insect control has recently been established by the Office of Scientific Research and Development.

The possibilities of DDT are sufficient to stir the most sluggish imagination, but even if all investigations should cease today, we already have a proud record of achievement. In my opinion it is the War's greatest contribution to the future health of the world.

Source: James Stevens Simmons. "How Magic Is DDT?" *Saturday Evening Post,* January 6, 1945. ©SEPS licensed by Curtis Licensing.

—∾—

Document 2: "Backfire in the War Against Insects," 1959

By the late 1950s, wildlife scientists and attentive members of the public were complaining about collateral damage to wildlife from indiscriminate use of DDT. The U.S. Department of Agriculture's disastrous pesticide campaign against the fire ant, in particular, drew wide condemnation. Much of the blame for these problems was attributed to incompetent behavior by government agencies, rather than to any inherent quality of the pesticide itself. While popular opinion had not yet turned against pesticides or for the environment, the critical tone of this Reader's Digest *article—a largely conservative publication—is illustrative of changing attitudes.*

The United States is engaged in an intensive war against destructive insects. The weapons employed are powerful and widespread, and so is the controversy they have engendered. Billions of pounds of poisons were broadcast over 100 million acres of cropland and forest. More billions of pounds are being spread across the nation this year—against spruce budworm in northern forests, grasshoppers in nine million acres of wheatland in the Midwest, white fringed beetle in the Southeast; against sand flies, gnats, Japanese beetles, corn borers and gypsy moths. The U.S. Department of Agriculture [USDA] is only one of the large-scale users of insecticides. State, county and even local groups also employ them, sometimes in cooperation with USDA, sometimes alone. The new insecticides, often used as massive sprays from planes, kill birds, fish and animals along with insects of all kinds, good as well as bad. The costs of the campaigns in money, destruction of wildlife and possible harm to human health are not adequately known. The need for them is hotly challenged and hotly defended. . . .

The first public outcry against massive spraying arose in 1957 during the USDA campaign against the gypsy moth in southern New York. Planes flew over at low levels, discharging a fog of DDT-impregnated kerosene on three million acres, including densely populated communities in Westchester County and on Long Island. Commuters awaiting their trains were sprayed, as were dairy farms, ponds, vegetable gardens and children, some of them three times.

Tempers flared, and fourteen citizens charging careless use and official arrogance went into federal court demanding an injunction against aerial spraying. After an extended hearing their application was denied.

Another and louder outcry was in the making. According to reports, twenty-seven million acres in nine Southern states from eastern Texas to South Carolina were "teeming" with South American fire ants. These quarter-inch-long ants, it was said, had captured much of the South's best farm land and were eating their way north and west, sucking plant juices, killing young wildlife and swarming in vicious assault on men in the fields. Their onslaught, if unchecked, might not stop short of California and Canada.

To combat the menace Congress voted an emergency appropriation of $2,400,000 for USDA. Plant Pest Control Crews, without prior field testing, started an aerial broadcast of heptachlor, a powerful chlorinated hydrocarbon of the DDT family. They treated 700,000 acres before the appropriation ran out. The USDA now has asked Congress for another $2,400,000 for the second step in a long-range poisoning program. Does the fire ant justify this costly campaign?

To get a firsthand view I went to Alabama, where fire ants have flourished for forty years, and talked with people for, against and in the middle of the program. Some remarkable facts emerged.

The foremost is this: the fire ant is not a serious crop pest at all. Dr. F. S. Arant, chief of the zoology-entomology department at Alabama Polytechnic Institute, told me, "Damage to crops by the imported fire ant in Alabama is practically nil. This department has not received a single report of such damage in the past five years. No damage to livestock has been observed. The ant eats other insects, including the cotton boll weevil. It is a major nuisance, but no more." . . .

Farmers and cattlemen detest the fire ants because their ugly two-foot-high mounds clog mowing machines, and the ants bite when the farmer gets down to clear the blades. But none of the farmers I talked with had suffered any crop damage from the ants. . . .

What was the effect of the 1957–58 fire ant campaign on wildlife? Dan Lay, Texas wildlife biologist, reported from Hardin County: "On May 12, before the poisoning, the fields were noisy with birds singing for territorial establishment. Dickcissels, red-winged blackbirds and meadow larks were building nests and laying eggs. Forty-one nests with eggs were found in one clover field."

Then the planes came, scattering tiny pellets of clay containing 10 percent heptachlor. The poison covered the ground, seven to twelve sugar-size granules to the square inch. The birds ate poisoned insects, pulled worms through poisoned soil or absorbed the poison through their feet. Within a day they began to tremble, went into convulsions and died. Orphan broods hatched and died in their nests. By June 3 only three of the forty-one nests in the clover field remained occupied. Birds along the roads were reduced 95 percent.

It was the same in other areas sprayed: quail and killdeer wiped out; doves, woodpeckers, snipe, mockingbirds, cardinals, woodcock, hawks, wild turkeys, shrikes and many other species almost exterminated.

Animals died, too. A raccoon which had been seen rolling frenziedly in the road was later found dead by the roadside. Four fox pups were found dead in their den, poisoned by food brought in by their mother. Fish, turtles, snakes, rabbits, opossums, squirrels, armadillos were killed.

Today fish and game commissions in most of the afflicted states, finding the cure worse than the disease, have demanded a halt to aerial spraying. "It's like scalping yourself to cure dandruff," said Clarence Cottam, former official in the Fish and Wildlife Service.

"Sickening," said Charles Kelley of the Alabama Conservation Department. "These people can kill more game in a month than our department can build up in twenty years." Kelly handed me one of the USDA warnings given people whose lands are about to be doused:

> Cover gardens and wash vegetables before eating them; cover small fish-ponds; take fish out of pools and wash pools before replacing the fish; don't put laundry out; keep milk cows off treated pastures for 30 days, and beef cattle 15 days; cover beehives or move them away; keep children off ground for a few days; don't let pets or poultry drink from puddles.

"How can any official read that and still say losses of wildlife are insignificant?" he demanded. . . .

Our forests flourished without chemical help through eons of time, and man has practiced agriculture with reasonable success for 100 centuries of recorded history. The new pesticides have been in general use for fifteen years. "Surely," says Dr. Fairfield Osborne, noted conservationist, "we would be wise to halt massive spraying until we know what effects the toxins are having on ourselves and our animal co-heirs to this planet."

Source: Robert S. Strother. "Backfire in the War Against Insects." *Reader's Digest* (June 1959).

—⁂—

Document 3: *Silent Spring,* 1962

Published in 1962, Rachel Carson's Silent Spring *was one of the most influential books of the 20th century and an important foundation of the environmental movement, as well as the movement against DDT and other persistent chemicals. Carson's book did not present original research but rather explained what was then known about the undesirable impacts of pesticides. In this opening chapter, Carson paints a vivid and disturbing picture of what might be.*

> There was once a town in the heart of America where all life seemed to live in harmony with its surroundings. The town lay in the midst of a checkerboard of prosperous farms, with fields of grain and hillsides of orchards where, in spring, white clouds of bloom drifted above the

green fields. In autumn, oak and maple and birch set up a blaze of color that flamed and flickered across a backdrop of pines. Along the roads, laurel, viburnum and alder, great ferns and wildflowers delighted the traveler's eye through much of the year. Even in winter the roadsides were places of beauty, where countless birds came to feed on the berries and on the seed heads of the dried weeds rising above the snow. The countryside was, in fact, famous for the abundance and variety of its bird life, and when the flood of migrants was pouring through in spring and fall people traveled from great distances to observe them.

Then a strange blight crept over the area and everything began to change. Some evil spell had settled on the community: mysterious maladies swept the flocks of chickens; the cattle and sheep sickened and died. The farmers spoke of much illness among their families. In the town the doctors had become more and more puzzled by new kinds of sickness appearing among their patients. There had been several sudden and unexplained deaths, not only among adults but even among children, who would be stricken suddenly while at play and die within a few hours. There was a strange stillness. The birds, for example—where had they gone? Many people spoke of them, puzzled and disturbed. The feeding stations in the backyards were deserted. The few birds seen anywhere were moribund; they trembled violently and could not fly. It was a spring without voices. On the mornings that had once throbbed with the dawn chorus of robins, catbirds, doves, jays, wrens, and scores of other bird voices there was now no sound; only silence lay over the fields and woods and marsh.

On the farms the hens brooded, but no chicks hatched. The farmers complained that they were unable to raise any pigs—the litters were small and the young survived only a few days. The apple trees were coming into bloom but no bees droned among the blossoms, so there was no pollination and there would be no fruit.

The roadsides, once so attractive, were now lined with browned and withered vegetation as though swept by fire. These, too, were silent, deserted by all living things. Even the streams were now lifeless. Anglers no longer visited them, for all the fish had died.

In the gutters under the eaves and between the shingles of the roofs, a white granular powder still showed a few patches; some weeks before it had fallen like snow upon the roofs and the lawns, the fields and streams.

No witchcraft, no enemy action had silenced the rebirth of new life in this stricken world. The people had done it themselves.

This town does not actually exist, but it might easily have a thousand counterparts in America or elsewhere in the world. I know of no community that has experienced all the misfortunes I describe. Yet every one of these disasters has actually happened somewhere, and many real communities have already suffered a substantial number of them. A grim specter has crept upon us almost unnoticed, and this imagined tragedy may easily become a stark reality we all shall know.

What has already silenced the voices of spring in countless towns in America? This book is an attempt to explain.

Source: Rachel Carson. "A Fable for Tomorrow." Chapter 1 of *Silent Spring.* Boston: Houghton Mifflin, 1962. Copyright © 1962 by Rachel L. Carson, renewed 1990 by Roger Christie. Reprinted by permission of Houghton Mifflin Harcourt Publishing Company. All rights reserved.

—m—

Document 4: "Silence, Miss Carson," 1962

Critics of Rachel Carson's Silent Spring *accused Carson of exaggerating, of creating unnecessary panic, and of distorting the truth. William Darby, chairman of the department of biochemistry and director at Vanderbilt University school of medicine, as well as a member of the National Research Council of the National Academy of Sciences, provided an early and scathing review of the book in the leading journal of the chemical industry.*

Silent Spring starts with a bit of dramatic description which the author then acknowledges does not actually exist. It then orients the reader to its subject matter by stating that "only within . . . the present century has man . . . acquired significant power to alter the nature of his world." It identifies as irrevocable and "for the most part irreversible" the effects of "this now universal contamination of the environment [in which] chemicals are the sinister and little recognized partners of radiation in changing the very nature of the world, the very nature of life itself." Man has, according to Miss Carson, now upset that ideal state of "adjustment and balance" of life on this planet through "synthetic creations of man's inventive mind, brewed in his laboratory, and having no counterpart in nature." These products, the reader is told, are "staggering in number," have "power to kill," have "incredible potential for harm," represent a "train of disaster," result in a "chemical death rain," and are being used with "little or no advance investigation of their effect on soil, water, wildlife, and man himself." She further warns the reader that all of these sinister chemicals will not only extinguish plant life, wild life, aquatic life, and man, but they will produce cancer, leukemia, sterility, and cellular mutations. . . .

Its bulk will appeal to those readers who are as uncritical as the author, or to those who find the flavor of her product to their taste. Those consumers will include the organic gardeners, the antiflouride leaguers, the worshipers of "natural foods," those who cling to the philosophy of a vital principal, and pseudo-scientists and faddists. . . .

The author ignores the sound appraisals of such responsible, broadly knowledgeable scientists as the President of the National Academy of Sciences, the members of the President's Scientific Advisory Committee, the Presidents of the Rockefeller Foundation and Nutrition Foundation, the several committees of the National Academy of Sciences-National Research Council (including the Food and Nutrition Board, the Agricultural Board, the Food Protection Committee) who have long given thoughtful study to these questions, and the special advisory committees appointed by the governors of California and Wisconsin. . . .

All of these groups of scientists have recognized the essentiality of use of agricultural chemicals to produce food required by the expanding world population and to sustain an acceptable standard of living and health. They have recognized the safety of proper use of agricultural chemicals and, indeed, the benefits to the consumer which accrue from their proper use in food and agricultural production. . . .

Miss Carson's book adds no new factual material not already known to such serious scientists as those concerned with these developments, nor does it include information essential for the reader to interpret the knowledge. It does confuse the information and so mix it with her opinions that the uninitiated reader is unable to sort fact from fancy. In view of the mature, responsible attention which this whole subject receives from able, qualified scientific groups, such as those identified in the foregoing (and whom Miss Carson chooses to ignore); in view of her scientific qualifications in contrast to those of our distinguished scientific leaders and statesmen, this book should be ignored. . . .

Such a passive attitude [toward nature] . . . coupled with the pessimistic (and to this reviewer, unacceptable) philosophy . . . means the end of all human progress, reversion to a passive social state devoid of technology, scientific medicine, agriculture, sanitation, and education. It means disease, epidemics, starvation, misery, and suffering incomparable and intolerable to modern man. Indeed, social, educational, and scientific development is prefaced on the conviction that man's lot will be and is being improved by a greater understanding of and thereby the increased ability to control or mold those forces responsible for man's suffering, misery, and deprivation. . . .

The public may be misled by this book. If it stimulated the public to press for unwise and ill-conceived restrictions on the production, use, or development of new chemicals, it will be the consumer who suffers. If, on the other hand, it inspires some users to read and heed labels more carefully, it may aid in the large educational effort in which industry, government, colleges, and many other groups are engaged (despite Miss Carson's implication that they are not).

The responsible scientist should read this book to understand the ignorance of those writing on the subject and the educational task which lies ahead.

Source: William J. Darby. "Silence, Miss Carson." *Chemical & Engineering News,* October 1, 1962.

—∿∿—

Document 5: President's Science Advisory Committee, 1963

Public reaction to Silent Spring *was such that federal officials were forced to respond. President Kennedy asked the President's Science Advisory Committee (PSAC) to investigate the issue and compile a report, which was released in 1963. The report reviewed available evidence and called for more systematic investigation and monitoring of pesticides. Although the report was cautious, it provided the most comprehensive and critical government analysis of pesticides to date. Significantly, its findings validated many of the arguments in* Silent Spring.

Evidence of increasing environmental contamination by pesticide chemicals has generated concern which is no longer limited to citizens of affected areas or members of special-interest groups. During two decades of intensive technical and industrial advancement we have dispersed a huge volume of synthetic compounds, both intentionally and inadvertently.

Today, pesticides are detectable in many food items, in some clothing, in man and animals, and in various parts of our natural surroundings. Carried from one locality to another by air currents, water runoff, or living organisms (either directly or indirectly through extended food chains), pesticides have traveled great distances and some of them have persisted for long periods of time. Although they remain in small quantities, their variety, toxicity, and persistence are affecting biological systems in nature and may eventually affect human health. The benefits of these substances are apparent. We are now beginning to evaluate some of their less obvious effects and potential risks. . . .

The Panel is convinced that we must understand more completely the properties of these chemicals and determine their long-term impact on biological systems, including man. The Panel's recommendations are directed toward these needs, and toward more judicious use of pesticides or alternate methods of pest control, in an effort to minimize risks and maximize gains. They are offered with the full recognition that pesticides constitute only one facet of the general problem of environmental pollution, but with the conviction that the hazards resulting from their use dictate rapid strengthening of interim measures until such time as we have realized a comprehensive program for controlling environmental pollution. . . .

The Panel's recommendations are directed to an assessment of the levels of pesticides in man and his environment; to measures which will augment the safety of present practices; to needed research and the development of safer and more specific methods of pest control; to suggested amendments or public laws governing the use of pesticides; and to public education. . . .

To enhance public awareness of pesticide benefits and hazards, it is recommended that the appropriate Federal departments and agencies initiate programs of public education describing the use and the toxic nature of pesticides. Public literature and the experiences of Panel members indicate that, until the publication of *Silent Spring* by Rachel Carson, people were generally unaware of the toxicity of pesticides. The Government should present this information to the public in a way that will make it aware of the dangers while recognizing the value of pesticides.

Source: "Use of Pesticides." President's Science Advisory Committee. Washington, D.C.: Government Printing Office, 1963.

―⚒―

Document 6: "DDT Ban Takes Effect," 1972

On June 14, 1972, Environmental Protection Agency (EPA) administrator William Ruckelshaus issued an order banning all remaining uses of DDT for agriculture, with minor exceptions. The magnitude of the change required some time to implement, which provided users—especially cotton growers—some time to switch over to other products. However, it would be another year before industry appeals were finally resolved in the courts.

The general use of the pesticide DDT will no longer be legal in the United States after today, ending nearly three decades of application during which time the once-popular chemical was used to control insect pests on crop and forest lands, around homes and gardens, and for industrial and commercial purposes.

An end to the continued domestic usage of the pesticide was decreed on June 14, 1972, when William D. Ruckelshaus, Administrator of the Environmental Protection Agency, issued an order finally cancelling nearly all remaining Federal registrations of DDT products. Public health, quarantine, and a few minor crop uses were excepted, as well as export of the material.

The effective date of the EPA June cancellation action was delayed until the end of this year to permit an orderly transition to substitute pesticides, including the joint development with the U.S. Department of Agriculture of a special program to instruct farmers on safe use of substitutes.

The cancellation decision culminated three years of intensive governmental inquiries into the uses of DDT. As a result of this examination, Ruckelshaus said he was convinced that the continued massive use of DDT posed unacceptable risks to the environment and potential harm to human health.

Major legal challenges to the EPA cancellation of DDT are now pending before the U.S. Court of Appeals for the District of Columbia and the Federal District Court for the Northern District of Mississippi. The courts have not ruled as yet in either of these suits brought by pesticide manufacturers.

DDT was developed as the first of the modern insecticides early in World War II. It was initially used with great effect to combat malaria, typhus, and the other insect-borne human diseases among both military and civilian populations.

A persistent, broad-spectrum compound often termed the "miracle" pesticide, DDT came into wide agricultural and commercial usage in this country in the late 1940s. During the past 30 years, approximately 675,000 tons have been applied domestically. The peak year for use in the United States was 1959 when nearly 80 million pounds were applied. From that high point, usage declined steadily to about 13 million pounds in 1971, most of it applied to cotton.

The decline was attributed to a number of factors including increased insect resistance, development of more effective alternative pesticides, growing public and user concern over adverse environmental side effects—and governmental restriction on DDT use since 1969.

Source: "DDT Ban Takes Effect." EPA Press Release, December 31, 1972.

5

TELLICO DAM:
Should the Tellico Dam Have Been Built?

—∿∿—

THE CONTROVERSY

The Issue

Throughout the 1970s, environmentalists and others repeatedly sued the federal government in order to stop construction of the Tellico Dam, a project that would turn the lower 33 miles of the Little Tennessee River into a flat water reservoir. The project was pursued by the Tennessee Valley Authority (TVA), a federal corporation created during the Great Depression to promote resource conservation and economic development for impoverished regions of the Tennessee Valley. In the mid-1960s, the TVA initiated the Tellico project with the stated goals of attracting industrial development to the region, stimulating population growth, creating new recreation opportunities, and reviving the corporation's historical, multipurpose mission. Opponents of the project criticized the loss of rich farmland and historical sites, as well as prime trout fishing areas and river recreation opportunities. With the passage of new environmental laws, such as the National Environmental Policy Act of 1969 (NEPA) and the Endangered Species Act of 1973 (ESA), opponents were able to file suit in court against the TVA for alleged violations of law. Of particular significance was the discovery of the snail darter, a local species of fish that the U.S. Fish and Wildlife Service (FWS) declared would be in danger of extinction if the Tellico Dam was completed. Opponents of the dam argued that such a threat was a direct violation of the ESA and therefore required that construction of the dam be halted. Supporters of the Tellico Dam argued that this was unreasonable because the project had been started long before these laws had been enacted and too much time and money had already been invested. More important, supporters argued, Congress did not intend for the law to be used in this way. The debate made its way to the Supreme Court and then back to Congress. The question before them was: Should the Tellico Dam be completed?

- ◆ *Arguments against the dam:* Critics of the Tellico project argued that the dam was unnecessary and that its construction would eliminate rich farmland, deprive residents of their rightful property, eliminate popular

154

river recreation, and destroy historical archaeological sites. Critics also charged that the Tellico Dam violated federal environmental law and would result in the extinction of an endangered species of fish and the destruction of its habitat, which was contrary to the public interest. They argued that an injunction against completion of the project was the only way to comply with the law.

♦ **Arguments for the dam:** Supporters of the Tellico project argued that the dam would generate needed economic development for the region by attracting water-based industry, stimulate population growth, provide new recreational opportunities, and generally improve the standard of living for people in the region. They disputed the applicability of environmental laws, arguing that the project preceded the passage of these laws and that Congress never intended to apply such restrictions to the Tellico project. They argued that it was in the public's interest to finish a project near completion into which so much money had already been invested.

—m—

INTRODUCTION

In 1963, the TVA, a federal corporation charged with promoting resource conservation and economic development in the Tennessee Valley, decided to pursue construction of the Tellico Dam on the Little Tennessee River, about 20 miles southwest of Knoxville, Tennessee. The proposed dam would be an extension to the nearby Fort Loudon Dam, constructed in the early 1940s. The TVA argued that the Tellico Dam and its reservoir would contribute to flood control, hydroelectric power generation, and, most important, promote industrial development and economic growth for the area. In 1966, Congress and President Lyndon B. Johnson gave funding approval, and construction began in the spring of 1967.

Opposition to the TVA plans appeared almost as soon as they were announced. Early opponents included local residents concerned about the taking of private land, as well as those who decried the loss of prime trout fishing areas and historically significant sites that would be inundated by the resulting reservoir. This initial resistance was uncoordinated and had little legal or political leverage. In the early 1970s, however, opposition to the Tellico Dam was strengthened by new federal environmental legislation and the involvement of a new group of environmental and legal professionals who set out to define and use these legal tools.

The legal and political fight over the Tellico Dam began in earnest in 1971 and lasted for eight years, as leading environmental organizations and local lawyers repeatedly sued the TVA for violating the newly passed NEPA and later the ESA. While NEPA lawsuits caused a significant delay in construction, the ESA proved to be the most potent obstacle for the TVA and other proponents of the Tellico project. In 1975, Dr. David Etnier discovered a previously unknown species of fish in the Little Tennessee River, which he named the snail darter. The FWS subsequently declared the snail darter to be an endangered species, and the river to be its critical habitat. Local lawyers and the Environmental Defense Fund (EDF) filed suit to stop completion of the Tellico Dam based on the presence of an endangered species that would be threatened with extinction if the river was impounded.

The Tellico Dam case was the first significant test of the ESA, and it pitted the new wave of environmental legislation against older concepts of resource conservation and institutions focused on economic growth and infrastructure development. When it was created in the 1930s, the TVA embodied the popular notion of resource conservation as wise use and productive management of natural resources, but the nation's ideas about conservation had changed. The proliferation of new environmental legislation in the late 1960s and early 1970s seemed to signify a serious reordering of national priorities. However, Congress had clearly not anticipated such a use of the ESA—either to interrupt a project into which so much time and money had already been invested or to preserve such an unremarkable creature. At stake was the meaning and intent of the law. How strictly was the law to be interpreted, and how far would the government go to protect wildlife and uphold the values espoused in the law?

Critics of the Tellico project argued that the dam was unnecessary and that its completion would cause serious environmental disruption, both for people and for wildlife. Since the dam was first proposed, local opponents argued that its construction would deprive residents of their rightful property, eliminate popular river recreation, including some of the best trout fishing in the region, and destroy historical archaeological sites. They also took aim at the justification for the dam, questioning the TVA's assertions about the balance of benefits and costs of one more dam and reservoir in a region that was already saturated with dams and reservoirs. After passage of NEPA in 1969 and the ESA in 1973, critics charged that the Tellico Dam violated federal environmental law. Completing the dam, they argued, would result in the extinction of an endangered species and the destruction of its habitat, an outcome that the law had strictly forbidden.

Supporters of the Tellico project argued that the dam would improve economic prospects for the region and that the basis of the opposition was unreasonable. The TVA argued that construction of the dam and its reservoir would promote industrial development through improved transportation access and increase the availability of high-value jobs in an area still dominated by agriculture. In addition, it would provide new recreational opportunities and generally improve the standard of living for people in the region. They disputed the applicability of environmental laws, arguing that the project preceded the passage of these laws and that Congress never intended to apply such restrictions to the Tellico project. Indeed, many members of Congress joined the TVA in this argument and asserted that such a strict application of the law was unreasonable and contrary to the intent of Congress when it passed the ESA.

The Tellico Dam, completed in 1979, stands 129 feet high and reaches 3,238 feet across the Little Tennessee River. Tellico Reservoir stretches 33 miles along the Little Tennessee River into the mountains of east Tennessee. (Photo by Marcos Luna)

Between 1975 and 1978, opponents of the Tellico project filed a series of lawsuits in federal court to stop construction. While the courts initially ruled that the TVA was, strictly speaking, in violation of the ESA, it was not necessarily clear if this meant that completion of the dam had to be stopped. The question eventually made its way to the Supreme Court and then back to Congress. Was the ESA to be interpreted so strictly? More specifically, should the Tellico Dam be completed?

BACKGROUND

The Tennessee Valley is the area drained by the Tennessee River and its tributaries and encompasses an area of 41,000 square miles, including parts of seven states—Tennessee, Kentucky, Virginia, North Carolina, Georgia, Alabama, and Mississippi. The largest portion of the valley lies within Tennessee. The valley is bounded to the east by the Appalachian Mountains and to the west by the Cumberland Plateau and Cumberland Mountains. Although it is one of the oldest settled parts of the country, it was also one of the poorest and least developed at the beginning of the 20th century. By the early 1930s, the Tennessee Valley was suffering from severe economic and environmental problems as a result of rapid population growth, poor natural resource management, exploitative farming practices, and stagnant economic growth. While much of the nation was impoverished by the Great Depression, the Tennessee Valley was especially hard hit.

On May 18, 1933, President Franklin D. Roosevelt signed into law the Tennessee Valley Authority Act, which created a unique federal corporation—the TVA. In an address to Congress on April 10, 1933, Roosevelt charged the TVA with "the broadest duty of planning for the proper use, conservation and development of the natural resources of the Tennessee River drainage basin and its adjoining territory for the general social and economic welfare of the Nation." Specifically, the TVA was tasked with improving navigability and providing flood control for the Tennessee Valley, generating and selling electricity, reforestation and improved use of marginal agricultural lands, and providing for agricultural and industrial development. The TVA was one of Roosevelt's most ambitious and unique New Deal programs, an effort to restart the nation's economy during the Great Depression and to demonstrate the government's ability to bring a comprehensive and rational approach to the interrelated problems of economic development and conservation of natural resources.

While the TVA was given a broad mandate, it focused much of its efforts on improving agriculture and reducing soil erosion, developing flood control, and, especially, power development. Between 1933 and 1944, the TVA completed 16 dams on the Tennessee River and its tributaries. It was the largest hydroelectric construction program the nation had ever seen. At its peak in 1942, one dozen dams and a steam power plant were simultaneously under construction, with nearly 28,000 people employed. This ambitious pace of construction was spurred in part by wartime needs for electricity to produce aluminum, an essential material for airplanes, as well as to provide power for the processing of uranium for nuclear weapons development at the Oak Ridge National Laboratory in Oak Ridge, Tennessee. However, the development of so much electricity-generating capacity also allowed the TVA to become the chief provider of abundant and cheap power to rural households in the region, which did not otherwise have access to electricity. Indeed, rural electrification was an important part of the TVA's mission. President Roosevelt and others believed that access to electricity was essential to economic development and to the improvement of the population's quality of life.

The TVA's efforts transformed the Tennessee Valley. New agricultural practices greatly reduced soil erosion and increased yields, which revived the viability of farming in the region. However, the most significant physical changes came from controlling the rivers. Flooding was greatly reduced by an extensive system of dams, reservoirs, and levees. Navigation of the Tennessee River was greatly improved. By 1945, a system of dams and locks on the Tennessee River had created a 650-mile-long navigation channel, allowing ships to travel from the Ohio River up the Tennessee River, all the way to Knoxville, Tennessee, which dramatically increased the amount of cargo that could be transported by river. The dams and the reservoirs themselves became popular tourist attractions, both for the feats of engineering that they represented, as well as the recreational possibilities of their reservoirs, such as boating and fishing. No less important, the TVA had emerged as the nation's largest public power producer.

The TVA's development program slowed considerably in the 1950s. While the TVA continued to develop new sources of electricity generation, these increasingly came from coal-fired power plants rather than from hydroelectric projects. (See the sidebar "TVA's Coal Controversy" on page 162.) All of the best dam sites had already been constructed, both for hydropower and for flood and navigation control. In addition, Congress was increasingly reluctant to fund water and power projects. In 1959, the TVA's funding limitation was partially solved by new legislation that allowed it to issue its own bonds to finance power-generation facilities. The bonds would be sold to the public and then paid back with revenue from the generation of electricity. However, the TVA still needed to seek congressional appropriations for other public works projects. Moreover, it now had to provide detailed justification and numbers to show that the benefits of these projects would exceed their costs. If the TVA wanted to be more than simply a provider of electricity, it would have to develop a proposal whose projected benefits exceeded the projected costs, and it would have to convince Congress of the merits of that project.

In 1963, the TVA planning board decided to revive the organization's historical, multipurpose mission by proposing an ambitious new project that would combine dam construction, industrial development, and recreation. The centerpiece of this new proposal was the resurrection of an old one—the Fort Loudon extension project. In the 1930s, the TVA developed plans to increase the hydroelectric capacity of the Fort Loudon hydroelectric dam on the Tennessee River by constructing another, smaller dam at the mouth of the Little Tennessee River—the Fort Loudon extension project—which would increase the reservoir of water available for power production at the Fort Loudon Dam. However, plans for the Fort Loudon extension project were shelved in 1942 when the War Production Board (WPB) refused to support the project because of the scarcity of materials during the war. The TVA renamed this revived proposal the Tellico Dam project. Although it too revolved around the construction of a dam near the mouth of the Little Tennessee River, the primary purpose of the Tellico Dam and its reservoir was not electricity generation or flood control, but economic and industrial development.

The TVA proposed to construct the Tellico Dam at the mouth of the Little Tennessee River, just above the confluence where the Little

Tennessee River joins the Tennessee River. However, the dam itself was actually a minor part of the whole project. It would contain no hydroelectric generating turbines and the concrete portion would be only a few hundred feet wide and rise to a maximum height of 129 feet. Earthen levees extending a mile north from the dam would stop the flow of a narrow second channel of the Little Tennessee River, helping to create the Tellico reservoir. A canal would carry water from the Tellico reservoir to the nearby Fort Loudon reservoir, increasing the latter's hydroelectric capacity (though the increase in electrical-generating capacity was less than 1 percent). More important, the canal would connect the two reservoirs and allow barge traffic to travel from the Tellico reservoir to the Fort Loudon reservoir, which would then provide access to the entire Tennessee River.

Improved water access was an important part of the justification of the project. The TVA argued that the Tellico reservoir would stimulate industrialization along the shoreline by creating all of the conditions necessary for industrial growth: easy transportation access to the Tennessee River and to rail and highways, an abundant labor supply, and cheap electricity. The TVA estimated that shoreline industries would create 6,000 jobs, which in turn would generate another 9,000 supporting service sector jobs in the area. In addition, the TVA claimed that these jobs would stimulate population growth and the construction of homes for 25,000 people. Finally, the reservoir itself would provide more opportunities for water-related recreation. These projected benefits were welcomed by political representatives for the area, as well as many in the business community. However, others were much less enthusiastic about the gains and more concerned about what would be lost.

By the 1960s, the Little Tennessee River already had four dams along its 135-mile length, the largest being the Fontana Dam (480 feet high and the tallest dam in the eastern United States) in western North Carolina, which the TVA constructed in 1944. The nearest existing dam on the Little Tennessee River was the Chilhowee Dam, 33 miles upstream from the proposed Tellico Dam site. The Chilhowee Dam was constructed in 1957 in order to provide hydroelectricity for the nearby Aluminum Company of America (ALCOA) plant. The cold water released by the Chilhowee created ideal conditions for coldwater fish downstream of the dam, and the Tennessee Game and Fish

TVA'S COAL CONTROVERSY

By the end of World War II, the Tennessee Valley Authority (TVA) had emerged as the nation's single largest producer of electricity. Although the TVA was known principally for its generation of hydroelectric power from dams, it had reached the limit of this potential energy source with the construction of the Kentucky Dam in 1944. Thereafter, the TVA turned to coal-fired steam power plants in order to generate electricity to meet the rapidly rising demand from homes and industry. Congress appropriated more than $1 billion during the first half of the 1950s so that the TVA could construct these coal-fired steam generators. By 1961, more than 70 percent of the TVA's electric power generation came from six coal-fired power plants, while the remainder came from its 26 hydroelectric-producing dams. The TVA had become the nation's single largest consumer of coal for electricity production. Although coal was mined nearby in Tennessee, the TVA's appetite for coal was such that it turned to sources farther away in Kentucky and Illinois to meet its needs. Equally important, the TVA strove to keep electricity-generating rates low by seeking out the lowest-priced coal. The cheapest coal came from strip-mining in the Appalachian Mountains.

Underground mining, common in coal-rich Pennsylvania, involves the construction of narrow tunnels deep into the ground to extract minerals. This process requires numerous miners and is slow and dangerous. By contrast, strip-mining employs large machinery to literally scrape off the surface soil in order to expose shallow beds of coal beneath, often along the sides of steep hills or mountains. While strip-mining is quicker and more efficient, it also results in large quantities of waste material, which are often allowed to simply slide down the slopes of mountains or are dumped into nearby streams or river valleys. Much of this waste contains noxious chemicals, which leach out into waterways. Moreover, without adequate restoration efforts, areas that are strip-mined are left as treeless slopes and exposed soil, which erode rapidly with rain, resulting in mudslides and silted streams and

Commission regularly stocked the river with trout. As a result, the lower stretch of the Little Tennessee River had become a popular fishing destination throughout the East. The last 33 miles of the Little Tennessee River Valley was also significant for its long history of human rivers. In the mid-1960s, residents of eastern Kentucky, where much of the TVA's coal was mined, protested that strip-mining of coal was devastating their landscape, destroying waterways and agricultural land, and even damaging homes and upending graveyards. In response to growing complaints and public criticism by the governor of Kentucky, the TVA advocated stronger regulations on strip-mining and, in summer 1965, instituted new rules in its coal-purchasing contracts, which required coal-mining companies to restore and replant strip-mined areas. Although the TVA was the first coal consumer in the country to institute land reclamation stipulations in its coal-purchase contracts, critics found these efforts inadequate, especially as strip-mining increased to meet demand.

In March 1971, three environmental organizations—the Natural Resources Defense Council, the Environmental Defense Fund, and the Sierra Club—filed suit in federal court against the TVA, charging that it violated NEPA when it failed to file an environmental impact statement for each of its coal-purchase contracts. The plaintiffs sought to force the TVA to cease its purchases of strip-mined coal, which accounted for nearly half of the coal consumed by the TVA. The environmentalists' argument was rejected by the court in April 1973, but controversy around the impact of strip-mining continued to draw attention. Congress attempted to pass legislation to regulate mining in 1974 and 1975, but these bills were rejected by President Gerald Ford. In 1977, President Jimmy Carter signed into law the Surface Mining Control and Reclamation Act of 1977, which gave the federal government power to control permitting, inspections, and enforcement of regulations on surface-mining activities. Although strip-mining is controlled by both federal and state laws, the practice continues to draw strong objections by environmental organizations and many residents of affected areas. In spite of complaints, coal production in the United States has increased steadily since the late 1970s, and more than half of all electricity produced in the nation today is generated from coal. Surface mining is used to produce most of the coal in the United States because it is less expensive than underground mining.

occupation and farming activity. Chota, a Cherokee capital during the 1700s, and Tanasi, the origin of the name Tennessee, along with the remnants of other Cherokee villages, were important archaeological sites within the valley. Similarly, the valley was home to Fort Loudon, the westernmost British fort constructed in 1756 to protect British and Cherokee inhabitants during the French and Indian War. The fort was constructed at the confluence of the Tellico and Little Tennessee Rivers. Although it had been abandoned for nearly two centuries, it was reconstructed by the Works Progress Administration in the 1930s and later designated a historic landmark in 1965. Preservationists reconstructed the fort atop land 17 feet higher to avoid being flooded by the reservoir. Across the river from Fort Loudon were the ruins of the Tellico Blockhouse, an early American outpost constructed in 1794. The valley provided some of the richest farming land in eastern Tennessee and many families traced their ancestors back to the 1830s when President Andrew Jackson authorized the forcible removal of the original Cherokee inhabitants. All of these were threatened by the Tellico project.

The earliest opponents of the Tellico Dam included those who wanted to protect historic sites, to preserve prime trout fishing areas, and landowners upset about losing their land. The Tellico project would require the acquisition of 38,000 acres in the Little Tennessee River Valley. However, only 16,500 of these acres would actually be inundated by the reservoir. The remaining 21,500 acres would be acquired by the TVA and later resold to developers for shoreline development of recreation and industry. This expansive taking of land outside of the reservoir itself was a departure from the TVA's traditional land acquisition policy and generated considerable consternation for landowners. In some cases, entire farms had to be sold even though only a small portion of the property would actually be inundated by the reservoir. Moreover, landowners could not refuse to sell their land. Under the TVA Act, Congress gave the TVA the power of eminent domain, allowing the TVA to condemn properties if the owners refused to sell. Landowners could appeal these decisions, which caused some delay, but in the end, all appeals were rejected.

Some opponents formed the Association for the Preservation of the Little Tennessee River in order to block the project, but they had little success. Defenders of trout fishing on the Little Tennessee River managed to attract the attention of prominent allies and dam opponents, including Trout Unlimited, a national conservation organization, and Supreme Court justice William O. Douglas, an avid trout fisherman. Justice Douglas made highly publicized visits to the area in 1965 and again in 1969 in order to show his support for opponents, and he publicly ridiculed the proposed dam verbally and in print. (See "'This Valley Waits to Die,' 1969," on page 187 in the Primary Sources section.) Opponents to the Tellico Dam also launched a letter-writing campaign and appeared before Congress to voice their opposition, but to no avail. The opponents had little legal leverage, and the TVA had made a more convincing case to local political leaders and to Congress. In fall 1966, President Lyndon Johnson signed into law the 1967 Public Works Appropriation Act, which authorized $3.2 million to begin work on the Tellico project. In March 1967, the TVA began construction. Work on the concrete portion of the dam was largely completed by March 1969, although there remained considerable work to be done in gaining rights to private land, moving and reconstructing bridges and highways, and, no less important, contending with new legal challenges.

A New Era of Environmental Legislation

The late 1960s and early 1970s witnessed an explosion of public interest in environmental issues, from pollution to wildlife protection. Although the country had a long tradition of interest in conservation and even preservation, the widespread and intense public interest in environmental issues that began in the 1960s was unprecedented. Much of this concern erupted after 1962 with the publication of Rachel Carson's *Silent Spring*, which focused public attention on the widespread and indiscriminant use of pesticides and the destructive and unforeseen consequences to wildlife and human health. Carson's critique gave voice to general anxieties about rapid development, the transformation (and degradation) of the environment, and the inadequate attention paid to what was being lost. Environmental organizations experienced a dramatic increase in membership and donations, which strengthened their ability to influence both public and political opinion.

Congress responded to this outpouring of public concern and political pressure by passing many new environmental laws that changed the legal landscape, especially for government agencies. Of particular significance were NEPA and the ESA. These laws declared new priorities for the United States with regard to the environment, and they created new legal tools for those who sought to delay, and possibly even halt, questionable projects.

The TVA was a prime target of environmental critiques that were now backed by public sentiment and the law. The TVA had come under increasing criticism since the mid-1960s for the air pollution and environmental degradation created by the mining and burning of coal to power its growing number of steam-driven electricity-generating plants. The first disruptive legal challenge came from an early application of NEPA to the Tellico Dam project. Shortly after the law came into effect on January 1, 1970, the Council on Environmental Quality (CEQ)—the agency charged with overseeing NEPA—asked the TVA if it planned to file an environmental impact statement (EIS) on the Tellico project. The TVA initially replied that it did not have to, arguing that the law did not apply since the project had begun before the law was passed. Nevertheless, in an effort to preclude public criticism, the TVA submitted an EIS to the CEQ in June 1971. The TVA's report to the CEQ emphasized the benefits of the Tellico project and downplayed or ignored the negative consequences. It drew heavily on the benefit-cost analysis it had prepared to justify the project to Congress and local supporters and even expanded its predictions for jobs created and the estimated value of recreational and economic improvements.

Opponents of the Tellico project lost no time in criticizing the TVA's claimed benefits and the EIS. In August 1971, EDF—a newly established environmental organization focused on using the courts to pursue its environmental agenda—joined with local opponents and filed suit in federal court against the TVA, asking that construction on the Tellico Dam be halted until an adequate EIS was prepared. The plaintiffs argued that the EIS was inadequate and violated NEPA because it failed to adequately describe the environmental impacts of the project and failed to identify alternatives to completion of the project. After a two-day hearing in January 1972, Judge Robert Taylor of the eastern district of Tennessee ruled in favor of the plaintiffs and ordered that construction on the dam be halted until an adequate EIS was prepared. By this point, the TVA had completed construction on the concrete portion of the dam, had finished a four-lane steel span bridge over the proposed reservoir, had acquired two-thirds of the land needed, and had expended over $29 million of the estimated $69 million cost of the project. The TVA filed a final EIS a month later, but the injunction against further construction lasted until October 1973 when Judge

Taylor ruled in a second hearing that the agency had met its procedural obligations under NEPA and lifted the injunction.

Despite the delay, it seemed that the Tellico Dam was headed inexorably toward completion. While the TVA had lost more than a year of construction time due to the NEPA injunction, it was permitted to continue surveying work and to acquire properties. Equally significant, it continued to seek and receive funding from Congress for the project as a whole. Opponents were dismayed by the court's decision to lift the injunction, but they persisted in their search for opportunities to halt the project. Their opportunity arrived with the discovery of a new species and the passage of a new law.

The Snail Darter and the ESA

As plaintiffs prepared for the second NEPA hearing in summer 1973, one of their expert witnesses, Dr. David Etnier, an ichthyologist in the zoology department at the University of Tennessee, was searching the Little Tennessee River in order to document rare fishes in order to bolster his testimony in the NEPA case. In August 1973, while snorkeling in the Little Tennessee, he came upon a small, brown three-inch fish which he quickly realized was a previously unknown species of darter or perch. He named the fish the snail darter because one of its principal food sources is aquatic snails. He eventually gave the fish the scientific name *Percina (Imostoma) tanasi,* and he believed that it was unique to the Little Tennessee River. Etnier was convinced that his discovery would prove valuable, but the NEPA case ended before he had a chance to present his finding to the court. However, Etnier's discovery gained new significance in December 1973 when President Richard Nixon signed the ESA into law. The new law substantially strengthened previous federal efforts to protect wildlife and, more important, declared a prohibition against actions that threatened species with eradication. (See the sidebar "Origins of the Endangered Species Act" on page 174.)

In fall 1974, Hiram Hill, a law student at the University of Tennessee, was searching for an environmental law issue to research for class when he heard about Etnier's discovery from students in the zoology department at the university. Hill asked his law professor Zygmunt Plater if the new ESA and the snail darter were appropriate subjects. Plater approved the topic and by the end of the semester the two had become convinced that the new law prohibited completion of the Tellico Dam. As they researched the case, they were joined by Joseph Congleton, a Knoxville attorney opposed to the Tellico project. In January 1975, the three filed a petition asking the secretary of the interior to list the snail darter as an endangered species and for an expedited consideration given the impending completion of the dam. In March, the acting director of the FWS—the agency to which administration of the law was delegated—issued a notice in the *Federal Register* that the agency was considering listing the snail darter as endangered. The FWS notified the TVA, and TVA officials responded by arguing to the FWS that more time should be allowed for study of the snail darter and its habitat. The TVA explained that it was currently funding a study of the snail darter in order to document its biology before the dam was completed. Nevertheless, in October 1975, the FWS declared the snail darter to be an endangered species based solely upon the threat presented by completion of the dam. The FWS wrote: "The proposed impoundment of water behind the proposed Tellico Dam would result in total destruction of the snail darter's habitat."

Although the FWS listed the snail darter as endangered, it made no attempt to enforce the law against the TVA. However, the ESA contains a citizen suit provision that allows individuals to sue anyone, including the government, for violation of the law. It requires only that the plaintiffs give written notice to the secretary of the interior and the violator 60 days before any action is taken. Less than two weeks after the FWS declared the snail darter to be endangered, Plater, Hill, and Donald Cohen—associate dean at the University of Tennessee Law School—sent separate letters to the secretary of the interior and to the TVA notifying them that the Tellico Dam threatened the existence of the snail darter and was thus in violation of the ESA. They requested that the secretary of the interior enforce the law and that the TVA comply with the law by stopping construction. Not surprisingly, the TVA did no such thing. In fact, the TVA actually accelerated the pace of work. Similarly, Congress continued to approve funding for the Tellico project despite the announced listing by the FWS and its implications for the dam. In December 1975, President Gerald Ford signed into law the 1976 Public Works Appropriation Act, which included over $23 million for the Tellico Dam. Two months later, Hill, Plater, and Cohen, along with the Audubon Council of Tennessee and the Association of

Southern Biologists, filed suit against the TVA in federal district court, seeking an injunction against completion of the dam. Court hearings on the case began in April 1976.

THE DEBATE

Arguments for and against the Tellico Dam had been going on since the mid-1960s, but the use of new environmental laws after 1970 narrowed the scope of the debate. While critics and defenders of the Tellico Dam continued to make their arguments in broad terms about the merits of the project, government officials and agencies such as the FWS and, especially, the courts, were concerned with much more specific questions. Did the Tellico project violate the ESA? If so, should completion of the dam be stopped? These were the questions that plaintiffs and defendants had to answer.

The Case Against the Dam

The plaintiffs argued that completion of the Tellico Dam threatened the existence of the snail darter and therefore violated the ESA. Moreover, they argued that the only appropriate solution was for the court to issue an injunction stopping completion of the dam. The plaintiffs brought forth a number of scientific experts, including Etnier, who explained how the dam threatened the existence of the snail darter. The snail darter is a tan, three-and-half-inch fish that feeds on freshwater snails found at the bottom of free-flowing rivers. The snail darter and its prey require shallow, swift-moving water in order to maintain high oxygen levels and a clean streambed. Surveys of the fish indicated that its habitat was restricted to the lower 17 miles of the Little Tennessee River. A search of nearby rivers with similar ecological conditions supported the argument that almost the entire species was restricted to the Little Tennessee, with an estimated population of 10,000 to 15,000 fish. Shortly before the trial began, the FWS issued a ruling designating the lower 17 miles of the Little Tennessee as critical habitat for the snail darter. Witnesses for the plaintiff explained that the river habitat would be inundated by the dam's reservoir, changing the average depth from two to three feet to 30 to 40 feet. The great increase in depth combined with the lack of water movement would result in much lower oxygen levels and the buildup of silt. Such conditions would smother snail darter eggs and eliminate its principal food source. Thus, the reservoir would destroy the snail darter's only significant habitat and the species itself.

The plaintiffs argued that the TVA was in direct violation of the ESA. Specifically, they cited section 7 of the ESA that directed all federal agencies to cooperate with the secretary of the interior and to do what was "necessary to insure that actions authorized, funded, or carried out by them do not jeopardize the continued existence of such endangered species and threatened species or result in the destruction or modification of habitat of such species which is determined by the Secretary, after consultation as appropriate with the affected States, to be critical." Not only was the TVA conducting actions that threatened the existence of an endangered species, but they had done so without proper consultation with the secretary of the interior and refused to consider alternative courses of action. The plaintiffs requested that the court impose an injunction against completion of the dam in order to prevent destruction of the snail darter and its habitat and to uphold the law. An injunction, they argued, was the only way to ensure compliance with the ESA, and an injunction was in the public interest. The plaintiffs argued that the preservation of ecological habitats and species was important for aesthetic and scientific reasons, and that Congress had recognized this importance when it passed the law.

The Case for the Dam

The TVA denied that its actions violated the ESA. However, even if it was in technical violation, the defendants argued that an injunction would be contrary to the will of Congress and would be unreasonable given the advanced stage of the project. The TVA argued that it was not in violation of the ESA because the law gave the TVA, not the Department of the Interior, the authority to make final decisions on whether or not to proceed with its projects, regardless of whether or not these actions threatened species. According to TVA officials, the ESA required federal agencies to take reasonable measures, in consultation with the Department of the Interior, to conserve endangered or threatened species of wildlife, but it did not override the TVA's prerogative or mission. The TVA pointed out that it had made sincere efforts to conserve the

The snail darter (*Percina tanasi*) is shown next to a paperclip for scale. The snail darter is native to the waters of eastern Tennessee and was declared an endangered species in 1975, nearly halting completion of the Tellico Dam. Its status was lowered to threatened in 1984. (U.S. Fish and Wildlife Service)

snail darter. At the request of Etnier in December 1973, the TVA had agreed to fund a biological study of the snail darter, including its life history and habitat. The TVA had also instituted a program to transplant the snail darter to other suitable river habitats, with the cooperation of the FWS, although Etnier had since expressed his doubts about the success of this attempt. Nevertheless, the TVA insisted that it was making every reasonable effort to conserve the snail darter, short of abandoning the project. More important, the defendants argued that Congress had not intended for the ESA to apply to the Tellico project, let alone halt its completion through an injunction.

The question of congressional intent was central to the TVA's argument. The defendants maintained that the ESA was not applicable to the Tellico project because the law was passed more than seven years after Congress had authorized construction of the dam and nearly six years after construction had begun. Indeed, the TVA was fairly close to completion of the project by the time the snail darter was listed on the endangered species list in late 1975. They argued that Congress had not intended for the law to be applied retroactively to a project into which so much time and money had already been invested. More important, the TVA asserted that Congress had clearly and repeatedly expressed its will regarding the Tellico project through its continued appropriations. Congress had consistently funded the Tellico project since 1966, despite passage of environmental laws such as NEPA and the ESA and repeated lawsuits based upon these laws. Since the Tellico project had been approved, over $78 million had been spent on the project, and, the TVA argued, approximately $53 million would be lost if the project was abandoned. It was simply unreasonable, they argued, to halt completion of the Tellico project at this stage in the face of clear signals from Congress.

Court Rulings

In May 1976, Judge Taylor for the U.S. District Court for the Eastern District of Tennessee ruled that the Tellico project was indeed in violation of the ESA. The court found that the Tellico project was subject to the ESA as interpreted by the FWS and that completion of the dam would likely eradicate the snail darter and its habitat, and therefore the TVA was in violation of the law. However, Judge Taylor refused to issue an injunction against completion of the dam. He determined that the TVA had acted in good faith by consulting with the FWS and by making every reasonable effort to conserve the snail darter, short of abandoning the project. However, the judge argued that halting the project was unreasonable given the amount of resources already invested and its advanced stage of construction. Judge Taylor wrote: "At some point in time a federal project becomes so near completion and so incapable of modification that a court of equity should not apply a statute enacted long after inception of the project to produce an unreasonable result. . . . Where there has been an irreversible and irretrievable commitment of resources by Congress to a project over a span of almost a decade, the Court should proceed with a great deal of circumspection." Finally, the judge accepted the TVA's argument that Congress had made its will clear that the ESA should not apply to the Tellico project by continuing to authorize funding despite awareness of the lawsuits over the ESA. (See "Ruling by Judge Robert Taylor, 1976," on page 189 in the Primary Sources section.)

Plater and the other plaintiffs appealed the district court's ruling to the U.S. Court of Appeals for the Sixth Circuit, asking that court to reconsider Judge Taylor's decision not to issue an injunction. The plaintiffs also requested a preliminary injunction to prevent further work on the Tellico Dam while the appeal was pending. In August 1976, the appeals court granted a limited injunction against closure of the dam, although it allowed other activities to continue. In the interim, congressional appropriations committees in the House and Senate continued to approve the TVA's funding for the 1977 fiscal year in spite of the injunction. The Senate Appropriations Committee went so far as to declare its support for the Tellico project in its appropriations committee report: "The Committee does not view the Endangered Species Act as prohibiting the completion of the Tellico project at its advanced stage and directs that this project be completed as promptly as possible in the public interest."

Hearings before the appeals court took place in October 1976, and the court issued its decision on January 31, 1977. The appeals court reaffirmed the district court's finding that construction of the Tellico project violated the ESA. However, the appeals court disagreed with Judge Taylor's rationale for denying the plaintiff's request for an injunction. More specifically, the court rejected the TVA's argument that an injunction was unreasonable given the amount of resources invested and the advanced stage of the project. Writing for the court, Judge Anthony Celebreeze argued, "Whether a dam is 50% or 90% completed is irrelevant in calculating the social and scientific costs attributable to the disappearance of a unique form of life. Courts are ill-equipped to calculate how many dollars must be invested before the value of a dam exceeds that of the endangered species." Judge Celebreeze asserted that it was not the place of the courts to weigh the costs and benefits of a course of action in search of fairness; the court's role was to apply the law as written. In addition, the appeals court rejected the argument that continued funding by congressional appropriations committees represented the will of Congress or was an adequate basis on which to exempt the Tellico project from a strict application of existing law. The court ordered that a permanent injunction against the dam be imposed "until Congress, by appropriate legislation, exempts Tellico from compliance

(continues on page 176)

ORIGINS OF THE ENDANGERED SPECIES ACT

The United States has long experience with the problem of species over-exploitation. By the 1870s, bison were nearly exterminated from the Great Plains, largely due to excessive hunting. Congress responded in 1894 by prohibiting hunting within Yellowstone National Park in order to provide a safe haven for the few remaining herds. In 1914, the last known passenger pigeon in existence died in a Cincinnati zoo. Passenger pigeons were one of the most abundant birds in North America until the 19th century, reportedly traveling in flocks more than a mile wide and hundreds of miles long and consisting of up to a billion birds. They were wiped out by a combination of excessive hunting and habitat loss. The unique threats to birds were such that the United States signed the Migratory Birds Treaty with Canada in 1916 to protect the habitat and migratory routes of various bird species. While these early federal efforts were significant, they were also exceptional.

Beginning in the 1960s, there was an explosion of concern over environmental degradation and the loss of wildlife. Congress responded with a raft of new environmental laws:

Wilderness Preservation Act of 1964, which established a system for the preservation of wilderness areas for future generations.

Endangered Species Preservation Act of 1966, which created a National Wildlife Refuge System and directed federal agencies to protect endangered species "insofar as is practicable and consistent" with their primary missions.

Endangered Species Conservation Act of 1969, which banned the importation, sale, or transport of any species or product of a species (e.g., jaguar fur) listed as endangered.

In 1971 and 1972, Congress passed additional laws protecting specific species, including wild horses and burros in the West and threatened marine mammals such as dolphins and whales. In 1972, President Richard Nixon called on Congress to create even stronger protections for endangered species. Congress obliged with the Endangered Species Act (ESA). The ESA directed the secretaries of interior and commerce to list species as either threatened or endangered "solely on the basis of the best scientific and commercial data available." Moreover, species were defined expansively and could include all mammals, fish, plants, birds, amphibians, reptiles, mollusks, crustaceans, arthropods, or other invertebrates. Endangered species were defined as those in danger of extinction throughout all or a significant part of their range, while threatened species were defined as likely to become endangered in the near future. The law prohibited federal agencies from pursuing any action that might harm a listed species.

The ESA was almost universally praised as it wound its way through Congress in 1973. No one anticipated or voiced aloud concerns about how such a law might conflict with economic activity or public works. Members of Congress and the news media referred exclusively to the salvation of large and spectacular animals—wolves, grizzly bears, jaguars, ocelots, elephants, and eagles. None mentioned fish, let alone plants or invertebrates. Assumptions about the major threats to species survival were also relatively simplistic—assigning blame to overhunting and direct exploitation—and ignoring the more complicated factors that led to habitat loss, such as land development.

The significance of the ESA was not apparent until after 1975 when a three-inch fish with no known economic or aesthetic value threatened to delay, and possibly stop, a public works project on which millions of government dollars had already been spent. To critics, this application of the ESA seemed patently ridiculous and a perversion of the law's original intent. According to the New York Times, one congressional staffer said, "When they voted for the act, Congressmen thought they were voting to protect warm and cuddly animals, or bold and beautiful things like the bald eagle, and not little slimy, scaly things and invertebrates." Environmental organizations saw the ESA as a powerful new legal weapon to preserve habitat and stop destructive development. Critics came to see the ESA as emblematic of environmental extremism run amok. Interestingly, public opinion polls in the late 1970s showed that most people continued to value the preservation of wildlife even if it came at an economic cost.

(continued from page 173)
with the Act or the snail darter has been deleted from the list of endangered species or its critical habitat materially redefined." (See "Ruling by Judge Anthony Celebreeze, 1977," on page 191 in the Primary Sources section.)

The ruling by the appeals court caused quite a bit of consternation for the TVA and for many members of Congress. However, the TVA wasted no time in pursuing a variety of options. It sent a formal petition to the FWS asking that the snail darter be removed from the endangered species list and that the designation of "critical habitat" be removed for the lower stretch of the Little Tennessee River. The FWS refused. The TVA appealed directly to Congress to resolve the issue by exempting the Tellico project from the ESA. Many members of Congress were quite receptive to the TVA's appeals. Some were incensed that a small, unremarkable fish with no known economic value could disrupt a public works project into which so much had already been invested and which was so close to completion. In addition, the country was in the midst of an energy crisis as a result of oil embargoes from the Middle East. Critics of the ESA argued that the country could not afford to delay any domestic projects related to energy generation. By spring 1977, members of the Senate were drafting an amendment to the ESA that would create a separate committee with the power to exempt certain projects from the ESA. (See "Senate Report on the Endangered Species Act, 1978," on page 193 in the Primary Sources section.) Extensive congressional hearings on the ESA and proposed amendments were conducted in April 1978. Finally, the TVA appealed the Sixth Circuit ruling to the Supreme Court. Although the Supreme Court takes up only a very small fraction of the many requests for review, it agreed to review the Tellico case, subsequently referred to as *TVA v. Hill.*

In June 1978, the Supreme Court issued its ruling in *TVA v. Hill,* upholding the appeals court decision and the permanent injunction. For the Supreme Court, there were two substantive questions to be resolved: 1) Was an injunction against a nearly completed dam required under the ESA; and 2) did congressional appropriations for the dam mean that Congress had effectively granted an exemption to the Tellico project? Writing for the Court, Chief Justice Warren Burger stated: "One would be hard pressed to find a statutory provision whose terms were any plainer than those in § 7 of the Endangered Species Act. . . . This language admits of no exception."

The Court drew attention not only to the language of the law itself, but to the long history of congressional deliberations that led to its passage. The chief justice wrote, "Congress was concerned about the *unknown* uses that endangered species might have and about the *unforeseeable* place such creatures may have in the chain of life on this planet. . . . The legislative history undergirding § 7 reveals an explicit congressional decision to require agencies to afford first priority to the declared national policy of saving endangered species. . . . [The legislative history] reveals a conscious decision by Congress to give endangered species priority over the 'primary missions' of federal agencies."

Finally, the Supreme Court rejected the argument that congressional appropriations represented the will of Congress or that they were a sufficient basis on which to grant the Tellico project an exemption from the law. In fact, the Court pointed to explicit rules in the House and Senate that specifically prohibited the use of appropriations acts to alter existing law. (See "Ruling by Chief Justice Warren Burger," 1978, on page 194 in the Primary Sources section.)

The Supreme Court decision only added fuel to the anti-ESA fire in Congress. By the summer of 1978, proposed amendments to the ESA had gained significant traction. Defenders of the ESA were forced to support more modest amendments to the law in hopes of fending off more radical changes. In November 1978, Congress reauthorized the ESA with an amendment that created an Endangered Species Committee with authority to grant exemptions to the ESA. The cabinet-level committee included the secretaries of agriculture, army, and interior, administrators of the Environmental Protection Agency and the National Oceanic and Atmospheric Administration, the chairman of the Council of Economic Advisers, and a representative of each state affected. The committee was jokingly referred to as the God Squad because of its authority over the life and death of listed species. When the committee met for the first time on January 23, 1979, it voted unanimously against exemption for the Tellico Dam.

The basis of its decision had less to do with preservation of the snail darter and more to do with the economics of the Tellico project. By this time, more than $103 million had been spent on the Tellico project, which was estimated to be 95 percent complete. Only about one-fifth of this amount had been spent on the dam itself, with the bulk spent on land acquisition and road construction. The committee took particular note of the loss of so much valuable farmland and existing recreational opportunities of the river. Charles Schultze, chairman of the Council of Economic Advisers and a member of the committee, explained that the benefits of the project were so marginal when compared to the costs that they did not even justify the expense of completing the remaining 5 percent. Interior secretary Cecil Andrus, also a committee member, later told the *New York Times*, "Frankly, I hate to see the snail darter get the credit for stopping a project that was ill-conceived and uneconomic in the first place."

In the face of apparent defeat, supporters of the Tellico project orchestrated a surprising, if controversial, resurrection of a project that seemed all but dead. During a normally quiet June afternoon in the House chamber, Representative John Duncan (R-Tenn.) rose to propose an amendment to the Energy and Water Development Appropriation Act of 1980 allowing the Tellico Dam to be completed, notwithstanding the Endangered Species Act "or any other law." The few House members in attendance at the time voted to suspend a reading of the amendment, and the bill passed the House without opposition. On the Senate side, Tennessee senators Howard Baker and Jim Sasser managed to rally just enough votes so that the Senate accepted the appropriations bill as amended by the House of Representatives. President Jimmy Carter threatened to veto the entire appropriations bill if it contained the amendment to allow completion of the Tellico Dam. However, in the end, and despite promises to dam opponents, President Carter signed the Energy and Water Development Appropriation Act of 1980 into law on September 25, 1979.

The unconventional victory for dam supporters was vilified in the popular press, and both the president and Congress were flooded with angry letters. In a last-ditch attempt to stop the dam, the Eastern Band of the Cherokees filed a lawsuit contending that the reservoir would violate the Native American Religious Freedom Act by preventing them from accessing sacred sites. However, the courts ruled that such rights did not override government projects. Despite the fact that all properties for the Tellico project had been legally acquired by the TVA, three former property owners remained at their homes. On November 13, 1979, a CBS news crew televised the awkward scene as federal marshals forcibly evicted the squatters, including a tearful 84-year-old woman who could not speak when asked where she would go now. A little over two weeks later, the TVA closed the gates to the Tellico Dam and began filling the reservoir.

OUTCOME AND IMPACT

The legacy of the Tellico project controversy is ambiguous, and much of what occurred in subsequent years has lent support to both sides of the issue. Although the snail darter was eliminated from the Little Tennessee River when it was turned into a flat water reservoir, the species was not eradicated. In 1980, Dr. Etnier discovered another population of snail darters in South Chickamauga Creek, a small stream near Chattanooga, Tennessee, 80 miles from the Tellico Dam. Subsequent searches revealed snail darter populations in other tributaries of the Tennessee River, which prompted the FWS to change the snail darter's status in 1983 from endangered to threatened.

The TVA's predictions of a water-based, industrial boom in the region were not accurate either. In 1982, it sold over 11,000 acres to the Tellico Reservoir Development Agency (TRDA), a public corporation created by the Tennessee legislature to help the TVA develop the land acquired for the Tellico project. In its last report, posted in 2008, the TRDA claimed a little over 3,600 jobs created in industry, though none of this industry used water transportation. Other projects included upscale resort communities and some residential development.

Despite its ambiguity, scholars have interpreted the battle over the Tellico project as one of the most significant events in the history of environmental law. The Supreme Court's strict interpretation of the ESA as allowing "no exceptions" established it as one of the nation's most powerful environmental statutes. And while Congress amended the ESA to allow for exceptions, exceptions have been rare in practice. Very few disputes over endangered species have risen to such a level as to attract the attention of Congress or the courts. The vast majority of cases involving the ESA are negotiated or resolved at the state or local level. In the few cases that have drawn widespread public attention, the ESA has been a lightning rod for controversy and criticism. Nevertheless, it has remained in place and served as a potent tool for delaying or even threatening to delay controversial activities or projects.

WHAT IF?

What if the Supreme Court had overruled the court of appeals and supported the original decision of the district court to allow completion of the dam?

If the Supreme Court had overruled the court of appeals and favored the opinion of the district court, the Tellico Dam would have been completed just the same, though likely much sooner. Moreover, Congress would not have felt compelled to amend the ESA, nor would individual members of Congress have inserted language bypassing the ESA in the appropriations act for 1980.

However, the Supreme Court's decision and Congress's reaction were actually quite important for later interpretations of the law. Had the Supreme Court rejected the appeals court's decision and upheld the rationale of the district court, the ESA would have been weakened substantially. Exempting the Tellico project on the basis that it was already underway and giving the courts or the agency the power to determine what was reasonable would have opened the door for later courts and agencies to make similar arguments about what was reasonable, regardless of the impact on endangered species. Under this alternative scenario, the ESA might have become just another paper tiger—something that appears threatening but really is not.

The Supreme Court's actual decision in *TVA v. Hill* provided for a very strict interpretation of the law. If a species is determined to be endangered, the only solution is either to change the project so as not to endanger the species or else to seek an unlikely exemption from the God Squad. This interpretation of the law has not allowed for alternative determinations of reasonability; one is either in compliance with the law or one is not in compliance. Though the ESA has generated considerable controversy, it has also stood as one of the strictest environmental laws in the nation.

CHRONOLOGY

1933   *May 18:* President Roosevelt signs into law the Tennessee Valley Authority Act of 1933, creating the Tennessee Valley Authority (TVA).

1935   *August 31:* President Roosevelt signs into law an amendment to the TVA Act, authorizing the TVA to provide electricity generation from its dams and to create a nine-foot navigation channel from Knoxville to the mouth of the Tennessee River.

1936   The TVA identifies a potential dam site at the mouth of the Little Tennessee River.

1942   *August 3:* The TVA board of directors withdraws its proposal for the Fort Loudon extension project, which included the building of a dam near the mouth of the Little Tennessee River.

1963   *April 15:* The TVA board of directors decides to seek congressional appropriations to pursue the Tellico Dam project.

1965   Supreme Court justice William O. Douglas makes a high-profile visit to the Little Tennessee River to fish for trout to show his opposition to the proposed Tellico Dam.

1966   *October 15:* Endangered Species Preservation Act becomes law. *October 19:* President Lyndon Johnson signs into law the 1967 Public Works Appropriation Act, which includes the initial $3.2 million appropriation to begin work on the Tellico Dam.

1967   *March 7:* The TVA begins construction on the concrete portion of the Tellico Dam.

1969   Congress amends the Endangered Species Preservation Act of 1966, extending protection to species in danger of "worldwide extinction" by prohibiting their importation and subsequent sale in the United States. The amended law calls for an international meeting to adopt a convention to conserve endangered species. One amendment to the act changes its title to the Endangered Species Conservation Act.
February 28: The TVA completes construction of the concrete portion of the Tellico Dam.
April: Supreme Court justice William O. Douglas revisits the Little Tennessee River to support opponents of the Tellico Dam and draw public attention.

1970 *January 1:* President Richard Nixon signs the National Environmental Policy Act (NEPA) into law.

1971 *March 3:* The Natural Resources Defense Council, Environmental Defense Fund (EDF), and Sierra Club file suit in the U.S. District Court for the Southern District of New York, charging the TVA with violating NEPA through its contracting for strip-mined coal.

June 18: The TVA submits its draft environmental impact statement on the Tellico Dam to the Council on Environmental Quality (CEQ).

August: Economics professor Keith Phillips and his class at the University of Tennessee complete a report critical of the TVA's benefit-cost analysis for the Tellico Dam.

August 11: EDF and others file a suit against the TVA for failing to file an adequate environmental impact statement on the Tellico Dam in district court.

December 7: Tennessee governor Winnfield Dunn sends a letter opposing construction of the Tellico Dam to the TVA.

1972 *January 11:* Judge Robert Taylor of the Eastern District of Tennessee issues a preliminary injunction against dam construction in the NEPA suit, *Environmental Defense Fund, Inc. v. TVA,* halting most work on the Tellico Dam.

February 10: The TVA files its final environmental impact statement on the Tellico Dam with the CEQ.

August 25: President Nixon signs into law the 1973 Public Works Appropriation Act, which includes $11.25 million for the Tellico Dam as recommended by the House and Senate appropriations committees.

1973 *August 12:* Dr. David Etnier discovers the snail darter, *Percina (Imostoma) tanasi,* in the Little Tennessee River.

August 16: President Nixon signs into law the 1974 Public Works Appropriation Act, which includes $7.5 million for the Tellico Dam as recommended by the House and Senate appropriations committees.

October 25: Judge Taylor rules that the TVA has complied with NEPA and the National Historic Preservation Act and lifts the injunction in *Environmental Defense Fund v. TVA* and dismisses the NEPA suit.

November 12: Construction resumes on the Tellico Dam.

December 28: President Nixon signs into law the Endangered Species Act (ESA).

1974   *August 28:* President Gerald Ford signs into law the 1975 Public Works Appropriation Act, which includes $16.9 million for the Tellico Dam as recommended by the House and Senate appropriations committees.

1975   *January 20:* Joseph Congleton, Zygmunt Plater, and Hiram Hill petition the U.S. Fish and Wildlife Service (FWS) to list the snail darter as endangered.

March 7: The FWS sends a letter to inform the TVA that there is "substantial evidence" to support further investigation of the need to list the snail darter as endangered and the possible consequences of that listing for the Tellico project.

March 12: The TVA general manager responds to the FWS's March 7 letter and disputes the FWS's interpretation of the ESA.

June 17: The FWS publishes a proposed rule to list the snail darter as endangered in the *Federal Register.*

October 9: Secretary of the interior issues a final rule listing the snail darter as an endangered species (effective November 10 in the *Code of Federal Regulations*).

October 20: Zygmunt Plater, Donald Cohen, and Hank Hill send letters notifying the TVA and the Department of the Interior that the TVA's work on the Tellico Dam violates the ESA and requesting that they take appropriate action.

December 15: The FWS publishes in the *Federal Register* a proposed rule to designate the lower 17 miles of the Little Tennessee River as a critical habitat of the snail darter.

December 26: President Ford signs into law the 1976 Public Works Appropriation Act, which includes $23.7 million for the Tellico Dam as recommended by the House and Senate appropriations committees.

1976   *February 18:* Hiram Hill, Zygmunt Plater, Donald Cohen, the Audubon Council of Tennessee, and the Association of Southern Biologists file an ESA citizen suit in the district court for the

Eastern District of Tennessee seeking an injunction to prevent completion of the Tellico Dam.

April 1: The FWS publishes in the *Federal Register* the final rule designating the lower 17 miles of the Little Tennessee River as critical habitat for the snail darter.

April 22: The FWS circulates guidelines to assist federal agencies in complying with the ESA.

April 29: Trial on *Hill v. TVA* commences.

May 25: Judge Taylor issues his decision in the ESA suit, *Hill v. TVA,* finding that the Tellico Dam does violate the ESA, but the judge refuses to issue an injunction.

June 17: The Senate Appropriations Committee report on the 1977 Public Works Appropriation Act recommends a $9.7 million appropriation for the Tellico Dam and directs the dam "be completed as promptly as possible in the public interest."

July 12: President Ford signs into law the 1977 Public Works Appropriation Act, which includes $9.7 million for the Tellico Dam as recommended by the House and Senate appropriations committees.

July 26: The U.S. Court of Appeals for the Sixth Circuit issues an injunction against completion of the Tellico Dam pending a decision on the appeal in *Hill v. TVA.*

October 14: The Sixth Circuit hears oral arguments in appeal of *Hill v. TVA.*

1977   *January 31:* The Sixth Circuit issues its decision in *Hill v. TVA* and orders an injunction forbidding completion of the Tellico Dam.

February 28: The TVA petitions the FWS to remove the snail darter from the endangered species list and to remove the designation of the Little Tennessee River as the critical habitat of the snail darter.

May 31: The TVA files a petition asking the U.S. Supreme Court to review the ESA suit, subsequently referred to as *TVA v. Hill.*

June 2: The House Appropriations Committee report on the 1978 Public Works Appropriation Act declares the committee's view that the ESA was not intended to halt the Tellico Dam project.

June 25: The Senate Appropriations Committee report on the 1978 Public Works Appropriation Act declares the committee's disagreement with the Sixth Circuit's interpretation of the ESA.

October 14: The General Accounting Office releases a critical review of the benefit-cost analysis prepared by the TVA for the Tellico Dam. It recommends that construction not proceed until a new benefit-cost analysis is prepared.

November 14: The Supreme Court agrees to review *TVA v. Hill.*

December 5: The FWS denies the TVA petition to delist the snail darter or to remove the designation of the Little Tennessee River as the snail darter's critical habitat.

1978 *April 13–14:* The Senate Committee on Environment and Public Works conducts hearings on §7 of the ESA.

April 18: The Supreme Court hears oral arguments in *TVA v. Hill.*

May 15: The Senate Committee on Environment and Public Works issues a report recommending addition of an exemption procedure for §7 of the ESA.

June 18: The Supreme Court issues its decision in *TVA v. Hill,* affirming the Sixth Circuit decision to issue an injunction against completion of the Tellico Dam.

November 10: President Jimmy Carter signs into law the ESA amendments of 1978, which add an exemption procedure to §7 and create an Endangered Species Committee to make exemption determinations.

1979 *January 23:* The Endangered Species Committee unanimously refuses to grant the Tellico Dam an exemption from §7 of the ESA.

June 18: Representative John Duncan inserts into the Energy and Water Development Appropriation Act of 1980 a rider allowing the Tellico Dam to be completed notwithstanding the ESA "or any other law."

September 25: President Jimmy Carter signs into law the Energy and Water Development Appropriation Act of 1980, including the rider allowing completion of the Tellico Dam.

November 29: The TVA closes the Tellico Dam and begins to fill the Tellico Reservoir.

1980 *November:* Dr. David Etnier finds another population of snail darters in South Chickamauga Creek, a small stream near Chattanooga, Tennessee, 80 miles from the Tellico Dam.

1983 *February:* U.S. Department of the Interior announces that the snail darter will be downgraded from endangered to threatened after populations were found in six tributaries of the Tennessee River.

DISCUSSION QUESTIONS

1. Should the Tellico Dam have been constructed? Why or why not?
2. What were the main criticisms of the Tellico project? How did supporters of the Tellico project respond to these criticisms?
3. Was it unreasonable to stop construction on the Tellico Dam after so much time and money had been invested in the project? Why or why not?
4. Many critics complained that the ESA was misapplied on the snail darter—a small, unremarkable fish with no known economic value. Should the ESA be used to defend any or all species? Are some species more deserving of protection from extinction than others? Why or why not?
5. Why do you think Congress continued to fund the Tellico project even after the courts had issued an injunction? Was Congress being inconsistent by continuing to fund the project or was it expressing its will?
6. How should the government balance the value of endangered species against other values, such as economic activity?

WEB SITES

New Deal Network. The Tennessee Valley Authority: Electricity for All. Available online. URL: http://newdeal.feri.org/tva/index.htm. Accessed March 24, 2011.

Tennessee Valley Authority. From the New Deal to a New Century: A Short History of TVA. Available online. URL: http://www.tva.gov/abouttva/history.htm. Accessed March 24, 2011.

United States Fish & Wildlife Service. Endangered Species Program. Available online. URL: http://www.fws.gov/endangered. Accessed March 24, 2011.

BIBLIOGRAPHY

Curtis, Jeff, and Bob Davison. "The Endangered Species Act: Thirty Years on the Ark." *Open Spaces Quarterly* 5, no. 3 (April 7, 2007). Available online. URL: http://www.open-spaces.com/article-v5n3-davison.php.

Doremus, Holly. "The Story of *TVA v. Hill:* A Narrow Escape for a Broad New Law." Chapter 4 in *Environmental Law Stories.* Eds. Richard J. Lazarus and Oliver A. Houck. New York: Foundation Press, 2005.

Murchison, Kenneth M. *The Snail Darter Case: TVA versus the Endangered Species Act.* Lawrence: University Press of Kansas, 2007.

Wheeler, William Bruce, and Michael J. McDonald. *TVA and the Tellico Dam 1936–1979: A Bureaucratic Crisis in Post-Industrial America.* Knoxville: University of Tennessee Press, 1986.

PRIMARY SOURCES

Document 1: "This Valley Waits to Die," 1969

The Tennessee Valley Authority (TVA) announced plans to dam the Little Tennessee River in the mid-1960s, and the proposal was quickly met by criticism from local people who stood to lose land, as well as by recreational fishers who valued the river for its excellent trout fishing. The controversy drew the attention of Supreme Court justice William O. Douglas, an avid trout fisherman. Justice Douglas made two high-profile visits to the area and, in this article, gave voice to his lament at the potential loss.

How do you save a jewel of a river which has become the plaything of a superpowerful government agency? Hopefully, with publicity. Let it be known, therefore, that 33 miles of a clear, lovely, wild river are facing extinction after a series of maneuverings that date back 30 years. Perhaps there is yet time for this priceless heritage to be saved . . . if the public will listen and react.

The river is the Little Tennessee, which rises in mountainous north Georgia and flows northward into North Carolina, then northwest through Great Smoky Mountains National Park into Tennessee, a distance of some 160 miles. The "Little T," as it's affectionately called by people who live along its banks, ends at its confluence with the Tennessee River about 15 miles west of Knoxville.

The government agency is the Tennessee Valley Authority—the TVA—which recently completed its concrete work for Tellico Dam. This 105-foot dam will flood out hundreds of families now living along the last 33 miles of the Little T, *the last remaining wild part of the river.* The lake resulting from the dam will forever ruin the Little T as Tennessee's finest trout river, and as a picturesque free-flowing river enjoyed by canoeists and a host of others seeking an escape to an unspoiled natural setting. Finally it will forever flood historic sites sacred to the Cherokee Indians—places as revered to them as are Williamsburg and Plymouth Rock to us.

Before I go further, I do not mean to imply that TVA has not done good deeds. Thirty years ago, TVA was the common man's hope against exploitation by private utility companies. Its dams brought cheap electricity and held back floods in a large area.

But the TVA also became manned by political hacks and its engineering staff, while competent, developed a compulsion for make-work projects for the purpose of self-perpetuation. The TVA engineering staff apparently feels it must build dams *whether they are needed or not....*

I visited several of the 300 families occupying some 16,500 acres of rich river bottomland which will be flooded, if the dam is completed. This land, washed and fertilized by floods over the centuries, is so rich it will produce 175 bushels of corn per acre, though the average is a bit lower. It is a land of corn, squash, watermelons and peas. Dairy cattle thrive there and are an important part of the Knoxville milkshed.

This agricultural land under the threat of TVA condemnation—and it will have started as you read this—produces $11 million annually in dairy income, $14 million in beef, $3 million in tobacco. According to soil-bank experts, this is Grade A-1 soil along the bottomlands. Naturally, no one wants to leave....

The Wier Valley (pronounced "Ware") is river bottomland originally owned by Col. Samuel Wier. It now consists of 150 acres and is operated by Mrs. Mayme Wier, a grandmotherly, bespectacled widow. She stood under the shade of one of several giant oak trees in front of her little white frame house. Miss Mayme, as she is known, spoke softly and despairingly, "I'se rather lost hope about saving the farm. If I lose the farm I jes' don't know where to go." Pointing toward a clump of trees by the river, she said all her husband's ancestors were buried there, the old headstones dating back to 1790. "Twenty-some years I'se been worryin' about TVA floodin' this land."

Will they give you enough to get into an old-folks' home, Miss Mayme? . . .

The Graham farm has a house that is 150 years old and has the original hand-planed pine floors and log walls, some of which is exposed for the décor. The John Grahams bought the farm in 1935 after the Norris Dam of TVA ran them out of Jefferson County.

"I built this place outta the bushes," John Graham told me. "I don't have time left to build another. Anyway, this kind of river-bottom farmland is extinct. TVA has done a lot of good, bringing electricity and all. But it seems TVA is buildin' this dam jes' to stay in the buildin' business."

Has a TVA man come around to discuss condemnation yet, Mr. Graham?

Source: William O. Douglas. "This Valley Waits to Die." *True,* May 1969.

—*m*—

Document 2: Ruling by Judge Robert Taylor, 1976

In February 1976, University of Tennessee law student Hiram Hill, along with his professor Zygmunt Plater and local environmental organizations, sued the Tennessee Valley Authority (TVA) for violating the Endangered Species Act. They argued that completion of the Tellico Dam would result in the extinction of the snail darter. In this excerpt from the ruling, Judge Robert Taylor of the district court ruled that halting the project would be unreasonable and contrary to the will of Congress.

The Endangered Species Act of 1973 became effective on December 28, 1973 more than seven years after the Tellico Project was authorized by Congress and nearly seven years after construction began. At that time more than $45 million had been appropriated for the project and over $35 million had been invested in it. . . . The snail darter was discovered several months before this Court approved TVA's final environmental impact statement. It was not listed as an endangered species until November 1975 and its critical habitat was not determined until April 1976.

Under these circumstances, and others heretofore outlined, is it reasonable to conclude that Congress intended the Act to halt the Tellico Project at its present stage of completion? We think not. The Act should be construed in a reasonable manner to effectuate the legislative purpose. . . . We recognize the rule that congressional approval of appropriations does not, standing alone, repeal provisions of law in effect at the time the appropriations are approved. . . . Nevertheless we believe that additional funding of the Tellico Project and a House Committee's direction to complete the project "in the public interest" after being informed by TVA that it did not construe the Endangered Species Act as preventing the project's completion is persuasive that such an interpretation of the Act is consistent with congressional intent. . . . We are convinced that Congress was thoroughly familiar with the project when additional appropriations were made since it had been dealing with the project over a number of years. . . .

This case must be viewed in the context of its particular facts and circumstances. We go no further than to hold that the Act does not operate in such a manner as to halt the completion of this particular project. A far different situation would be presented if the project were capable of reasonable modifications that would insure compliance with the Act or if the project had not been underway for nearly a decade.

If plaintiffs' argument were taken to its logical extreme, the Act would require a court to halt impoundment of water behind a fully completed dam if an endangered species were discovered in the river on the day before such impoundment was scheduled to take place. We cannot conceive that Congress intended such a result. . . .

Finally, we conclude that TVA has not acted arbitrarily, capriciously or otherwise not in accordance with the law in continuing further implementation of the Tellico Project. . . . It has acted within the scope of authority given it by Congress and has informed Congress, through its committees, about the snail darter and its position on the application of the Endangered Species Act to the project.

TVA has made a good faith effort to conserve the snail darter and has consulted with other agencies about the problem rather than taking the immutable position that it was not required to comply with the Act. . . .

For the foregoing reasons, we conclude that plaintiffs' prayer for a permanent injunction must be denied and the action dismissed.

Source: Tennessee Valley Authority v. Hill, 419 F. Supp. 753 (E.D. Tenn. 1976).

—∞—

Document 3: Ruling by Judge Anthony Celebreeze, 1977

When the district court refused to halt construction of the Tellico Dam, the plaintiffs appealed the decision to the United States Court of Appeals for the Sixth Circuit. In the excerpt from his decision in January 1977 below, court of appeals judge Anthony Celebreeze directly addressed the defendant's arguments about what constitutes a reasonable interpretation of the law and the will of Congress.

Although this legal controversy may well enjoy a modicum of notoriety because it appears to pit the survival of an obscure fish against completion of a $100 million reservoir . . . Only three questions need be addressed:

Does Tellico Dam completion violate the Endangered Species Act?

Assuming a violation, are there adequate grounds for exempting Tellico from compliance?

If no exemption is justified, is injunction the proper remedy to effectuate the purposes of the Act?

We are satisfied that TVA's continued preparations to dam the Little Tennessee violate § 1536 of the Endangered Species Act. . . .

We cannot condone non-compliance on the theory propounded by TVA that congressional approval of Tellico appropriations, upon full disclosure of the plight of the snail darter, constitutes legislative acquiescence in or express ratification of TVA's laissez faire interpretation of the Act. . . . Advisory opinions by Congress concerning the "proper" application of an existing statute cannot influence our review because they lack the force of law. To credit them would be tantamount to permitting the legislature to invade a province reserved to the courts by Article III of the constitution. The meaning and spirit of the Act are clear on its face. We need not refer to legislative history to rationalize our independent assessment of its impact. . . .

With no cause to exempt the Tellico project from strict compliance with the Act, we find that the District Court abused its discretion in refusing to permanently enjoin all further actions by TVA which may detrimentally alter the critical habitat of the snail darter. We cannot accept TVA's contention that, even if Tellico completion is technically in violation of the law, halting further construction pending intervention by Congress or additional rule making by the Secretary of the Interior constitutes an inequitable remedy.

TVA claims to have done everything possible to save the snail darter, short of abandoning work on the dam. That alternative is deemed by TVA to be innately unreasonable. We do not agree. It is conceivable that the welfare of an endangered species may weigh more heavily upon the public conscience, as expressed by the final will of Congress, than the writeoff of those millions of dollars already expended for Tellico in excess of its present salvagable value. . . .

Although we must reverse the district court's decision, we are sympathetic to its analysis of the equitable factors present here which would normally militate against granting injunctive relief. TVA has not acted in bad faith. Its efforts to preserve the snail darter appear to be reasonable. As we have already demonstrated, only Congress or the Secretary of the Interior can properly exempt Tellico from compliance with the Act. The separation of powers doctrine is too fundamental a thread in our constitutional fabric for us to be tempted to preempt congressional action in the name of equity or expediency. . . .

Therefore, we reverse the district court's order of dismissal and remand the cause with instructions that a permanent injunction issue halting all activities incident to the Tellico Project which may destroy or modify the critical habitat of the snail darter. This injunction shall remain in effect until Congress, by appropriate legislation, exempts Tellico from compliance with the Act or the snail darter has been deleted from the list of endangered species or its critical habitat materially redefined.

Source: Hill, et al. v. Tennessee Valley Authority, 549 F.2d 1064 (6th Cir. 1977).

—∭—

Document 4: Senate Report on the Endangered Species Act, 1978

*After the court of appeals ordered a permanent injunction against com-
pletion of the Tellico Dam in 1977, Congress proposed amendments to
the Endangered Species Act to create an Endangered Species Committee
with the power to grant exemptions. Below are excerpts from a Senate
report in May 1978 accompanying an early version of that amendment.*

The bill . . . contains a provision which is intended to provide a mechanism
for the resolution of conflicts which might arise between the Endangered
Species Act's mandate to protect and manage endangered and threatened
species and other legitimate national goals and priorities such as providing energy, economic development and other benefits to the American
people. . . . Testimony received by the committee indicates that a substantial number of Federal actions currently underway appear to have all the
elements of an irresolvable conflict within the provisions of the act.

This number may increase significantly in the future as the Fish and
Wildlife Service continues to list additional species and critical habitats. . . . It has also been brought to the committee's attention that the
General Accounting Office suspects, but has not confirmed, that the
Fish and Wildlife Service has refrained from listing species which may
pose a conflict with a Federal action, for fear of provoking the Congress
into weakening the protective provisions of section 7.

The committee believes that these circumstances clearly illustrate
the need for an amendment to the act which will provide flexibility in its
administration, while maintaining protection of threatened and endangered species. . . .

[T]he final decision to grant an exemption must be based on criteria
set forth in section 7 (e) (2) as follows:

There is no reasonable and prudent alternative to such action.
The action is of national or regional significance.
The benefits of such action clearly outweigh the benefits of alter-
native courses of action consistent with conserving the species

or its critical habitat, and that such action is in the public interest. . . .

In the balancing process the Endangered Species Committee is not expected to balance simply the importance of a species against the value of a Federal action. The criteria expressly mandate that the balancing which is to take place is between the benefits of a proposed Federal action and the benefits of alternative courses of action which will not result in harm to the species or its critical habitat. The committee recognized the difficulty of simply comparing species value with a proposed Federal action. The balancing of the benefits of alternative courses of action mandated by the criteria will allow a more logical comparison of the available options. Although the balancing process is difficult the Endangered Species Committee should note that the decision to allow the extinction of a species or destroy all or parts of its critical habitat should not be taken lightly and great care must be applied in trying to decide finally, in cases of conflict, what future course of action is in the public interest.

Source: U.S. Senate Committee on Environment and Public Works. "Endangered Species Act Amendments of 1978." Senate Report 95-874. May 15, 1978.

—⁓—

Document 5: Ruling by Chief Justice Warren Burger, 1978

After the court of appeals issued a permanent injunction against completion of the Tellico Dam, the Tennessee Valley Authority requested that the Supreme Court review the case, and the Supreme Court accepted. In June 1978, the Court issued its ruling upholding the appeals court and the injunction. In the excerpt below, Chief Justice Warren Burger explained the main issues of concern for the Supreme Court, and he declared a strict interpretation of the Endangered Species Act.

We begin with the premise that operation of the Tellico Dam will either eradicate the known population of snail darters or destroy their critical habitat. . . . Starting from the above premise, two questions are presented: (a) would TVA be in violation of the Act if it completed and operated the Tellico Dam as planned? (b) if TVA's actions would offend the Act, is an injunction the appropriate remedy for the violation? For the reasons stated hereinafter, we hold that both questions must be answered in the affirmative.

(A)

It may seem curious to some that the survival of a relatively small number of three-inch fish among all the countless millions of species extant would require the permanent halting of a virtually completed dam for which Congress has expended more than $100 million. The paradox is not minimized by the fact that Congress continued to appropriate large sums of public money for the project, even after congressional Appropriations Committees were apprised of its apparent impact upon the survival of the snail darter. We conclude, however, that the explicit provisions of the Endangered Species Act require precisely that result.

One would be hard pressed to find a statutory provision whose terms were any plainer than those in § 7 of the Endangered Species Act. Its very words affirmatively command all federal agencies "to *insure* that actions *authorized, funded,* or *carried out* by them do not *jeopardize* the continued existence" of an endangered species or "*result* in the destruction or modification of habitat of such species. . . ." . . . This language admits of no exception. . . .

Concededly, this view of the Act will produce results requiring the sacrifice of the anticipated benefits of the project and of many millions of dollars in public funds. But examination of the language, history, and structure of the legislation under review here indicates beyond doubt that Congress intended endangered species to be afforded the highest of priorities. . . .

The plain intent of Congress in enacting this statute was to halt and reverse the trend toward species extinction, whatever the cost. This is reflected not only in the stated policies of the Act, but in literally every section of the statute. . . . [T]he legislative history undergirding § 7 reveals an explicit congressional decision to require agencies to afford first priority to the declared national policy of saving endangered species. The pointed omission of the type of qualifying language previously included in endangered species legislation reveals a conscious decision by Congress to give endangered species priority over the "primary missions" of federal agencies. It is not for us to speculate, much less act, on whether Congress would have altered its stance had the specific events of this case been anticipated. In any event, we discern no hint in the deliberations of Congress relating to the 1973 Act that would compel a different result than we reach here. Indeed, the repeated expressions of congressional concern over what it saw as the potentially enormous danger presented by the eradication of *any* endangered species suggest how the balance would have been struck had the issue been presented to Congress in 1973. . . .

Expressions of committees dealing with requests for appropriations cannot be equated with statutes enacted by Congress, particularly not in the circumstances presented by this case. First, the Appropriations Committees had no jurisdiction over the subject of endangered species, much less did they conduct the type of extensive hearings which preceded passage of the earlier Endangered Species Acts, especially the 1973 Act. We venture to suggest that the House Committee on Merchant Marine and Fisheries and the Senate Committee on Commerce would be somewhat surprised to learn that their careful work on the substantive legislation had been undone by the simple—and brief—insertion of some inconsistent language in Appropriations Committees' Reports.

Second, there is no indication that Congress as a whole was aware of TVA's position. . . .

(B)

Having determined that there is an irreconcilable conflict between operation of the Tellico Dam and the explicit provisions of § 7 of the Endangered Species Act, we must now consider what remedy, if any, is appropriate. . . .

Here we are urged to view the Endangered Species Act "reasonably," and hence shape a remedy "that accords with some modicum of common sense and the public weal." . . . But is that our function? We have no expert knowledge on the subject of endangered species, much less do we have a mandate from the people to strike a balance of equities on the side of the Tellico Dam. Congress has spoken in the plainest of words, making it abundantly clear that the balance has been struck in favor of affording endangered species the highest of priorities, thereby adopting a policy which it described as "institutionalized caution."

Our individual appraisal of the wisdom or unwisdom of a particular course consciously selected by the Congress is to be put aside in the process of interpreting a statute. Once the meaning of an enactment is discerned and its constitutionality determined, the judicial process comes to an end. We do not sit as a committee of review, nor are we vested with the power of veto. The lines ascribed to Sir Thomas More by Robert Bolt are not without relevance here:

> The law, Roper, the law. I know what's legal, not what's right. And I'll stick to what's legal. . . . I'm not God. The currents and eddies of right and wrong, which you find such plain-sailing, I can't navigate, I'm no voyager. But in the thickets of the law, oh there I'm a forester. . . . What would you do? Cut a great road through the law to get after the Devil? . . . And when the last law was down, and the Devil turned round on you—where would you hide, Roper, the laws all being flat? . . . This country's planted thick with laws from coast to coast—Man's laws, not God's—and if you cut them down . . . d'you really think you could stand upright in the winds that would blow them? . . . Yes, I'd give the Devil benefit of law, for my own safety's sake."

R. Bolt. *A Man for All Seasons,* act I, p. 147 (*Three Plays,* Heinemann ed., 1967).

We agree with the Court of Appeals that in our constitutional system the commitment to the separation of powers is too fundamental for us to pre-empt congressional action by judicially decreeing what accords with "common sense and the public weal." Our Constitution vests such responsibilities in the political branches.

Affirmed.

Source: Tennessee Valley Authority v. Hill, et al., 437 US 153 (S. Ct. 1978).

6

HAZARDOUS WASTE:
Who Should Pay for the Cost of Cleaning Up Hazardous Waste Sites?

—ᴍ—

THE CONTROVERSY

The Issue

In the late 1970s, the nation awoke to the issue of uncontrolled hazardous waste. The discovery of chemical wastes buried beneath a residential community in upstate New York aroused near panic as the public, industry, government officials, and scientists grappled with questions about threats to health, safety, cleanup, and liability. As a result of this and other discoveries, a national debate developed around the question of responsibility and liability for cleanup, proper disposal, and compensation to affected individuals. Who should pay for the costs of cleanup of hazardous waste sites?

- ♦ *Arguments that the chemical industry should cover most costs:* Affected residents, environmentalists, and some officials argued that the government should address the issue of hazardous waste, and that the chemical industry, which profited directly from the production and cheap disposal of hazardous wastes, should shoulder most of the cost and liability.

- ♦ *Arguments that the federal government should cover most costs:* The chemical industry and others argued that all of society benefited from the production and cheap disposal of chemical products, and, therefore, the burden of the nation's hazardous wastes should be borne equally by all, not just by one sector of industry, and that the federal government should cover most costs. Only those individuals or firms that were egregiously negligent or criminal, they argued, should be held liable for improper disposal or handling of hazardous waste.

—ᴍ—

INTRODUCTION

On August 2, 1978, New York State health commissioner Robert Whalen announced that there existed "a great and imminent peril to the health of the general public . . . as a result of exposure to toxic substances." Initial health studies indicated an increased risk of birth defects and miscarriages, as well as liver problems. He urged that children under two years of age and pregnant women evacuate the area adjacent to an abandoned chemical waste site known as Love Canal, which was buried beneath a suburban neighborhood in Niagara Falls, New York, near the Canadian border. The commissioner made the announcement to a remarkably small audience, but the import of his announcement grew dramatically as national and international news outlets picked up the story. Reporters descended on the Love Canal community and transmitted images and words of beleaguered residents in various states of confusion, panic, fear, and anger. This was not the only place where abandoned hazardous waste was discovered, but Love Canal came to symbolize the issue like no other.

Over the next two years, the drama of Love Canal dominated the news as residents, government officials, and industry representatives struggled over how to respond. Residents demanded to be evacuated and compensated. Local, state, and federal officials argued over responsibility and cost. The company that had buried the wastes denied culpability, arguing that it had behaved responsibly. This and similar events touched a nerve of public unease over the hidden dangers of chemical contamination and pollution. Pressure quickly mounted on local, state, and federal government officials to respond.

Even before the eruption of the Love Canal crisis, the federal government had begun to consider ways to address the environmental problems of handling and disposing of hazardous waste. Now, the Love Canal controversy placed renewed pressure on officials to act. In the wake of Love Canal and other hazardous waste crises, Congress took up consideration of a number of bills that sought to address the problem through the creation of a dedicated fund, described as a superfund, to pay for the cost of cleaning up chemical spills and hazardous waste sites. The bills varied in detail, but two major questions faced members of Congress: 1) How should the cleanup fund be supported?;

and 2) how should liability for the cleanup of hazardous waste sites be assigned? These were high-stakes questions with important ramifications for public health, the environment, and the economy.

Environmental leaders and the newly created Environmental Protection Agency (EPA) argued for aggressive federal involvement in identifying and initiating cleanup of hazardous waste sites. The EPA estimated that there were tens of thousands of sites throughout the country where hazardous waste was improperly dumped or abandoned, threatening public health and the environment. They estimated that it would take years and cost billions of dollars to identify and clean them all up. Environmental advocates argued that the polluters—the chemical and petroleum industries—were primarily responsible for the problem and should be forced to foot the bill for cleanup. These industries, they argued, profited most directly from the production, sale, and cheap disposal of these chemical products and should therefore shoulder the bulk of the costs. The chemical industry and its allies countered that it was unfair to hold the chemical industry solely responsible, since all of society benefited from the industrial products. Critics of aggressive government intervention also argued that the problem of abandoned hazardous waste sites was exaggerated, that it was not as large a problem as some feared, and that the health threat was unproven and therefore questionable. Moreover, they argued, it was unfair to hold chemical producers, transporters, and waste handlers retroactively guilty of violating newly created standards, when much of the disposal had taken place years earlier in ways that were common and not illegal at the time. The central policy debate that faced the nation boiled down to a relatively simple question: Who should pay for the cleanup of the nation's hazardous waste sites?

BACKGROUND

As in the industrial revolution that preceded it, the chemical revolution of the early 20th century changed manufacturing processes and the everyday life of the nation. The hallmark of this revolution was the dramatic increase in the use of synthetic organic chemicals and the replacement of natural materials—cotton, wood, rubber, metals, soap, manure, and natural solvents—with synthetic products made from petrochemicals, such as plastics. Following World War II, there was

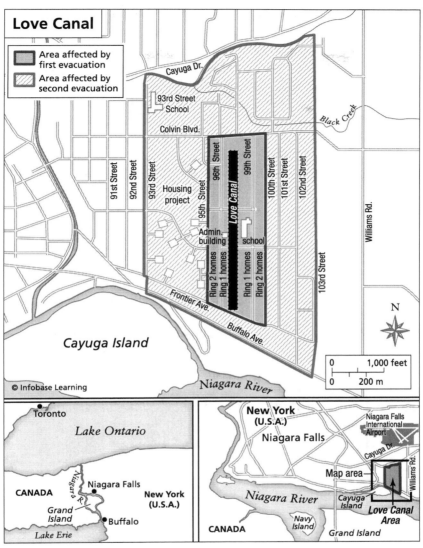

Love Canal

Legend:
- Area affected by first evacuation
- Area affected by second evacuation

Cayuga Dr.

Black Creek

93rd Street School

Colvin Blvd.

91st Street
92nd Street
93rd Street
95th Street
96th Street
99th Street
100th Street
101st Street
102nd Street

Housing project

Love Canal

Williams Rd.

Admin. building
school

103rd Street

Ring 2 homes
Ring 1 homes
Ring 1 homes
Ring 2 homes

Frontier Ave.

Buffalo Ave.

Cayuga Island

© Infobase Learning

Niagara River

N

0   1,000 feet
0   200 m

Toronto

Lake Ontario

CANADA
Niagara Falls
Grand Island
Buffalo
New York (U.S.A.)
Lake Erie

New York (U.S.A.)
Niagara Falls

Niagara Falls International Airport

Cayuga Dr.

Map area

Niagara River

Cayuga Island
Navy Island

CANADA
Grand Island

Love Canal Area

Williams Rd.

In the late 1970s, investigations by environmental officials revealed the presence of toxic chemicals in Love Canal—an abandoned industrial waste pit buried beneath a residential community in Niagara Falls, New York. In 1978, the federal government declared the community a disaster area, and New York State evacuated and purchased the 236 homes nearest to the canal (Ring 1). Continued lobbying by remaining residents forced the federal government to issue a second state of emergency in 1980 and to broker a deal with New York State to evacuate and purchase a second group of homes around Love Canal (Ring 2). The Love Canal controversy prompted a national debate on toxic chemicals and spurred passage of the nation's strictest environmental laws to control hazardous waste.

substantial growth in synthetic organic chemical production: Approximately 1 billion pounds were produced in 1940, increasing to 30 billion pounds by 1950, and to 300 billion pounds by 1976.

The chemical revolution of the post–World War II period coincided with the rise of the modern American economy. Increased industrial output of new synthetic products was matched by the growth of a consumer culture. Americans of all walks of life availed themselves of the abundance of new products—from fabrics like rayon, nylon, and polyester to new forms of paints, cleaners, fertilizers, and pesticides. These new synthetic products were versatile and cheap with many advantageous properties, but their effects on health and the environment were largely unknown, or at least underappreciated. The increased production of these substances also created large volumes of waste products, many of which were toxic. With little government oversight, the handling of these wastes was left largely to the industries themselves. Aside from dumping into surface waters such as lakes and rivers, which was increasingly frowned upon, most industries used a variety of land-based facilities for hazardous waste disposal: landfills, surface impoundments (lagoons or ponds of liquid waste), deep well injection, aboveground tank and drum storage, piles (exposed mounds of waste), and land farms (spreading and mixing of waste over large areas of open land to allow organic breakdown of the waste). While widely practiced, the significance of these disposal choices did not become apparent until the latter part of the 20th century. As American industries grew across the country, so did their waste disposal sites.

In the early 1900s, an entrepreneur by the name of Elon Huntington Hooker set up the Hooker Electrochemical Company in Niagara Falls, New York, in order to take advantage of the cheap hydroelectric power generated by the nearby falls. Hooker Electrochemical (later Occidental Chemical Corporation) used electricity to turn brine into chlorine and caustic soda. These chemicals are used for a wide variety of products and manufacturing processes—pulp and paper production, processing and dying of textiles, the manufacture of soaps and detergents, aluminum production, and as intermediate chemicals in the production of everything from pharmaceuticals to plastics.

Beginning sometime in the early 1940s, Hooker began using a nearby canal to dispose of its chemical wastes. The canal was the remnant of a failed business venture in the late 19th century by William T.

Love. The uncompleted project left behind a trench 10 feet deep, 80 feet wide, and 3,200 feet long, which came to be known as Love's Canal or Love Canal. As the canal filled with water, it became a recreation space and public swimming hole for local residents. In 1947, Hooker Electrochemical purchased the canal and the land surrounding it for disposal of its chemical wastes. When Hooker acquired the 16-acre site, the surrounding area was largely undeveloped. Between 1947 and 1953, Hooker dumped approximately 25,000 tons of chemical wastes, some sealed in drums, into the canal.

At that time, the disposal of industrial waste, as for any waste, was largely a local matter and not a subject of federal regulations. No national standards existed to determine appropriate disposal practices, and there were few if any laws that distinguished between regular household or municipal rubbish and industrial or chemical wastes. In the early 1950s, the Niagara Falls Board of Education approached Hooker and asked to purchase a portion of the land for the construction of a new school to serve a rapidly growing population. The expanding City of Niagara Falls had in fact begun to encroach on the once isolated grounds of the Hooker Electrochemical Company. Hooker initially refused to sell, but later changed its mind and in 1953 sold the entire property to the Niagara Falls Board of Education for the token price of one dollar.

Hooker later contended that it had been pressured by the city to sell the land and threatened with the use of eminent domain to take the property, but city officials deny this contention. The final sale agreement stipulated that Hooker would not be liable for injury or damage resulting from the chemical wastes buried on the site. Moreover, Hooker representatives recommended that the land immediately above the buried canal not be disturbed or used for anything except a park or playground. Board members were apparently not too concerned about the presence of the buried waste at the time of sale, which is not surprising. In 1953, few Americans had any knowledge of the danger of chemical wastes; environmental consciousness and stigma or fear of such wastes or contamination were still years away. More than 20 years would pass before the term *hazardous waste* became familiar to the general public. Thus, despite Hooker's disclosure of the presence of buried chemicals, as well as concerns by the board's own engineers about the instability of the soil, an elementary school was erected almost directly on top of the buried canal in 1955. Over the next two decades, the area, including portions of the buried canal, was further developed with streets, sewers, utilities, and residential housing, though few residents knew anything about the site's history.

Concern about toxic chemicals did not really take hold until the emergence of the modern environmental movement, which gained popular momentum in the early 1960s with the publication of Rachel Carson's *Silent Spring* in 1962. *Silent Spring* raised an alarm about the indiscriminate use of pesticides and other dangerous, man-made chemicals and the threats to human health and ecosystems posed by the uncontrolled spread of these and similar toxins. This new ecological consciousness affected popular thought and government activity and reached a crescendo in 1970 with the celebration of the first Earth Day on April 22, an event in which millions around the world participated. That same year also witnessed a frenzy of federal activity as both Congress and the White House rushed to create new environmental policies and institutions. In 1970, President Richard Nixon signed the National Environmental Policy Act (NEPA) into law and created the EPA and the National Oceanic and Atmospheric Administration. With the issue of pollution high on the agenda for lawmakers, Congress passed a series of laws to control air and water pollution in the early 1970s. In particular, lawmakers sought to place strict controls on the use of bodies of water or the atmosphere for the disposal of industrial or commercial wastes. Regulations and rules regarding land-based disposal of wastes, however, were slower in coming.

As early as 1970, Congress passed the Solid Waste Disposal Act, but this law simply authorized the study of the issue of solid waste disposal practices and their environmental impacts. The delay in federal approaches to land-based disposal was partly due to the fact that solid waste disposal was historically a local or municipal responsibility. Moreover, some policy makers worried that federal involvement in municipal waste disposal was too much of an intrusion into local prerogatives.

In the years before the discovery of Love Canal, the issue of hazardous waste was not high on the agenda of either environmentalists or lawmakers. However, Congress had passed two pieces of legislation in 1976 that had a direct bearing on the control of toxic industrial materials and wastes—the Toxic Substances Control Act (TSCA) and the Resource Conservation and Recovery Act (RCRA). TSCA gave the EPA authority to regulate the production and distribution of industrial chemicals that posed a potential hazard to the public. This law was prompted by widespread concerns about the growing number of industrial chemicals whose toxic properties were unknown. At the time, scientists estimated that there were more than 70,000 industrial chemicals in circulation, but less than 2 percent had been evaluated to determine their effects on human health or the environment. RCRA charged the EPA with identifying and classifying hazardous chemicals and creating a system to regulate and track them from "cradle to grave" throughout the country.

However, advocates of TSCA and RCRA severely underestimated the complexity of identifying substances that were hazardous, let alone devising safe ways to handle and dispose of them. As a result of the sheer complexity of the task, the EPA was unable to make rules to implement RCRA for more than two years after the law had been passed. Nonetheless, Congress viewed these laws as advances in the crusade to bring pollution under control. Moreover, while the nation had taken bold steps in the prevention and regulation of air and water pollution, land pollution was, until then, still unaddressed. By the EPA's own estimates, land pollution had actually been exacerbated by laws that prevented air and water pollution. As new laws and regulations required industries to capture wastes before they entered the air and prohibited the disposal of wastes into bodies of water, industries sought affordable land-based solutions for waste disposal. TSCA promised to tackle the proliferation of toxic chemicals and products by controlling their production in the first place, while RCRA offered a way to control the present and future management of hazardous waste disposal. Just before RCRA became law in 1976, one congressional committee concluded, somewhat prematurely, that the last loophole in pollution control had been closed.

Early Warnings

As early as the 1960s, some Love Canal residents began to complain about noxious fumes and black, oily residue seeping into basements. Heavy precipitation in spring 1975 literally brought the issue to the surface as the buried canal began to overflow. Houses next to the canal showed signs of the chemical presence as grass and shrubbery died off, backyards began to sink, and rusting drums poked out of the earth. There were also reports of chemical burns to children and pets that had come into contact with chemical residues in and around the buried

CHEMICAL CONTROL, INC.

In 1976, Congress passed the Resource Conservation and Recovery Act (RCRA), the first national attempt to directly regulate and control the handling and disposal of hazardous wastes—"from cradle to grave." RCRA was directed at a variety of issues having to do with solid waste, with hazardous waste being only one among many. Hazardous waste was not yet on the public agenda—that would wait for the eruption of Love Canal two years later. The hazardous waste sections of the 1976 law directed the Environmental Protection Agency (EPA) to develop criteria for what constituted hazardous waste, as well as to establish standards for regulating their transportation and the issuance of permits for the proper operation of hazardous waste disposal facilities. The complexity and enormity of these tasks took both Congress and the EPA by surprise. In the spring of 1980, nearly four years after RCRA had been signed into law, the EPA was finally ready to publish a large section of the RCRA rules. A press conference to announce the new rules was scheduled at a New Jersey chemical waste dump that had recently come under government control. A week before the scheduled press conference, the dump exploded.

The dump in question was a 3.4-acre waste disposal facility in Elizabeth, New Jersey, formerly owned by Chemical Control, Inc. The waste facility had only started operation in 1970 but faced problems early on when the company's president was indicted in 1977 for illegally dumping chemical wastes on vacant city lots and into city sewers and creeks. Two years later, he was sentenced to a three-year prison term. When state officials investigated the Chemical Control facility site in May 1979, they found more than 40,000 leaking drums of highly toxic, corrosive, and combustible chemical wastes. Many of the rusted 55-gallon drums were unlabeled, and in some places they were stacked in teetering columns five drums high. In one section of the facility, investigators discovered quantities of explosive picric acid, several pounds of radioactive material, bottles of nitroglycerin, containers of explosive compressed gases, cylinders of mustard gas, and 10 pounds of infectious biological waste. Upon discovery of the materials stored at the site, the mayor of Elizabeth declared a state of emergency and restricted public canal. Residents who lived next to the buried canal described a black, tarry substance oozing out of basement walls, overpowering chemical odors, and a variety of health ailments.

access to within a half-mile. Because of the imminent risk of fire or explosion, state officials took control of the site and began the process of removing the most dangerous or unstable substances.

At 10:54 P.M. on April 21, 1980, the Chemical Control site exploded into flames. Witnesses described thunderous booms and an explosion like an "atomic blast." One resident who lived across the parking lot from the site said, "I looked out and saw these big barrels flying in the air like they were soda cans." Flames reached heights of 200–300 feet, and clouds of acrid, black smoke billowed out for 15 miles. Four fire crews responded to the fire, which took more than 10 hours to contain. Sixty-six people, including 59 firefighters, were treated for injuries during and after the blaze. By most accounts, the conflagration could have been much worse. By sheer luck, prevailing winds carried the toxic smoke out to sea and away from the most populated areas. No less important, a yearlong state cleanup had already removed more than 8,000 barrels of the most hazardous and volatile materials. As the Elizabeth health director later remarked, "We were within a hair's breadth of a disaster."

The Chemical Control fire had a political impact as well, occurring as it did when the EPA was just preparing to announce rules for RCRA and in the midst of congressional hearings on Superfund bills. A week after the fire, the EPA announced that it had cancelled its planned press conference at the site. New Jersey environmental officials warned that the nearly 100 people expected to attend the press conference would have needed to wear protective clothing just to get near the site. An EPA spokesperson explained, "Because that would require hundreds of asbestos suits and respirators, we decided against it." This did not stop some members of Congress who donned the appropriate gear—white protective suits, thick yellow gloves, and full face respirators—in order to tour the site and draw attention to the need for Superfund legislation. Indeed, the Chemical Control fire was repeatedly cited as a glaring example of the need for the nation as a whole to take more aggressive action and make available adequate resources to deal with the problem of hazardous waste sites. Two months after the April 1980 blaze, the Chemical Control site caught fire again.

In 1976, a joint commission of the U.S. and Canadian governments traced pesticide contamination of Lake Ontario to Niagara Falls and eventually to the buried wastes in Love Canal. Following a series of articles by a local journalist exposing the history of the Love Canal site, city and state officials launched an investigation that revealed widespread groundwater contamination. In early 1978, the EPA and the New York Department of Environmental Conservation began testing air and water samples inside basements of homes abutting the canal. These tests confirmed the presence of carcinogenic chemicals from the buried dump site. On May 15, 1978, the EPA announced its discovery of toxic benzene in the air inside of basements nearest the canal, suggesting a serious health threat.

At public meetings following the EPA's announcement, state and local officials asked residents to cooperate with health and environmental studies, though there was significant confusion and frustration when state and local officials publicly disagreed over the severity of the threat. The state health official reported excessive levels of toxic substances and warned residents about the hazards of exposure. The county health commissioner attempted to repudiate these warnings and belittled residents for their fears. Nevertheless, over the next two months, the New York Department of Health conducted health surveys that revealed elevated rates of miscarriage and birth defects in families living in some parts of the neighborhood adjacent to the canal.

On August 2, 1978, New York State health commissioner Robert Whalen declared a public health emergency. He ordered that an engineering plan be put in place to stop further spread of the wastes from the canal, that the fall opening of the 99th Street School (which sat atop the canal) be delayed, and that further health and environmental studies be conducted. He also urged that children under two years of age and pregnant women living on streets adjacent to the canal evacuate as soon as possible. (See "'Evacuation of Kids Urged,' August 2, 1978," on page 227 in the Primary Sources section.) The residents' distress was heightened by the fact that the commissioner and the state had no authority to help families with the costs of such a sudden move. The announcement, which the *New York Times* reported, became national and international news almost immediately. Intense media coverage of distressed families and irate residents put severe pressure on government officials.

Lois Gibbs, president and founder of the Love Canal Homeowners Association in Niagara Falls, New York, trims a Christmas tree on December 21, 1978, with decorations naming chemicals found in the Love Canal dump. Gibbs emerged as the most outspoken community leader in the controversy over Love Canal. (Associated Press)

As soon as public officials announced that the hazardous waste in Love Canal represented a potential threat, cost and responsibility became serious areas of contention. Residents demanded assistance. They feared not only for the health of their families, they were also deeply anxious about the costs of moving and the loss of their homes and property values—their largest economic assets. With little experience and no formal procedures in place to handle such crises, government officials were similarly hamstrung and unsure. When the state health commissioner announced that Love Canal posed "a great and imminent peril," his purpose was not to arouse panic but to formally activate a state statute and money allocated to contain the site and determine the extent of the health threat. However, he had neither the authority nor the resources to help residents directly. City and county officials declared that they were unable to do anything because of tax restrictions. New York's congressional delegation rushed to create ad hoc emergency legislation to provide money for assistance with the cleanup.

The day after Whalen's announcement, New York governor Hugh Carey asked President Carter to declare the Love Canal community a disaster area in order to make federal assistance available. However, the head of the Federal Disaster Assistance Administration (later renamed the Federal Emergency Management Agency), who toured the neighborhood that week, was reluctant to declare an emergency. "This isn't a flood or a tornado," he said. "It's unique. I think it will take a somewhat creative interpretation of the disaster legislation to fix." Five days after the health commissioner's announcement, Governor Carey held a press conference at the 99th Street School during which he announced that the state had a plan to halt the spread of contaminants from the canal. He promised that the state would purchase the houses closest to the canal that had been made uninhabitable by the contamination. "You will not have to make mortgage payments on homes you don't want or cannot occupy," he said. "Don't worry about the banks. The state will take care of them." That same day, President Carter declared the community a disaster area, although the federal government would only provide funds to help with remediation of the site, not with evacuation or permanent relocation of families.

With White House promises of emergency federal aid for remediation of the site, the state purchased 236 homes nearest to the buried canal over the following three months (at an eventual cost of $10.7 million). Hooker Electrochemical representatives were quick to deny legal responsibility, arguing that the board of education assumed responsibility when it purchased the property. They pointed out that Hooker had explicitly warned the board about the buried chemicals and claimed that the contamination was a result of the board's mismanagement of the site. Nevertheless, Hooker volunteered to provide $280,000 toward remediation. At the same time, state and federal officials began to consider legal action against the company. While homes closest to the canal were purchased and remediation efforts initiated soon after the 1978 declaration of disaster, the Love Canal saga would continue for another two years as more and more residents demanded to be bought out and as both government and private parties initiated lawsuits to assign blame and recover damages.

The Love Canal crisis drew the attention of federal lawmakers. By March 1979, Congress began to seriously consider new legislation to address the problem of abandoned hazardous waste sites. Representatives from Hooker Electrochemical were some of the first witnesses to appear at congressional hearings on the issue. By this time, few people contested that hazardous waste was a national problem. Proposed legislation was submitted by the EPA, members of the House of Representatives, and the Senate. The bills before Congress, while differing significantly in detail, all addressed one centrally important question: Who should pay?

THE DEBATE

The EPA, along with environmental organizations and prominent members of Congress, argued that the problem of improperly maintained or abandoned hazardous waste sites presented a dire threat to public health and the environment. Some described hazardous waste as the most important environmental problem facing the nation. Indeed, by 1979, Congress was familiar not only with Love Canal, but other recently discovered sites such as the Valley of the Drums and Toone, Tennessee. The Valley of the Drums was a 13-acre site in Brooks, Kentucky, 12 miles south of Louisville, where in 1979 authorities discovered over 17,000 drums of unidentified waste that had been illegally and surreptitiously dumped in pits and trenches on a farm. As the drums deteriorated, contaminated liquids from the site flowed into a creek that ran directly into the Ohio River. In Toone, Tennessee, the Velsicol Chemical Corporation maintained a landfill for the disposal of pesticides and volatile organic compounds manufactured at its plant in Memphis. Over the course of a decade, the company had dumped 130,000 drums of plant waste at the site. Leachate from the landfill contaminated the groundwater, making some local residents ill and rendering their drinking water wells permanently unusable. As a result of EPA investigations, the issue drew both public and congressional attention. Following congressional hearings in October 1978, the company offered compensation to Toone residents and paid to reconnect affected homes to a temporary water supply. While these and other recent experiences

Shortly after announcement of the threat posed by leaking chemicals, the Love Canal dump site in Niagara Falls, New York, was fenced off. (Str/Associated Press)

made congressional advocates sensitive to the issue of hazardous waste, the true extent of the problem was as yet unknown.

The Case for Making Industry Pay

The EPA contracted with Fred C. Hart Associates, an environmental consulting firm headed by former New York City air resources commissioner Fred C. Hart, to determine the extent of the hazardous waste problem. The Hart study, completed in February 1979, estimated that there were approximately 30,000 to 50,000 active and inactive hazardous waste sites throughout the country and that approximately 30,000 of these posed significant problems. The estimated cost to clean up all of these sites was more than $44 billion. Moreover, the consultant warned that the EPA would likely only be able to recover half of that amount from the operators of these facilities, leaving the federal government with a bill of at least $22 billion.

Advocates of an aggressive federal response argued that action needed to be taken as quickly as possible and those responsible for the mess should be made to clean it up or pay for cleanup. With the backing of the White House, the EPA drafted legislation that proposed the creation of a dedicated fund to pay for cleanup in emergency situations or in cases where no responsible parties could be found. The fund would be supported through federal contributions and, most important, by a tax on oil and chemical feedstocks—the raw materials of the chemical industry. Advocates of such a fund—dubbed "Superfund"—argued that dedicated monies were needed in order to assure that funds would be available for this expensive undertaking in a timely manner. They argued that the alternative—an open-ended reliance on the federal Treasury and congressional appropriations—would put an unfair burden on taxpayers for the cleanup of industries' mess, increase the federal deficit, and be subject to the whims of congressional and public interest. Advocates argued that chemical and petroleum companies had directly profited from the production and cheap (some said irresponsible) disposal of hazardous wastes and therefore bore the bulk of the responsibility for the cost of cleanup.

Critics argued that it would make more sense to tax companies or individuals who generated hazardous wastes through use of these chemicals, rather than the companies who supplied the feedstocks. However, the EPA reasoned that it would be more practical, from an administrative perspective, to manage fees levied against less than 1,000 large and stable companies than to try and administer fees against more than 250,000 generators. Moreover, advocates of a tax on feedstocks argued that such a fee could easily be passed on to generators, thus sparing the feedstock suppliers financial hardship.

Intimately related to the issue of funding was the determination of liability. Superfund supporters favored a system of strict, joint and several liability. Strict liability meant that individuals or companies who had owned or contributed to a hazardous waste site could be held liable for the costs of cleanup whether or not they had acted negligently. Advocates argued that strict liability would free the government from the expensive and often insurmountable standards required to prove negligence under traditional tort law. Moreover, supporters wanted to preclude the possibility that generators of hazardous waste might try to avoid responsibility by passing the wastes off to waste transporters and handlers.

Joint and several liability meant that all contributors to a site could be held equally liable, regardless of their individual contributions. The rationale for joint and several liability was that it would be nearly impossible in many cases (e.g., Valley of the Drums) to determine who had contributed what and in what amount, especially in cases where the suspected contributors were uncooperative, could not be identified, or no longer existed. In addition, the EPA anticipated situations in which many if not most of the identified contributors to a hazardous waste site would not have the financial ability to pay for cleanup. However, chances were that at least one of the identified contributors would be a larger company with more substantial financial resources. Joint and several liability thus increased the odds that the federal government would be able to recover the costs of cleanup from someone.

Indeed, at the heart of the proposal for strict, joint and several liability was the concern that the government and, thus ultimately, the taxpayers would be left holding the bill for cleanup if burdened by the extreme difficulty of proving responsibility and negligence. Advocates argued that previous attempts to recover costs or damages for negligent handling or disposal of hazardous wastes were often unsuccessful under traditional norms of proof and liability. As a result, the nation's hazardous waste sites were not being cleaned up.

The Case for Making Government Pay

Chemical and petroleum industries did not dispute the need to manage hazardous wastes responsibly, nor did they dispute the need to clean up uncontrolled hazardous waste sites. However, the Chemical Manufacturers Association (CMA), an organization representing many of the

nation's chemical companies, along with other industrial representatives, such as the National Association of Manufacturers, opposed the
Superfund proposals and hotly disputed the premises for its funding
and liability schemes. Opponents argued that problems such as Love
Canal were certainly tragic, but they were unusual and there was no
national crisis. They dismissed EPA estimates about the extent of the
problem as pure guesswork.

Following the Hart study and its multibillion dollar estimates for
cleanup, the CMA announced the results of its own national study of
hazardous waste sites. According to the CMA, there were 4,800 sites
nationwide that contained hazardous wastes and only 400 of these
posed significant problems—a far cry from the 30,000 estimated by the
EPA's consultant. CMA cost estimates for cleanup for all of these problem sites approximated $400 million. While few in Congress took the
CMA study seriously (in part because they refused to share the evidence for their conclusions), the issue of uncertainty about the scope
of the problem was real enough. Other critics, including editors of the
Wall Street Journal, argued that the actual public health threat of hazardous waste was still unproven and quite likely overblown.

A central argument of the CMA was that blame for hazardous
waste was misplaced and that all of society bore responsibility, not just
the chemical industry. In an op-ed in the *Washington Post,* CMA president Robert A. Roland, wrote:

> One of the things that we must all realize in discussing the solid-
> waste disposal problem, including toxic or hazardous wastes, is
> that it is not just the problem of the chemical industry. It is a
> result of society's advanced technology and pursuit of an increas-
> ingly complex lifestyle. Man always has been a messy animal . . .
> certain amounts of waste are inevitable. . . . Everyone should
> realize that the blame does not belong to a single company, or a
> single industry, but to all of us as individuals and as an advanced
> society. Rather than looking for scapegoats, we should recognize
> the dilemma . . . and consider new ways to encourage the dis-
> closure of dumpsite information and ways to limit the crushing
> liabilities that could result.

The CMA was quite sensitive to the symbolic significance of putting the onus of cost and liability on the chemical industry, which,

they reasoned, would simply reinforce public perception that they were to blame. They argued that a tax on feedstocks was inequitable and punitive and did not reflect society's responsibility for problems that everyone had contributed to and everyone had a responsibility to help resolve. They repeatedly pointed out that many hazardous waste sites throughout the country were owned by nonprofit institutions such as hospitals and the government itself. The CMA proposed that the costs of cleanup should be financed by the federal

---

STRINGFELLOW ACID PITS: "LOVE CANAL OF THE WEST"

In 1956, James Stringfellow purchased an old granite quarry in a steep sided canyon of the Jarupa Mountains in Riverside County, California, 50 miles east of Los Angeles. Geologists had concluded (mistakenly) that the site was underlain by impermeable bedrock and would therefore act as a natural barrier to the migration of liquid wastes. The Stringfellow Quarry Company, Inc., subsequently opened a legal industrial waste dump that came to be known as the Stringfellow Acid Pits. Between 1956 and 1972, more than 200 companies deposited 34 million gallons of liquid industrial waste, primarily from metal finishing, electroplating, and pesticide production. Much of the waste was kept in 20 unlined evaporation ponds on the site.

The Stringfellow waste dump was fairly isolated, though it sat about a mile upstream of the small suburban communities of Glen Avon Heights, Pedley, and Mira Loma. Few residents complained about the site until heavy rains in 1969 caused an overflow of the waste ponds, which released all manner of noxious and caustic chemicals into the local Pyrite River. The overflow required extensive remediation efforts, and nearby residents began to complain about a variety of health symptoms. As a result of repeated complaints and state investigations of groundwater contamination, the Stringfellow dump ceased operations in 1972. It was taken over by the state when a subsequent owner of the site failed to pay taxes. Heavy rains returned in November 1978, and state officials were forced to release 800,000 gallons of chemical wastes into the Pyrite River and flood-control channels in order to avert a much larger and uncontrolled release of wastes. The flood-control channels ran through the downstream community of Glen Avon. One resident described flooding of his property. "It was like a river, foul and foamy. . . . It dried, and the earth

Treasury, cost recovery from responsible parties, and a state matching contribution.

The proposal for strict, joint and several liability standards was even more objectionable. While the CMA and others certainly agreed that those who had illegally dumped hazardous wastes should be held responsible for the cost of cleanup, they argued that the proposed Superfund liability standards would result in highly inequitable outcomes. Because individual contribution to a site would not be considered,

was a weird gray like a moonscape." Unaware of what the rushing brown water contained, children in nearby schools and neighborhoods waded and played in the toxic wastes. Residents later recalled how tennis shoes and blue jeans disintegrated after contact with the contaminated waters.

Shortly after the Comprehensive Environmental Response, Compensation, and Liability Act of 1980 (commonly known as the Superfund) was passed in 1980, some declared the Stringfellow Acid Pits the most polluted waste site in California. One state senate staffer described the site as the "Love Canal of the West." The Stringfellow site was one of the first sites in the nation to be considered under the Superfund program. However, federal money and remedial activity on the site were delayed when it became the center of a political scandal. In 1983, congressional critics accused Environmental Protection Agency administrator Anne M. Burford of delaying a $6 million federal cleanup grant for the site in an effort to prevent then-and-now governor Edmund G. (Jerry) Brown, Jr., a Democrat, from claiming credit for it. The scandal was part of a larger revolt against the Reagan administration's attempts to undermine environmental programs, including Superfund. Burford and many other high-ranking EPA appointees were forced to resign. The Stringfellow site was shortly after added to Superfund's national priority list. Federal and state prosecutors initiated lawsuits against 30 of the largest contributors to the waste dump, including such notable companies as McDonnell Douglas, Montrose Chemical, General Electric, Hughes Aircraft, Northrop, and Rockwell International. Many of the wastes and contaminated soils were removed and hauled to another approved waste facility 20 miles away. Unfortunately, the latter site was itself discovered to be leaking in 1984 and subsequently became a candidate for federal cleanup.

strict, joint and several liability meant that companies could essentially be held liable for the wrongs committed by others—a violation of basic tenets of common law. In addition, CMA representatives speculated that in the pursuit of cost recovery for abandoned sites where multiple parties were found to be responsible, the government would inevitably focus on companies with deeper pockets. As a result, liability would be based more on ability to pay than actual culpability. Even more problematic was the retroactive liability inherent in the proposed standards. Companies could be held liable for past dumping practices that were acceptable, or at least not illegal, at the time they were done. This, the CMA argued, violated the principle against ex post facto laws. The latter point was particularly applicable in the Love Canal case. According to Zoltan Merzei, vice chairman of Occidental (owner of Hooker Electrochemical), "They [Hooker] were no more negligent than any other companies." The problem, he argued, was in "trying to judge yesterday's practices with today's rules." (See "'The Other Side of Love Canal,' July 31, 1980," on page 229 in the Primary Sources section.)

OUTCOME AND IMPACT

Congress initiated hearings on Love Canal, hazardous waste disposal, and the Superfund bills beginning in March 1979. (See "Love Canal Testimony, March 28, 1979," on page 230 in the Primary Sources section.) These hearings lasted for more than a year and half. During that tumultuous period, events seemed to conspire against opponents of greater federal regulation. On March 28, 1979, just as Love Canal residents were testifying before a Senate subcommittee, a nuclear power plant on Three Mile Island in central Pennsylvania suffered an ominous accident. The partial meltdown of one of the reactors, the release of radioactive steam, and the brush with catastrophe at the plant put the entire country on edge.

A year later, in April 1980, midway through hearings on the Superfund bills, a hazardous waste disposal site in Elizabeth, New Jersey, exploded. (See the sidebar "Chemical Control, Inc." on page 206.) Luckily for nearby communities, including New York City, the billowing clouds of toxic smoke were blown out to sea, though the event dramatized the sense of urgency in controlling hazardous wastes. (See "'Every

Mother Is Scared to Death,' April 27, 1980," on page 232 in the Primary Sources section.)

A month later, in May 1980, Love Canal once again grabbed national headlines when an EPA study of chromosome damage to residents was leaked to the press. (See "Linking Chemicals and Illness, June 8, 1980," on page 233 in the Primary Sources section.) When two EPA officials visited the community to explain the results, residents took them hostage in front of the media and demanded that the government evacuate those families that had been left behind. While the standoff was short-lived, the residents had made their point. President Carter issued a second emergency declaration for the area and brokered a deal with New York State to pay for the evacuation and eventual purchase of the homes for the remaining 700-plus families living around Love Canal.

In the November elections of 1980, President Carter lost by a landslide to Ronald Reagan and Republicans took control of the Senate, which seemed to dim the prospects of approval for a Superfund program. (See "Pressing for Passage of Superfund, September 11, 1980," on page 235 in the Primary Sources section.) In the last weeks of a lame-duck session of Congress, however, members reached a compromise and passed the Comprehensive Environmental Response, Compensation, and Liability Act of 1980 (CERCLA)—otherwise known as the Superfund. On December 11, 1980, outgoing president Carter signed it into law.

The final Superfund legislation created a five-year, $1.6 billion fund for cleanup of inactive or abandoned hazardous waste disposal sites. The fund money was only to be used for emergency removal when a site posed an imminent hazard to public health or when the responsible party would not or could not take action. Chemical and petroleum industries were required to pay for the bulk of the fund through feedstock fees, with 85 percent of these payments coming from the chemical industry. States were required to contribute 10 percent of the cost of cleanup (50 percent if the site was owned by the state or a municipality), and they were to provide long-term maintenance of the site as well as the removed waste. (See the sidebar "Stringfellow Acid Pits: 'Love Canal of the West'" on page 216.)

Strict liability was retained, although it was modified to allow responsible parties to reduce their liability if they could show that damage was caused by a third party over which they had no control, while exercising due diligence themselves. While references to joint and several liability were removed from the wording of the final legislation, the courts nevertheless upheld this interpretation in later rulings on enforcement actions against responsible parties. The legislation also mandated the creation of the Agency for Toxic Substances and Disease Registry, which was given the job of studying the health impacts of the substances found at Superfund sites.

CERCLA was the most expensive environmental legislation the country had yet seen. Equally important, it codified two important principles of environmental policy: the idea that polluters should pay (through the feedstock tax and liability standards) and the primacy of protecting public health (the primary criteria by which to assess hazards). While ambitious, CERCLA was not responsible for the cleanup of all contaminated or hazardous waste sites across the country, but rather only the most severely contaminated. The EPA created a system for ranking hazardous waste sites, so that only the most serious were added to a national priority list (NPL). The states were responsible for sites that did not make it onto the NPL. In fact, most states created their own hazardous waste programs, often modeled after the federal Superfund law.

When CERCLA was signed into law in December 1980, the federal government and New York State had spent or committed over $60 million for evacuation, home purchases, health and environmental testing, and remedial construction at Love Canal. As early as 1979, the EPA initiated a lawsuit against Hooker in order to recover costs. In April 1980, New York State also sought to recover costs, as well as to assign an additional $250 million in punitive damages.

In 1983, Love Canal was formally added to the Superfund NPL. In 1988, the district court in New York found Hooker liable under CERCLA and ordered it to pay the federal and state governments for their costs incurred in the cleanup. While the court found that Hooker had created a "public nuisance," it dismissed the state's accusations that Hooker had acted recklessly, thus relieving the company of punitive damages. Nevertheless, in 1994, Hooker agreed to pay $98 million to settle New York's claims for cleanup costs, as well as to assume responsibility for the operation and maintenance of the leachate collection system installed at the Love Canal landfill. A year later, Hooker agreed to pay the federal government $129 million (for both cleanup of the site and evacuation of residents).

In 2003, the EPA reported that the Love Canal site was under control, and in 2004, it was removed from the Superfund's NPL. While the Love Canal landfill remains permanently fenced off and monitored, 240 formerly boarded-up homes in the once abandoned neighborhood have been renovated and sold to new owners and 10 newly constructed apartment buildings have been occupied.

Between 1980 and 2010, more than 1,600 hazardous waste sites across the country were placed on the Superfund NPL. Remediation has been completed at more than two-thirds of these sites. Since 1980, the EPA's enforcement program managed to secure more than $32.6 billion from private parties who were found responsible for cleanup costs.

Despite this substantial progress, the EPA estimates that one in four Americans still lives within three miles of a Superfund site. The Superfund program was not universally welcomed, and the arguments regarding the fairness of funding have continued. As specified in the original legislation, the Superfund tax has to be reauthorized by Congress every five years in order to continue. In 1995, Congress allowed the chemical feedstock taxes to expire. As a result, the Superfund monies were rapidly depleted, and taxpayers have paid an increasing proportion of the cleanup costs. Between 1991 and 1995, the portion of Superfund spending coming from the federal Treasury averaged 17 percent; in 2000–02, it was 50 percent. By 2003, the fund for cleanup was exhausted. Since then, the program for cleanup has relied on annual congressional appropriations of $1.2–$1.3 billion. The EPA estimates that the costs for cleanup will grow by 50–200 percent over the next decade. Thus, it appears that the argument over who should pay remains unsettled.

WHAT IF?

What if the Superfund program had not been passed by Congress in December 1980? Would the federal government have been left with the entire cost of cleanup? Would the issue of hazardous waste simply have been forgotten or ignored?

If Congress had not passed CERCLA on the eve of its adjournment in December 1980, passage in the subsequent session of Congress would have been doubtful. However, it was quite likely that some form of legislation or regulatory program would have been created to deal with the problem of abandoned hazardous waste sites and that lawmakers would have found a way to spread the costs and responsibility so that the taxpayer was not left holding the bill. President Ronald Reagan and the new majority of Senate Republicans had been elected in 1980 with the avowed goal to reduce the size, cost, and burden of the federal government. The Reagan administration was particularly hostile to the environmental regulation that had proliferated during the 1970s. Indeed, in the first two years of its term, the Reagan administration did everything in its power to undermine the Superfund program. It appointed business-friendly administrators to head the EPA and its programs, slashed funding and staffing, withheld Superfund monies for cleanup, reduced the EPA's enforcement activities, and negotiated settlements that were highly favorable to industry. While Reagan had been elected on a wave of popular support for deregulation and reduced government, the environment was not an area where the public or Congress was willing to cut back. Polls showed consistent support for environmental programs and aggressive enforcement of environmental laws, despite the cost. The problem of hazardous waste was still high on the public agenda as a result of the new environmental consciousness, media attention to ongoing crises, and the EPA's own efforts at promoting the problem since the mid-1970s.

When members of Congress launched an investigation into the Reagan EPA's lackluster enforcement, the ensuing confrontation erupted into a scandal that forced the resignation of top Reagan EPA appointees, including the EPA administrator, and resulted in the conviction of the head of the Superfund program on charges of perjury. The administration was forced to appoint new leaders to the EPA in order to salvage the reputation of both the EPA and itself. From that point on, the EPA adopted a more aggressive stance in its enforcement of Superfund. When the Superfund program was reauthorized by Congress in 1986, the fund was increased to $8.5 billion. While the Reagan administration was loathe to impose new taxes on industry, it was even more unwilling to allow the federal government to assume the heavy costs of cleanup. As a result, the greatly expanded fund was to be supported by new fees imposed on the oil industry as well as new corporate environmental taxes. Thus, even under a hostile administration opposed to federal regulation and new taxes, pressure from the public, environmental advocates, and legislators to deal with the problem of uncontrolled hazardous waste sites remained dominant.

Even if the Superfund program had not been created, it is likely that some form of federal program would have been implemented to deal with problems that resulted from hazardous waste sites. Public and congressional concern about toxic waste was high in the 1980s. There was strong support for government activity to monitor and clean up these problems, regardless of cost. However, while the federal government would likely have embarked on an expensive program to contain and clean up hazardous waste sites, it is less likely that Congress would have imposed such a sweeping tax on the chemical industry to pay for the program. While the most egregious and negligent polluters would certainly have been sued for cleanup costs, the bulk of costs would have fallen on the taxpayers. Without a stable source of dedicated funding and as Congress and the public became increasingly critical of the sheer expense of the program, it is quite likely that fewer sites would have been cleaned up.

CHRONOLOGY

1890s William T. Love partially constructs and then abandons canal in Niagara Falls.

1942–1953 Hooker Electrochemical buries 25,000 tons of industrial wastes in the abandoned Love Canal.

1953 Hooker sells Love Canal site to Niagara Board of Education for one dollar with disclaimer about buried chemicals.

1953–1970s Homes, streets, and utilities are constructed on and around the buried Love Canal site.

1955 Niagara Board of Education erects 99th Street School on Love Canal site.

1962 Rachel Carson publishes *Silent Spring,* sparking environmental consciousness about pollution and toxic chemicals.

1970 National Environmental Policy Act is signed into law.

The first Earth Day is celebrated.

Environmental Protection Agency (EPA) is created.

1976 Joint Canadian-American commission traces pesticide contamination in Great Lakes to Love Canal site.

Heavy rains cause Love Canal chemicals to surface, and residents complain about odors, chemical seepage, and health impacts.

Niagara Gazette begins reporting on history of Love Canal and associated problems.

First federal laws directly addressing handling and disposal of toxic industrial substances—the Toxic Substances

Control Act and Resource Conservation and Recovery Act—are signed into law.

1978   *March:* EPA investigates basements of homes nearest canal and reports presence of toxic chemicals.

August 2: State health commissioner declares a state of emergency at the Love Canal and orders closing of 99th Street School and evacuation of pregnant women and children under two.

August 7: New York governor Hugh Carey announces that the state will purchase homes of residents living nearest the canal. President Jimmy Carter declares Love Canal a disaster area and approves emergency financial aid.

October: Congress holds hearings on Velsicol Chemical Corporation's leaking hazardous waste disposal site in Toone, Tennessee.

1979   *March:* Congress begins to hear testimony on problem of abandoned hazardous waste sites, such as Love Canal, as well as proposed legislation to deal with the problem.

March 28: Partial meltdown of reactor at Three Mile Island nuclear power plant in central Pennsylvania occurs.

1980   *April 21:* Hazardous waste dump in Elizabeth, New Jersey, explodes.

May 17: EPA study of chromosome damage to Love Canal residents is leaked to the press and reported in the *New York Times.*

May 19: Demanding immediate action on evacuation of another 710 families, members of Love Canal Homeowners Association take two EPA officials hostage.

May 21: President Carter declares an emergency at Love Canal, permitting officials to offer temporary relocation of 700 families with federal funds administered by New York State.

September 15: U.S. House of Representatives begins debate on legislation to establish a $1.2 billion Superfund to clean up abandoned hazardous waste sites.

October 1: President Carter and Governor Carey sign $20 million state/federal relocation agreement, allowing purchase of remaining homes around Love Canal.

December 11: President Carter signs Comprehensive Environmental Response, Compensation, and Liability Act into law.

1983	Love Canal site is added to the Superfund national priority list (NPL).
1988	District court in New York finds Hooker Electrochemical liable for cleanup costs at Love Canal.
1994	Hooker settles with federal government and New York State for cleanup and relocation costs totaling more than $220 million.
1995	Congress allows Superfund chemical feedstock tax to expire.
2004	Love Canal is removed from Superfund's NPL.

DISCUSSION QUESTIONS

1. Did Hooker Electrochemical relieve itself of liability by disclosing potential risks when it sold the Love Canal property to the Niagara Falls Board of Education? Was the Board of Education irresponsible in its use of the Love Canal property?
2. Should the government have assumed the cost of permanently relocating all of the residents of Love Canal?
3. Should Congress have included liability for personal injury or illness from exposure to hazardous chemicals in the Superfund legislation?
4. Was the formula to share the cost of Superfund between taxpayers and industry fair? Why or why not?
5. Was the standard of strict, joint and several liability for hazardous waste sites fair? Why or why not?

WEB SITES

"Despite Toxic History, Residents Return to Love Canal." CNN, August 7, 1998. Available online. URL: http://www.cnn.com/US/9808/07/love.canal. Accessed March 28, 2011.

"Learning from Love Canal: A 20th Anniversary Retrospective." Available online. URL: http://arts.envirolink.org/arts_and_activism/LoisGibbs.html. Accessed March 28, 2011.

Love Canal Collections—University at Buffalo. Available online. URL: http://ublib.buffalo.edu/libraries/specialcollections/lovecanal. Accessed March 28, 2011.

Love Canal—New York State Department of Health. Available online. URL: http://www.health.state.ny.us/environmental/investigations/love_canal. Accessed March 28, 2011.

Love Canal: Press Releases and Articles. Available online. URL: http://www.epa.gov/history/topics/lovecanal/01.htm. Accessed March 28, 2011.

"Love Canal: The Truth Seeps Out." Reason.com (February 1981). Available online. URL: http://www.reason.com/news/printer/29319.html. Accessed March 28, 2011.

Superfund 365: Video clips of Lois Gibbs commenting on Love Canal and Superfund. Available online. URL: http://transition.turbulence.org/Works/superfund/video.html. Accessed March 28, 2011.

Superfund's 30th Anniversary: 30 Years of Protecting Communities and the Environment. Available online. URL: http://www.epa.gov/superfund/30years. Accessed March 28, 2011.

BIBLIOGRAPHY

Barnett, Harold C. *Toxic Debts and the Superfund Dilemma.* Chapel Hill: University of North Carolina Press, 1994.

Brown, Michael H. *Laying Waste: The Poisoning of America by Toxic Chemicals.* New York: Pantheon, 1980.

"Cleaning Up Hazardous Wastes." *CQ Researcher* 6, no. 32 (1996): 745–768.

Collin, Robert W. *The Environmental Protection Agency: Cleaning Up America's Act.* Westport, Conn.: Greenwood, 2006.

Colten, Craig E., and Peter N. Skinner. *The Road to Love Canal: Managing Industrial Waste before the EPA.* Austin: University of Texas Press, 1996.

Epstein, Samuel S., Lester O. Brown, and Carl Pope. *Hazardous Waste in America.* San Francisco: Sierra Club Books, 1982.

Landy, Marc K., Marc J. Roberts, and Stephen R. Thomas. *The Environmental Protection Agency: Asking the Wrong Questions from Nixon to Clinton.* New York: Oxford University Press, 1994.

Layzer, Judith A. "Love Canal: Hazardous Waste and the Politics of Fear." In *The Environmental Case: Translating Values into Policy*, pp. 54–80. Washington, D.C.: CQ Press, 2006.

Levine, Adeline Gordon. *Love Canal: Science, Politics, and People*. Lexington, Mass.: Lexington Books, 1983.

Magoc, Chris J. "Love Canal and the Grassroots Movement against Toxic Waste." In *Environmental Issues in American History: A Reference Guide with Primary Documents*, pp. 247–268. Westport, Conn.: Greenwood, 2006.

Mazur, Allan. *A Hazardous Inquiry: The Rashomon Effect at Love Canal*. Cambridge, Mass.: Harvard University Press, 1998.

PRIMARY SOURCES

Document 1: "Evacuation of Kids Urged," August 2, 1978

In late summer 1978, New York State health commissioner Robert Whalen held a press conference in Albany, New York, during which he declared a public health emergency in the area immediately surrounding the buried Love Canal dump in Niagara Falls, New York. The story, originally reported by the local Niagara Gazette, *soon caught national attention.*

ALBANY—State Health Commissioner Robert Whalen today declared the Love Canal situation in Niagara Falls an official emergency and urged that young children and pregnant women move away from the area immediately.

In a 12-page order issued to federal, state, county and city officials, Whalen recommended that two pregnant women known to be living in the area temporarily relocate.

He also urged 20 families with children under two years of age to have the youngsters move out of the homes along 97th and 99th streets as well as Colvin Boulevard as soon as possible.

No evacuation order was served, but a spokesman for Whalen said his advice is "very strong."

No state funds were immediately made available to assist the families, but that possibility was left open for future study.

The health commissioner also asked that the Niagara Falls Board of Education temporarily delay the opening of 99th Street School "to minimize exposure of school-age children to waste chemicals while corrective construction activity takes place."

Dr. Whalen described the situation as "a public nuisance and an extremely serious threat to health, safety and welfare."

"A review of all the available evidence respecting the Love Canal landfill site has convinced me of the existence of a great and imminent peril to the health of the general public residing at or near the said site as a result of exposure to toxic substances eminating from such site," Dr. Whalen said.

At the special meeting in Albany, it was revealed that the risk of spontaneous abortion in the area is nearly double normal. Most of such occurrences have been in the southern section of the canal during summer months. The state order also directs the Niagara County Board of Health to take remedial actions designed to alleviate the hazards. . . .

The state will oversee further studies aiming at the following:

- Delineation of chronic diseases inflicting all residents who have lived adjacent to the old Hooker Chemical Corp. landfill, with particular emphasis on the frequency of spontaneous abortions, congenital defects and other illnesses including cancer.
- A study of the full limits of the Love Canal with respect to the location of toxic chemicals.
- Continued air, water and ground sampling in the area.
- Identification of groundwater that may have been contaminated by chemical leachate.
- Determination of whether customized ventilation systems, carbon filters and special sumps should be employed in the area.

It has already been determined that residents near the canal have suffered an abnormal number of birth defects and miscarriages. A number of residents also have what appear to be liver problems.

Hooker had three technical advisers at Whalen's meeting acting as observers, a spokesman for the firm said.

He said "we're waiting to hear from them" and indicated there would be no official reaction until they reported back.

Residents from the Love Canal area were also present at the meeting.

Source: Mike Brown. "Evacuation of Kids Urged." *Niagara Gazette,* August 2, 1978.

—m—

Document 2: "The Other Side of Love Canal," July 3, 1980

Not everyone believed that the chemicals at Love Canal were responsible for illnesses experienced by residents or even that there was any real threat. On July 31, 1980, the president and chief operating officer of Hooker Chemical Corporation, David L. Baeder, gave a presentation before representatives of the financial community at the Waldorf Astoria Hotel in New York City. Baeder defended the company's actions and questioned the veracity of health claims at Love Canal.

Love Canal was an appropriate waste disposal site. Hooker's use of the canal site as a landfill from 1942 to 1952 was not an irresponsible operation, as some have suggested. Even with all the advantages of hindsight, a task force of the American Institute of Chemical Engineers recently concluded that the design of the canal site back in the 1940's and early 1950's would essentially conform to most provisions of pending federal regulations. . . .

There have been suggestions that Hooker "foisted" the site upon an unsuspecting local school board, that adequate warnings were not given that the property had been used as a chemical landfill and that care needed to be exercised to avoid disturbance of the protective cover we had placed upon the property. The deed to the school board, the minutes of the school board meeting, correspondence between Hooker and the school board and articles from the local Niagara Falls newspaper clearly reflect that adequate warnings were given by the company regarding the condition of the property and the proper precautions to be taken in its use. . . .

What went wrong? The problem of chemicals migrating from the Love Canal . . . was in large part attributable to the failure of others to properly maintain the site during the twenty-seven years since Hooker relinquished control of it. In direct disregard of Hooker's public warnings, three streets together with storm drains and sewer lines were built across the property by the city of Niagara Falls and the state of New York. The school board's records reflect that thousands of cubic yards of materials were authorized by the board staff to be removed for use as fill at other locations. Eventually these intrusions permitted surface waters to seep into the site and, in 1978, after there had been record precipitation, the canal, like a bathtub, overflowed permitting chemicals to migrate onto the properties adjoining the canal. . . .

With respect to exposure levels to chemicals among Love Canal residents, media coverage has created strong perceptions, many of which are wrong.

Based upon analysis of data we've recently obtained under the Freedom of Information Act from the Environmental Protection Agency, exposure to chemicals in Love Canal homes was very low. These exposure levels should not have been used as a basis for relocation. . . .

As a result of inadequate and often misleading information, Love Canal area residents have been led to believe that chemicals were present in their homes and in their neighborhood in dangerously high concentrations and that health problems in their neighborhood were rampant. They have responded predictably with ever-increasing demands for permanent relocation. I have sincere sympathy for the residents. The government has frightened these people.

Source: "The Other Side of Love Canal: Facts vs. Fallacies." Donald L. Baeder, president and chief operating officer of Hooker Chemical Corporation. Proceedings of presentation to financial community representatives in New York City, July 31, 1980.

—ɷ—

Document 3: Love Canal Testimony, March 28, 1979

In March 1979, Congress held hearings to investigate the Love Canal problem. Below is an excerpt of testimony to a Senate committee by resident Anne Hillis describing her experience with Love Canal and the death of her son, which she blamed on chemical contamination.

My name is Anne Hillis. I am a Wife, a Mother, I live in Niagara Falls, New York. I also live close to a "Dump." A dump called Love Canal. I don't want to live there anymore. I hate Love Canal, I hate my life at Love Canal. It's a strange life that I lead now, it is filled with disruptions, frustrations, sleepless nights and a grip of fear that only those in similar situations can understand.

My family and I live in a historically wet area, east of Love Canal.

From State, air testing my home, like most homes, shows chemical contamination.

Homes along the Canal edge are empty—a green fence surrounds them now. The fence is far too late, because the contaminated water has been running in our homes (cellars) and yards for years.

We've lived in the home for 13 ½ years. We lost a child there. My 10-year-old son went to 99th Street School, as did other children in the neighborhood, some of those children are gone now after the August 1978 emergency was declared by Dr. Whalen . . . and President Carter.

But the remaining children are still in the same houses, the same bad air, and the same horrible environment.

Despair, hopelessness, we ask—What are we doing to our children and to our own bodies, staying? The stress alone is enough to break anyone.

I think many of us are at this point. Our homes are valueless, we can't sell, who would buy a home like this?

Some have thoughts of trying to rent, but how can we rent a contaminated house. A house we ourselves fear to live in—not I cannot. . . .

Knowing the chemicals were there—Hooker knew—Why did they not stress this to the School Board?

They are a big Company, they produce their chemicals—surely they had some idea of what the chemicals could do.

The people of Love Canal know now what they have done—they have produced children with extra fingers, extra toes, double rows of teeth, cleft palate, enlarged hearts, vision and hearing impairment and retardation. . . .

I believe most Americans assume that the Government would be there when they need help, but the people of the Love Canal area are now very disillusioned. Is this belief wrong? For the people of Love Canal feel a hopelessness. Are we not Americans?

Our City, our State has done nothing to help the people in the areas outside the 99th and 97th streets, if our Federal Government does not help us, we are all doomed at Love Canal.

May God help us and our Country, for we need help, desperately.
Anne Hillis

Source: Testimony of Anne Hillis to Joint Senate Subcommittee on Environmental Pollution and Hazardous Waste, March 28, 1979.

—⁓—

Document 4: "Every Mother Is Scared to Death," April 27, 1980

One of the key concerns of residents who lived next to Love Canal was government assistance with evacuation. In this letter sent to New York governor Hugh Carey, residents urged the governor to take responsibility for an adequate and timely response to a problem that threatened health.

The Love Canal is a man-made disaster that won't stop. The Love Canal can no longer be covered up and pushed aside, covered with half-truths and clay caps. The health effects are real. Miscarriages, birth defects that last a lifetime and illness are only the beginning.

In October 1979 Senator Daly and Assemblyman Murphy presented and passed a bill to allow New York State to purchase at fair market value the homes of Love Canal residents desiring to leave the neighborhood. It has been six months and not one home has been purchased. The appraisals have begun. Residents are ready to leave. Dozens of families have signed sales contracts for the purchase of new homes. But we sit and wait while the political football games of pass the buck continues. It has become a game of pricetags versus the lives of the Love Canal victims. . . . If you think that the passing of the Murphy-Daly bill has relieved you of any further responsibility to the Love Canal residents, you are wrong. The need to declare a health emergency is greater than ever.

On Tuesday, April 15, Lois Gibbs' four-year-old daughter, Missy, was admitted as an emergency patient to Buffalo Childrens Hospital. She was covered with bruises from head to foot. Her blood was not clotting and she was a very sick child. Tests for leukemia began immediately. . . . What chemicals was Missy exposed to at the Love Canal that could now be threatening her very life? . . . Every mother in the Love Canal is scared to death, wondering who will be the next one with leukemia symptoms. Will it be her child, her neighbors' child or even herself? Every family watches and wonders what the spring thaw is washing to the surface, scared of what their children might be walking in, playing in, or falling in. Is it dioxin? Or something worse? . . . Your responsibility to the Love Canal residents is greater than ever. I urge you PLEASE immediately reevaluate New York State's role in the Love Canal. . . . It is imperative that New York State take charge. It is obvious that the local governments have failed miserably. It is not too late to declare an immediate health hazard. It is not too late to move everyone out now before any more lives are lost.

You, personally, know there is a very real health hazard in the Love Canal. Dr. Axelrod has said that no level of dioxin is safe. You can stop this political football game. The lives and health of 500 families are too important to play politics. Use your influence to get us out of here now! We cannot live another day in this hell! Failure to act now will leave skeletons in your closet. The skeletons of the Love Canal victims. A needless waste!

Mr. & Mrs. Joseph Dunmire
Niagara Falls

Source: "Every Mother Is Scared to Death," by Mr. and Mrs. Joseph Dunmire. A letter to Governor Hugh Carey reprinted in the *Niagara Gazette,* April 27, 1980.

—∞—

Document 5: Linking Chemicals and Illness, June 8, 1980

A central concern of Love Canal residents and many officials was that chemical exposure led to a variety of illnesses. However, conclusive proof was inherently difficult if not impossible to find. Some argued that these inconclusive findings showed that concern over Love Canal was overblown, but officials remained sympathetic to residents' concerns. The following article from the Niagara Gazette *encapsulates the fears and uncertainties surrounding the Love Canal site.*

ALBANY—Despite spending million of dollars and conducting thousands of tests on Love Canal residents, New York State Health Department officials say they may never be able to prove the medical problems of residents are caused by the poisonous chemicals stored there.

Gov. Hugh Carey and his top health officials say the 23,000 tons of toxic waste buried in the canal pose a greater threat to the mental health of residents than they do to the physical. Carey last week appointed a blue-ribbon panel to review the massive test data.

But several studies have indicated a link between the chemicals and a variety of health problems, although state health officials say these links are only suggestive. Among them:

- State studies involving thousands of blood samples the last two years showed evidence of an unusual number of blood and liver disorders among Love Canal residents.
- An independent study commissioned by the U.S. Environmental Protection Agency and conducted by Houston scientist Dr. Dante Picciano suggested that nearly a third of 36 residents tested suffered chromosomal aberrations.
- A study by Dr. Stephen Barron, a University of Buffalo neurologist, suggested nerve damage in 75 percent of a group of 33 persons tested.
- A study by Beverly Paigen, a cancer research scientist at Roswell Park Memorial Institute, indicated a variety of medical problems, including a high rate of miscarriages, deformities, birth defects, stillborn children, kidney disease, suicides and cancer.

Some have labeled the Picciano, Barron and Paigen studies inconclusive and preliminary. Dr. David Axelrod, commissioner of the State Health Department, says that none of the tests provide scientific proof that Love Canal chemicals have caused human illness. "We may never be able to draw an absolute conclusion with regard to a cause-effect relationship," he said.

"If we do find a high correlation between adverse health effects and chemicals found, or if we don't, it won't necessarily confirm or deny a cause-effect."

Despite that, Axelrod and Dr. Nicholas Vianna, the health department's director of environmental epidemiology (study of disease patterns), say they wouldn't risk living in the area. Vianna said that, while as a scientist he can't conclude that the canal neighborhood is hazardous to human health, as a citizen he would avoid any area where chemical contaminants were thought to be buried.

"I'd be yelling and screaming as loud as anybody to get out," he said. "Would you believe me if I told you otherwise? I don't think the way people in Love Canal have responded is an indication of anything but them being human. . . . "The biggest thing we worry about is what we don't know. These people have a lot of questions, and the situation is such that we in the scientific arena don't have the answers."

Source: Jack Jones. "Link between Canal Chemicals, Illnesses May Never Be Proven." *Niagara Gazette,* June 8, 1980.

—⚹—

Document 6: Pressing for Passage of Superfund, September 11, 1980

In September 1980, Environmental Protection Agency (EPA) administrator David M. Costle testified before the Senate Finance Committee to urge passage of the Comprehensive Environmental Response, Compensation, and Liability Act, commonly known as the Superfund. As the following EPA press release explains, Costle argued that numerous crises across the country showed that hazardous waste was a national problem. Congress passed the legislation on December 11, 1980.

"The situation concerning hazardous waste disposal sites is grim," said Costle. "The past few years have brought to public attention an unforgettable series of incidents resulting from improper hazardous waste management—the continuing tragedy of Love Canal, the pollution of the water supply of over 300,000 people in Iowa, and the discovery of up to 20,000 to 30,000 discarded and leaking barrels of chemical wastes in the "Valley of the Drums" in Kentucky. In 1979, EPA estimated the number of hazardous waste sites to range between 32,000 and 50,000, and the number of sites posing a significant health or environmental problem to be between 1,200 and 2,000.

"A recent and incomplete EPA survey of 250 hazardous waste disposal sites found 32 sites where 452 drinking water wells had to be closed because of chemical contamination, 130 sites where water supplies and groundwaters had been contaminated but wells have not been closed, 27 sites with actual damages to human health (kidneys, cancer, mutations, aborted pregnancies, etc.), 41 sites where soil contamination made the land unfit for livestock or human uses, and at least 36 sites where income loss could be expected as a result of loss of livestock, fish kills, crop damage and similar losses," said Costle.

"Of some 1,000 sites investigated to date, we have found more than 250 that need remedial action. We still have more than 6,000 candidate sites to investigate, and we are becoming aware of about 200 more every month. In July alone, we learned of 671 more. This legacy of many years of uncontrolled hazardous waste disposal may well be the most serious environmental problem facing the nation today.

"Existing legal authorities are inadequate to deal with these problems in many ways."

Superfund would be funded by a small non-inflationary fee on various segments of the petrochemical industry. "This feedstock approach would impose fees or taxes at the beginning of the commercial chain of production, distribution, consumption, transportation, and disposal of hazardous substances," said Costle. "It would do this by assessing 11 primary petrochemicals, 34 inorganic raw materials, and crude oil produced domestically, imported, or exported. These 46 substances are either hazardous themselves or they are the basic building blocks used to generate all major inorganic and synthetic organic hazardous products and wastes.

"The feedstock system distributes costs broadly, evenly, and efficiently among all those who produce and consume hazardous substances and generate hazardous wastes. It can be implemented quickly and with much less red tape than other options. It would involve fewer than 700 companies and just 46 substances, instead of hundreds of thousands of firms and hundreds of substances as in other options.

"We felt and feel strongly that funding for the program should come as broadly as possible from those segments of industry which are the most responsible for imposing risks on society and have the greatest knowledge of and control over these risks and received the greatest direct economic benefits."

Source: "Costle Presses for Immediate Passage of Superfund," EPA press release, September 11, 1980.

7

Bhopal:
Who or What Was Responsible for the Bhopal Disaster?

—ᴍ—

THE CONTROVERSY

The Issue

In December 1984, the world's worst industrial disaster struck the city of Bhopal, India. In the middle of the night, a pesticide plant accidentally released deadly methyl isocyanate (MIC) gas into the crowded city, killing thousands and condemning tens of thousands to debilitating injury and illness for years to come. The disaster shocked the world and raised questions about government and corporate responsibility for industrial accidents that devastate human life and the environment. In the United States, the Bhopal tragedy prompted new policy for public oversight in the handling of hazardous materials to prevent a similar tragedy from happening at home. The government of India eventually settled out of court with Union Carbide Corporation (UCC), the parent company of the pesticide plant, absolving the company of further liability. However, many victims of the disaster and their advocates condemned the settlement arrangement, arguing that UCC and its officials should be held criminally liable. UCC argued that it was neither at fault nor responsible. Who or what was responsible for the Bhopal disaster?

♦ **Arguments that UCC was responsible:** Critics of UCC argued that the disaster was due to poor planning, gross negligence, and a dangerously defective plant design. Critics argued that the company had imperiled residents of Bhopal by improperly handling and storing large quantities of hazardous materials and failing to develop a system for proper communication and emergency preparedness in the event of an accident. They argued that UCC was legally and morally responsible for the accident and should be fined heavily and its officers held criminally responsible.

♦ **Arguments that UCC was not responsible:** UCC argued first and foremost that the Indian pesticide plant was a separate corporate entity and that the government of India was also responsible for its oversight and safe operation. The company argued that the accident was due to an unforeseeable coincidence of events or possibly even sabotage. UCC argued that it had fulfilled its legal and moral obligations by doing everything it could to help and that the issue was settled by the Indian courts and government settlement.

—*m*—

INTRODUCTION

Just after midnight on December 3, 1984, thousands of tons of poisonous gas spewed into the night air from a pesticide plant in Bhopal, India. Workers inside the plant scrambled to try to contain the gas leak, but their efforts were ineffective. All the major safety systems had been disabled earlier as part of cost-cutting measures and plans to dismantle and sell the plant; they could not control the chemical reaction that had caused the gas leak. Many fled the plant, heading upwind as they had been warned in order to avoid the toxic fumes. Outside the plant, however, there was no warning. A thick, yellowish-white cloud descended on the neighboring residential slums that had developed around the plant and then spread out into other parts of the old city. Residents woke up breathless and confused by the sharp odor of fumes that choked them and stung their eyes and made them cough and vomit. Many died in their homes, but thousands fled, unsure of the source of the threat or where to run. Sunrise revealed thousands of dead and dying people and animals littered throughout the city and its streets and even extending into the surrounding countryside and forests. Local hospitals were overwhelmed by thousands suffering from a confusing variety of debilitating symptoms, and there was little that could be done. Though it would take years to do a final accounting, it is believed that more than 500,000 people were exposed to the toxic gases, which led to the deaths of 7,000 to 10,000 people in just the first three days; the effects would persist for decades. It was the world's worst industrial disaster.

In the immediate aftermath of the disaster, Indian authorities and the public demanded accountability and compensation from those responsible. The pesticide plant belonged to Union Carbide India Limited (UCIL), an Indian subsidiary of the multinational company UCC, based in Danbury, Connecticut, and one of the largest chemical companies in the world. Investigations by Indian authorities and UCC engineers traced the catastrophic leak to the introduction of water into a tank containing MIC, a toxic substance used in the manufacture of a popular pesticide. The introduction of water into the tank was variously attributed to faulty plant design, mistakes by workers, or possibly even sabotage. Indian authorities and many groups representing the victims placed blame and responsibility on UCC. They argued that UCIL and its Bhopal plant were ultimately under the control and responsibility of UCC, which had maintained majority ownership in the Indian subsidiary and exercised decision-making influence. Thus, the faulty plant design, mismanagement of the plant, and even the decision to store dangerous quantities of toxic chemicals in the midst of a dense city were ultimately the responsibility of the parent corporation. UCC disputed these claims, arguing that UCIL was a separate corporate entity with responsibility for its own day-to-day decision making, which was outside UCC's control. Moreover, UCC argued that the Indian government was just as responsible, since it was intimately involved in licensing and oversight of the pesticide plant and safety of the surrounding community. Finally, UCC pointed to controversial evidence of worker sabotage, which no amount of planning could prevent.

The legal dispute over responsibility began early in 1985 with hundreds of lawsuits filed against UCC in both U.S. and Indian courts. Victims' representatives and the Indian government hoped to have their case heard in American courts, where compensation and penalties would be higher. However, a federal district court judge in New York ultimately ruled that the case should be handled by the Indian courts. Thus, in late 1986, the case against UCC began in Indian courts where the government of India claimed sole power to represent the victims. In early 1989, the Indian supreme court announced that the parties had reached agreement on an out-of-court settlement in which UCC would pay the Indian government $470 million, and all further liabilities or claims against the company would be dropped. While UCC and the Indian government claimed victory, victims' groups and others were outraged by the low amount and the fact that UCC had been absolved of all legal responsibility. Moreover, the ordeal for victims of the gas leak was far from over. The extent of injuries and their persistence would only grow with time. Compensation from the legal settlement would not even begin to arrive until years after the disaster and would take more than two decades to complete. Although UCC considered the issue closed with the 1989 settlement, victims' groups and the Indian

The UCC chemical plant in Bhopal, Madhya Pradesh, India, sits idle after the uncontrolled release of deadly chemicals that killed thousands in 1984. (Pablo Bartholomew/Liaison/Getty Images)

government have continued to revisit the question: Who or what was responsible for the Bhopal disaster?

BACKGROUND

Bhopal is the capital city of the Indian state of Madhya Pradesh, located in the geographic center of India. Bhopal is an old city, established nearly 1,000 years ago by Raja Bhoj. Bhopal is also known as the City of Lakes because of its many natural and artificial lakes. On the western edge of the city is Upper Lake, the largest artificial lake in Asia, which was constructed in the 11th century. Plans for the modern layout of the city were established by Dost Mohammad Khan, an Afghan nobleman who took control of Bhopal and the surrounding region in the early 1700s. During British rule of India from the 18th to early 20th centuries, the Bhopal principality became a protectorate of Britain and a gathering point for Muslims, which distinguished it from the rest of the largely

Hindu nation. Indeed, the Islamic influence on the city is apparent in its many mosques, palaces, and other public architecture. After India gained independence from Britain in 1947, Bhopal was established as the capital city of the new state of Madhya Pradesh.

Following independence, the government of India embarked on an ambitious program to rapidly industrialize a largely rural and cash-poor nation. Bhopal was an early site of importance because of its centralized location and existing rail infrastructure. In 1959, Bhopal began its transformation into an industrial center with the establishment of Bharat Heavy Electrical Limited just outside the city. The new facility employed 50,000 people in the manufacture of electrical equipment. Other industries were soon attracted to the area by favorable tax incentives, as well as by its centralized location, established infrastructure, and abundant supply of labor. As more industries located in and around Bhopal, its population swelled with impoverished rural immigrants seeking employment. However, many of these rural immigrants were hard pressed to find sufficient employment and often found themselves relegated to slums and squatter settlements. By some estimates, nearly 20 percent of the city's population lived in these patchwork squatter settlements, many of which developed immediately adjacent to the many factories.

India's drive for industrialization and modernization was accompanied by a program to improve domestic agriculture, which would not only address recurring famines but also reduce the country's dependence on the importation of food grains and improve agricultural exports. Traditional agriculture in India, as in most parts of the world, depended on labor-intensive practices, seasonal precipitation patterns, and organic fertilizers. While these methods were well known and time tested, crop yields were relatively low and even erratic by modern standards. Beginning in the early 1960s, India embraced the Green Revolution, a campaign to improve agriculture with modern technology and the use of scientifically developed, high-yielding hybrids of rice, wheat, and other crops. These new high-yield varieties promised dramatic improvements in productivity, but they required heavy inputs of synthetic fertilizers, irrigation, and chemical pesticides. In 1969, scientists at the All India Rice Improvement Project demonstrated that yields of some hybrid rice varieties could be increased by nearly 200 percent with the use of insecticides. Indian officials announced plans to dramatically increase the use of pesticides. With the expectation of a dramatic expansion in the pesticides market, UCIL decided to take advantage of this potentially lucrative opportunity.

As previously stated, UCIL was a subsidiary of UCC, a multinational company incorporated in New York and headquartered in Danbury, Connecticut. UCC boasted locations in 40 countries around the globe—one of the largest multinational corporations in the world. It had maintained a corporate presence in India since 1905. UCC's Indian subsidiary, UCIL, had begun as a battery-manufacturing company but had expanded into plastics and chemicals. Until the mid-1950s, UCC had maintained 100 percent ownership in its Indian subsidiary. However, the newly independent country was eager to reduce foreign influence by encouraging domestic industry and severely restricting foreign ownership. As a condition of continuing to do business in India, UCC was forced to reduce its share of ownership in the Indian subsidiary, although it was allowed to retain a controlling majority ownership in UCIL because of the sophisticated nature of the technology involved.

In 1966, UCIL applied for permission from the government of India to establish a pesticide plant in the country in order to produce SEVIN, a brand-name carbaryl pesticide that was rapidly rising in popularity as a substitute for DDT. The latter was becoming much less effective due to growing insect resistance. UCIL's proposal was well received by the Indian government, which was eager to reduce dependence on imports. The application was quickly approved, and UCIL obtained a lease to site the plant in an industrial zoned area on the northern edge of Bhopal, less than two miles from the city's busy train station and commercial center. UCIL's Bhopal pesticide plant began production of the carbaryl pesticide in 1969 with permission to produce up to 5,000 tons annually. While the Bhopal plant formulated the pesticide, it still needed to import the raw ingredients, such as MIC and alpha-naphthol, from the UCC plant in Institute, West Virginia. In 1970, the general manager of UCIL's Agricultural Products Division applied for a license to manufacture up to 2,000 pounds of MIC at the Bhopal plant annually, thereby avoiding the need to import this raw material. After the application was approved, the Bhopal plant expanded to accommodate construction of the new MIC production facility, which was completed in 1979. The Bhopal plant began to manufacture MIC on February 5, 1980—the only plant outside of the United States using UCC technology to do so. By 1980, the 80-acre plant had a regular workforce of 1,000 people, although many others from surrounding shantytowns worked informally to provide a variety of services.

Problems and Accidents

While the Indian government and UCC had high hopes for UCIL's pesticide endeavor, the Bhopal plant encountered growing financial, technical, and safety problems early on. UCIL was able to successfully manufacture MIC, but it failed to develop the capability to manufacture alpha-naphthol, the second major ingredient in the formulation of carbaryl pesticides. After spending four years and nearly $3 million on an alpha-naphthol manufacturing facility, UCIL was forced to abandon this effort in 1982 and continue importing this expensive raw component. At the same time, the market for its carbaryl pesticide never materialized. New, cheaper pesticide products, as well as a proliferation of smaller companies, severely undercut demand for MIC-based pesticides. In addition, a series of droughts in India from the late 1970s and into the early 1980s had left many Indian farmers indebted and unable to purchase expensive pesticide products. Without sufficient demand for its products, the Bhopal plant never exceeded a third of its capacity. As a result of these financial problems, UCIL's Bhopal plant was compelled to cut costs and reduce its workforce through layoffs and transfers. The weakened financial state of the company and its efforts to reduce costs led to low morale among the remaining workers, high employee turnover that led to the loss of many experienced engineers, and a general weakening of the quality and safety of its operations.

After 1981, UCIL's Bhopal pesticide plant was under severe financial stress, and this stress was compounded by a series of accidents. In the early hours of the morning on December 24, 1981, two workers were performing maintenance operations on the piping system. Because of the potential presence of toxic gases in the pipes, they wore gloves, hard hats, and air-masks connected to an air supply source. One of the workers, Ashraf Khan, was unexpectedly splashed with cold liquid phosgene from one of the pipes. In his surprise and panic, Khan removed his mask and inhaled toxic phosgene gas. He was rushed to the plant infirmary and then to the nearby Hamidia hospital, where he died after 72 hours. Khan's death rattled his fellow workers and alarmed the surrounding community. Most residents in the surrounding communities were unaware that the plant dealt with such poisonous substances. At least one journalist, as well as other concerned citizens, wrote to complain about the danger of working with such toxic materials in close vicinity to densely populated parts of Bhopal (See "'Bhopal Sitting at the Edge of a Volcano,' 1982," on page 263 in the Primary Sources section.) Even before publicity around Khan's death had died down, the Bhopal plant was struck by a second high-profile accident. On February 10, 1982, a leak of phosgene gas sent 25 workers to the hospital. A state factory inspector and plant managers determined that the leak was caused by the use of the wrong type of seal on a pipe. A subsequent minor accident two months later involving electricians was attributed to worker carelessness. The issue of safety at the Bhopal plant came to the attention of Madhya Pradesh's state legislators, but the state labor minister assured them that he had personally inspected the plant and found it to be safe. Workers' unions at the Bhopal plant complained about mismanagement at the plant and inadequate training or safety measures, and a few attempted to launch public protests. However, these efforts failed to gain wider support from the community or from many workers who feared for their jobs.

In May 1982, UCC sent a team of engineers from its Institute, West Virginia, plant to perform a safety audit of the Bhopal plant. This was the third such audit since the MIC unit at the Bhopal plant had come online in 1980. UCC engineers inspected the plant, reviewed logs, and interviewed workers and management. In their report, issued a month later, the UCC engineers reported numerous problems with the plant, many of which could result in fire or dangerous exposure to toxic chemicals. However, the report concluded that none of these problems constituted imminent danger. Five months later, on October 6, 1982, a leak of a mixture of chloroform, MIC, and hydrochloric acid resulted in chemical burns to three employees. Fifteen other employees were exposed and reported severe irritation of their eyes, although they returned to work shortly after. In April 1983, UCIL submitted a report to UCC claiming that it had addressed most of the deficiencies identified in the May 1982 safety audit. By June 1984, UCC and UCIL's board of directors had decided that the Bhopal plant was simply unprofitable and a drain on the larger company. Plans were made to either sell the plant or dismantle it and ship it to another country. In preparation for closure, the Bhopal plant produced its last batch of MIC in late October 1984. The remaining MIC was stored in two 15,000-gallon tanks to be used in one-ton increments, reacted with alpha-naphthol to produce carbaryl, and then formulated into the SEVIN pesticide. However, all of these plans became moot in early December 1984.

The Disaster

At around 11 P.M. on December 2, 1984, night-shift workers at the Bhopal plant noticed the stinging odor of MIC, which they traced to a leak of yellowish-white gas from an upper area of the MIC unit. They informed their supervisor, and the supervisor responded that they would address the issue after their tea break. In the meantime, workers continued to inspect the area until teatime at 12:15 A.M. By 12:45 A.M., the MIC fumes had become unbearable, and the workers had become very concerned. The MIC control room operator noticed that the temperature and pressure gauges for one of the MIC tanks had risen far beyond safe limits. When he went to visually inspect the MIC tank, he heard a loud rumbling sound and observed that a six-inch-wide crack had developed along the length of the concrete shell that encased the 40-foot MIC tank. The MIC was undergoing an uncontrolled reaction, rising to dangerous temperatures and generating enormous pressure. Workers attempted to contain the problem, but crucial safety systems were offline. MIC was supposed to be maintained at low temperature, but the MIC refrigeration unit had been offline for weeks and the coolant removed for use in another part of the plant. The plant contained systems to neutralize escaping gas, but these too were inoperable. As gas began to shoot skyward from the MIC unit, the plant's fire brigade attempted to smother it with water but found that the water pressure was inadequate to reach the vent stack. Alarms within the factory were sounded at 12:50 A.M. to alert plant workers, many of whom fled in panic.

The toxic cloud drifted out over surrounding communities, and nearby residents were the first to wake to choking fumes and stinging eyes. Disoriented, unable to breathe or see, people stumbled out of their homes and into the dark streets. Though there was no official alarm or news, residents nevertheless realized the threat, and panic ensued as thousands attempted to flee from the toxic fumes. Many died in their sleep or collapsed along the roads. Local police were notified of a gas leak at the plant some time after 1 A.M., though they were unable to contact personnel at the plant to find out what was going on. Sometime after 2 A.M., the plant's public siren finally began to wail. Police officials initially advised residents to stay indoors, but later the decision was made to evacuate the city. The commander at a nearby military base mobilized all available vehicles in order to aid with the evacuation and suffered injury himself from gas exposure during the evacuation. At Bhopal's normally busy train station, the stationmaster and another employee endured the choking fumes in order to divert trains from coming into the station. He and others at the train station later died from exposure to the toxic fumes.

Daylight revealed thousands of dead and severely injured people and animals strewn throughout the city and surrounding countryside. Local hospitals were inundated with injured and dying patients suffering from a bewildering array of symptoms: intense irritation of eyes and temporary blindness, severe respiratory distress and even asphyxiation, nausea and vomiting, spasms and loss of muscle control, coma, and death. Without information on the cause, medical personnel were at a complete loss over how to treat the poisoning or what to expect in the future for those exposed or injured. More than 500,000 people were exposed to the poisonous gases. In the first three days following the gas leak, 7,000 to 10,000 people died, though initial government estimates placed the death toll at less than 2,000. In the rush to cope with the calamity, little effort was made to record the full extent of death and injury. Many died in surrounding forests or in the communities to which they had fled. Corpses were indiscriminately buried in mass graves, dumped in the Narmada River far from the city, or burned in funeral pyres in order to avert a worsening of the public health crisis.

As news of the disaster spread around the world, all eyes turned to UCC for answers. U.S. journalists were particularly interested in the possibility of a similar disaster at UCC's MIC plant in Institute, West Virginia. (See the sidebar "Could It Happen Here?" on page 256.) In a press conference organized immediately after the gas leak, UCC officials assured the media that the cause of the leak would be thoroughly investigated, but that definitive answers would take some weeks. Three days after the disaster, UCC's chief executive officer (CEO), Warren Anderson, led a team of engineers to Bhopal in order to investigate the disaster and to meet with Indian officials. However, upon arriving in Bhopal, the UCC team was turned away from the plant, and Anderson and his crew placed under house arrest for criminal negligence. After six hours and a bail of $2,000, Anderson was quickly ushered out of the country. The question of culpability was high on the minds of Indian officials and the public. Senior managers of UCIL's Bhopal plant had already been arrested on charges of criminal negligence. Indian and American lawyers began to interview thousands of victims in order to prepare for lawsuits against UCC, both in India and the United States. The government of India and UCC officials launched investigations into the cause of the disaster. In the United States, Congress initiated hearings during which UCC officials testified about Bhopal and the safety of its sister plant in Institute, West Virginia. While the Bhopal disaster was centered in India, the disaster prompted U.S. officials to look more closely at how such a disaster could be averted. Indeed, the Bhopal disaster and fear of a similar catastrophe prompted U.S. lawmakers to pass landmark legislation forcing chemical companies to disclose information about the chemicals they handled, as well as to work with surrounding communities to create plans in the event of a disaster. (See the sidebar "Emergency Planning and Community Right to Know" on page 248.)

Numerous lawsuits were filed in both Indian and American courts. By the end of January 1985, more than 45 lawsuits had been filed against UCC in U.S. state and federal courts. Approximately 1,200 suits were filed in Indian courts, including 482 personal injury suits against UCIL in Bhopal, a $1 billion representative suit against UCC and UCIL, and a suit in India's supreme court against UCIL and the governments of India and Madhya Pradesh. In an effort to bring some order to the many lawsuits, a judicial panel for the U.S. federal courts consolidated all federal suits against UCC in the U.S. District Court of the Southern District of New York under Judge John F. Keenan. In March 1985, the government of India passed a law that gave the Indian government the sole power to represent victims in court and to manage all aspects of registering and processing claims. The following month, the government of India filed suit in U.S. federal court charging Union Carbide with liability for the deaths of 1,700 individuals, injury to more than 200,000 people, and property damages. The lawsuit sought punitive damages "in an amount sufficient to deter Union Carbide and any other

(continues on page 250)

EMERGENCY PLANNING AND COMMUNITY RIGHT TO KNOW

Shortly after the Bhopal catastrophe in 1984, Union Carbide Corporation (UCC) officials testified before Congress that such an accident could not happen on American soil because of superior safety standards. However, a growing body of evidence showed that serious accidents involving hazardous chemicals were not uncommon. In fall 1985, the Environmental Protection Agency (EPA) released a study showing that more than 6,900 accidents involving spills or releases of toxic chemicals had occurred in the United States over the previous five years, including 135 deaths and 1,500 injuries. Most of these accidents happened in or near industrial plants.

Growing awareness influenced public opinion. A survey of 3,100 communities in 1985 by the Federal Emergency Management Agency (FEMA) reported that 93 percent of respondents identified hazardous materials as a significant threat to their communities. Industries sought to reassure the public and the government that they were making every effort to ensure safety, but a series of high-profile accidents, as well as increased media attention and government scrutiny, called into question the credibility of voluntary action by industry. In response, Congress made emergency planning for a chemical disaster mandatory. In October 1986, Congress passed the Emergency Planning and Community Right-to-Know Act (EPCRA) as Title III of the Superfund Amendments and Reauthorization Act (SARA).

The purpose of EPCRA was "to provide the public with important information on hazardous chemicals in their communities, and to establish emergency planning and notification requirements that would protect the public in the event of a release of hazardous chemicals." EPCRA consists of two core programs: 1) Emergency Planning and Notification, which requires each state to provide for emergency planning in the event of chemical releases from industrial facilities; and 2) Reporting Requirements, which provides for public access to mandatory reports filed by industries handling, disposing, or releasing significant quantities of hazardous chemicals.

Under the first component—Emergency Planning and Notification—the governor of each state must appoint a State Emergency Planning Commission (SEPC), which in turn supervises and coordinates Local Emergency

Planning Commissions (LEPCs). The LEPCs, made up of local residents, municipal officials, and public health and safety representatives, must design and implement local emergency plans in the event of a chemical accident. Facilities must notify the SEPC, the LEPC, and the local fire department if they possess a chemical substance listed as an extremely hazardous substance (EHS) in an amount exceeding a specific threshold. If a facility releases an EHS above the threshold, it must immediately notify the SEPC and LEPC.

The second component of EPCRA—Reporting Requirements—is commonly known as the "community right-to-know" provision and is arguably the law's most significant aspect. Under this provision, facilities handling or releasing significant quantities of listed chemicals must file reports listing and describing chemicals used at their industrial plants. These chemical reports are to be made accessible to the public. Moreover, the law mandated an innovative program for disseminating such information—the Toxic Release Inventory (TRI). Industrial facilities meeting specific size and chemical thresholds are required to submit annual reports relaying information on hazardous chemical releases into all environmental media—air, water, or land. EPCRA mandated that TRI reports be made available to the public via a national toxic chemical database that must be accessible by computer telecommunication (i.e., the Internet)—the first law to do so.

EPCRA did not require a reduction in toxic chemicals, nor did it require a material change in the way these substances are handled. However, the mandate to make information about chemical usage publicly available had a profound impact on industry behavior, and it provided public advocates and the government with powerful new tools to aid planning, regulation, and sometimes, enforcement and litigation. Prior to EPCRA, members of the public and government officials could make only rough estimates about the amount of chemicals released into the environment, and these estimates were easily disputed. When the TRI reports became available after 1988, both government and industry were astounded by the sheer amount of chemicals being released into the environment. Public pressure to reduce the volume of toxic chemicals has since resulted in steady reductions in the amount of chemicals released into the environment.

(continued from page 247)

multinational corporation from the willful, malicious and wanton disregard of the rights and safety of the citizens of those countries in which they do business." UCC initially offered to pay $200 million as an out-of-court settlement, but the government of India rejected the offer. By some estimates, compensation and penalties would more likely be in the realm of $3 billion.

In July 1985, UCC filed a motion to have the case dismissed from U.S. courts, arguing that the case should be under the jurisdiction of Indian courts. Lawyers for the Indian government, as well as civil society groups speaking on behalf of victims, opposed this move, arguing that the complexity of the case was beyond the capacity of the Indian court system and that compensation to victims would be far less than could be recovered in American courts. Nevertheless, in May 1986, Judge Keenan ruled that the case was properly under the jurisdiction of Indian courts. (See *"Re Union Carbide Corporation Gas Plant Disaster at Bhopal, India, in December 1984,"* on page 264 in the Primary Sources section.) In September 1986, the government of India filed suit against UCC in the district court for Bhopal.

THE DEBATE

As the lawsuits wound their way through American and then Indian courts, investigations by UCC engineers and by Indian researchers concluded independently that the gas leak had been caused by the introduction of water into the MIC tank. As water came into contact with MIC, it initiated a runaway chemical reaction that caused the temperature and pressure in the tank to rise beyond safe limits. In addition, inoperative or inadequate safety systems prevented containment of the release. When UCC publicly released its findings in March 1985, it refrained from explaining how the water had entered the MIC tank, stating only that the water was introduced "inadvertently or deliberately." Use of the word "deliberately" raised suspicions of sabotage. However, journalist interviews of plant personnel and later investigations by the Indian authorities concluded that the water had been introduced accidentally as plant workers were attempting to flush out pipes with water in order

Demonstrators in Bhopal, India, on February 1, 1989, protest that the settlement for $470 million with Union Carbide to compensate victims of the 1984 chemical accident was too low. Many continue to call for criminal prosecution of former Union Carbide officials. (Robert Nickelsberg/Time Life Pictures/Getty Images)

to clear clogs. Although the flushing of pipes was a routine procedure, these reports concluded that leaky pipes and failure to observe proper safeguards had caused the water contamination. The exact mechanisms by which water had been introduced into the tank became the subject of intense scrutiny and debate, although it was only part of the larger question: Who was responsible for the disaster?

The Case that UCC Was Responsible

Critics of UCC charged that it was liable for the death, injury, and destruction caused by the gas leak at the Bhopal plant. Specifically, they charged that the accident "occurred as the result of unreasonable and highly dangerous and defective plant conditions." Critics argued that UCC had encouraged and permitted the storage of dangerous quantities of MIC in a densely populated area, had failed to provide even basic information with regard to protection against or appropriate medical treatment in the event of MIC exposure, had failed to install or maintain adequate safety systems, had neglected to properly design or maintain emergency relief systems, and had failed to disclose known safety concerns, including the possibility of such a runaway reaction. (See "An Account by Worker V. D. Patil, 2004," and "An Account by Worker M. L. Verma, 2004," on pages 266 and 267 in the Primary Sources section.)

Fundamentally, the Indian government maintained that UCC, as the parent company of UCIL, bore full and final responsibility for the disaster created by its subsidiary. It argued that because multinational corporations act as one entity accomplishing a global purpose, the parent corporation must be responsible for preventing disaster—and eventually be liable in the event of a disaster. Moreover, they pointed out that UCC maintained a controlling ownership (50.9 percent) in UCIL and was actively engaged in the design and management of UCIL and its Bhopal pesticide facility. Plaintiffs argued that the parent company designed the Bhopal plant, wrote the performance specifications, trained technical personnel at its facilities in the United States, and "warranted that the design was based upon the best manufacturing information available and that the drawings and design instructions were sufficiently detailed and complete so as to enable competent technical personnel to detail, design, erect, commission and operate the Bhopal plant."

Humanitarian and aid groups, as well as environmental organizations, both within and without India, also argued that UCC was responsible for the disaster. They pointed to the dramatic difference in the quality and standards of safety between the Bhopal plant and the one in Institute, West Virginia. While the latter was equipped with the latest computer-monitoring systems, the Bhopal plant had been equipped only with antiquated analog monitoring devices, which required more manual intervention. Critics were also angered by UCC's response in the immediate wake of the disaster, its failure to provide details about the chemical composition of the gases to which people were likely exposed, as well as its initial attempts to downplay the danger of exposure to MIC gas. Finally, critics found UCC's initial offers of compensation to be grossly inadequate and a cynical attempt to evade responsibility.

The Case that UCC Was Not Responsible

UCC officials denied responsibility or legal liability for the disaster. They argued that the Bhopal plant was under the control and management of UCIL, an Indian company incorporated in India and managed by Indians. UCC's relationship with UCIL, they argued, operated at "arms length" and was largely financial and advisory. UCC argued that it provided technology and training services to UCIL on a contract basis, but that UCIL bore the ultimate responsibility in making decisions about the organization and operation of the plant. Shortcomings and failures in proper operation and safety at the plant were due to mismanagement by UCIL's Indian managers, improper training of staff, incompetence or unprofessional behavior of workers, and lack of proper oversight by the Indian government.

In December 1986, UCC responded to the Indian government's civil suit with a countersuit against the government of India and the state of Madhya Pradesh. UCC charged that the state of Madhya Pradesh had allowed illegal squatter settlements on public land next to the Bhopal plant, which exacerbated the crisis. They argued that had people not been allowed to live so close to the plant, the casualties from the release would have been much lower. UCC also argued that the central government of India was intimately involved in the design and construction of the plant, from decisions about where the plant could be sited to decisions about the size and scope of the plant's MIC production. Finally, UCC increasingly advanced its theory that the introduction of water into the MIC tank was a deliberate act by a disgruntled worker and was thus an unforeseeable act of sabotage. Details of the last argument were formally unveiled in May 1988 by Arthur D. Little (ADL), a private consulting firm, which UCC had hired to investigate the disaster. (See "'Investigation of Large-Magnitude Incidents,' 1998," on page 268 in the Primary Sources section.)

ADL's report disputed the accounts given by plant workers, citing inconsistencies between their stories and the physical evidence later analyzed from the plant. The ADL report concluded that an individual had deliberately introduced water into the MIC tank to spoil its contents, though this person may not have anticipated the magnitude of the disastrous consequences. In any case, the report alleged, fellow workers later lied about subsequent events in order to distance themselves from any wrongdoing. ADL's sabotage theory contradicted reports by Indian scientists, India's Central Bureau of Investigation (CBI), as well as reports by various investigating journalists.

OUTCOME AND IMPACT

Between fall 1986 and early spring 1989, UCC and the government of India wrangled over the issues of responsibility and liability in Indian courts. Representatives from each side met repeatedly in an effort to secure an out-of-court settlement that would bring relief more quickly to the victims. Indeed, judges in the United States and India, as well as UCC and the government of India, repeatedly argued for a quick settlement, or at least interim relief, for the many thousands of Bhopal victims, many of whom were not only ill but destitute. In response to Judge Keenan's plea, UCC offered $5 million in interim relief, although the Indian government rejected the offer because UCC's requirements for detailed documentation were too onerous under the circumstances. In December 1987, the district judge of Bhopal ordered UCC to pay approximately $270 million in interim relief while the court case was still being argued, although the payment did not indicate a judgment or liability. UCC appealed the order to the high court of Madhya Pradesh, arguing that the judge had no such authority and that the issue would simply complicate and extend the case. The high court upheld the district court's order but reduced the amount to approximately $192 million and argued that this amount actually represented a ruling against the company. However, in September 1988, the supreme court of India took over jurisdiction of the case against UCC. On February 14, 1989, the supreme court of India announced that UCC and the government of India had reached an out-of-court settlement. UCC would pay the government of India $470 million ($45 million of which would come from UCIL) in "full settlement of all claims, rights and liabilities related to and arising out of the Bhopal Gas disaster." UCC described the court's decision as "fair and reasonable," but many victims and their representatives were outraged by the low figure and the fact that the court's ruling absolved the company of any further liability or criminal prosecution.

(See "'Bhopal: What We Learned,' 1990," on page 269 in the Primary Sources section.) Throughout India, as well as other countries, activist groups launched demonstrations to protest the settlement, criticizing UCC and the government of India.

Following national elections in November 1989, a new Indian government announced that it would review the fairness of the settlement and consider petitions filed by victims' groups. In October 1991, India's supreme court upheld the settlement, although it allowed for reconsideration of criminal wrongdoing. India's CBI also reopened criminal investigations and began discussions about an extradition request for UCC CEO Warren Anderson on the basis of criminal negligence. In December 1991, the chief judicial magistrate in Bhopal issued a proclamation ordering Anderson and Union Carbide Eastern (the division of UCC with oversight of UCIL and other subsidiaries in Asia) to appear in court in February 1992 to face charges of culpable homicide not amounting to murder in connection with the gas leak. Neither Anderson nor any other representative of UCC appeared before Indian courts. Anderson was declared an absconder from justice in India, but neither the Indian nor the U.S. government made a serious effort at extradition. In order to raise cash for its settlement, UCC sold UCIL to McLeod Russell Ltd. in 1994. UCIL was subsequently renamed Eveready Industries India Limited. In February 2001, UCC was purchased by Dow Chemical Company, the largest chemical multinational corporation in the world. Dow has since denied any remaining liability or responsibility over the Bhopal disaster.

Compensation and aid to the Bhopal victims was slow in coming. Medical care was hampered by still incomplete understanding about the chemicals involved, as well as grossly inadequate resources to provide health care assistance or rehabilitation to the many thousands affected. Subsequent studies of the disaster revealed serious ongoing health complications for those exposed, including evidence of genetic damage to children born to women who were exposed.

Following the out-of-court settlement in 1989, the Indian government struggled to put together a relief and compensation system to determine eligibility and an appropriate level of individual compensation. Compensation awards to the first few individuals were announced in October 1992, nearly eight years after the disaster. Victims' groups

(continues on page 258)

COULD IT HAPPEN HERE?

In the wake of the Bhopal disaster, many communities looked closer to home and asked, "Could it happen here?" Union Carbide Company (UCC) representatives were quick to assure the American public and government officials that such an accident could not happen in the United States because of superior safety systems and training. Nevertheless, one community was especially concerned: Institute, West Virginia, where UCC operated the only pesticide plant in the nation to manufacture and store methyl isocyanate (MIC)—and it was 10 times larger than the plant in Bhopal. Located ten miles west of Charleston, West Virginia, the small community of Institute consisted of 300 permanent residents, along with 4,000 students at West Virginia State College, which is adjacent to the pesticide plant. The UCC plant was the largest employer in the Kanawha Valley, although it was only one of over a dozen chemical companies in the area.

Immediately after the Bhopal accident, UCC suspended further production of MIC at the Institute plant until the cause of the Indian accident was identified. UCC officials repeated assurances that the American plant was completely safe, but a report by the Environmental Protection Agency (EPA) in January 1985 revealed that the company had repeatedly failed to report leaks of MIC. UCC later admitted that it had experienced 61 leaks of MIC at the Institute plant over the previous five years, although none had caused injury. Representative Henry Waxman of California, a particularly vociferous critic of the company, subsequently released a confidential UCC memo that said that an inspection of the Institute plant revealed that a runaway reaction could occur in an MIC storage tank and that the response would not be enough to prevent catastrophic failure of the tank and that a real potential for a serious accident existed. UCC officials responded that as a result of the memo the company had made modifications to avert such a possibility.

Between December 1984 and April 1985, the UCC Institute plant spent more than $5 million in new safety equipment, invited local leaders inside the plant, commissioned a safety test by an independent consulting company, and hired a local public relations firm to convince the community that the plant posed no threat. In April 1985, the EPA announced that it was satisfied with the safety of the Institute plant and would allow production of MIC to resume. In a *Washington Post* article in 1985, Thad Epps, a UCC spokesperson, was quoted as saying to reporter Michael Isikoff, "There's no question that we're being extra careful. We know the whole world is watching." Some residents were still concerned, especially when it came to what many considered an inadequate emergency notification system. A few weeks before production resumed, the plant tested a new siren to alert the community in case of an emergency, but it was barely audible. In the same *Washington Post* article, Isikoff quotes an Institute resident, "They told everybody it was going to be earth-shattering, but it failed miserably. It sounded like a ruptured duck." UCC subsequently donated a new $10,000 siren to the local volunteer fire department.

On the morning of August 11, 1985, a large cloud of toxic gas escaped from the Institute plant and no alarm sounded. Shortly after 9 A.M., a large yellow cloud of gas erupted from the plant, darkening skies and, according to some residents, smelling "like a dead skunk." Authorities were first alerted to the leak by residents complaining of a foul smell and choking fumes. Emergency broadcasts interrupted local TV and radio and advised 20,000 residents within a 10-mile radius of the plant to stay indoors with windows shut. The thick gas cloud even interrupted traffic on nearby Interstate 64. Approximately 135 people in the area were sent to local hospitals, most suffering from breathing difficulty, eye irritation, nausea, dizziness, and headaches. Six plant workers were the most seriously affected. UCC engineers later revealed that they were aware of the leak when it happened but did not alert the community because their computer systems indicated that the cloud would stay confined to the plant premises. Later investigation revealed that the plant computer system was not programmed for the specific chemicals that leaked out. In April 1986, the Occupational Safety and Health Administration (OSHA) fined UCC nearly $1.4 million for 221 violations at the Institute plant—the largest such fine in OSHA history. However, subsequent negotiations between UCC and OSHA reduced the final settlement to $408,000.

(continued from page 255)
complained that the compensation system placed unreasonable demands on victims to prove their eligibility in a complex bureaucratic maze, especially since many were very poor and often illiterate. Many complained that the compensation awards were too low and were not being awarded fairly. A 1995 assessment revealed that maximum average compensation was approximately $545 for personal injury and approximately $1,605 for death, though many received far less. By 2004, over $334 million had been disbursed to 570,000 victims (an average of less than $600 per person), though another $327 million still remained to be disbursed as a result of interest accrued on the original deposit, devaluation of the Indian currency, and the slowness with which compensation claims were granted. In July 2004, the supreme court of India ordered that the remaining money be disbursed. Victims' groups continue to organize for better compensation and assistance by the Indian government, as well as criminal prosecution of UCC and its officers. Since December 1985, the tragedy of Bhopal has been observed annually with demonstrations, calls for action, and the burning of effigies of UCC's Warren Anderson and Indian officials.

WHAT IF?

What if the lawsuits against UCC had been heard in U.S. courts, rather than being sent to India?

If the lawsuits against UCC had been retained under the jurisdiction of U.S. courts, it is likely that they would have taken at least a decade to resolve, if not longer. However, legal cases in the United States would have involved many more plaintiffs than just the government of India. Before the case was sent to India, U.S. federal courts recognized the lawsuits filed on behalf of Bhopal victims by numerous private lawyers and other organizations, despite the Indian government's claim to be the sole legitimate representative of Bhopal victims. In fact, many victims' groups were unhappy with the Indian government's claim at sole representation. They argued that the Indian government had usurped the right of victims to represent themselves and that their claim represented a conflict of interest since many felt that the Indian government was itself negligent and culpable.

The involvement of so many parties in U.S.–based lawsuits would have vastly complicated negotiations, and it is unlikely that the parties would have been able to come to a resolution or out-of-court settlement, especially since victims' groups held very different ideas than the Indian government about what would constitute fair compensation. What is less clear is whether U.S. courts would have found UCC liable for the disaster. Once again, however, even this deceptively simple question would have been complicated by separate civil and criminal suits. It is likely that UCC would have settled separately with some individuals or groups and been found liable in civil suits, since the standard of proof in tort cases is much lower than in criminal cases. The company would have been forced to pay out millions in damages to a variety of different parties, including the Indian government.

Disbursement of that compensation to the victims, however, would not necessarily have proceeded any more quickly or smoothly than it did in reality. American courts would be powerless to control the disbursement of compensation to victims in another country. It is less likely that UCC and especially CEO Warren Anderson would have been found criminally culpable for the disaster, since the standards of proof for criminal negligence are so much higher.

CHRONOLOGY

1966   Union Carbide India Limited (UCIL) proposes the establishment of a facility to produce pesticide in Bhopal, Madhya Pradesh, India.

1970   The UCIL Bhopal pesticide plant is opened.

1976   UCIL is granted a license to manufacture methyl isocyanate (MIC) at Bhopal.

1977   *September:* Bhopal pesticide plant begins manufacturing the pesticide SEVIN using imported MIC.

1980   *February:* Bhopal pesticide plant begins to manufacture MIC on site, in addition to other chemicals such as Aldicarb, phosgene, and monomethylamine.

   December: A maintenance worker at the Bhopal pesticide plant dies after accidentally inhaling phosgene gas.

1982   *January:* 25 workers at Bhopal plant are hospitalized as a result of a phosgene gas leak.

   May: An operational survey of the Bhopal plant site conducted by Union Carbide Corporation (UCC) personnel from the

United States finds numerous safety problems and maintenance issues.

October 5: Leak at Bhopal plant results in hospitalization of hundreds of nearby residents.

1984 *September:* An operational safety/health survey of the MIC II Unit at UCC's Institute, West Virginia, plant warns of the possibility of an uncontrollable chemical reaction.

December 3: Shortly after midnight, MIC gas leaks from a tank at the UCIL plant in Bhopal. Thousands are killed or severely injured.

1985 *March:* A UCC technical team and the government of India independently conclude that the gas leak was caused by the accidental introduction of water into the MIC tank.

March 29: The government of India passes the Bhopal Gas Leak Disaster Act.

August 11: The UCC pesticide plant in Institute, West Virginia, experiences a gas leak leading to 135 hospitalizations.

1986 *May 12:* U.S. district court judge John Keenan dismisses the Bhopal litigation from U.S. courts.

September 5: The government of India files suit against UCC in Bhopal district court.

October 16: President Ronald Reagan signs into law the Emergency Planning and Community Right-to-Know Act of 1986.

1988 *May:* Arthur D. Little, Inc., publishes a report that asserts that the gas leak was caused by sabotage.

1989 *February:* The supreme court of India directs a final settlement of all Bhopal litigation in the amount of $470 million.

1991 *October 3:* The supreme court of India upholds the civil settlement of $470 million and dismisses all outstanding petitions seeking review of the settlement but directs that the criminal proceedings be revived.

December: The chief judicial magistrate in Bhopal issues a proclamation ordering UCC CEO Warren Anderson and Union Carbide East to appear in court in February 1992 to face charges of culpable homicide.

1992 *February 1:* The chief judicial magistrate of Bhopal declares Anderson and Union Carbide as proclaimed offenders.

1994   *September:* UCC's shares in UCIL are sold to McLeod Russell Ltd. UCIL is renamed Eveready Industries India Limited.

1998   *September:* Madhya Pradesh government takes control of land around Bhopal and posts notices in nearby residential areas warning against drinking the water from wells.

2001   *February 5:* The Federal Trade Commission approves the merger of Union Carbide with the Dow Chemical Company.

2002   *January:* Shrishti and Toxics Link, a Delhi-based environmental organization, issues a report finding contamination in vegetables grown around the Bhopal factory site, as well as a bioconcentration of contaminants in breast milk samples taken from women in the surrounding areas.

2003   Madhya Pradesh Gas Relief and Rehabilitation Department reports that 15,248 have died from the Bhopal gas leak, and 554,985 compensation claims for varying degrees of injuries or disability have been medically assessed or approved. Activists and survivors' organizations estimate that over 20,000 people have died since 1985 as a result of the Bhopal disaster.

2004   *May:* The supreme court of India orders the Madhya Pradesh government to supply fresh drinking water through tankers to people whose potable water supplies were contaminated by pollutants from the Bhopal plant.
      July: The supreme court of India orders the government of India to release all additional settlement funds to the Bhopal victims.

2005   *January 6:* The chief judicial magistrate orders that the Dow Chemical Company be made a party in the criminal case since UCC is a fully owned subsidiary of that company.

2006   *September:* The Bhopal Welfare Commission reports that all cases of initial compensation claims by victims have been cleared and no more are pending.

DISCUSSION QUESTIONS

1. Who was responsible for the Bhopal disaster? Why?
2. Should the lawsuit against UCC have been heard in India or the United States? Why?

3. Why did the government of India and other critics assign blame to UCC, rather than to Union Carbide India Limited?
4. Who did Union Carbide blame for the disaster?
5. Was the out-of-court settlement between UCC and the government of India fair? Why or why not?
6. How could the Bhopal disaster have been avoided?

WEB SITES

Amnesty International. Bhopal—End 25 Years of Injustice. Available online. URL: http://www.amnesty.org. Accessed March 28, 2011.

Bhopal Information Center. Union Carbide Company. Available online. URL: http://www.bhopal.com/. Accessed March 28, 2011.

The Bhopal Medical Appeal. Funding Free Clinics for Bhopal. Available online. URL: http://www.bhopal.org/. Accessed March 28, 2011.

The Bhopal Memory Project. Human Rights Project at Bard College. Available online. URL: http://bhopal.bard.edu/. Accessed March 28, 2011.

International Campaign for Justice in Bhopal. Available online. URL: http://bhopal.net/2010dharna/blog/. Accessed March 28, 2011.

BIBLIOGRAPHY

Chouhan, T. R. *Bhopal: The Inside Story.* New York: Apex Press, 2004.

D'Silva, Themistocles. *The Black Box of Bhopal: A Closer Look at the World's Deadliest Industrial Disaster.* Victoria, B.C.: Trafford Publishing, 2006.

Fortun, Kim. *Advocacy after Bhopal.* Chicago: University of Chicago Press, 2001.

Hanna, Bridget, Ward Morehouse, and Satinath Sarangi, eds. *The Bhopal Reader.* New York: Apex Press, 2005.

Morehouse, Ward, and M. Arun Subramaniam. *The Bhopal Tragedy: What Really Happened and What It Means for American Workers and Communities at Risk.* New York: Council on International and Public Affairs, 1986.

Shrivastava, Paul. *Bhopal: Anatomy of a Crisis.* Cambridge, Mass.: Ballinger Publishing Company, 1987.

PRIMARY SOURCES

Document 1: "Bhopal Sitting at the Edge of a Volcano," 1982

Rajkumar Keswani, a local Bhopal journalist, was one person who wrote a series of articles in the Rapat Weekly, *a Hindi newspaper, warning Bhopal of potential disaster.*

Bhopal a pile of dead humans in one to one and a half hour.

Wake-up, people of Bhopal, sitting at the edge of a volcano! No savior will save you from this foreign death! Those who used to talk about our rights have pawned their voice and those who could relieve us from this misery are themselves in chains in golden cages that were made for parrots.

Union Carbide's Phosgene storage tank laughs at the fate of Bhopal and Bhopal is lost in Nero's flute.

Union Carbide established the demon MIC plant in 1980 after obtaining its license in 1977 and it has played with many lives since then. Some time back 24 people were hanging between life and death due to Phosgene leak and after suffering for several months are back fighting death to earn their bread.

In 1967–68 when Union Carbide was established, the site of the factory was outside the municipal limits. The area later was brought within the municipal limits and in 1975 the then Administrator of the Municipal Corporation Mr. Mahesh Neelkanth Buch served a notice on Carbide asking them to relocate their factory outside the municipal limits. . . . [H]e was transferred and the matter was buried and then at the same time as per a deal, the General Manager of Carbide, at the time Mr. C. S. Ram, donated a sum of Rs. 25,000 to build the Vardhaman Park.

Thus the notice was sent to the freezer.

This matter dates back to 1977 when the erection of the MIC plant began and to 1980 when the plant started operations. Prior to this, this chemical used to come from the corporation's plant in the USA.

Accidents began in the plant from the time it started. Many accidents were covered up. On December 26, 1981 Mohammad Ashraf was killed due to leakage of Phosgene gas while he was working in the Carbon Products Division of Union Carbide from USA that led to acute sickness of 24 persons who had to be hospitalized and for many months the workers suffered. Right after they got out of the hospital the workers went back to their fight with death.

In our last issue we had informed about the threat posed by this factory to the entire city and the hazards for the workers. Phosgene gas that was used by Hitler in his gas chambers, and this is used for the production of methyl isocyanate, is stored in a tank in this factory and if that leaks or explodes it will take one to one and half hour for the death of the entire population of the city. . . . While this threat on human lives continues to loom over us our leaders, officials, our government and other people choose to be silent. But the silence has its reason. Union Carbide pays for this silence.

According to reliable sources Union Carbide has made a room of their Guest House in Shyamla Hills available to the Chief Minister [i.e. Governor of the state of Madhya Pradesh] on a permanent basis where he carries out his personal affairs. Usually he arrives there between 11 o'clock and 1 o'clock but he goes there at different hours too. Under such circumstances, what has Carbide to fear? . . .

This is an awful conspiracy against humanity. People who are busy with their own affairs are unmindful. Those who know, remain silent. Death is creeping in. For now Bhopal sleeps, till the next morning and possibly to never get up some morning.

Source: Rajkumar Keswani. "Bhopal Sitting at the Edge of a Volcano." *Rapat Weekly*, October 1, 1982. Issue 2, Year 5. Excerpted from *The Bhopal Reader.* 2005. Bridget Hanna, Ward Morehouse, and Satinath Sarangi, eds. New York: Apex Press.

—∞—

Document 2: *Re Union Carbide Corporation Gas Plant Disaster at Bhopal, India, in December 1984*

On May 12, 1986, U.S. district court judge John F. Keenan dismissed the case against Union Carbide from U.S. federal courts on the basis of forum non conveniens, *a legal doctrine that declares that significant decisions leading to the case were made elsewhere, making it inconvenient to secure witnesses and evidence in the proposed forum (i.e., the United States).*

CONCLUSION

It is difficult to imagine how a greater tragedy could occur to a peacetime population than the deadly gas leak in Bhopal on the night of December 2–3, 1984. . . . This Court is firmly convinced that the Indian legal system is in a far better position than the American courts to determine the cause of the tragic event and thereby fix liability. Further, the Indian courts have greater access to all the information needed to arrive at the amount of the compensation to be awarded the victims. . . .

The Bhopal plant was regulated by Indian agencies. The Union of India has a very strong interest in the aftermath of the accident which affected its citizens on its own soil. . . . The Indian interests far outweigh the interests of citizens of the United States in the litigation.

Plaintiffs, including the Union of India, have argued that the courts of India are not up to the task of conducting the Bhopal litigation. They assert that the Indian judiciary has yet to reach full maturity due to the restraints placed upon it by British colonial rulers who shaped the Indian legal system to meet their own ends. Plaintiffs allege that the Indian justice system has not yet cast off the burden of colonialism to meet the emerging needs of a democratic people. The Court thus finds itself faced with a paradox. In the Court's view, to retain the litigation in this forum, as plaintiffs request, would be yet another example of imperialism, another situation in which an established sovereign inflicted its rules, its standards and values on a developing nation. This Court declines to play such a role. The Union of India is a world power in 1986, and its courts have the proven capacity to mete out fair and equal justice. To deprive the Indian judiciary of this opportunity to stand tall before the world and to pass judgment on behalf of its own people would be to revive a history of subservience and subjugation from which India has emerged. India and its people can and must vindicate their claims before the independent and legitimate judiciary created there since the Independence of 1947. . . .

Therefore, the consolidated case is dismissed on the grounds of *forum non conveniens* under the following conditions:

Union Carbide shall consent to submit to the jurisdiction of the courts of India, and shall continue to waive defenses based upon the statute of limitations;

Union Carbide shall agree to satisfy any judgment rendered by an Indian court, and if applicable, upheld by an appellate court in that country, where such judgment and affirmance comport with the minimal requirements of due process;

Union Carbide shall be subject to discovery under the model of the United States Federal Rules of Civil Procedure after appropriate demand by plaintiffs.

SO ORDERED.

Source: Re Union Carbide Corporation Gas Plant Disaster at Bhopal, India, in December 1984. MDL No. 626; Misc. No. 21–38 (JFK) ALL CASES. United States District Court for the Southern District of New York. 634 F. Supp. 842 (May 12, 1986.)

—ɷ—

Document 3: An Account by Worker V. D. Patil, 2004

In this excerpted testimony on the Bhopal disaster, V. D. Patil, a former worker at Union Carbide India Limited (UCIL), described deteriorating working conditions and the loss of experienced personnel. He and others argued that mismanagement of the plant led directly to the disaster.

I joined UCIL on 6 November 1978 as part of the first group for the MIC unit. I had eight months of classroom training, one month on the job in the Sevin plant and then began work in pre-commissioning the plant. Out of 32 who joined with me, ten had resigned before the start up of the plant at end of 1979. In 1981, another ten of my colleagues resigned. In 1982, another ten resigned. Only two persons, myself and R. K. Yadav, remained. My colleagues joined UCIL believing in the name of Union Carbide but when they saw the working conditions, the facilities provided, the promotion policy and the behavior of the management, they realized that they were not up to good standards. We also saw that senior operators from other units were no better off and were being treated like labor-class workers. As my fellow workers are all science graduates and diploma holders, they started planning to leave UCIL soon after joining. As they got other opportunities, they joined other offices or factories. I did not get another opportunity until February 1984, when I was offered a job in Bombay Dyeing as a foreman. . . .

After I joined UCIL, other batches of trainees came and also quickly left. As a result, by 1982 the plant was mostly run by the trainees since many senior operators had resigned. In 1981, they stopped giving training for the MIC unit and transferred operators from other units who did not have training in the MIC process. Up to 1982, the supervisory staff was well trained and did not change too often. After 1982, however, supervisory staff was also transferred in from other units without any additional training. The quality of the operating personnel became worse and worse, and the condition of the plant was also deteriorating. . . . No one in the plant had sufficient training and experience, leading to increasingly unsafe conditions. The disaster should have been no surprise to anyone.

Source: V. D. Patil. Excerpted from "Other Workers Speak Out: Testimonies from Union Carbide Bhopal Plant Personnel." T. R. Chouhan et al. 2004. *Bhopal: The Inside Story.* New York: Apex Press.

—⚊—

Document 4: An Account by Worker M. L. Verma, 2004

When Union Carbide Corporation began to advance its sabotage theory, it did not provide the name of the suspected saboteur, but the description pointed to M. L. Verma, a worker at the Union Carbide India Limited plant. Verma and fellow workers disputed the accusation, though Verma was never publicly named or formally charged.

Around 11:30 P.M., we felt MIC [methyl isocyanate] irritation so we came out from the [tea] room to locate the source of the leak. We saw that some water was dropping from the MIC plant structure. Near that water, the MIC was in greater concentration. . . . We reported the MIC leak to production assistant S. Qurashi. The plant superintendent was also sitting there in the control room. They replied that the MIC plant is down and thus there is no chance of leak. They did not take our report seriously. . . .

Around 12:50 A.M., the leak became vigorous and started coming out from the vent gas scrubber atmospheric line. I was standing in front of the control room when the siren started. After a few minutes, the plant superintendent came back to the MIC unit. As he met me, he asked, 'What happened?' I told him MIC was pouring from the top of the vent gas scrubber.

Because of the siren, the emergency squad came to the MIC unit. They tried to control the leak by massive water spraying. I also helped them until the conditions in the area became unbearable. Then along with other workers, I left the MIC unit in the opposite wind direction. The MIC production assistant also fled. When the plant superintendent came back from smoking, he ordered that the loud siren be stopped. This was around 1:00 A.M. Around 2:00 A.M. when we learned that the toxic release was affecting the communities outside the plant, we argued with the plant superintendent to restart the loud siren. He refused saying it would serve no purpose, but we insisted until he switched it on again. Around 2:15 A.M., the gas leak stopped so we returned to the MIC unit. . . .

Around 3:00 A.M., I saw many people from outside coming for medical help. Many were in dying condition. . . . When I came to know that the area in which my family was living was also affected, I rushed home. This was around 5:00 A.M. Outside the plant, I saw how badly the gas had affected people.

Source: M. L. Verma. Excerpted from "Other Workers Speak Out: Testimonies from Union Carbide Bhopal Plant Personnel." T. R. Chouhan et al. 2004. *Bhopal: The Inside Story.* New York: Apex Press.

—⋙—

Document 5: "Investigation of Large-Magnitude Incidents," 1988

In May 1988, a member of the Bhopal investigation team from Arthur D. Little (ADL), a private consulting firm hired by Union Carbide Corporation (UCC), released their assessment of the Bhopal disaster at an international conference. ADL proposed that the disaster had been caused by deliberate sabotage.

The results of this investigation show, with virtual certainty, that the Bhopal incident was caused by the entry of water to the tank through a hose that had been connected directly to the tank. It is equally clear that those most directly involved attempted to obfuscate these events. . . .

We believe that . . . a disgruntled operator entered the storage area and hooked up one of the readily available rubber water hoses to Tank 610, with the intention of contaminating and spoiling the tank's contents. It was well known among the plant's operators that water and

MIC should not be mixed. He unscrewed the local pressure indicator, which can be easily accomplished by hand, and connected the hose to the tank. The entire operation could be completed within five minutes. Minor incidents of process sabotage by employees had occurred previously at the Bhopal plant, and, indeed, occur from time to time in industrial plants all over the world. . . .

Shortly after midnight, several MIC operators saw the pressure rise on the gauges in the control room and realized that there was a problem with Tank 610. They ran to the tank and discovered the water hose connection to the tank. . . . They decided upon transferring about one ton of the tank's contents to the SEVIN unit as the best method of getting the water out. The major release then occurred. . . .

Not knowing if the attempted transfer had exacerbated the incident, or whether they could have otherwise prevented it, or whether they would be blamed for not having notified plant management earlier, those involved decided upon a cover-up. They altered logs that morning and thereafter to disguise their involvement. As is not uncommon in many such incidents, the reflexive tendency to cover up simply took over. . . .

Because the investigation [by UCC] was blocked, a popular explanation arose in the media as to the cause of the tragedy. A thorough investigation . . . was ultimately conducted over a year later. That investigation has established that the incident was not caused in the manner popularly reported, but rather was the result of a direct water connection to the tank.

Source: Ashok S. Kalelkar. "Investigation of Large-Magnitude Incidents: Bhopal as a Case Study." Presented at the Institution of Chemical Engineers Conference on Preventing Major Chemical Accidents in London, England. Cambridge, Mass.: Arthur D. Little, Inc., 1988.

—⚭—

Document 6: "Bhopal: What We Learned," 1990

Six years after the Bhopal disaster, former Union Carbide Corporation (UCC) chief executive officer Warren Anderson circulated a statement praising the out-of-court settlement agreement between UCC and the government of India. He argued that a speedy settlement was paramount to the interests of humanitarianism.

For decades, at Carbide, safety has been a paramount concern and even a single critical injury or death has always been considered a major calamity which immediately receives urgent attention at the highest levels of the company. You can imagine our horror, then, when we began to receive initial reports from India that hundreds of people had died in a gas release from UCIL's Bhopal plant. When the full magnitude of what had happened became known that day, the entire company was shaken to its core. . . .

We saw Bhopal for what it was—a terrible tragedy involving real people who had either lost family members or had suffered injuries, in some cases serious injuries. They needed medical relief, prompt aid in any form possible, and an early settlement which would help restore their lives and bring long-term relief. They didn't need what they ultimately got—armies of lawyers and politicians who spent years claiming to represent them and deciding what was in their best interests. We saw Bhopal in moral—not legal—terms. Although we had good legal defenses—the plant wasn't ours and it later was established that the tragedy had been caused by employee sabotage—we didn't want to spend years arguing those issues in court while the victims waited.

We therefore said immediately that Union Carbide Corporation would take moral responsibility for the disaster. . . . We then set about trying to do two things, bring immediate relief to the victims, and effect a prompt and fair settlement of the matter. . . .

Oddly enough, the problem was not money. We believe that the government negotiators realized early on that the amount on the table was very generous and more than adequate to fully compensate all of the victims. Notwithstanding, they still wouldn't settle. The problem was political, both at the government level and on an individual level. Multinationals such as Carbide are widely disliked in India, as is the case in much of the Third World. . . . There was therefore a large body of opinion in India that was opposed to any settlement with us, irrespective of the amount. In addition, it was also clear to the government that—politics being politics—the opposition would inevitably claim that the amount of any settlement was far too low. . . .

What ultimately settled the matter was the courage of the Indian Supreme Court . . . willing to take full responsibility for the settlement, which eliminated the major obstacle to a resolution from the Indian government's point of view. The judges knew that they would face tremendous criticism from activist groups—and they did—but they were willing to face it because they also knew that in the end the case was about poor people who needed relief, and not about politics, lawyers, grand legal doctrines or multinationals in the Third World.

Source: "Bhopal: What We Learned." Warren M. Anderson, former chairman, Union Carbide Corporation. Circulated in Bhopal in April 1990. Excerpted from Kim Fortun. *Advocacy after Bhopal.* Chicago: University of Chicago Press, 2001.

8

EXXON VALDEZ DISASTER:
Was the Decision to Levy Punitive Damages Against Exxon Fair?

—m—

THE CONTROVERSY

The Issue

Shortly after midnight on March 24, 1989, the *Exxon Valdez* oil tanker struck an underwater reef and released nearly 11 million gallons of crude oil into the pristine waters of Prince William Sound, Alaska. It was the largest oil spill in U.S. history at the time, and neither the private companies involved nor the government was prepared to deal with a disaster of this magnitude. The oil slick eventually spread out across the sound and into the Gulf of Alaska, affecting more than 1,200 miles of Alaska's southern coast. Tens of thousands of seabirds were killed, along with many other creatures, including sea otters, harbor seals, bald eagles, and even killer whales. The oil spill caused the cancellation of the fishing seasons for salmon and herring, vital to the livelihoods of the area's commercial fishermen and Native Alaskan villagers. Exxon Corporation, owner of the *Exxon Valdez*, launched a massive cleanup effort, employing thousands of workers to recover the oil and clean beaches, but the damage could not be undone. In 1994, a federal jury imposed a punitive fine against Exxon for $5 billion, one of the largest such civil penalties in the nation's history. Was this punitive fine fair?

♦ **Arguments that the punitive damages were fair:** Critics of Exxon argued that the oil spill into Prince William Sound damaged one of the nation's most pristine and sacred environments. The spill caused massive disruption to the lives of the area's residents. They argued that the oil spill was the result of a pattern of reckless behavior on the part of the Exxon management and a callous attitude toward the welfare of people and the environment. Specifically, they pointed to Exxon's decision to employ a captain with known problems with alcohol and the company's failure to adequately prepare for such a disaster. Finally, critics argued that a punitive fine against Exxon had to be unusually large in order to change the attitudes and behavior of the massive multinational corporation.

272

♦ ***Arguments that the punitive damages were not fair:*** Exxon's defenders
argued that a punitive fine was unnecessary and unwarranted. The company assumed responsibility for the spill without hesitation and made an
exemplary effort to contain and clean up the spill. Exxon argued that it
had deployed every available resource, spending more than $2 billion on
the cleanup effort. In addition, Exxon voluntarily paid out hundreds of
millions of dollars in compensation to affected residents and had already
settled civil and criminal fines of another $1 billion with the state and
federal governments. Finally, they argued that the spill was caused by the
unusual mistakes of the individuals piloting the ship and not by the decisions or actions of the Exxon Corporation or its leadership.

INTRODUCTION

Shortly after midnight on March 24, 1989, a 987-foot-long oil tanker
named *Exxon Valdez* struck a rocky reef in Prince William Sound,
Alaska, puncturing the ship's hull and releasing almost 11 million gallons of crude oil into the coastal waters. It was the largest oil spill in U.S.
history at the time. Although authorities were alerted to the problem
almost immediately, lack of equipment and preparation coupled with
worsening weather delayed effective response and allowed the escaped
oil to spread. As days turned into weeks, the oil slick extended throughout the sound and onto the coasts. It eventually covered hundreds of
square miles of ocean and affected over 1,200 miles of Alaskan coastline. The *Exxon Valdez* oil spill was one of the largest environmental
catastrophes the United States had ever experienced, and it occurred
in one of the country's most fragile environments. The oil disaster
seemed especially tragic because it affected an area celebrated for its
pristine beauty, which symbolized the last remaining unspoiled frontier
of America. Birds and fish died by the tens of thousands. Many mammals died as well, including sea otters, seals, and killer whales. For residents of the communities around Prince William Sound, however, the
spill was much more than a loss of beautiful scenery; it was a threat to
their very livelihoods. For Native Alaskans living in traditional villages,
harvests from the sea were central to their culture and material sustenance. For thousands of commercial fishermen and related businesses,
the sea was their only source of income. For residents of Prince William

Sound as a whole, the normal rhythms of life came to a standstill and the future looked bleak.

By summer 1989, the largest oil disaster also became one of the largest cleanups. At peak activity, over 10,000 people were employed by Exxon Corporation to help with cleaning up the oil and with environmental restoration. The devastation in Prince William Sound and cleanup response dominated the news and stimulated national debates about energy, the environment, and about corporate and government responsibility. Offshore oil activity was curtailed by the president, and Congress passed new, stricter legislation to regulate oil transportation to try to prevent future disasters. However, the focus of concern in Prince William Sound was on compensation and accountability.

Although a number of major oil companies were responsible for the transport of oil across Alaska and through Prince William Sound, it was the Exxon Corporation—the owner of the ill-fated *Exxon Valdez*—that drew the public's ire and legal challenges. Thousands of lawsuits, both civil and criminal, were filed against Exxon and the captain of the *Exxon Valdez*, Joseph Hazelwood. Many of the civil lawsuits were resolved in out-of-court settlements in which Exxon agreed to compensate individuals or businesses for their losses. One of the largest was with state and federal governments for over $1 billion to settle criminal charges. However, the question of civil liability and possible punitive fines loomed large. In 1994—more than five years after the spill—the civil trial against Exxon and Captain Hazelwood began in a federal district court in Anchorage, Alaska. The jury found that Exxon and the captain of the *Exxon Valdez* had acted recklessly, clearing the way for consideration of possible punitive damages.

Lawyers for the plaintiffs—representing more than 30,000 people in Prince William Sound's fishing industry—argued that Exxon should be punished for its reckless behavior, and the only way to do this was with a multibillion dollar fine. The plaintiffs argued that Exxon had a history of reckless and callous behavior toward the environment, and that the accident, as well as its slow and inadequate response to the spill, was a reflection of this problem. Although Exxon had paid out hundreds of millions for compensation and cleanup, the plaintiffs asserted that the environment of Prince William Sound had been permanently altered, and no amount of compensation could undo the damage. People's lives, they argued, would be interrupted for decades to come. The plaintiffs

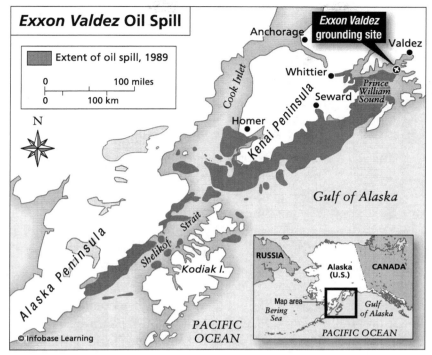

Exxon Valdez Oil Spill

Extent of oil spill, 1989

0   100 miles
0   100 km

N

Anchorage

Exxon Valdez grounding site

Valdez

Whittier

Cook Inlet

Prince William Sound

Seward

Homer

Kenai Peninsula

Gulf of Alaska

Shelikof Strait

Alaska Peninsula

Kodiak I.

RUSSIA

Alaska (U.S.)

CANADA

Map area

Bering Sea

Gulf of Alaska

PACIFIC OCEAN

PACIFIC OCEAN

© Infobase Learning

Oil from the grounded *Exxon Valdez* tanker eventually drifted nearly 500 miles from the spill site and affected more than 1,000 miles of coastline. (Map by Dale Williams)

argued that punitive fines were justified and had to be large enough to hurt in order to change Exxon's corporate culture and to send a message to other companies that careless treatment of the environment and people's lives would not be tolerated. Exxon countered that punitive damages were unwarranted because the company's response to the spill was exemplary. Exxon argued that it was not responsible for the reckless behavior of the captain and that it acted aggressively to contain the spill, using every available resource and employing thousands of workers, including many locals, to fight the spill and do the cleanup. Exxon's lawyers pointed out that the company had already paid out billions in cleanup and settlement agreements in a good-faith effort to correct the mistake and fairly compensate those who were harmed. They asserted that the company had changed its policies to prevent future disasters, and the evidence indicated that Prince William Sound and its fisheries were already recovering. Exxon's lawyers argued that nothing would be accomplished by levying punitive fines against the company. The question before the 11-member jury was: Should Exxon be punished with punitive fines and, if so, how much?

BACKGROUND

Opening the Trans-Alaska Pipeline System

Beginning in the late 1960s, Alaska emerged as an important domestic source of oil for America. It also became an early battleground over commercial resource exploitation and rising environmental sensitivity. In 1968, a consortium of oil companies announced the discovery of a large oil deposit beneath Prudhoe Bay on Alaska's North Slope. With an estimate of some 20 billion barrels of oil, it was the largest oil field in North America.

In order to transport oil to market from Alaska's remote Arctic coast, the oil company consortium proposed the construction of a pipeline from Prudhoe Bay through the interior of Alaska, terminating at the port of Valdez on Alaska's southern coast—the northern-most, ice-free port. From the Valdez terminal, tanker ships could transport the oil to refineries on the West Coast or in Japan. By 1970, the oil company consortium had incorporated as the Alyeska Pipeline Service Company in order to pursue the massive project, but the plan was brought to a standstill in April 1970 when environmental organizations sued to halt the project, arguing that it should prepare a thorough environmental impact statement before the government granted approval. New legislation, such as the National Environmental Policy Act (NEPA) of 1969, required such reviews and reflected a growing national concern about environmental degradation.

Concern over oil pollution in particular was at a high point. In January 1969, an oil well five and a half miles off the coast of Santa Barbara, California, ruptured, leaking 4.2 million gallons of oil into the water and coating 35 miles of some of the most attractive and expensive coastal property in the nation. The outcry over the Santa Barbara oil blow-out, spurred by images of oil-coated birds and other dead and dying sea life, galvanized criticism and opposition to further oil development in sensitive coastal areas. Critics of the Trans-Alaska Pipeline System

(TAPS) argued that the oil companies should consider alternative ways to transport the oil. As planned, the oil tankers would be carrying millions of gallons of oil through treacherous, iceberg-laden waters in one of the world's most ecologically rich and fragile environments.

While environmental concern was high, concerns over energy and national security took precedence. Beginning in spring 1973, there was growing national concern over an impending energy crisis, as domestic oil producers struggled to meet skyrocketing demand and energy prices rose. Advocates of TAPS, including the Nixon administration, argued that increasing domestic oil production was essential to preventing an energy crisis and to reducing American dependence on imported oil from the politically volatile Middle East. By summer 1973, several bills were being considered in Congress to authorize construction of TAPS, although there was considerable controversy over how to deal with environmental challenges, especially those stemming from NEPA.

Geopolitical developments changed the balance of the debate. On October 6, 1973, Egypt and Syria invaded Israel, initiating the Yom Kippur War. On October 20, the Arab members of the Organization of the Petroleum Exporting Countries (OPEC)—an organization of the world's leading oil-producing nations—sharply cut world oil production and announced an embargo against the United States and other countries for providing military support to Israel. The price of oil jumped dramatically and oil-dependent countries scrambled to make up the shortfall. In the United States, the impact was felt most acutely in the price and supply of home heating oil and gasoline. Prices doubled, and in some parts of the country there were even shortages, forcing worries about winter heating and long lines of angry motorists.

The energy crisis had finally arrived, and it provided the final push for TAPS and domestic energy development. In mid-November 1973, Congress passed the Trans-Alaska Pipeline Authorization Act, which halted all legal challenges against construction of the pipeline and exempted it from further environmental review. Nevertheless, in an effort to assuage environmental concerns, oil company officials promised to exercise the highest environmental safety precautions, including the establishment of a dedicated monitoring and emergency oil spill response plan, which the authorizing legislation required.

Construction of TAPS began in spring 1974 and was completed on May 31, 1977. At a final cost of more than $8 billion, it was the largest and most expensive privately funded project in history. The pipeline itself was an engineering marvel—steel pipe, four feet in diameter, running 800 miles through the Alaskan wilderness, crossing three mountain ranges and numerous rivers and streams. In some places, the pipeline had to be supported on stilts to keep it from melting the frozen tundra and buckling.

Oil began flowing through TAPS on June 22, and on August 1, 1977, the *ARCO Juneau* carried the first tanker load of North Slope oil from the Valdez terminal. Within a few years, the volume of oil flowing through TAPS would constitute one-quarter of U.S. oil production. Oil production was an economic boon for Alaska. Taxes on oil production and property soon constituted the largest single source of revenue for the state and eventually allowed Alaska to abolish its state income tax and even issue annual royalty checks to its residents. Alaskans were reaping the economic rewards of the oil boom.

During its first 12 years of operation, TAPS experienced relatively few oil spills and no major oil spills on water. Those that did occur happened on land along the length of the pipeline itself. Consistent with its promises, the Alyeska Pipeline Service Company initially maintained a dedicated oil spill response team. Acting much like firefighters, the Alyeska team ran drills, maintained its equipment for rapid response, and was on duty 24 hours a day. Beginning in 1981, however, Alyeska began looking for ways to cut costs and eliminated the dedicated oil response team. From 1982 onward, oil spills would be handled by regular staff at the terminal. Under agreement with the coast guard and the state of Alaska, Alyeska's oil response team was supposed to run regular practice drills, but after 1982 these training exercises were infrequent and perfunctory.

Globally, as oil consumption and production increased, so did oil spills. (See "Top 65 Oil Spills in the World, 1964–1989," on page 302 in the Primary Sources section.) A year after TAPS began operating, the American supertanker *Amoco Cadiz* ran aground three miles off the coast of Brittany, France, spilling 68 million gallons of crude oil. The oil covered 125 miles of shoreline and was the largest spill in history at the time. The following year, a Pemex well 150 miles off the coast of the Yucatán Peninsula suffered an explosion and uncontrolled blowout. The gushing offshore well leaked 140 million gallons of crude oil into the Gulf of Mexico for nearly a year before it could be capped, surpassing the size of the *Amoco Cadiz* spill. Luckily for coastal communities, most of the oil drifted out to sea where it eventually broke apart.

In spite of an increasing number of devastating oil spills, petroleum continued to grow as the world's most important fuel source. Like most industrialized countries, the United States was increasingly dependent on imported oil in order to meet domestic demand. With the 1973 OPEC oil embargo still in memory, however, this dependency was a constant cause for concern. By the late 1980s, the United States was importing approximately half of the oil it consumed. Promoters of domestic oil development argued that this dependency on foreign sources of oil was dangerous, and they pushed for further exploitation of potentially rich and untapped oil fields on Alaska's North Slope. However, some of the proposed areas were designated as protected wildlife refuges, sparking heated political debate over the importance of resource development and wilderness preservation. In spring 1989, an ecological crisis changed the terms of the debate. (See the sidebar "The Battle for ANWR" on page 280.)

Disaster at Home

By 6:00 P.M. on March 23, 1989, the *Exxon Valdez* oil tanker was loaded with more than 53 million gallons of crude oil at the Alyeska Marine Terminal. The 987-foot ship—longer than three football fields—was only three years old, one of the newest and most technologically sophisticated in Exxon's 20-tanker fleet. After loading was complete, the *Exxon Valdez* was bound for Long Beach, California, a five-day trip. The ship's captain, Joseph Hazelwood, had been piloting Exxon ships for 19 years and had little cause to worry. Indeed, in the 12 years that TAPS had been operating, tankers had carried oil from Valdez and through Prince William Sound more than 8,700 times without a major accident. On this evening, however, things would change.

Prior to boarding his ship on Thursday evening, March 23, 1989, Captain Hazelwood had been in the nearby town of Valdez shopping, taking care of business, and having drinks with some of his fellow shipmates. Just before the scheduled departure time, Hazelwood and the other crewmembers returned to the ship. When the *Exxon Valdez* left its mooring at 9:12 P.M., it was piloted for the first seven miles through

THE BATTLE FOR ANWR

The discovery of North America's largest oil field in Prudhoe Bay in 1968 invigorated interest in Alaska as an important source of petroleum for the United States. Since the late 1940s, America's domestic oil production had steadily declined while its dependence on foreign oil had continued to increase. Alaska's strategic significance as a domestic source of oil increased after the OPEC oil embargo in 1973. However, Alaska's North Slope and Arctic shore have longstanding significance for their unique values as wilderness.

Beginning in the early 1950s, conservationists and wilderness enthusiasts launched a campaign to draw attention to the area's natural, unspoiled beauty and its scientific value as the largest and last remaining undisturbed wilderness on the continent. Massive mountain ranges, wide vistas of undisturbed tundra, and large populations of charismatic mammals, such as herds of caribou, inspired a movement for preservation. In 1960, the U.S. Department of the Interior obliged by designating 8.9 million acres of northeast Alaska as the Arctic National Wildlife Range, "For the purpose of preserving unique wildlife, wilderness and recreational values."

After an unsuccessful bid to halt construction of the Trans-Alaska Pipeline in the early 1970s, environmentalists intensified their efforts to protect remaining areas of undisturbed Alaskan wilderness. In December 1980, President Jimmy Carter signed into law the Alaska National Interest Lands Conservation Act, which redesignated the area as the Arctic National Wildlife Refuge (ANWR) and more than doubled the area protected as wilderness to 18 million acres—an area larger than the state of West Virginia—making it the largest national wildlife refuge in the nation. Although the newly added area was protected wilderness, the 1980 legislation nevertheless acknowledged continued interest in natural resource extraction. Section 1002 of the 1980 law singled out 1.5 million acres along Alaska's northeast Arctic coastal plain by requiring studies of potential petroleum resources and analyses of the impacts of natural gas and oil exploration. This particular area also

Valdez Narrows by a local tugboat pilot, consistent with company policy and federal law. Shortly after 11:00 P.M., the tugboat pilot turned the ship back over to Hazelwood and left the ship. With approval from the coast guard, the captain steered the ship outside of its normal shipping happened to be a region important to caribou migration and calving and for subsistence resources for Native Alaskan villagers. The area designated by Section 1002 would become ground zero in repeated battles over drilling in ANWR.

The 1980s saw a dramatic increase in U.S. dependence on imported oil and a growing political conservatism that was hostile to environmental regulation. In 1987, President Ronald Reagan advocated opening Section 1002 of ANWR to oil drilling in the interests of boosting domestic oil production and reducing U.S. vulnerability to foreign oil supply disruptions. By law, however, drilling in ANWR required an act of Congress. After repeated attempts, a Senate committee approved leasing of the coastal plain for oil exploration and development in March 1989. Ten days later, the *Exxon Valdez* ran aground on Bligh Reef and spilled nearly 11 million gallons of North Slope crude oil into the pristine waters of Alaska's Prince William Sound. In the immediate wake of America's greatest oil spill, general support for drilling in ANWR evaporated—but not for long.

Over the following two decades, advocates of oil development would make repeated attempts to advance legislation in Congress to allow oil exploration and development in ANWR's Section 1002. In fact, support or opposition for drilling in ANWR was both a lightning rod for controversy and a litmus test of political ideology. It has been a perennial debate. In 1995, Congress passed legislation enabling oil exploration in ANWR, but President Bill Clinton vetoed it. In 2001, President George W. Bush pushed for opening ANWR to oil development in his national energy plan but enabling legislation was blocked in the Senate. Numerous attempts were once again made by members of Congress in 2005 through budget amendments, but disagreement between the House of Representatives and the Senate prevented these amendments from moving forward. In 2008, presidential candidate Barack Obama and congressional leaders declared their opposition to drilling in ANWR, but the issue is likely to resurface.

lane in order to avoid icebergs that were floating into the normal outbound shipping lane. At around 11:52 P.M., Hazelwood placed the ship on autopilot, revved the engine up to full oceangoing speed, and turned control over to Third Mate Gregory Cousins. He instructed his third mate to return the ship to its proper lane after they had skirted the float-ing ice. The timing of this maneuver was important in order to avoid a collision with Bligh Reef, which lay directly in the ship's current path.

Cousins was not aware that the ship had been placed on autopilot or that it was speeding up. Hazelwood left the deck to go below, leav-ing Cousins as the only officer on the bridge—a violation of coast guard regulations and company policy. Cousins was already working beyond the legal six-hour shift, having elected to take over for another ship-mate who was scheduled to relieve him for the midnight to 5:00 A.M. shift. A few minutes after midnight, Cousins realized that his attempt to maneuver the ship back into its normal shipping lane was not going to work—the huge ship could not turn quickly enough and was headed straight toward Bligh Reef. He called the captain to come to the bridge, but it was too late. The ship shuddered with a series of sharp jolts and came to a halt atop the submerged rocks. Captain Hazelwood took con-trol and repeatedly attempted to work the ship free, but it was no use.

At 12:26 A.M. on Friday morning, Hazelwood radioed the Val-dez traffic center and told the coast guard personnel on duty: "We've fetched up, ah, hard aground north of Goose Island, off Bligh Reef and, ah, evidently leaking some oil and we're going to be here a while, and, ah, if you want, ah, so you're notified." Eight of the ship's 11 cargo tanks had been ruptured. Within the first three and a half hours of the acci-dent, approximately 5.8 million gallons of crude oil spilled out. Worse, the ship itself appeared to be in danger of breaking apart, threatening to lose the remaining 48 million gallons of cargo.

Response

The first few hours after an oil spill at sea are crucial if the oil is going to be contained or recovered before it spreads too far or becomes too weathered for chemical treatment or burning. Unusually calm weather during the first two days after the spill provided responders with ideal conditions for containment and recovery. Unfortunately, this window of opportunity was lost due to slow response, conflicts over authority, and a lack of adequate equipment.

Under the national contingency plan that had been approved to deal with oil spills, Alyeska had the responsibility of first response to a spill, while state and federal officials were tasked with oversight. Despite these plans, Exxon took charge of the response from Alyeska—much to the surprise of state and federal officials. It soon became apparent that neither Alyeska nor Exxon was prepared to respond to such a disaster. However, state and federal officials were no more capable of responding to the spill because they too lacked the resources or even a clear plan.

Officials from the coast guard and Alaska's Department of Environmental Conservation (DEC) arrived on the grounded ship by 3:30 A.M.—about three hours after the ship's distress call. A coast guard official reported that oil was bubbling violently from beneath the ship, splashing four feet above the surface, and the smell of petroleum was overpowering. Alyeska's oil response boat was unable to arrive until about noon on Friday—11 hours after notification. In the original contingency plan, Alyeska had promised a response within five hours.

The first order of business was to transfer the remaining oil from the *Exxon Valdez* to another ship in order to prevent the disaster from getting any worse. This required considerable time for the relief ships to maneuver next to the disabled *Exxon Valdez*—without striking the nearby reef themselves—and then connect hoses to begin transfer. With limited personnel and resources, Alyeska's response team was not able to lay out containment boom (floating barriers to corral the oil) around the leaking ship until Saturday morning—more than a day and a half later. The coast guard and Alyeska personnel eventually stabilized the ship so that it could be safely towed to harbor without fear of breakup or loss of more oil. Nevertheless, nearly 11 million gallons of crude oil had spilled into Prince William Sound. The oil slick covered an area three by five miles around the ship. As Alyeska's slow and inadequate response became painfully apparent, the president of Exxon Shipping publicly declared that Exxon Corporation would assume responsibility for containment and cleanup of the oil spill. State and federal officials were surprised by Exxon's announcement, but they nevertheless deferred to Exxon's lead. However, conflict erupted almost immediately over strategies to contain the spill.

Exxon requested permission from the DEC and the coast guard to begin a massive application of chemical dispersants in order to break up and dilute the oil as quickly as possible. DEC officials and many fishermen were wary of heavy use of chemical dispersants; no one could predict how toxic the chemicals might be for sea life. State officials and local residents preferred the use of mechanical containment and recovery before resorting to potentially toxic chemicals, but Exxon was insistent that chemical dispersants were the only way to quickly and effectively mitigate the oil's impact. Federal and state officials had the final say, but there was very little objective research on the effectiveness or toxicity of these chemicals to inform their decision. At the same time, the dispute was somewhat academic since neither Exxon nor any other organization had sufficient chemical dispersants in stock to make an appreciable dent in the extensive oil slick. Nevertheless, after a number of tests, state and federal officials finally approved the application of chemical dispersant on Sunday afternoon—three days into the oil spill.

That evening and into Monday morning, a sudden spring blizzard put a halt to cleanup plans. By this time, only about 1.5 percent of the oil had been recovered, dispersed, or burned. Winds over 70 miles per hour and waves 20 feet high spread the oil over a 500-square-mile area of Prince William Sound and churned the oil into a thick, mousse-like consistency that was immune to burning or even chemical attack. Oil was pushed onto the shores of a number of islands and threatened numerous other coastal areas. Reports of oiled and dead seabirds were now arriving. It was no longer possible to contain the spill. Efforts turned toward protecting select coastal areas and eventually cleanup.

From the very beginning of the disaster, local residents and especially fishermen were eager to assist in any way they could. Within hours of the grounding, fishermen from the town of Cordova had assembled 75 fishing boats ready to assist and notified Alyeska and Exxon of their readiness to help. The coastal communities around Prince William Sound had a vital interest in the health of the waters. Fishing and related industries, as well as tourism, were the economic lifeblood of the region.

Moreover, early spring was a critical period for fishing. Herring season was about to begin. The state's salmon hatcheries were preparing to release more than 100 million salmon fry from their pens and into the sound so that they could feed on the plankton that bloom in April. The oil threatened to destroy the year's fish harvest, which could mean economic ruin for tens of thousands of people. For traditional Native Alaskan villages, the sea was their main source of subsistence. In a rare instance of cooperation, Exxon, government officials, and fishermen combined forces to protect the bays of five critical salmon hatcheries. Using miles of boom, they managed to deflect the oncoming oil as it made its way south through Prince William Sound. While the vital hatcheries were saved, the oil catastrophe was still unfolding for the rest of Prince William Sound.

The oil spill devastated the sound's wildlife. Rather than floating out to sea, the oil collected along the shores and shallows where wildlife was most abundant and vulnerable. Tides and waves brought oil onto the beaches, coating the rocks and soaking deep into the rocky shores. Spring is the season of migration when millions of birds descend on Prince William Sound, feeding on the area's normally abundant fish and other sea life. Birds died by the tens of thousands. Oil coated their feathers as they landed on the waters or dove for fish, making it impossible to fly or even stay afloat. Many were poisoned from ingesting the toxic oil as they attempted to preen their feathers. Marine mammals—sea otters, harbor seals, killer whales—died as well. Fumes from the oil blinded them and stung their lungs as they surfaced within the thick, black crude. Like the birds, sea otters ingested oil as they attempted to clean their fur, vital for maintaining buoyancy and insulation in the frigid waters.

The beaches of Prince William Sound were blackened by oil and littered with the bodies of birds, sea otters, and other creatures. Eagles and bears that scavenged on the oiled carcasses were also poisoned. Volunteers from around the world joined local residents in attempts to save oiled birds and sea otters, though resources were woefully short and the area affected immense. Efforts were also made to dispose of oiled carcasses as quickly as possible before they were eaten by other creatures.

As the catastrophe unfolded, the Exxon Corporation was faced with the daunting task of saving beaches and its reputation. From mid-April through the summer and early fall of 1989, efforts turned toward cleanup of oil-stained shores and containment of the myriad smaller slicks of oil that continued to threaten beaches throughout the sound. With federal and state approval, Exxon hired thousands of local workers and outside contractors to clean the shores and recover what oil they could. They skimmed oil from the water, hauled away oily debris and animal carcasses, used high-powered jets of hot water to clear oil from the surface of rocky beaches, and even wiped individual rocks and stones with paper towels.

By June 1989, the oil covered more than 10,000 square miles. Although Exxon and its contractors expended enormous effort and sums of money, Alaska's DEC and many local residents complained about the inadequacy of cleanup efforts. While the surfaces of some beaches appeared to be clear of oil, in many cases it remained thick and easily disturbed only inches below the surface. Disputes erupted over which beaches to clean and the level of cleanup needed. However, later research suggested that some cleanup efforts may have been counterproductive. High-pressure hosing of rocks with hot water certainly washed oil away, but it also washed away any organisms on the rocks, retarding ecological recovery. Thousands of cleanup workers stomped through fragile shoreline ecosystems, trampling delicate organisms and stressing others and leaving behind their own litter. In early August, Exxon officials proudly declared that more than 700 miles of shoreline had been treated and 16,000 tons of oily debris collected. By mid-September, as winter approached, Exxon declared cleanup activities concluded for the season. Cleanup activities would continue for two more summers into 1992. According to Exxon officials, more than 1,000 miles of shoreline were treated at an overall expense of more than $2 billion.

Cleanup efforts in the sound brought diminishing returns. Much damage had already occurred and could not be undone. Exxon had managed to recover less than 10 percent of the spilled oil. Nearly half of the oil ended up on the shores of Prince William Sound. The oil slick traveled for more than 600 miles from the spill site at Bligh Reef, affecting more than 1,200 miles of coastline. Cleanup crews recovered the carcasses of thousands of marine birds and mammals, although the recovered bodies represented only a small portion of the actual mortality. The oil spill killed an estimated 250,000 seabirds, 2,800 sea otters, 300 harbor seals, 250 bald eagles, and as many as 22 killer whales.

The total ecological disruption was harder to quantify, but apparent. The economic and cultural impact on residents dependent on fishing was substantial. In early April 1989, Alaska's Department of Fish and Game canceled the herring fishing season because of damage to the spawning area. Fisheries for salmon, herring, crab, shrimp, rock fish, and sable fish were closed throughout Prince William Sound, Cook Inlet, the outer Kenai Coast, Kodiak, and Alaska Peninsula. Shrimp and salmon fisheries would remain closed in parts of Prince William Sound through 1990. Pacific herring, which was already experiencing low numbers, worsened, resulting in repeated cancellations of the fishing season for the next two decades. Commercial fishermen experienced serious economic disruption. Some found temporary employment in the cleanup effort with Exxon and its contractors. Exxon's claims office, set up days after the spill, paid claims to those who could show a direct economic loss, although there were numerous complaints about disparities in who was compensated or how much.

The disruption for Native Alaskan villagers was both economic and cultural because the oil affected many of their subsistence hunting and fishing grounds. For these villagers, harvesting of fish, shellfish, birds, seals, and sea creatures was a way of life and a necessity. The oil spill contaminated these subsistence resources and led to debilitating anxiety for years because they did not know what food sources were safe to eat or when they might be safe. In the immediate wake of the disaster, Exxon delivered emergency food supplies to the villages. Although the material aid was welcome, it could not substitute for the socially important process of harvesting and the unique foods that were so central to their cultures.

The *Exxon Valdez* oil spill dominated national news and prompted government officials to address concerns about oil pollution. By February 1990, the state-appointed Alaska Oil Spill Commission had released its report analyzing the *Exxon Valdez* oil spill and making policy recommendations. (See "Foreword to the Alaska Oil Spill Commission Report, 1990," on page 306 in the Primary Sources section.) In late June 1990, President George H. W. Bush declared a 10-year moratorium on offshore oil drilling off the coasts of Oregon, Washington, and most of California, as well as the Florida Keys and Georges Bank fishing grounds off the New England coast. The president argued that the moratorium was meant to allow further study of the environmental impact of offshore oil activity, but it was fairly clear that he was responding to an upsurge in public concern over environmental degradation from oil extraction and development.

A more significant move was made shortly after when Congress passed the Oil Pollution Act of 1990 (OPA), which incorporated some of the lessons from the *Exxon Valdez* disaster. The OPA expanded the federal government's authority to plan for and respond to oil spills. It increased the financial liabilities of companies that handle and transport oil and created a national Oil Spill Liability Trust Fund, which could provide up to $1 billion per spill incident. The legislation also declared that all oil tankers in U.S. waters would need to be double-hulled by

2015. The debate over double-hulled tankers had raged since the 1970s. Following the *Exxon Valdez* spill, the Coast Guard released estimates that up to 60 percent of the oil spilled could have been prevented if the ship had been double-hulled. In addition, the OPA set new rules limiting the number of hours tanker crews could work in order to reduce errors caused by fatigue. The law required all oil tankers and barges to carry enough equipment to start cleanup operations at the first sign of a spill. Further, each tanker must have a response plan to deal with accidents. (See the sidebar "A History of Marine Oil Pollution" on page 290.) Finally, and quite controversially, the legislation included a clause prohibiting any vessel that, after March 22, 1989, had caused an oil spill of more than 1 million gallons in any marine area from operating in Prince William Sound—effectively banning the *Exxon Valdez* from ever returning to the sound.

Culpability and Restitution

The questions of culpability and compensation for the oil spill figured high in the minds of residents of Prince William Sound and government officials. Although a number of parties were sued in connection with the oil spill and response (including the oil companies comprising Alyeska), Captain Hazelwood and the Exxon Corporation drew the most scrutiny. Shortly after the *Exxon Valdez* grounded on Bligh Reef, news emerged that the captain may have been intoxicated and that Exxon knew about his drinking problems. As the owner of the ship that caused the oil spill, Exxon was also the most obvious subject of litigation. In late summer 1989, the state of Alaska filed suit in State Superior Court against Exxon Corporation and the oil companies that comprised the Alyeska Pipeline Service Company. The state also charged Hazelwood with felonies and misdemeanors in connection with the spill. In February 1990, a federal grand jury in Anchorage indicted Exxon for violations of at least five environmental laws: the Clean Water Act, the Refuse Act of 1899, the Migratory Bird Treaty Act, the Ports and Waterways Act, and the Dangerous Cargo Act. Finally, Exxon faced tens of thousands of civil lawsuits from private parties.

Government lawsuits against Exxon threatened to drag on for years. In January 1991, Alaska governor Walter Hickel proposed dropping all federal and state charges against Exxon over damages in exchange for $1.2 billion to restore and enhance Prince William Sound. By October 1991, the state of Alaska, the federal government, and Exxon reached a court-approved settlement and plea agreement that resolved criminal charges as well as civil claims by the government for restoration of damages to natural resources. As part of the criminal plea agreement, Exxon was fined $150 million for violations of the Clean Water Act and the Migratory Bird Treaty Act—the largest fines ever levied for environmental crimes. However, the court forgave $125 million in recognition of Exxon's cooperation in the spill cleanup and for paying certain private claims. Exxon was fined $100 million as restitution for injuries caused to fish, wildlife, and the lands affected by the spill. Finally, Exxon agreed to a civil settlement of $900 million, to be paid out over 10 years. The latter would be used for restoration and monitoring of injured natural resources and to reimburse the state and federal governments for expenses associated with response and cleanup.

In 1992, the Alaska DEC declared cleanup activities complete. Exxon had spent more than $2.1 billion on cleanup activities and another $300 million in its voluntary compensation program. However, it still faced a storm of both civil and criminal suits. These lawsuits addressed the physical and economic damages suffered from the oil spill, but they also addressed the outrage and widespread sense of violation expressed by residents of Prince William Sound and the wider public. While Exxon's expenditures and the billion dollar settlement were momentous, they did not relieve Exxon of the myriad civil lawsuits filed by private parties. Indeed, hostility against Exxon was still very high. In summer 1993, fishermen in Prince William Sound staged a three-day blockade of Valdez port in order to draw attention to their still unpaid claims for damages. The blockade was ended only after the personal intervention of Secretary of the Interior Bruce Babbit.

DEBATE

The largest civil trial by private citizens against Exxon Corporation and Captain Hazelwood began in Anchorage federal district court in May 1994. More than 32,000 fishermen, cannery workers, landowners, and others filed civil lawsuits against Exxon for compensation and punitive damages. In order to bring order to so many lawsuits, the district court combined the suits into a class composed of 32,677 fishermen, Native Alaskans, landowners, municipalities, and others. Judge Russel Holland, the presiding magistrate, further limited compensation

A HISTORY OF MARINE OIL POLLUTION

Since the late 19th century, one of the largest sources of oil pollution into the marine environment has been through marine transportation. The first bulk oil tanker began operating successfully in the Caspian Sea in 1878. Oil spills at sea were a problem from the very beginning. Oil tankers lost their cargo at sea during storms, by running aground, or through collisions. During periods of war, ships carrying oil were often targeted as a way to deprive the enemy of needed fuel and to wreak havoc.

The frequency and severity of marine oil spills worsened in the 1960s. This was a result of the increased amount of transported oil and, equally significant, a dramatic increase in the size of oil tankers. Until the 1950s, slightly more than 2,000 oil tankers of 15,000 deadweight tons or less plied the world's oceans. In terms of cargo-carrying capacity, these ships had changed relatively little since the late 19th century. In the 1960s, however, Japanese shipmakers developed a new class of oil tankers using high-efficiency diesel engines and light, high-strength steel. By 1965, the average size of an oil tanker had increased to 27,000 deadweight tons. By 1968, the year that oil was discovered in Alaska's Prudhoe Bay, there were 60 tankers of 150,000 deadweight tons or more—10 times the average size of only a decade before.

These new supertankers made transportation of oil more economically efficient, but they also resulted in more catastrophic oil spills. One of the earliest such catastrophes was the grounding of the *Torrey Canyon* (118,000 deadweight tons) in 1967, which spilled more than 36 million gallons of crude oil into the English Channel. These larger tankers also experienced a high accident rate. In 1969, there were 1,416 tanker accidents in a world fleet of 6,103 ships. In 1970, a Marine Science Affairs Committee reported that oil was a major source of pollution in the marine environment and estimated that 300 million gallons of oil was spilled or leaked into the marine to economic claims by commercial fishermen and Native Alaskans. In order to make the massive case more manageable, the court divided the civil trial into phases. In the first phase, the jury would decide whether or not Exxon and Captain Hazelwood were reckless. In the second phase, the jury had to determine the amount of compensatory

environment annually. In 1973, as Congress debated legislation to enable construction of the Trans-Alaska Pipeline System (TAPS) and marine transport of oil through Prince William Sound, it was estimated that 11,250 oil spills occurred annually in the United States alone.

During debates over TAPS in the early 1970s, concerns over the possibility of oil spills in Prince William Sound were repeatedly raised. One idea that attracted significant attention was the proposal that oil tankers be required to have double hulls. In a double-hulled ship, the bottom or sides are surrounded by a second skin of steel, with an air space between the two, which can greatly reduce the possibility that the ship's outer hull will be breached and release oil in the event of a collision or grounding. Few ships at the time were double-hulled. Oil companies did not favor double hulls because they reduced the amount of oil that a ship could carry and increased its weight, making the shipping of oil less profitable and more expensive. Moreover, they worried that such a requirement would put American vessels at a competitive disadvantage since other countries did not have these requirements. Nevertheless, in anticipation of such a legal requirement, ARCO constructed two double-hulled oil tankers for the Alaska oil trade. However, Congress included no such requirement in the final legislation that approved construction of TAPS in 1973. Without an explicit legal requirement, the practice of constructing double-hulled tankers was not followed.

Public debate over double-hulled tankers was not revived until the grounding of the *Exxon Valdez* in 1989. Shortly after the accident, the coast guard estimated that 60 percent of the Prince William Sound oil spill could have been prevented if the *Exxon Valdez* had been double-hulled. A little more than a year later, Congress passed the Oil Pollution Act of 1990, which finally wrote into law a requirement that all oil tankers in United States waters be double-hulled by 2015. By February 2010, all of the oil tankers in Prince William Sound were double-hulled. Numerous other countries, as well as the European Union, have since adopted similar requirements.

The *Exxon Valdez* oil tanker lies atop Bligh Reef two days after grounding on March 24, 1989. More than 10 million gallons of crude oil leaked out of the ship and into the waters of Prince William Sound, Alaska. (Natalie B. Fobes/National Geographic/ Getty Images)

payments to 10,000 fishermen and 4,000 Alaskan Natives. However, it was the third phase that was on everyone's mind, presenting the question that captivated the rest of the nation. Should Exxon face punitive damages and, if so, how much?

The Case for Punitive Damages

Lawyers for the plaintiffs argued that punitive damages were certainly warranted and that they should be between $5 and $15 billion—large enough to hurt such a large corporation and to change its behavior. The plaintiffs described Exxon as a faceless, multinational company that behaved recklessly with the health and welfare of people and the environment. Plaintiffs reiterated that Exxon knew that Hazelwood had a drinking problem and yet still put him in charge of a supertanker loaded with 53 million gallons of crude oil in one of the most treacherous and fragile waterways in the world. Moreover, no manager had ever asked Hazelwood personally about his drinking problem or recovery. The captain's intoxication was the basis of a series of bad decisions that resulted in the grounding on Bligh Reef: the decision to bring the ship up to full speed while still in the ice-laden waters of Valdez Narrows and his failure to notify other officers that he had done this; his decision to leave the bridge at a critical point of navigation and to leave third mate Gregory Cousins—an unqualified junior officer—alone and in charge; and his decision to try to work the ship free after it had already grounded on the reef, risking catastrophic damage to the ship and possibly making the oil spill worse.

Plaintiffs asserted that Exxon was a powerful and arrogant corporation with an uncaring view of anything except profit. They pointed out that Exxon Corporation's chairman Lawrence Rawl never even visited Prince William Sound or met with victims of the oil spill in spite of the fact that it was the largest oil spill in the country and in his company's history. Worse, Exxon executives had even received bonuses after the spill. Plaintiffs highlighted the size of the company and its assets and the need for a high penalty. The plaintiffs' attorney declared, "[W]hat is punishment for a poor man can be nothing for a rich man." Exxon was the 26th largest company in the world (fifth largest industrial corporation) with average annual revenues of $111.6 billion, annual net cash flow from operations of $10.1 billion, and annual average net income (i.e., profit) of $4.83 billion. Plaintiffs argued that the monies already paid out by Exxon were not only inadequate but far less than they appeared. In particular, the plaintiffs pointed out that Exxon's billion dollar settlement with the state and federal governments was actually worth less than half its face value because it would be paid out over the course of a decade; the economic value of the award would be less because of inevitable deflation in the real value of each dollar over time. Moreover, Exxon would be able to deduct the cleanup and court expenses from its federal and state tax liability. Finally, Exxon could never really fully compensate or restore the pristine quality and sanctity of Prince William Sound. Nor could it compensate for the noneconomic harm to plaintiffs—disturbance of the social fabric of communities, increased social conflict, cultural disruption, and psychological stress. (See "An Address by Walter Meganack, Sr., 1989," on page 307 in the Primary Sources section.) For these reasons and others, the plaintiffs argued that the jury should charge Exxon with punitive damages that would hurt the large multinational corporation and send a message that such behavior would not be tolerated. Although Captain Hazelwood was also subject to punitive damages, the plaintiffs allowed that he had already suffered economic hardship and public shame. They suggested that he be fined only one dollar.

The Case Against Punitive Damages

Exxon's defense lawyers acknowledged that Hazelwood drank before he boarded his ship on that fateful night, but they denied that he was drunk or that alcohol was responsible for the wreck. They argued instead that the third mate was at fault for failing to carry out the captain's command to simply turn the ship before approaching the reef.

Defense lawyers argued that Exxon officials had monitored Hazelwood's alcoholism since his hospitalization but maintained that alcohol was not the cause of the accident. (See "An Interview with Joe Hazelwood, 2007–2008," on page 308 in the Primary Sources section.) More important, Exxon argued that the accident was the result of errors in judgment by individuals and it should not be held responsible for the actions of those individuals.

Exxon's lawyers argued that punitive damages against the company were unnecessary and unwarranted. First and foremost, Exxon maintained that it was not fair to hold it accountable or at fault for the errors made by individuals piloting the ship. Captain Hazelwood had violated not only the law but company policy with his actions. Exxon's response to the oil spill, they argued, was exemplary and far beyond its legal obligation. Exxon assumed responsibility for containment and cleanup without hesitation. It acted aggressively to contain and clean up the oil, working cooperatively with state and federal officials, as well as with local residents and volunteers. If anything, the company had been hampered in a more effective response because of delays by government officials in the use of chemical dispersants before the weather made their use impossible. The government bore a significant amount of responsibility for the company's inability to mount a more successful attack on the spill.

Nevertheless, the company had launched an unprecedented cleanup response, employing more than 10,000 people to recover spilled oil, clean beaches, and perform other environmental cleanup work, sparing little expense in the immediate wake of the spill. All told, Exxon argued that it had already spent $3.4 billion responding to the oil spill: $2.1 billion for direct cleanup efforts, $1 billion in a civil settlement with the federal and state governments for damages to the natural environment and to pay for expenses incurred, and over $300 million in voluntary compensation to over 11,000 residents and businesses in the Prince William Sound region. Indeed, Exxon had voluntarily set up a claims office in Valdez within days of the spill in order to provide economic relief to those who were directly harmed. This, they argued, was a major loss to the company and showed that the company had made a substantial and sincere effort to mitigate the accident and its effects. The leadership at Exxon had been stung by the disaster and its costs and had since implemented new, stricter policies to prevent such a thing from ever happening again. (See "'An Open Letter to the Public,' 1989," on page 309 in the Primary Sources section.) Nothing would be accomplished, they argued, with punitive fines. No more could be done for the sound than had already been done, and injured parties had been fairly compensated.

OUTCOME AND IMPACT

In June 1994, the jury found that the *Exxon Valdez* oil spill was caused by the recklessness of Captain Hazelwood and the Exxon Corporation. The finding of recklessness opened the way for punitive damages.

At the conclusion of the second phase of the trial, the jury awarded the plaintiffs $286.8 million in compensation—less than one-third of what they had sought but nearly three times what Exxon had offered. It was the second largest civil damage award against a U.S. company after the $470 million damage award against the Union Carbide Corporation for the 1984 Bhopal pesticide tragedy in India, and the largest ever for a pollution case. Nevertheless, the defense greeted the reduced award with relief.

In a separate settlement reached before the second phase had concluded, Exxon agreed to pay Alaskan Natives $20 million for damages to fish, seals, kelp, and other foods that Native Alaskans in 18 villages harvested from areas of Prince William Sound and other regions of Alaska polluted by the oil spill.

Hearings and testimony for the punitive damages phase of the trial lasted less than five days. However, the jury's deliberations dragged on for more than three weeks, sparking fears of a hung jury and the need for a retrial. On September 16, 1994, the jury announced that it had reached a consensus. It awarded $5,000 in punitive damages against Captain Hazelwood and $5 billion in punitive damages against the Exxon Corporation. It was the second largest punitive damage award in U.S. history, although the jurors were apparently not aware of this precedent. Plaintiffs celebrated the decision, while the defendants expressed disappointment. Exxon's treasurer informed the court that "the full payment of the judgment would not have a material impact on the corporation or its credit quality." Indeed, shortly after the judgment was announced, the value of Exxon stock actually rose. Nevertheless, Exxon was sure to appeal.

Joseph Hazelwood faced four criminal charges in connection with the spill, but he was eventually convicted of only one—a misdemeanor for negligent discharge of oil. Notably, the jury was not convinced that Hazelwood was drunk. In March 1990, he was sentenced to wipe rocks and clean beaches in Prince William Sound for 1,000 hours and to pay $50,000 as a "token restitution." However, he never cleaned any beaches. His appeals of the guilty verdict lasted until 1998, when it was finally upheld. He finished his community service at a soup kitchen in Anchorage in the summer of 2001 and submitted a check for $50,000 to the state of Alaska in May 2002.

Exxon appealed the damage award, arguing that it was excessive and out of keeping with traditional maritime law that limited the liability of ship owners. Moreover, it continued to argue that it was inappropriate to hold the company liable for the actions of the ship's captain. The appeal was denied by Judge Holland in 1997, at which point Exxon appealed to the ninth circuit court of appeals in San Francisco. In 2002, the ninth circuit court remanded the case back to Judge Holland with instructions to reconsider the size of the award. Judge Holland subsequently reduced the award to $4 billion, but Exxon appealed to the ninth circuit again. Once again, the ninth circuit remanded the case back to Judge Holland with instructions to reconsider the size of the award. In 2004, Judge Holland *raised* the award to $4.5 billion. On third appeal in 2006, the ninth circuit reduced the punitive damage award to $2.5 billion. Exxon then petitioned the U.S. Supreme Court to consider the constitutionality of the punitive damages. The Supreme Court accepted the case, and oral arguments were heard in February 2008. In June 2008, the Supreme Court reduced the damages to $507.5 million, arguing that punitive damages should not exceed compensatory claims as a matter of principle. (See *"Exxon Shipping Company v. Baker,* 2008," on page 310 in the Primary Sources section.) Fourteen years after the original civil case and nearly two decades after the disaster the case against Exxon for the *Exxon Valdez* oil spill in Prince William Sound was finally concluded. Damages could finally be paid, although nearly 20 percent of the original plaintiffs were no longer living.

In 2009, the Exxon Valdez Oil Spill Trustee Council, the organization created to oversee the restoration of Prince William Sound with monies from the 1991 settlement, issued a 20-year annual update and retrospective report revisiting the disaster and reporting on the progress made since then. Of 28 affected species, the trustees reported that at least seven species of wildlife had met recovery objectives, including bald eagles, harbor seals, river otters, pink and sockeye salmon, and several species of seabirds, such as loons, murres, and cormorants. Others species were still recovering, including killer whales, sea otters, clams, mussels, and harlequin ducks. Pacific herring still showed little or no recovery since the spill, and the status of many other species was simply unknown. Although the sound would eventually recover, the length of time involved was unknown. Nearly two decades after the spill, oil could still be found a few inches beneath the rocky soil on shores throughout the sound.

Until 2010, the *Exxon Valdez* oil spill remained the largest oil spill in U.S. waters—an infamous and unbroken record in American environmental history. On April 20, 2010, this record was shattered when the *Deepwater Horizon,* an oil-drilling rig 50 miles off the coast of Louisiana, exploded and sank. Eleven men were killed, and the underwater well was broken, releasing an uncontrollable and unprecedented volume of oil into the Gulf of Mexico—up to 2.5 million gallons of crude oil per day. This was nearly equivalent to the *Exxon Valdez* spill every

In the aftermath of the *Exxon Valdez* oil spill off the coast of Alaska, Exxon hired thousands of workers to clean oil residue off local beaches. (Michio Hoshino/ Getty Images)

four days. When the well was finally capped in July 2010, an estimated 210 million gallons of oil had been spilled. Once again, a catastrophic oil spill has shone a spotlight on the inadequacies of the oil production system and the consequences of the nation's petroleum dependency.

WHAT IF?

What if the oil spill had had been caused by a smaller shipping company, one without the vast resources of the Exxon Corporation?

If the oil spill in Prince William Sound had been caused by a small shipping company, rather than the multinational Exxon Corporation, it is likely that fewer resources would have been mobilized and the response would have been slower. Under agreements made in the late 1970s, the state of Alaska and the federal government expected the Alyeska Pipeline Service Company—the consortium of oil companies that own and operate TAPS—to take charge of oil spill containment and cleanup.

Alyeska, however, was woefully unprepared to respond quickly or adequately to a major oil spill at sea. It lacked both personnel and equipment and was unable to mobilize resources quickly. Neither the state of Alaska nor federal officials had the ability to mobilize resources quickly. Without a preapproved plan and resources in place, government procedures for procuring equipment or personnel are notoriously slow relative to private industry. However, it is likely that many of the same problems would have plagued any response, resulting in a rapidly spreading oil slick throughout the sound and onto its shores. Neither private industry nor the government had adequate resources to control an oil spill of this magnitude, forcing most efforts to focus on saving a few important areas, such as the salmon hatcheries. Moreover, many communities throughout the sound would, once again, have been left to fend for themselves. Without the involvement of Exxon or a similarly large and resource-rich company, however, it is likely that federal officials—the coast guard in particular—would have been compelled to assume control of the oil spill response.

Although the coast guard did not have the resources of Exxon, it is possible that its response may have been more efficient and possibly even more effective. In later examinations of the accident and its aftermath, the Alaska Oil Spill Commission identified conflict and confusion over command between government officials and Exxon as one of several key organizational issues that hindered a more effective response. Exxon's greatest contribution to the oil spill response was in the massive deployment of equipment and personnel to clean oil from beaches and in payments made for civil and criminal fines, as well as compensation.

CHRONOLOGY

1968 *March 13:* Atlantic Richfield Company (ARCO) and Humble Oil and Refining Company (later Exxon Company, U.S.A.) announce Prudhoe Bay discovery well.

1969 *February 10:* Atlantic Pipe Line, Humble Pipe Line, and BP Pipe Line Corporation announce plans to build an 800-mile trans-Alaska pipeline.

1970 *January:* President Nixon signs the National Environmental Protection Act into law.

April: Environmental groups sue to block Alaska pipeline construction.

1972 *January:* Court of appeals upholds injunction against permitting the Trans-Alaska Pipeline System (TAPS) until a proper environmental impact statement is filed.

1973 *October 20:* OPEC cuts oil production and announces embargo against the United States and other western countries for supporting Israel.

November 16: President Richard Nixon signs into law the Trans-Alaska Pipeline Authorization Act, canceling environmental legal challenges and clearing way for construction.

1974 *March:* Construction of TAPS begins.

1977 *May 31:* Construction of TAPS is completed.

June 20: Oil begins to flow in TAPS.

August 1: First tanker carrying North Slope crude oil *(ARCO Juneau)* leaves the Valdez terminal.

1989 *March 24:* Supertanker *Exxon Valdez* runs aground on Bligh Reef and spills 10.8 million gallons of crude oil into Prince William Sound.

1990 *June:* President George H. W. Bush suspends offshore drilling rights off the coasts of Oregon, Washington, and most of California, as well as the Florida Keys and the Georges Bank fishing grounds off the New England coast until the year 2000.

August 18: Oil Pollution Act of 1990 is signed into law in response to public concern over *Exxon Valdez* oil spill.

1991 *September 30:* Alaska governor Walter J. Hickel signs a $1 billion agreement settling federal and state claims against Exxon stemming from the *Exxon Valdez* spill.

1992 State of Alaska and the coast guard declare cleanup complete.

1994 *September 16:* Eleven-member jury in federal district court in Anchorage, Alaska, awards $5 billion punitive damages against Exxon.

2001 *November:* Federal appeals court overturns $5 billion punitive damages award.

2006 *December 22:* Panel of the United States Court of Appeals for the Ninth Circuit in San Francisco reduces punitive damages against Exxon Mobil to $2.5 billion.

2008 *June 25:* U.S. Supreme Court reduces $2.5 billion punitive damages award against Exxon Mobil to $507.5 million.

2010   *April 20:* Explosion and fire sinks *Deepwater Horizon* oil drill-
        ing platform 50 miles off the Louisiana coast, killing 11 men and
        releasing more than 200 million gallons of oil into the Gulf of
        Mexico.

DISCUSSION QUESTIONS

1. Who was responsible for the *Exxon Valdez* oil spill? Why?
2. What factors allowed the oil spill to spread so far? Why wasn't it
   contained and cleaned up before it could spread?
3. How did the oil spill affect Prince William Sound? Wildlife?
   Humans?
4. How did government policy affect the disastrous oil spill?
5. Was it fair to assess punitive damages against Exxon? Why or why
   not?
6. Was Captain Joseph Hazelwood's punishment fair? Why or why
   not?

WEB SITES

Alaska Resources Library & Information Service (ARLIS). Exxon Valdez
    FAQs—Expanded. Available online. URL: http://www.arlis.org/news/
    exxon-valdez-faqs/. Accessed March 30, 2011.

Alyeska Pipeline Service Company. About Us. Available online. URL:
    http://www.alyeska-pipe.com/about.html. Accessed March 30, 2011.

Anchorage Daily News. Hard Aground: Disaster in Prince William
    Sound. Available online. URL: http://www.adn.com/evos/. Accessed
    March 30, 2011.

Exxon Valdez Oil Spill Trustee Council. Legacy of an Oil Spill. Avail-
    able online. URL: http://www.evostc.state.ak.us/. Accessed March 30,
    2011.

New York Times. Times Topics: *Exxon Valdez* Oil Spill (1989). Available
    online. URL: http://topics.nytimes.com/top/reference/timestopics/
    subjects/e/exxon_valdez_oil_spill_1989/ind ex.html. Accessed March
    30, 2011.

NOAA. Office of Response and Restoration. NOAA's National Ocean
    Service. *Exxon Valdez* Oil Spill. Available online. URL: http://

response.restoration.noaa.gov/topic_subtopic_entry.php?RECORD_
KEY%28entry_subtopic_topic%29=entry_id,subtopic_id,topic_id&
entry_id%28entry_subtopic_topic%29=700&subtopic_id%28entry_
subtopic_topic%29=2&topic_id%28entry_subtopic_topic%29=1.
Accessed March 30, 2011.

Prince William Sound Regional Citizens' Advisory Council. Citizen
Oversight. Available online. URL: http://pwsrcac.info/citizen-over-
sight/. Accessed March 30, 2011.

BIBLIOGRAPHY

Alaska Oil Spill Commission. Final Report. "SPILL: The Wreck of the
Exxon Valdez." (February 1990). Available online. URL: http://www.
arlis.org/docs/vol1/B/33339870.pdf.

Coates, Peter A. *The Trans-Alaska Pipeline Controversy: Technology,
Conservation, and the Frontier.* Cranbury, N.J.: Associated University
Press, 1991.

Cooper, Mary H. "Oil Spills: Increasing U.S. Dependence on Oil Imports
Heightens Risks to Environment." *Congressional Quarterly Researcher*
2, no. 2 (1992).

Davidson, Art. *In the Wake of the EXXON VALDEZ: The Devastating
Impact of the Alaska Oil Spill.* San Francisco: Sierra Club Books, 1990.

Jones, Stan, Sharon Bushell, and Ellen Wheat. *The Spill: Personal Stories from the* EXXON VALDEZ *Disaster.* Kenmore, Wash.: Epicenter
Press, 2009.

Ott, Riki. *Not One Drop: Betrayal and Courage in the Wake of the* Exxon
Valdez *Oil Spill.* White River Junction, Vt.: Chelsea Green Publishing,
2008.

PRIMARY SOURCES

Document 1: Top 65 Oil Spills in the World, 1964–1989

*Below is the listing of the world's largest uncontrolled releases of oil at
the time of the* Exxon Valdez *oil spill. In December 1989, it ranked as the
34th largest oil spill in the world.*

TOP 65 OIL SPILLS, 1964–1989

No.	Date	Spill	Location	Volume × 1,000 barrels
1	Jun 79–Mar 80	Ixtoc I, well blowout	Mexico	3,300–10,200
2	Feb–Dec 83	Norwag Oil Field, well blowout	Persian Gulf	1,900–4,400
3	Aug 6, 83	*Castilo de Bellver*, fire	South Africa	1,200–1,900
4	Mar 16, 78	*Amoco Cadiz*, grounding	France	1,600–1,800
5	Jul 19, 79	*Aegean Captain/ Atlantic Empress*	Off Tobago	1,162
6	Aug 80–Jan81	D-103 Libya, well blowout	Libya	1,000
7	Aug 2, 79	*Atlantic V Empress*, fire	Barbados	988
8	Mar 18, 87	*Torrey Canyon*, grounding	England	850–920
9	Feb 23, 80	*Irene's Serenade*, fire	Greece	292–871
10	Dec 19, 72	*Sea Star*, collision, fire	Gulf of Oman	840
11	Aug 20, 81	Kuwait Nat. Petrol. Tank	Gulf of Oman	743
12	May 12, 78	*Urquiola*, grounding	Spain	642–730
13	Mar 20, 70	*Othello*, collision	Sweden	438–730
14	Feb 25, 77	*Hawaiian Patriot*, fire	N. Pacific	723
15	Nov 15, 79	*Independence*	Turkey	688
16	May 25, 78	No. 128, wellpipe	Iran	667
17	Jan 29, 75	*Jakob Maersk*	Portugal	595
18	Jul 6, 85	BP storage tank	Nigeria	569
19	Aug–Oct 85	*The Nova*, Kgarg Island	Iran	510
20	Dec 11, 78	BP, Shell fuel depot	Zimbabwe	478
21	Feb 27, 71	*Wafra*	South Africa	467
22	Aug 9, 74	*Metula*, Strait of Magellan	Chile	380
23	Jan 7, 83	*Assimi*, fire	Off Oman	376

(continues)

TOP 65 OIL SPILLS, 1964–1989 *(continued)*

No.	Date	Spill	Location	Volume × 1,000 barrels
24	May 5, 70	*Polycommander*	Spain	73–365
25	Jun 12, 78	Tohoku storage tanks, earthquake	Japan	357
26	Dec 31, 78	*Andros Patria*	Spain	348
27	Dec 10, 83	*Peracles GC*	Qatar	333
28	Nov 6, 85	Ranger, TX, well blowout	Texas	150–326
29	Jun 13, 68	*World Glory*, hull failure	South Africa	322
30	Jun 1, 70	*Ennerdale*, struck granite	Seychelles	299
31	Dec 18, 74	Mizushima Refinery, oil tank rupture	Japan	270
32	Jun 14, 73	*Napier*	SE Pacific	263
33	Dec 29, 80	*Juan A Lavelleja*	Algeria	262
34	Mar 24, 89	*Exxon Valdez*, grounding	Alaska	256
35	Oct 19, 78	Turkish Petroleum Corp.	Turkey	255
36	Nov 1, 79	*Burmah Agate*, collision, fire	Texas	31–255
37	Mar 27, 71	*Texaco Oklahoma*, 120 mi offshore	North Carolina	220–255
38	Jun 11, 72	*Trader*	Mediterranean	248
39	Feb 4, 76	*St. Peter*	SE Pacific	248
40	Jan 18, 77	*Irene's Challenge*	Pacific	248
41	Jan 28, 72	*Golden Drake*	NW Atlantic	226
42	Dec 28, 70	*Chryssi*	NW Atlantic	226
43	Nov 25, 69	*Pacocean*, broke in two	NW Pacific	219
44	May 27, 77	*Caribbean*	E Pacific	219
45	Dec 30, 76	*Grand Zenith*, disappearance	NW Atlantic	212
46	Jul 28, 76	*Cretan Star*	Indian Ocean	212

TOP 65 OIL SPILLS, 1964–1989 *(continued)*

No.	Date	Spill	Location	Volume × 1,000 barrels
47	Nov 5, 69	*KEO*, hull failure	Massachusetts	210
48	Nov 4, 69	Storage tank	New Jersey	200
49	Apr 22, 77	Exolink Bravo, well blowout	North Sea	110–195
50	Apr 1, 72	*Giuseppi Giuletti*	NE Atlantic	190
51	Dec 16, 77	*Vempet Venol*, collision	South Africa	175–190
52	Dec 15, 76	*Argo Merchant*, grounding	Massachusetts	183
53	Oct 15, 67	Humble Oil pipeline, offshore leak	Louisiana	150
54	Dec 21, 73	*JAWACTA*	Baltic Sea	146
55	Sep 6, 67	*R.C. Stoner*	Wake Island	143
56	Nov, 70	*Marlena*	Sicily	102
57	Apr 20, 70	Pipeline, NW shore Taru Bay	Saudi Arabia	100
58	Dec 2, 71	Oil well, 80 mi SW	Persian Gulf	100
59	Mar 7, 80	*TANIO*, broke amidship	France	99
60	Jan 2, 86	Ashland storage tank, rupture	Pennsylvania	90
61	Jan–Oct, 69	Santa Barbara Channel, well blowout	California	33–80
62	Feb 4, 70	*Arrow*, grounding	Nova Scotia	36–73
63	Nov 13, 70	Storage tank, Schuylkill River	Pennsylvania	71
64	Jul 30, 64	*Alvenus*, grounding	Louisiana	67
65	Mar 10, 70	Offshore platform, well blowout	Louisiana	65

Conversion Factors—7.3 barrels/ton; 42 gallons/barrel

Source: *Alaska Oil Spill Commission Final Report. Spill: The Wreck of the* Exxon Valdez. *Implications for Safe Transportation of Oil.* (February 1990).

Document 2: Foreword to the Alaska Oil Spill Commission Report, 1990

In February 1990, the Alaska Oil Spill Commission released its report, which recounted the Exxon Valdez *disaster and the individual and systemic factors that led to the accident and the inadequate response.*

This was the threatened tanker catastrophe residents of Prince William Sound had dreaded—but many had come to discount. . . . The system that carried 25 percent of America's domestic oil production had failed. So had the regulatory apparatus intended to make it safe. The promises that led Alaska to grant its right-of-way and Congress to approve the Alaska pipeline in June 1973 had been betrayed. The safeguards that were set in place in the 1970s had been allowed to slide. The vigilance over tanker traffic that was established in the early days of pipeline flow had given way to complacency and neglect. . . .

This disaster could have been prevented—not by tanker captains and crews who are, in the end, only fallible human beings, but by an advanced oil transportation system designed to minimize human error. It could have been prevented if Alaskans, state and federal governments, the oil industry and the American public had insisted on stringent safeguards. It could have been prevented if the vigilance that accompanied construction of the pipeline in the 1970s had been continued in the 1980s. . . .

This disaster could have been prevented by simple adherence to the original rules. Human beings do make errors. The precautions originally in place took cognizance of human frailty and built safeguards into the system to account for it. This state-led oversight and regulatory system worked for the first two years, until the state was preempted from enforcing the rules by legal action brought by the oil industry. After that, the shippers simply stopped following the rules, and the Coast Guard stopped enforcing them. . . .

The world's oil shipping companies, to the great benefit of consumers and corporate shareholders, have created a megasystem that carries oil from wellheads in the far corners of the earth to refineries in its major industrial centers. But this megasystem is fragile. It requires careful scrutiny from outside the industry in design, construction and operation. When it fails, as it has in tanker disasters around the world, entire coastlines are at risk. . . .

This is a huge risk, yet Alaskans assume such peril daily as super-tankers carry 2 million barrels of North Slope crude through Prince William Sound and out into the Gulf of Alaska. Other Americans on three coasts face just as ominous a threat as the world tanker fleet delivers 52 percent of U.S. oil consumption from foreign sources.

What will reduce these risks? Obviously, the present system, providing minimum penalties for creating massive environmental damage, has not deterred the industry from putting the coasts and oceans of the world at continual risk. The system calls out for reform.

Source: Alaska Oil Spill Commission Final Report. Spill: The Wreck of the Exxon Valdez. *Implications for Safe Transportation of Oil.* (February 1990).

—꿈—

Document 3: An Address by Walter Meganack, Sr., 1989

In June 1989, mayors representing coastal communities affected by two of the worst oil spills—the Amoco Cadiz *in 1978 and the* Exxon Valdez—*convened a conference in Valdez, Alaska, to discuss their common experiences and lessons learned. This excerpt is from a written speech submitted by Walter Meganack, Sr., village chief of Port Graham, Alaska.*

The Native story is different from the white man's story of oil devastation. It is different, because our lives are different, what we value is different; how we see the water and land, the plants and the animals, is different. What white men do for sport and recreation and money, we do for life: For the life of our bodies, for the life of our spirits, and for the life of our ancient culture. Fishing and hunting and gathering are the rythms [sic] of our tradition; regular daily lives, not vacation times, not employment times. . . .

The land and the water are our sources of life. The water is sacred. The water is like a baptismal font, and its abundance is the holy communion of our lives.

Of all the things that we have lost since non-Natives came to our land, we have never lost our connection with the water. The water is our source of life. So long as the water is alive, the Chugach Natives are alive. . . .

And then we heard the news: Oil in the water. Lots of oil. Killing lots of water. It is too shocking to understand. Never in the millennium of our tradition have we thought it possible for the water to die. But it is true.

We walk our beaches. But the snails and the barnacles and the chitons are falling off the rocks. Dead. Dead water. We caught our first fish, the annual first fish, the traditional delight of all—but it got sent to the state to be tested for oil. No first fish this year. We walk our beaches. But instead of gathering life, we gather death. Dead birds. Dead otters. Dead seaweed. . . .

The oil companies lied about preventing a spill. Now they lie about cleanup. Our people know what happens on the beaches. Spend all day cleaning one huge rock, and the tide comes in and covers it with oil again. Spend a week wiping and spraying the surface, but pick up a rock and there's four inches of oil underneath. Our people know the water and the beaches. But they get told what to do by ignorant people who should be asking, not telling. . . .

Will it end? After five years, maybe we will see some springtime water life again. But will the water and the beaches see us? What will happen to our lives in the next five years? What will happen this fall when the cleanup stops and the money stops? . . . A wise white man once said, "Where there is life, there is hope." And that is true.

But what we see now is death. Death—not of each other, but of the source of life, the water. We will need much help, much listening in order to live through the long barren season of dead water, a longer winter than ever before.

Source: Walter Meganack, Sr. Proceedings of the International Conference of "Oiled Mayors." Valdez, Alaska. (June 26–27, 1989). Available online. URL: http://www.pwsrcac.org/docs/pwsrcacinfo/003.OiledMayorsConf.pdf.

—⁓—

Document 4: An Interview with Joe Hazelwood, 2007–2008

The man at the center of the Exxon Valdez *oil spill, Captain Joseph Hazelwood, lost his job and endured 13 years in the Alaskan criminal courts. Below is an excerpt from an interview he conducted between 2007 and 2008 recounting his experience.*

The true story is out there for anybody who wants to look at the facts, but that's not the sexy story and that's not the easy story. People want to hear the news when they want it, and they don't want to delve into any complicated thought processes. They'll settle for quick sound bites. That's what happened, and we'll leave it at that. . . .

Occasionally people have called me a scapegoat, but I've never felt comfortable with that term when applied to me in regard to the oil spill. I was the captain of a ship that ran aground and caused a horrendous amount of damage. I've got to be responsible for that. There's no way around it. Some of the things that came later, the efforts at cleaning up, were really beyond my purview, but it still goes back to that: if my ship hadn't run aground and spilled part of its cargo, the event never would have happened.

I can't escape that responsibility, nor do I want to. I would like to offer an apology, a very heartfelt apology, to the people of Alaska for the damage caused by the grounding of a ship that I was in command of.

Source: "Joe Hazelwood: Captain of the Exxon Valdez" in *The Spill: Personal Stories from the* EXXON VALDEZ *Disaster* by Stan Jones, Sharon Bushell, and Ellen Wheat. Kenmore, Wash.: Epicenter Press, 2009.

—◊◊◊—

Document 5: "An Open Letter to the Public," 1989

In the first few weeks after the spill, Exxon published full-page ads in major newspapers throughout the country to assure the public that it was doing everything it could. Below is one ad published in the New York Times *on April 3, 1989.*

AN OPEN LETTER TO THE PUBLIC

On March 24, in the early morning hours, a disastrous accident happened in the waters of Prince William Sound, Alaska. By now you all know that our tanker, the *Exxon Valdez,* hit a submerged reef and lost 240,000 barrels of oil into the waters of the Sound.

We believe that Exxon has moved swiftly and competently to minimize the effect this oil will have on the environment, fish and other wildlife. Further, I hope that you know we have already committed several hundred people to work on the cleanup. We also will meet our obligations to all those who have suffered damage from the spill.

Finally, and most importantly, I want to tell you how sorry I am that this accident took place. We at Exxon are especially sympathetic to the residents of Valdez and the people of the State of Alaska. We cannot, of course, undo what has been done. But I can assure you that since March 24, the accident has been receiving our full attention and will continue to do so.

L. G. Rawl

Chairman

Source: "An Open Letter to the Public." Lawrence G. Rawl, chairman of the Exxon Corporation. *New York Times* (3 April 1989).

—ᴍ—

Document 6: *Exxon Shipping Company v. Baker,* 2008

The U.S. Supreme Court took up several questions about the Exxon Valdez *case, including whether or not Exxon could be held liable for the actions of its ship's captain. In their opinion issued on June 25, 2008, the justices were tied on the latter question, but a majority agreed that the punitive damages should be reduced, based largely on historical precedent and the idea that damages should be predictable.*

3. The punitive damages award against Exxon was excessive as a matter of maritime common law. In the circumstances of this case, the award should be limited to an amount equal to compensatory damages. . . .

(a) Although legal codes from ancient times through the Middle Ages called for multiple damages for certain especially harmful acts, modern Anglo-American punitive damages have their roots in 18th-century English law and became widely accepted in American courts by the mid-19th century. . . .

(b) The prevailing American rule limits punitive damages to cases of "enormity," . . . in which a defendant's conduct is outrageous, owing to gross negligence, willful, wanton, and reckless indifference for others' rights, or even more deplorable behavior. The consensus today is that punitive damages are aimed at retribution and deterring harmful conduct. . . .

(d) American punitive damages have come under criticism in recent decades, but the most recent studies tend to undercut much of it. Although some studies show the dollar amounts of awards growing over time, even in real terms, most accounts show that the median ratio of punitive to compensatory awards remains less than 1:1. . . . The real problem is the stark unpredictability of punitive awards. Courts are concerned with fairness as consistency, and the available data suggest that the spread between high and low individual awards is unacceptable. . . .

In this context, the unpredictability of high punitive awards is in tension with their punitive function because of the implication of unfairness that an eccentrically high punitive verdict carries. A penalty should be reasonably predictable in its severity, . . . And a penalty scheme ought to threaten defendants with a fair probability of suffering in like degree for like damage. . . .

(f) (iii) The more promising alternative is to peg punitive awards to compensatory damages using a ratio or maximum multiple. . . . The question is what ratio is most appropriate. An acceptable standard can be found in the studies showing the median ratio of punitive to compensatory awards. Those studies reflect the judgments of juries and judges in thousands of cases as to what punitive awards were appropriate in circumstances reflecting the most down to the least blameworthy conduct, from malice and avarice to recklessness to gross negligence. . . . In a well-functioning system, awards at or below the median would roughly express jurors' sense of reasonable penalties in cases like this one that have no earmarks of exceptional blameworthiness. Accordingly, the Court finds that a 1:1 ratio is a fair upper limit in such maritime cases. . . .

(iv) Applying this standard to the present case, the Court takes for granted the District Court's calculation of the total relevant compensatory damages at $507.5 million. A punitive-to-compensatory ratio of 1:1 thus yields maximum punitive damages in that amount. . . .

Source: Exxon Shipping Company v. Baker, 554 U.S. 471 (2008).

9

KYOTO PROTOCOL:

Should the United States Have Ratified the Kyoto Protocol on Climate Change?

—ᴍ—

THE CONTROVERSY ————————————————————————

The Issue

In December 1997, representatives of the world's governments gave tentative approval to the Kyoto Protocol, an ambitious international treaty to slow or halt global emissions of greenhouse gases. Scientists from around the world warned that the Earth's atmosphere was warming and that this warming was likely due to emissions of greenhouse gases, especially carbon dioxide—a basic by-product of burning of fossil fuels such as coal, oil, and natural gas. According to leading scientists, the increasing atmospheric concentrations of greenhouse gases and the resulting warming were unprecedented in human history and risked disruptive if not catastrophic changes to the global environment. The Kyoto Protocol would require significant and possibly expensive changes to society, though uncertainties still remained. Moreover, the treaty committed industrialized nations, such as the United States, to lead the world in making these changes. U.S. officials faced a contentious question: Should the United States ratify the Kyoto Protocol?

- ◆ **Arguments in favor of the Kyoto Protocol:** Supporters argued that the science was clear and action was needed now. The global nature of the problem required a global solution, and the Kyoto Protocol was an important first step. Moreover, changes made today would be less expensive and disruptive than changes made later. Finally, supporters argued that it was up to the wealthier, industrialized nations of the world, which were responsible for the greatest proportion of emissions, to lead by example.
- ◆ **Arguments against the Kyoto Protocol:** Opponents questioned the credibility of the science, accusing supporters of exaggeration. They argued that there were still too many uncertainties about the human contribution or the impacts to justify such drastic societal changes. The changes might even be beneficial. Critics argued that the Kyoto Protocol

threatened the U.S. economy and that it was unfair and counterproductive to exempt less developed countries from also having to restrict their greenhouse gas emissions.

—〰—

INTRODUCTION

In December 1997, representatives from more than 160 nations around the world met in Kyoto, Japan, in an attempt to come to an agreement on controlling emissions of greenhouse gases that scientists had concluded were contributing to a warming of the global climate. According to a variety of scientific evidence, humans were increasing the concentration of greenhouse gases in the Earth's atmosphere, which trapped more and more heat in the atmosphere, increasing the global average temperature. Unless these emissions were brought under control, the rising temperature threatened both society and the natural environment with catastrophic changes.

This was the largest environmental threat the world had ever faced and would require coordinated global action to control. However, the risks and costs of action were also high. Controlling human emissions of greenhouse gases meant altering the way the world used and produced energy—the foundation of modern society. Not everyone was convinced that such momentous action was warranted, and there was considerable resistance from both governments and various sectors of society to any action that might impose significant costs. Nevertheless, delegates at the Kyoto conference worked to develop an international treaty that would commit the nations of the world to reduce their greenhouse gas emissions with binding targets and a strict time line for action.

The tentative agreement that emerged was dubbed the Kyoto Protocol and represented the world's first attempt at a binding global agreement to address global warming. If ratified, the international treaty would commit the wealthier, industrialized nations of the world to reduce their greenhouse gas emissions by 5 percent below 1990 levels by 2012. Developing countries were exempted from the requirements in order to give them time to develop their economies and meet more basic social needs. Though a modest first step, and not nearly enough to arrest global warming, the targets nevertheless represented a politically significant and daunting goal.

For all practical purposes, reducing greenhouse emissions would mean using less energy from fossil fuels—coal, oil, and natural gas—the lifeblood of the modern, technological society. However, in order to make the agreement more acceptable, signatories to the Kyoto Protocol could meet their obligations in a variety of ways other than actually reducing their emissions, an important and contentious compromise. By sponsoring projects in developing countries, reducing deforestation, or trading for emissions credits, signatories to the treaty could claim credits to meet their promised targets. For all its imperfections, the Kyoto Protocol was a momentous achievement. However, its implementation was far from assured, even among the countries that played such a large role in its development, especially the United States.

As the single largest emitter of greenhouse gases in the world and the world's most influential political and economic force, the U.S. position on the Kyoto Protocol was considered central to the treaty's realization. However, the issue of global warming was a highly contentious one within the country and among policy makers. While President Bill Clinton's representatives were instrumental in drafting the Kyoto Protocol, the U.S. Senate declared in no uncertain terms that it would not ratify a treaty with binding limits on U.S. emissions, especially if it did not also require commitments by developing nations such as China and India. The split between the president and the Senate was illustrative of a persistent debate about global warming itself and the proposed policy responses.

Advocates of the Kyoto Protocol argued that the scientific evidence was clear. Without quick and decisive action, the world was headed for an unprecedented environmental and social catastrophe. Since the 1960s, scientists had built up increasingly precise and sophisticated analyses of human impacts on the atmosphere. Multiple forms of evidence showed that humans had dramatically increased the concentration of greenhouse gases in the atmosphere, especially carbon dioxide, and this increased concentration was clearly correlated with an unnatural rise in global average temperatures. Since 1990, an international panel of the world's most prestigious scientists had repeatedly affirmed these discoveries, and it predicted disastrous consequences if actions to significantly reduce global emissions were not taken soon. Supporters argued that the Kyoto Protocol was an important first step in the global effort to respond to the impending crisis, and they defended the structure of the agreement. They argued that it was up to the world's industrialized, developed nations to lead the way. These countries, especially Europe and the United States, were responsible for the vast bulk of the emissions that had accumulated in the atmosphere over the last two centuries, and these countries were most economically and technologically equipped to make the necessary changes. However, there were also advantages to early action. The effort to reduce greenhouse gas emissions would have numerous other environmental benefits, and the technological demands would spur entirely new and innovative industries that would benefit the world's economies.

The scientific evidence for global warming was central to debates about the nature of the threat and the courses of action that should be taken. However, the science itself was not the sole basis on which decisions could be made, since the science around such an incredibly complex phenomenon was inherently probabilistic and uncertain. Moreover, there were other values at issue, including competing social and economic costs and questions of trust and sovereignty.

Many critics of the protocol were fundamentally skeptical about the claims that humans were principally responsible for a warming of the climate or that climate change was happening or, even if it was, that it was necessarily a bad thing. Skeptics of global warming repeatedly questioned the veracity of the science, accusing the scientists behind the claims of exaggeration, unsupported statements riddled with uncertainty, and even bias. Indeed, the uncertainty of the science of climate change was a constant theme for those unconvinced about the nature of the problem or hostile to the proposed solution. Critics argued that the costs of the Kyoto Protocol were much more certain. Opponents argued that the treaty threatened American sovereignty by giving the international community control over America's economic activity. Equally important, they argued that the costs of compliance would be devastating to the U.S. economy, raising energy prices and forcing many businesses to close or relocate to countries with less stringent requirements. Indeed, the latter point was especially worrisome because the treaty exempted rapidly developing countries, which critics complained was unfair and would eventually put the United States at a competitive disadvantage.

In order to become official, the Kyoto Protocol had to be ratified by developed countries representing at least 55 percent of global greenhouse gas emissions. The eyes of the world rested on the United States, and policy makers faced a contentious question: Should the United States ratify the Kyoto Protocol?

BACKGROUND

Scientists had long speculated that it might be possible for human activity to alter the chemistry of the atmosphere. As early as 1896, the Swedish scientist Svante Arrhenius proposed that the tremendous amount of carbon dioxide gas released into the atmosphere from the burning of coal might someday lead to a warmer climate. Few took the idea seriously. Although scientists understood that the atmosphere was instrumental in keeping the Earth warm and that carbon dioxide was one of those gases that could retain heat, there were simply too many unknowns about how the atmosphere or the climate worked. At the same time, the idea that humans could alter so vast a thing as the global atmosphere hardly seemed possible. The idea was revived periodically in subsequent decades, but it was not until the late 20th century that scientific understanding and technology could begin to address such a complex question or that popular attitudes could even consider such a possibility.

The concern that humans might be inadvertently changing the atmosphere and the global climate system first emerged as a serious concern in the United States in the 1970s. This was a period of heightened concern about environmental degradation, and there was already ample evidence that humans were having global environmental impacts. In the early 1970s, researchers identified acid rain as a serious threat to forests and water bodies in states in the Northeast. (See the sidebar "Acid Rain and Emissions Trading" on page 318.) The problem was traced to sulfurous emissions from power plants far away in the Midwest, which were carried hundreds of miles east by high-altitude winds. Europe had been battling a similar problem since the 1960s. Emissions from industry and power plants in England and Germany blew east and north, combined with precipitation, and decimated forests in Norway and Sweden.

In 1974, scientists discovered that emissions of chlorofluorocarbons (CFCs), a common class of chemicals used in refrigeration and aerosol cans, were destroying stratospheric ozone, a thin layer of gas high in the atmosphere that protected life on Earth from the Sun's harmful radiation. This discovery would eventually lead to the first global environmental pollution control treaty, though that was more than a decade away. Scientists noted at the time that CFCs were also powerful greenhouse gases, with the potential to affect the retention of heat in the atmosphere. However, it was carbon dioxide that emerged as the more important consideration for global atmospheric warming because it was emitted in such vast quantities.

Since 1960, researchers had documented a clear and consistent rise in the global atmospheric concentration of carbon dioxide, and there was little doubt that human activity was responsible. Carbon dioxide is emitted naturally by plants and animals, but it is also emitted in large quantities from the burning of wood and fossil fuels, such as coal and oil. However, human activity was also responsible for many other forms of atmospheric pollution, some of which was suspected of having a cooling effect on the climate. It was not clear if the net influence of humans on the climate was toward warming or cooling. In 1976, Congress held dedicated hearings on the possibility of climate change as a result of atmospheric pollution, prompting more intensive studies. By the late 1970s, the balance of research, both domestic and international, leaned toward warming of the atmosphere. In the early 1980s, a series of U.S. government studies reaffirmed research pointing toward global warming as a result of increased concentration of greenhouse gases. Researchers projected that only a few degrees of warming—averaged across the entire planet—could be disruptive: a rise in sea levels from the melting of the polar ice caps and glaciers could inundate coastal cities; changes in precipitation could exacerbate both drought and flooding; and changes in growing seasons could affect agriculture and the availability of food. A 1983 report by the Council on Environmental Quality warned that, "the more rapidly the world increases fossil fuel use now, the sooner and more rapidly it must begin its reduction in order to avoid exceeding any given CO2 [carbon dioxide] ceiling."

Action to create policies to deal with the threat of climate change began with the international community. Since the early

(continues on page 320)

ACID RAIN AND EMISSIONS TRADING

Acid rain refers to precipitation that is highly acidic as a result of its mixture with nitric and sulfuric acids, which in turn form in the presence of air pollutants such as sulfur dioxide and nitrogen oxides. These pollutants are emitted into the atmosphere as a result of the burning of fuels such as coal and petroleum. This acidified precipitation—acid rain—can cause damage to forests and water bodies, such as ponds and lakes, by changing the chemistry of water and soil, making them unsuitable for many organisms. In some cases, acid rain may also cause damage to buildings and other structures, eating away at materials made of marble or limestone. By the mid-1800s, observant individuals had begun to notice that forests downwind of industrialized areas showed signs of deterioration. In 1872, the British scientist Robert Angus Smith coined the term *acid rain* to describe the phenomenon. He measured the acidity of precipitation in heavily industrialized centers of England and documented the damage caused to plants and other materials. As the intensity of coal- and petroleum-based industry increased, so did the phenomenon. However, acid rain would not be widely recognized as a problem for another century.

In the United States, acid rain emerged as an environmental issue in the late 1970s after a series of investigations of its effects on northeastern forests. Although the federal government had passed increasingly stringent laws to control air pollution since the late 1960s, the acid rain problem was unique because the environmental damage often occurred far from the source of the pollution. While acid rain was having its worst impacts on the forests and water bodies of the northeastern United States and southeastern Canada, the sulfuric and nitric air pollutants that created the acid rain were traced to large, coal-fired power plants hundreds of miles away in the U.S. Midwest. Utilities in the Ohio Valley were producing electricity by burning enormous quantities of low-grade coal, which contained high concentrations of sulfur impurities, resulting in high emissions of sulfur dioxide—the largest precursor to acid precipitation.

Ironically, the power plants had constructed ever taller smokestacks (some as high as a 1,000 feet) in order to better dilute their air emissions and prevent them from affecting the surrounding area (and largely in response to earlier air pollution regulations). However, this approach merely pushed the pollutants higher into the atmosphere, where they were picked up by the prevailing westerly winds (which blow from west to east) and carried hundreds of miles east. Officials and residents of the Northeast and Canada were alarmed by reports of the damage and frustrated by the fact that the source of the problem was out of their control.

Although understanding about the acid rain problem increased throughout the 1980s, opposition to environmental regulation by the Reagan administration prevented government action. President George H. W. Bush signed into law the Clean Air Act Amendments of 1990. The legislation ushered in new regulations to control a variety of air pollutants and introduced a novel regulatory program to control acid rain. Title IV of the legislation created an emissions trading program (known as the Acid Rain Program) in which utilities were required to purchase permits, or allowances, for each ton of sulfur dioxide or nitrogen oxides emitted. These permits could be purchased directly from the Environmental Protection Agency or traded between utilities. Utilities that found it more cost-effective to reduce their emissions than to buy allowances could trade or sell their allowances to other utilities for which reductions were more expensive. In this way, each facility was allowed to decide how to handle the cost of its pollutant emissions—a radically new approach in pollution regulation.

The goals of the legislation were to create flexibility in the regulation of pollution and to bring the total amount of acid rain–forming pollutants throughout the country down. In order to do the latter, the total number of available emissions permits was capped, and this number would decline each year. As a result, there would be fewer and fewer allowances to emit sulfur dioxide over time, and the total amount of the pollutants emitted would decline. The Acid Rain Program was initiated in phases, beginning in 1995 with the country's largest and dirtiest power plants, and later expanded after 2000 to cover most power plants. Since it began, the total amount of emissions of sulfur dioxide and nitrogen oxides has declined dramatically, more quickly and at a significantly lower cost than anticipated. The Acid Rain Program emissions-trading scheme was hailed as a model for future pollution regulation. Despite reductions in acid rain, affected forests and water bodies in the eastern United States and Canada have shown slow and incremental recovery.

(continued from page 317)

1970s, numerous international scientific conferences had focused on the possibility of climate change and its potential impacts. It was from these conferences that the research on climate change was forcefully brought to the attention of policy makers. In October 1985, the United Nations Environment Programme (UNEP), the World Meteorological Organization (WMO), and the International Council of Scientific Unions sponsored a climate change conference in Villach, Austria, called the International Conference on the Assessment of the Role of Carbon Dioxide and of Other Greenhouse Gases in Climate Variations and Associated Impacts. Delegates to the conference developed a consensus statement calling on government leaders to deal with the threat of climate change. The conferees suggested the development of a framework convention treaty modeled on the one recently developed to deal with the problem of stratospheric ozone depletion. (See the sidebar "A Hole in the Sky: Depletion of Stratospheric Ozone" on page 334.) The climate change conference occurred only a few months after the signing of the Vienna Convention for the Protection of the Ozone Layer, the international agreement that would form the legal foundation for the historic 1987 Montreal Protocol that resulted in a global ban on CFCs. Indeed, the dramatic discovery of a hole in the ozone layer in 1985 and the rapid development of a global treaty with binding limitations on emissions of CFCs would serve as an influential model on how to deal with a global atmospheric threat.

While climate change was increasingly familiar to scientists and those who were environmentally concerned, the issue did not really capture the attention of the American public until summer 1988. On an unusually hot June day, James Hansen, a leading scientist at the U.S. National Aeronautics and Space Administration (NASA) and longtime climate modeler, testified before the U.S. Senate Committee on Energy and Natural Resources that he was 99 percent certain that the Earth was warming and that this warming was due to the increasing concentration of greenhouse gases in the atmosphere. Ominously, he warned that the warming would likely lead to extreme weather events and that impacts would worsen if greenhouse gas emissions continued to grow over time as projected.

Hansen's testimony was front-page news and seemed to be borne out by events. The year 1988 was turning out to be the hottest in over a century of recorded temperatures. Many parts of the world, including the United States, were suffering from crippling droughts, and there was concern about damage to the year's crops. Inland water bodies also seemed to be threatened. The Mississippi River was at its lowest level since record keeping began in 1872. The congressional testimony and resulting media coverage elevated concerns about global warming, but it also stimulated a growing counterresponse from skeptics. Industry groups and politically conservative think tanks in the United States initiated their own campaign to challenge global warming claims and proposals for policy that might entail new and costly regulations on energy consumption and production—the most important source of carbon dioxide emissions. The growing controversy in the United States contrasted with a growing consensus in the international scientific community.

A few days after Hansen's testimony, delegates from around the world convened at the World Conference on the Changing Atmosphere in Toronto, Canada. The conference delegates discussed the most recent research and concluded that immediate and drastic action was needed if damaging climatic changes were to be avoided. They called for a reduction in global emissions of greenhouse gases to 20 percent below 1988 levels by 2005. Before policy action could be considered, however, UN members argued that the science had to be more clearly understood. A few months later in November 1988, UNEP and WMO established the Intergovernmental Panel on Climate Change (IPCC) to assess the complex science of climate change and to synthesize the vast body of available knowledge into more accessible information for policy makers and the global community. Specifically, the IPCC was charged with the tasks of 1) assessing the available scientific information on climate change; 2) assessing the environmental and socioeconomic impacts of climate change; and 3) formulating possible response strategies. The IPCC itself did not do climate research. Rather, it compiled, reviewed, and synthesized the world's available scientific knowledge into carefully worded summary reports whose language was painstakingly reviewed by hundreds of scientists and numerous committees, government representatives, and nongovernmental organizations (NGOs), such as environmental and industry groups.

Activists demonstrate in front of the U.S. Embassy in Brussels, Belgium, on June 12, 2001, to protest against the U.S. stance on the Kyoto Protocol on climate change, ahead of President George W. Bush's visit. (Etienne Ansotte/AFP/Newscom)

The IPCC is a unique organization that relies on the voluntary contributions of time from hundreds of top researchers from around the world. It also includes representatives from every interested country and makes a concerted effort to give members of developing countries equitable representation. The latter effort was important for maintaining legitimacy and the attention of policy makers.

The reports of the IPCC provide the scientific foundation for negotiations on international policies to address climate change. In October 1990, the IPCC released its First Assessment Report to the United Nations General Assembly. The IPCC reported that human activities were rapidly increasing the atmospheric concentrations of carbon dioxide and other greenhouse gases, enhancing the Earth's natural greenhouse effect and leading to a warming of the Earth's surface. The Earth had already warmed by 0.3° to 0.6° Celsius (approximately 0.5° to 1° Fahrenheit) over the last 100 years with the five warmest years—averaged over the globe—all occurring during the 1980s. Sea levels had also risen during this time by 10 to 20 centimeters (approximately four to eight inches). These observations were broadly consistent with the global climate models on which future projections were made, although there were still many uncertainties about the specific nature or timing of impacts, as well as how particular areas of the Earth would be affected.

If current trends continued, the IPCC projected that the increasing concentration of atmospheric greenhouse gases would accelerate the natural greenhouse effect and lead to a general warming of the globe at a rate of about 0.3° C (0.5° F) per decade—a rate of warming not seen on Earth since the end of the last ice age 10,000 years ago. The First Assessment Report acknowledged that natural climatic variability could not be ruled out as an explanation for the observed warming—this would require more observations and more time to disentangle. However, the evidence and analyses pointed increasingly toward human emissions as the important cause. More important, the longer the delay in action today, the more difficult the necessary reductions in the future would be as the gases accumulated. The worst impacts would be delayed for decades or even centuries. The First Assessment Report prompted the UN to initiate negotiations on an international policy to address climate change. The basic framework for an international treaty on climate change would be brought forth at a UN conference on the environment.

United Nations Framework Convention on Climate Change

In June 1992, the United Nations convened a Conference on Environment and Development (UNCED) in Rio de Janeiro, Brazil, that is informally known as the Earth Summit. The Rio conference was convened with the specific purpose of addressing global environmental problems and related issues of economic and social development. More than 170 countries were represented, as well as the media and more than 2,400 nongovernmental organizations—nearly 17,000 attendees in all. Although the conference was to address numerous global environmental issues—from biological diversity to deforestation to whaling—climate change was near the top of the list.

For most delegates, the IPCC's First Assessment Report represented the single most important and trustworthy source of information on scientific questions about global warming. Most delegates were ready to discuss actions to prevent global warming, which meant reducing anthropogenic—human-caused—emissions of greenhouse gases. However, the U.S. position was of unique importance. As the largest political and economic force in the world and as the single largest emitter of greenhouse gases (estimated at one-quarter of global emissions, though it represented only 5 percent of the world's population), U.S. cooperation was crucial for the success of an international agreement. Many delegates were ready to negotiate mandatory limits on greenhouse gases, but the U.S. delegation was not. President George H. W. Bush had demonstrated interest in combating environmental problems, but he was not prepared to accept binding limits that would hinder economic growth or put the United States at an economic disadvantage relative to other countries. The Bush administration was lobbied heavily by a consortium of industries that opposed policies that might increase environmental regulations or impose new costs on energy production or consumption. Industry representatives realized that any attempt to regulate or reduce greenhouse gas emissions would have costly consequences for businesses directly involved in the exploitation of fossil fuels and energy. The United States was severely criticized by its allies, especially European countries, for its opposition to binding limits but held fast.

A compromise agreement was developed that called for voluntary reductions in greenhouse gas emissions—the United Nations Framework Convention on Climate Change (UNFCCC). (See "Excerpt from the United Nations Framework Convention on Climate Change, 1992," on page 344 in the Primary Sources section.) UNFCCC was an international treaty that called on countries to halt the further buildup of greenhouse gases in order to prevent catastrophic global warming. Article 2 of the UNFCCC stated that the ultimate objective of the treaty was "stabilization of greenhouse gas concentrations in the atmosphere at a level that would prevent dangerous anthropogenic interference with the climate system." The UNFCCC made it clear that because the industrialized countries of the world produced most of the greenhouse gases, they should take the lead in reducing greenhouse gas emissions. The goal was to reduce emissions back to 1990 levels by the year 2000. However, compliance was entirely voluntary, and there were no specifics on how countries should achieve that goal. Nevertheless, the UNFCCC established a system to monitor progress and share information. In addition, the UNFCCC allowed for modification of the terms of the treaty as science improved and new information became available. The signatories, or parties, would meet each year in Conferences of the Parties to review progress and build on UNFCCC. More than 150 countries signed the convention, including the United States, and it was ratified by the U.S. Senate a few months later. The UNFCCC officially went into force two years later in 1994.

By the mid-1990s, it was apparent to most that the vague and voluntary approach of the UNFCCC was not adequate. Global emissions continued to grow with no sign of abating. At the first UNFCCC Conference of the Parties in Berlin, Germany, in March 1995, the delegates agreed that progress to control emissions would require a more aggressive approach, and they made plans to amend the treaty. In December 1995, the IPCC released its Second Assessment Report, which stated that the atmospheric concentrations of greenhouse gases—carbon dioxide, methane, and nitrous oxides—were nearly 30 percent higher than they had been in preindustrial times (before 1750 A.D.). The increased concentration was attributed mostly to fossil fuel use, land use change, and agriculture.

Earlier estimates of global warming were reinforced, and numerous observations of how the global climate had already changed during the past century were more apparent: warmest temperatures since recordings going back to 1860; rising sea levels; warmer nights; increases in precipitation over high northern latitudes.

More important, the report declared that "the balance of evidence . . . suggests a discernible human influence on global climate." Indeed, considerable progress had been made in distinguishing between natural and anthropogenic influences on climate. This point was widely quoted in the media as the definitive link between human activity and global warming and provided added justification for more aggressive policy. At the second Conference of the Parties in Geneva, Switzerland, in July 1996, the delegates adopted a declaration that "the continued rise of greenhouse gas concentrations in the atmosphere will lead to dangerous interference with the climate system."

There was broad agreement among the delegates that effective control of greenhouse gas emissions would require clear and legally binding targets. Preparations were begun to negotiate such an amendment, or protocol, at the next Conference of the Parties in Kyoto, Japan. While there was growing movement in the international community to address the threat of climate change, the issue grew more controversial within the United States. Since the late 1980s, new industry-funded organizations and politically conservative think tanks had launched their own campaigns to raise doubts about global warming and to slow or stop the push for new policies to control greenhouse gas emissions. With the aid of a few outspoken scientists, these groups highlighted the uncertainties of climate science and even called into question the motives of the IPCC scientists. Initially, these skeptics faced an uphill battle. When Bill Clinton became president in 1993, his Democratic administration brought a sympathetic ear to environmental issues such as climate change. Indeed, Vice President Al Gore was one of the earliest and most outspoken U.S. officials on the threat of global warming.

Then, in November 1994, Republicans won major victories in elections for the Senate and House of Representatives, effectively giving them control of Congress. The Republicans provided climate change skeptics and opponents of environmental regulations a powerful and authoritative platform for their message. While the scientific community was largely persuaded by the evidence for human-influenced climate change, industry groups and conservative think tanks took their message directly to policy makers and the public at large. The resulting media debates created significant doubt and confusion about climate change. Indeed, the confusion was such that even issues of settled science seemed to be open for debate. Although it was the president's prerogative to negotiate international treaties, no treaty could be binding on the United States without ratification by the Senate. Only months before the next UNFCCC Conference of the Parties in Kyoto, the U.S. Senate passed a resolution stating that it would not ratify any treaty that would negatively affect the U.S. economy or impose binding limits on U.S. greenhouse gas emissions without placing similar limits on developing countries. Support for the Senate resolution was unanimous. The U.S. delegation thus entered negotiations under significant limitations.

The Kyoto Protocol

In December 1997, more than 6,000 official delegates and countless other attendees convened for the third Conference of the Parties in Kyoto, Japan, with the explicit intention of crafting a protocol to the UNFCCC that would impose legally binding commitments. Among the most vociferous proponents of strict and immediate action were the representatives of small island nations. These countries, many of which were poor and only a few feet above sea level, were particularly alarmed by the prospect of expanding oceans and intensified storms. European countries were also eager to adopt aggressive limits on greenhouse gases and a clear timetable. By contrast, Australia, Canada, Japan, New Zealand, Russia, members of the Organization of the Petroleum Exporting Countries (OPEC), and the United States were resistant to aggressive targets. Two additional issues became the focus of serious contention: 1) the different responsibilities between developed and less developed countries, and 2) the way in which countries could meet their emissions reduction commitments.

Since the signing of the UNFCCC at the Earth Summit in 1992, the parties had agreed that the onus for action should rest (at least initially) on wealthier, industrialized countries as a matter of equity and practicality. By any estimate, developed countries were responsible for the vast bulk of greenhouse gases, which had accumulated in the Earth's atmosphere since the advent of fossil-fueled industry. These countries represented only a minority of the world's total population yet still accounted for the majority of present-day emissions. While developed countries had benefited greatly from industrialization, the impacts of the resulting climate change would fall most heavily on the people of poorer, less developed nations who had little if anything to do with the creation of the problem. Because of high population density in environmentally vulnerable areas, weak infrastructure, and lower capacity to respond to emergencies, it was the world's poor who would suffer the most from the effects of climate change. As a matter of practicality, the economic and technological changes that were needed to reduce greenhouse gas emissions would likely be costly and complex and thus beyond the capacity of poorer nations.

Despite the standing agreement to differentiate responsibilities between developed and less developed countries, U.S. negotiators attempted to reopen the issue. They argued that less developed, industrializing nations needed to make meaningful commitments as well. Countries such as China, India, Mexico, and Brazil were industrializing rapidly, and the emissions from their massive populations would eventually overshadow reductions made by industrialized countries. While a few other countries supported the United States, the vast majority of delegates were adamantly opposed to this proposal.

The U.S. delegation had more success on the issue of methods of accounting for greenhouse gas emissions. According to IPCC reports, the fundamental cause of the ongoing warming of the planet was a net increase in the atmospheric concentration of greenhouse gases. In order to slow or stop the climatic changes, greenhouse gas emissions would have to be greatly reduced. The most direct way to do this was to radically reduce the use of fossil fuels as a primary source of energy. However, the U.S. delegation proposed a variety of creative accounting mechanisms by which countries could meet their commitments to reduce net greenhouse gas emissions. U.S. negotiators argued that countries should be able to claim credit for reducing greenhouse gas emissions by use of natural carbon sinks, such as forests. Trees, like all plants, absorb carbon dioxide from the atmosphere and incorporate it into their structure, thus locking up (or sinking) the carbon. By maintaining or even expanding forests, it was argued, a substantial amount of carbon dioxide was essentially kept out of the atmosphere. Countries with large standing forests, such as the United States, Canada, and Russia, were especially supportive of this idea. The second accounting proposal was a system for the exchange or trade of emissions credits between countries. The idea was to allow countries that were able to bring their emissions below their reduction targets to sell their excess capacity—the difference between their actual emissions and the targeted cap—to countries that were not able to easily meet their targets. For example, if Sweden was committed to reducing its emissions by 5 percent, but managed to reduce its emissions by 8 percent, it could sell the excess 3 percent to other countries. Sweden would earn income, and the trade would also work to the advantage of a country for which the purchase of credits was less costly than actual reductions. While individual countries might avoid actual reductions, the overall result would still be a net reduction in global greenhouse gas emissions so long as these emissions credit swaps were carefully monitored and the over-all global emissions cap maintained. The idea was modeled on the program implemented in the United States to control the release of pollutants that caused acid rain.

It was also proposed that developed countries should be able to claim credit for investments in clean development programs—such as renewable energy projects—in developing countries, which would serve to offset greenhouse gas emissions. The U.S. proposals for these flexible mechanisms of greenhouse gas accounting were criticized by delegates who wanted more aggressive and direct action to reduce emissions. They argued that these flexible mechanisms were simply cynical attempts to skirt meaningful reductions or, worse, an effort to sabotage the already tense negotiations.

The Kyoto Conference began on December 1, 1997, and was scheduled to end on December 10. On the last day of the conference, however, there was still no agreement. While the conference was sup-posed to end on the afternoon of the last day, delegates pushed their negotiations deep into the night and well into the next morning. By the late morning of December 11, the exhausted attendees had man-aged to come to agreement on the Kyoto Protocol to the UNFCCC. Under the Kyoto Protocol, developed countries committed to reduc-ing their overall greenhouse gas emissions to at least 5 percent below 1990 levels by 2012. However, these commitments varied slightly by country: 8 percent reductions for the European Union, 7 percent for the United States, 6 percent for Japan, stabilization at 1990 levels for Russia and Ukraine, and slight increases for Iceland and Australia. The Kyoto Protocol incorporated the flexible mechanisms proposed by the United States: emissions trading, credit for carbon sinks, and credit for invest-ments in developing countries to offset greenhouse gas emissions. In order to become official, the protocol had to be ratified by at least 55 parties, including developed countries accounting for at least 55 per-cent of the total greenhouse gas emissions of all developed countries in 1990. The details and legal language of the international treaty still had to be worked out, but agreement on the major provisions was hailed as a significant event.

The Clinton administration supported the Kyoto Protocol. On November 12, 1998, the United States formally signed the treaty. How-ever, it still had to be ratified by the U.S. Senate. President Clinton faced a dilemma because the agreement contained provisions that the Senate had already explicitly rejected. However, U.S. support for the Kyoto Protocol was widely perceived as vital to the treaty's success. The eyes of the world were upon the United States. The country faced a contentious question: Should the United States ratify the Kyoto Protocol?

DEBATE

The Case for the Kyoto Protocol

Supporters of the Kyoto Protocol asserted that the treaty was a prudent and necessary step to address the threat of human-induced climate change. They argued that commitments under the treaty could be met at reasonable cost and would actually result in a number of ancillary benefits. First and foremost, they maintained that the weight of scientific authority indicated that climate change was a serious problem requiring timely action. According to the most recent report by the IPCC, the Earth had already warmed considerably over the last century as a direct result of anthropogenic emissions of greenhouse gases. (See "Excerpt from IPCC Second Assessment Report, 1995," on page 346 in the Primary Sources section.)

Concentrations were already 30 percent higher than they had been in preindustrial times and were projected to double by the end of the 21st century. The resultant warming of the atmosphere could create any number of disruptive changes to the global environment. Melting of the polar ice caps and glaciers would raise sea levels and inundate coastal cities, while at the same time depleting sources of freshwater for millions who depended on regular meltwater from mountain snowpack. Warmer temperatures, higher humidity, and more energy in the atmosphere could mean more intense storm activity, from damaging thunderstorms to more frequent and intense tornadoes and hurricanes. Normal weather patterns would likely be disrupted, exacerbating drought in drier areas and floods in wetter areas. These changes would also be disruptive for agriculture and natural resources, such as fisheries and forests. As ecosystems changed, many species would go extinct, while pests and other noxious organisms would move into new areas. Because the climate system is so complex, there were many possible changes that would likely come as a surprise and with the potential to prove catastrophic.

Advocates of the treaty asserted that action needed to begin sooner rather than later, even with remaining uncertainties. Carbon dioxide emissions remained in the atmosphere for centuries, while the effects were delayed or lagged. Thus, the full consequences of past emissions had yet to be felt, and the effects of today's emissions would last for decades, if not centuries, to come. The longer the delay, the worse and more extended the impacts and the harder and more costly it would be to make the needed changes. Decisions being made by today's governments and other institutions—such as whether to build a coal- or gas-fired power plant with an average operating life span of 20 to 30 years—would also have consequences for our ability to limit the buildup of greenhouse gases in the future.

Proponents of the treaty maintained that the costs of compliance were manageable and were outweighed by the potential costs of inaction. President Clinton's Council of Economic Advisers calculated that the costs of complying with the Kyoto targets for emissions reductions might amount to $7 to $12 billion per year between 2008 and 2012—approximately 0.1 percent of the nation's projected gross domestic product (GDP). For the average consumer, this would lead to an added cost of 4 to 6 cents per gallon of gasoline. For the average household, this would raise annual energy expenditures by about $70 to $110 per year—an amount well below the typical fluctuations in energy prices. (See "Administration Economic Analysis of Kyoto Protocol, 1998," on page 347 in the Primary Sources section.)

The Clinton administration took pains to emphasize that the costs of compliance would be low because of the flexibility mechanisms built into the Kyoto Protocol, largely at the insistence of the United States. These mechanisms would provide cost-effective ways for the country to meet its obligations. At the same time, the burden of these obligations would likely be lessened by domestic initiatives such as investments in renewable energy research, as well as energy efficiency and conservation. These efforts would not only help the United States lower its greenhouse gas emissions but have ancillary benefits such as less expenditure on energy and less pollution and even spur technological innovation.

More important, the short-term costs of mitigating climate change paled in comparison to the long-term costs of inaction. By some estimates, the monetary damages from environmental, health, and economic impacts of global warming over the next century ranged in the tens of billions of dollars per year. By one estimate, a doubling of the atmospheric concentration of greenhouse gases and the resultant impacts could cost the U.S. economy $86 billion per year—1.1 percent of annual GDP. More worrisome, however, was the potential cost of surprises—the effects of global warming might not be gradual and predictable, but relatively abrupt, unforeseen, and potentially catastrophic. Finally, supporters of the Kyoto protocol defended the spirit of the treaty, while acknowledging that it would not be the final solution. The protocol represented a first step toward global action. For reasons of fairness and practicality, it was up to the wealthier, developed nations of the world to lead by example.

The Case Against the Kyoto Protocol

Criticism of the Kyoto Protocol ranged from those who were sympathetic to the problem but dissatisfied with the policy's shortcomings to those who rejected the entire premise of global warming. Opposition was spearheaded by industry groups, politically conservative think tanks, and a few vocal scientists. At one end of the spectrum, critics continued to argue that the scientific evidence for anthropogenic climate change was weak or even wrong. At the very least, the science was too uncertain to justify such an ambitious and expensive policy. They argued that climate models, upon which so much was based, still suffered from holes and inconsistencies with regard to available evidence. Advocates of the global warming theory, skeptics argued, had yet to make a convincing case. Moreover, these critics took issue with assertions that there existed a scientific consensus or that such a claim was even relevant. Had not Galileo stood alone and ridiculed before the scholars of his day to argue that the Earth was not the center of the universe?

Others went so far as to question the objectivity and professional integrity of the IPCC and other climate researchers who supported the thesis of anthropogenic climate change. They accused the IPCC and its sympathizers of exaggerating claims and stoking fears in order to stimulate a greater flow of money for research or to advance liberal environmental agendas for greater government control of the economy. More generally, however, critics argued that the science of climate change was too uncertain. If anything, the issue deserved more time and more rigorous research.

Other critics of the protocol argued that global warming, if true, would not necessarily pose the catastrophic threat alleged by doomsayers. In spite of more than a century of industrial emissions of carbon dioxide and other greenhouse gases, the Earth's climate had changed only a little, and it was not certain that future changes would happen so abruptly as to be unmanageable. Humans had lived through greater variations of climate and managed to survive and even thrive. For a time, some opponents to the protocol argued that global warming would be beneficial over the long run. An increase in average global temperatures would improve the quality of life and health by lessening the more deleterious impacts of cold weather. In addition, the warmer climate and higher concentrations of carbon dioxide would stimulate plant growth, improving agriculture and making the world a greener place.

Critics of the policy itself argued that the Kyoto Protocol would likely do more harm than good. A binding international treaty would be harmful to the U.S. economy and its national sovereignty. Critics argued that the costs of compliance were woefully underappreciated and unacceptable. (See "The Undermining of American Prosperity, 1998," on page 349 in the Primary Sources section.) Competing estimates of the impact on the national economy ranged from $200 to $300 billion in losses to GDP to more than $3 trillion in total costs between 2001 and 2012. The business community would be hardest hit, which in turn would negatively affect workers and consumers. National sovereignty would also be threatened because the treaty would give international bureaucrats (i.e., the United Nations) power over American industry and energy policy.

Critics argued that the Kyoto Protocol was unfair and impractical. The treaty failed to include meaningful commitments by developing countries, which constituted most of the world. This was a significant part of the U.S. Senate's opposition. (See "Senate Resolution Expressing Opposition to Binding Limits on Emissions under the UNFCCC, 1997," on page 350 in the Primary Sources section.)

Of special concern were China and India. These countries were experiencing phenomenal economic growth and improvements in their standards of living, with corresponding growth in their energy use and emissions. Although the United States was constantly condemned for being the single largest emitter of greenhouse gases, all projections

A HOLE IN THE SKY: DEPLETION OF STRATOSPHERIC OZONE

In 1974, two chemists at the University of California, Irvine, discovered that CFCs, a common class of industrial chemicals used in everything from aerosol cans to refrigerators, appeared to threaten the integrity of stratospheric ozone. Ozone is a naturally occurring gas that is concentrated in a thin layer 10 to 20 miles up in the atmosphere that has the unique property of absorbing and blocking ultraviolet (UV) radiation from the Sun. Scientists had already determined that this ozone layer is vital to life on Earth, because UV radiation is harmful and even deadly to all forms of life.

Just prior to the discovery of the threat posed by CFCs, the country had been embroiled in a debate over threats to the ozone layer from high altitude aircraft and the oxides of nitrogen released in their exhaust. Concerns about damage to the ozone layer, as well as other issues, forced Congress to cancel plans to develop a fleet of supersonic airplanes that would have traveled within the stratosphere. However, analysis showed that CFCs were six times more effective at destroying stratospheric ozone than oxides of nitrogen. Follow-up studies supported these initial findings, and atmospheric scientists estimated a substantial loss in stratospheric ozone if the offending chemicals continued to be produced and used at the same rates, although these conclusions were based on unproven computer models. Nevertheless, the implications of a degraded ozone layer captivated the media and public attention. With a loss of protective ozone and an increase in the amount of UV radiation, scientists predicted increases in skin cancer and eye damage for humans, damage to crops, and substantial impacts on ecosystems. Government officials took the threat seriously, and by the spring of 1978, U.S. environmental regulators announced a ban on CFCs in aerosols and urged other countries to do the same. However, CFCs remained important chemicals in many other products and processes, and there were debates about a complete ban of CFCs and other industrial chemicals determined to deplete stratospheric ozone.

showed that China would soon surpass the United States in total emissions but yet would not be bound by any commitments. Industries in the United States that found the cost of business increasing because

The issue of ozone depletion gained new urgency in fall 1985 when ground-based and satellite measurements showed a vast region of severely depleted ozone over Antarctica. Although studies of the ozone layer had been increasing since the mid-1970s, the new evidence of catastrophic ozone depletion and satellite images of a vast hole in the sky over the South Pole spurred international action. The United States led the charge to convince other nations to phase out the chemicals and institute binding limits. In September 1987, 47 countries signed the Montreal Protocol on Substances That Deplete the Ozone Layer, an international treaty to control and phase out the production and use of CFCs and other ozone-depleting chemicals. The treaty was remarkable and precedent setting—the first international environmental agreement of its kind. Moreover, it had been accomplished in spite of significant scientific uncertainty and without any clear technological solution or substitute for CFCs, chemicals that were central to numerous industries and embedded in countless consumer products.

Under the initial version of the Montreal Protocol, nations agreed to reduce their annual production of CFCs by 50 percent by 1999, although developing countries were given another 10 years to comply with these targets. U.S. commitments were included in title VI of the 1990 Clean Air Act Amendments. The Montreal Protocol was amended several times in following years to speed up the phaseout of CFCs and other chemicals as the extent of damage to stratospheric ozone became more apparent. Indeed, the ozone hole over Antarctica continued to expand throughout the 1990s, and new evidence showed that the ozone layer was thinning over the high latitudes of the Northern Hemisphere, stoking concerns over increases in the incidence of skin cancer in areas with high populations of light-skinned people who are more susceptible. As international bans have taken effect, researchers have observed a decline in the concentration of CFCs and other ozone-depleting substances in the atmosphere, and the ozone layer has shown signs of stabilization. Atmospheric scientists estimate that the ozone layer will repair itself by the end of the 21st century.

of onerous restrictions on greenhouse gas emissions would cease to be competitive with their counterparts in the developing world where there were no such restrictions. American companies would go out of business or be forced to relocate. In order to meet its commitment to reduce emissions to 7 percent below 1990 levels, the United States would need to cut its projected 2012 emissions by 25 percent—a tremendous burden that would be ruinously expensive if it was even possible. Even if developed countries somehow managed to meet the Kyoto reduction targets, the impact on global warming would be miniscule and inconsequential because emissions reductions from developed countries would be offset by the projected growth in emissions from developing countries that were exempt. Critics seriously doubted that it was economically or even technologically feasible to reach the Kyoto Protocol reduction targets within the time frame specified. Thus, the treaty asked for too much with too little time and yet did not ask enough of the rest of the world.

OUTCOME AND IMPACT

Although the Clinton administration had repeatedly voiced support for UNFCCC and the Kyoto Protocol, it faced a conundrum in the Senate's opposition. With little prospect for ratification, President Clinton decided not to submit the treaty to Congress. When he left office, the Kyoto Protocol remained in limbo, neither ratified nor officially rejected.

When U.S. president George W. Bush assumed power in 2001, his attitude toward climate change and the Kyoto Protocol was still unclear. During the presidential election campaign the previous September, candidate Bush declared his willingness to pursue reductions of carbon dioxide from the nation's power plants. However, in March 2001, President Bush abruptly reversed his campaign pledge and informed Congress that he opposed the Kyoto Protocol and would not pursue reductions of carbon dioxide because of the potential for economic harm due to higher energy prices. (See "Letter to Members of the Senate on the Kyoto Protocol on Climate Change, 2001," on page 352 in the Primary Sources section.)

President Bush described the Kyoto Protocol as "fatally flawed" because it did not require reductions from developing countries and because it threatened the U.S. economy. Moreover, he emphasized the uncertainty of climate change science and called for more research. At the same time, he also gave assurances that he wanted the United States to continue to work with the international community and with UNFCCC. President Bush's unequivocal rejection of the Kyoto Protocol, as well as his questioning of the science, caused an uproar in Europe and among other allies. It also seemed to deliver a crippling blow to the Kyoto Protocol.

Although the Kyoto Protocol had been officially approved at the third Conference of the Parties, it faced two basic hurdles: 1) ratification by enough countries whose emissions amounted to at least 55 percent of 1990 levels, and 2) clarification of the agreement into specific legal language. The effective withdrawal of the United States from participation—the single largest source of greenhouse gases—lowered expectations of success. Nevertheless, the parties continued to meet in follow-up conferences to work out the details and lobby reluctant countries to officially ratify the treaty. Despite a climate of high uncertainty and low expectations, delegates were able to come to agreement on the specific terms and language to implement the treaty at the seventh Conference of the Parties in Marrakech, Morocco, in October 2001. In November 2004, Russia ratified the protocol, giving the treaty the minimum number of participants necessary to enable the treaty to come into force in February 2005.

Work under UNFCCC did not end with ratification of the Kyoto Protocol. The Kyoto Protocol was scheduled to expire in 2012, which meant that a new agreement would need to be created. Although the parties hoped to craft a new agreement before Kyoto expired, such agreement was elusive. The election of a new U.S. president— Barack Obama—in 2008 seemed to offer some hope to supporters of the Kyoto Protocol that the United States might rethink its position and assist in efforts to create binding agreements to address climate change. A potentially new precedent was set at the 17th Conference of the Parties in Durban, South Africa, in December 2011. For the first time, negotiators for both the United States and developing countries, such as China and India, agreed to be part of a legally binding treaty to address global warming. The terms of the future treaty were to be defined by 2015 and become effective in 2020.

The science around climate change has become more compelling and dire in its warnings. In 2007, the IPCC released its Fourth Assessment Report that declared that the evidence for global warming was unequivocal and that the effects were now clearly observable across the planet: warmer air and sea temperatures, retreating glaciers, rising sea levels, and disrupted ecosystems. Moreover, greenhouse gas emissions continued to grow rapidly, and atmospheric concentrations were now at levels not seen on Earth in 650,000 years.

In summer 2010, the U.S. National Oceanic and Atmospheric Administration released its own comprehensive report confirming that the previous decade was the warmest on record and that the Earth had grown warmer over the past 50 years. Indeed, over the past three decades, each succeeding decade was warmer than the last. The 1980s were the hottest on record at the time but were surpassed by the 1990s, and the 1990s in turn were surpassed by the 2000s. The effects of this warming have been clearly documented by numerous indicators across the planet: sea-level rise, longer growing seasons, changes in river flows, increases in heavy downpours, earlier snowmelt, and extended ice-free seasons.

WHAT IF?

What if the United States had ratified the Kyoto Protocol?

If the U.S. Senate had, by some miraculous change of heart, agreed to ratify the Kyoto Protocol, the action would have put substantial pressure on other countries to approve the protocol as well. In addition, U.S. approval would have also created stronger political leverage to convince rapidly developing countries such as China, India, Mexico, and Brazil to begin consideration of their own future commitments. The hesitancy and then rejection by the United States provided other reluctant countries with an effective excuse to delay decision making. If the world's wealthiest and largest emitter of greenhouse gases was unwilling to participate in a global agreement, why should anyone else? The U.S. rejection also cast doubt on the possibility of success for the entire endeavor. Only sheer tenacity by the other parties enabled the protocol to come into effect eight years after it had been approved.

Less clear is how U.S. ratification of the Kyoto Protocol would actually have affected greenhouse gas emissions. Though numerous countries ratified the protocol, very few have succeeded in actually reducing their emissions. Moreover, the problem of emissions from less developed countries still remains. Indeed, in 2006, China surpassed the United States as the single largest emitter of greenhouse gases on the planet—as predicted but several years ahead of projections. In 2009, the United States accounted for 18 percent of worldwide energy-related carbon dioxide emissions, though it was home to only 5 percent of the global population. China accounted for 25 percent of global carbon dioxide emissions and was home to 20 percent of the global population. If current trends continue, global greenhouse gas emissions will continue to grow, although most of the growth will occur in less developed countries. According to the U.S. Energy Information Administration, more than half of the global growth in carbon dioxide emissions between 2007 and 2035 is projected to come from China alone, followed distantly by India, the second most populous nation on Earth. The IPCC and other scientists have repeatedly warned that such increases are unsustainable and risk catastrophic disruption to the environment and human welfare.

CHRONOLOGY

1896   Swedish scientist Svante Arrhenius publishes the first calculation of potential global warming from human emissions of carbon dioxide (CO_2).

1955   *May 18:* The head of the U.S. Weather Bureau announces that a significant general rise in average temperature (3.6°F, that is, 2°C) has been seen in the previous 50 years.

1957   Oceanographer Roger Revelle testifies before Congress on the possibility that emissions of CO_2 may lead to dangerous changes in the climate.

1960   Charles D. Keeling accurately measures CO_2 in the Earth's atmosphere and detects an annual rise.

1965   President's Science Advisory Committee (PSAC) on environmental pollution publishes the first high-level government report to mention global warming.

1969   The World Meteorological Organization's Commission for Climatology passes a resolution calling for global monitoring of climate and atmospheric pollutants, including CO_2.

1971   Congress cancels supersonic transport program amid concerns about cost and noise and threats to stratospheric ozone.

1972   *June 5–16:* United Nations Conference on the Human Environment in Stockholm, Sweden, is the first major UN conference on international environmental issues.

1974   *June:* Chemists Mario J. Molina and F. S. Rowland at the University of California, Irvine, report that CFCs pose a significant threat to stratospheric ozone.

1977   *July:* A blue-ribbon panel for the National Academy of Sciences (NAS) warns of disruptive climate change due to increased concentration of CO_2 in the atmosphere.

Congress passes Clean Air Act, which includes restrictions on aerosol propellants in spray cans in order to reduce the threat to the ozone layer from CFCs.

1978   *March 15:* United States announces a ban on CFCs for all domestic aerosol products and urges other nations to take similar action to protect stratospheric ozone.

1979   *February:* World Climate Conference in Geneva, Switzerland, concludes there is a "clear possibility" that an increase of CO_2 "may result in significant and possibly major long-term changes of the global-scale climate."

Nations of western Europe adopt a Convention on Long-Range Transboundary Air Pollution.

1980   U.S. Congress passes the Acid Deposition Act, a 10-year research program to look at the effects of acid rain.

1981   *August 29: New York Times* publishes a front page article about NASA scientist's (James Hansen's) scientific predictions of potential sea level rise from global warming.

1983   *October:* Environmental Protection Agency and NAS release separate reports about possible effects of anthropogenic emissions of carbon dioxide.

1984   British scientists at Halley Bay in Antarctica discover alarmingly low concentrations of stratospheric ozone over Antarctica.

1985   The Villach Conference declares a consensus among experts that some global warming is inevitable and calls on governments to consider international agreements to restrict emissions.

1987   *September 16:* Montreal Protocol on Substances That Deplete the Ozone Layer is opened for signature.

President Reagan signs into law the Global Climate Protection Act, which requires the administration to prepare a plan to stabilize the level of greenhouse gases.

1988 *June 23:* NASA climate scientist James Hansen and his team report to Congress with near certainty that a long-term warming trend is underway and that the greenhouse effect is to blame. The Intergovernmental Panel on Climate Change (IPCC) is established by the World Meteorological Organization and United Nations Environment Programme.

1989 Leading U.S. industries form the Global Climate Coalition to counter arguments about global warming.

1990 President George H. W. Bush signs into law the Global Change Research Act of 1990, which establishes the U.S. Global Change Research program.

August: IPCC releases First Assessment Report, which concludes that average global temperatures have risen and are likely to keep rising.

1992 *June 3–14:* Representatives from 170 countries meet at the United Nations Conference on Environment and Development and adopt the United Nations Framework Convention on Climate Change (UNFCCC).

October 15: U.S. Senate ratifies UNFCCC.

1993 *April 20:* President Clinton announces a Climate Change Action Plan.

1994 *March 21:* UNFCCC enters into force after it has been ratified by the required 50 governments.

1995 *December:* IPCC releases the Second Assessment Report on climate change, which declares that the world is getting warmer and that warming is most likely caused in part by humans.

1996 *July 17:* At the second Conference of the Parties in Geneva, Switzerland, the United States announces that it will seek legally binding targets and timetables for reducing greenhouse gas emissions.

1997 *July 25:* U.S. Senate unanimously passes the Hagel-Byrd Resolution declaring that the Senate will not ratify any treaty that imposes greenhouse gas emissions reductions without also imposing such reductions for developing nations.

December 11: More than 160 nations agree to the Kyoto Protocol to the UNFCCC.

1998 *November 12:* The United States signs the Kyoto Protocol, but President Clinton says that he will not submit it for Senate ratification until developing countries agree to limit their emissions as well.

2001 *January 22:* The IPCC releases its Third Assessment Report concluding that warming over the last 50 years is attributable to human activities.

March: President George W. Bush announces that the United States will not ratify the Kyoto Protocol.

July: At an international conference in Bonn, Germany, 178 governments negotiate a compromise agreement for implementing the Kyoto Protocol.

2004 *August:* An annual report by the U.S. Climate Change Science Program and the Subcommittee on Global Change Research states that "emissions of carbon dioxide and other heat-trapping gases are the only likely explanation for global warming over the last three decades."

October: Russia ratifies the Kyoto Protocol, enabling the treaty to go into effect.

2005 *January:* European nations adopt a scheme that requires permits for carbon emissions and sets up a market for trading the permits.

February 16: The Kyoto Protocol enters into force with 141 signatory nations.

2007 *February:* IPCC issues its Fourth Assessment Report, which declares that warming of the earth's climate system is unequivocal.

Coalitions of northeastern, midwestern, southwestern and western U.S. states lay plans for mandatory regional systems to track and cut back their residents' CO_2 emissions.

2011 *December:* At the 17th Conference of the Parties in Durban, South Africa, the United States and developing countries agree to be part of a legally binding treaty on global warming by 2020.

DISCUSSION QUESTIONS

1. Should the United States have ratified the Kyoto Protocol? Why or why not?
2. What was the evidence for global warming? Was this evidence convincing? Why or why not?

3. When did the issue of global warming begin to concern policy makers and the general public? Why then?
4. Why was the U.S. Senate opposed to the Kyoto Protocol?
5. What was the justification for exempting developing countries from commitments to reduce greenhouse gases under the Kyoto Protocol? Was this exemption justified? Why or why not?

WEB SITES

American Institute of Physics. The Discovery of Global Warming. By Spencer Weart. Available online. URL: http://www.aip.org/history/climate/index.htm. Accessed March 31, 2011.

Intergovernmental Panel on Climate Change. Available online. URL: http://www.ipcc.ch/index.htm. Accessed March 31, 2011.

NOAA Climate Services. Available online. URL: http://www.climate.gov/#climateWatch. Accessed March 31, 2011.

PBS. NOW. Science and Health: The Political Climate. Available online. URL: http://www.pbs.org/now/science/climatedebate.html. Accessed March 31, 2011.

Pew Center on Global Climate Change. Available online. URL: http://www.pewclimate.org/. Accessed March 31, 2011.

United Nations Framework Convention on Climate Change. Available online. URL: http://unfccc.int/2860.php. Accessed March 31, 2011.

United States Global Change Research Program. Available online. URL: http://www.globalchange.gov/. Accessed March 31, 2011.

BIBLIOGRAPHY

"Acid Rain: New Approach to Old Problem." *CQ Researcher* 1 (March 8, 1991).

Benedick, Richard Elliot. *Ozone Diplomacy: New Directions in Safeguarding the Planet.* Cambridge, Mass.: Harvard University Press, 1991.

Bolin, Bert. *A History of the Science and Politics of Climate Change: The Role of the Intergovernmental Panel on Climate Change.* New York: Cambridge University Press, 1987.

Dessai, Suraje, Nuno S. Lacasta, and Katharine Vincent. "International Political History of the Kyoto Protocol: From The Hague to Marrakech and Beyond." *International Review for Environmental Strategies* 4, no. 2 (2003): 183–205.

"Global Warming Treaty: Should the U.S. Do More to Cut Greenhouse Gases?" *CQ Researcher* 11, no. 3 (2001): 41–64.

Grundmann, Reiner. "Ozone and Climate: Scientific Consensus and Leadership." *Science, Technology & Human Values* 31, no. 1 (2006): 73–101.

Leggett, Jeremy. *The Carbon War: Global Warming and the End of the Oil Era.* New York: Routledge, 2001.

McCright, Aaron M., and Riley E. Dunlap. "Defeating Kyoto: The Conservative Movement's Impact on U.S. Climate Change Policy." *Social Problems* 50, no. 3 (2003): 348–373.

Munton, Dan. "Dispelling the Myths of the Acid Rain Story." *Environment* 40, no. 6 (1998): 4.

Oppenheimer, Michael, and Annie Petsonk. "Article 2 of the UNFCCC: Historical Origins, Recent Interpretations." *Climatic Change* 73 (2005): 195–226.

Sarewitz, Daniel, and Roger Pielke, Jr. "Breaking the Global-Warming Gridlock." *Atlantic* (July 2000): 55.

Weart, Spencer R. *The Discovery of Global Warming.* Revised and expanded edition. Cambridge, Mass.: Harvard University Press, 2008.

PRIMARY SOURCES

Document 1: Excerpt from the United Nations Framework Convention on Climate Change, 1992

In June 1992, hundreds of world leaders convened for the United Nations Conference on Environment and Development in Rio de Janeiro, Brazil, and approved the United Nations Framework Convention on Climate Change, the first international treaty to combat the threat of anthropogenic climate change.

ARTICLE 2
OBJECTIVE

The ultimate objective of this Convention and any related legal instruments that the Conference of the Parties may adopt is to achieve, in accordance with the relevant provisions of the Convention, stabilization of greenhouse gas concentrations in the atmosphere at a level that would prevent dangerous anthropogenic interference with the climate system. Such a level should be achieved within a time frame sufficient to allow ecosystems to adapt naturally to climate change, to ensure that food production is not threatened and to enable economic development to proceed in a sustainable manner.

ARTICLE 3
PRINCIPLES

In their actions to achieve the objective of the Convention and to implement its provisions, the Parties shall be guided, *inter alia,* by the following:

The Parties should protect the climate system for the benefit of present and future generations of humankind, on the basis of equity and in accordance with their common but differentiated responsibilities and respective capabilities. Accordingly, the developed country Parties should take the lead in combating climate change and the adverse effects thereof.

The specific needs and special circumstances of developing country Parties, especially those that are particularly vulnerable to the adverse effects of climate change, and of those Parties, especially developing country Parties, that would have to bear a disproportionate or abnormal burden under the Convention, should be given full consideration.

The Parties should take precautionary measures to anticipate, prevent or minimize the causes of climate change and mitigate its adverse effects. Where there are threats of serious or irreversible damage, lack of full scientific certainty should not be used as a reason for postponing such measures, taking into account that policies and measures to deal with climate change should be cost-effective so as to ensure global benefits at the lowest possible cost. . . .

The Parties have a right to, and should, promote sustainable development. Policies and measures to protect the climate system against human-induced change should be appropriate for the specific conditions of each Party and should be integrated with national development programmes, taking into account that economic development is essential for adopting measures to address climate change.

The Parties should cooperate to promote a supportive and open international economic system that would lead to sustainable economic growth and development in all Parties, particularly developing country Parties, thus enabling them better to address the problems of climate change.

Source: United Nations Framework Convention on Climate Change. Opened for signature at the UNCED in Rio de Janeiro, Brazil, June 4–14, 1992.

—〰—

Document 2: Excerpt from IPCC Second Assessment Report, 1995

In December 1995, the Intergovernmental Panel on Climate Change (IPCC) released its Second Assessment Report on global climate change, which drew particular attention for stronger statements on the evidence linking global warming to anthropogenic activity.

ANTHROPOGENIC INTERFERENCE WITH THE CLIMATE SYSTEM
INTERFERENCE TO THE PRESENT DAY

2.2 The atmospheric concentrations of the greenhouse gases, and among them, carbon dioxide (CO_2), methane (CH_4) and nitrous oxide (N_2O), have grown significantly since pre-industrial times (about 1750 A.D.): CO_2 from about 280 to almost 360 ppmv, CH_4 from 700 to 1720 ppbv and N_2O from about 275 to about 310 ppbv. These trends can be attributed largely to human activities, mostly fossil-fuel use, land-use change and agriculture. . . . An increase of greenhouse gas concentrations leads on average to an additional warming of the atmosphere and the Earth's surface. Many greenhouse gases remain in the atmosphere—and affect climate—for a long time. . . .

2.4 Global mean surface temperature has increased by between about 0.3 and 0.6°C since the late 19th century, a change that is unlikely to be entirely natural in origin. The balance of evidence, from changes in global mean surface air temperature and from changes in geographical, seasonal and vertical patterns of atmospheric temperature, suggests a discernible human influence on global climate. There are uncertainties in key factors, including the magnitude and patterns of long-term natural variability. . . .

Possible consequences of future interference

2.6 In the absence of mitigation policies or significant technological advances that reduce emissions and/or enhance sinks, concentrations of greenhouse gases and aerosols are expected to grow throughout the next century. . . .

2.10 All model simulations . . . show the following features: greater surface warming of the land than of the sea in winter; a maximum surface warming in high northern latitudes in winter, little surface warming over the Arctic in summer; an enhanced global mean hydrological cycle, and increased precipitation and soil moisture in high latitudes in winter. . . .

2.11 Warmer temperatures will lead to a more vigorous hydrological cycle; this translates into prospects for more severe droughts and/or floods in some places and less severe droughts and/or floods in other places. Several models indicate an increase in precipitation intensity, suggesting a possibility for more extreme rainfall events. Knowledge is currently insufficient to say whether there will be any changes in the occurrence or geographical distribution of severe storms, e.g., tropical cyclones.

2.12 There are many uncertainties and many factors currently limit our ability to project and detect future climate change. Future unexpected, large and rapid climate system changes (as have occurred in the past) are, by their nature, difficult to predict. This implies that future climate changes may also involve "surprises."

Source: "IPCC Second Assessment Synthesis of Scientific-Technical Information Relevant to Interpreting Article 2 of the UN Framework Convention on Climate Change." *IPCC Second Assessment: Climate Change 1995. A Report of the Intergovernmental Panel on Climate Change.* December 1995.

—∿—

Document 3: Administration Economic Analysis of Kyoto Protocol, 1998

In July 1998, the Clinton White House released a report analyzing the costs and benefits of complying with the Kyoto Protocol on climate change. The report concluded that the United States could reach its Kyoto target at a relatively modest cost and that the benefits of mitigating climate change are likely to be substantial.

The Administration employed a variety of tools to assess the various possible costs and non-climate benefits of our emissions reduction policy.

Our overall conclusion is that the net costs of the Administration's policies to reduce emissions are likely to be relatively modest, assuming those reductions are undertaken in an efficient manner with effective international trading, the Clean Development Mechanism, meaningful developing country participation, and sound domestic policies. That potential small net premium, even excluding the benefits of mitigating climate change, purchases a partial insurance policy against a serious environmental threat. Further, although we think the economic benefits of mitigating climate change are subject to too many uncertainties to quantify, those benefits over time are likely to be real and large. . . .

EFFECTS OF CLIMATE CHANGE POLICY ON U.S. COMPETITIVENESS

Some have expressed concern that the Kyoto Protocol might adversely affect the competitive position of American industry. In general, structural changes in the economy have the effect of expanding some sectors and contracting others. But to provide some perspective on this issue, consider the following facts. First, on average, energy constitutes only 2.2 percent of total costs to U.S. industry. Second, energy prices already vary significantly across countries. . . . Third, roughly two-thirds of all emissions are not in manufacturing at all, but in transportation and buildings, sectors which, by their very nature, are severely limited in their ability to relocate to other countries.

Evaluating how the Kyoto Protocol could affect competitiveness of a few specific manufacturing industries—especially those that are energy-intensive, such as aluminum and chemicals—is complex. However, the modest energy price effects associated with permit prices of $14/ton to $23/ton would likely have little impact on competitiveness.

Further, there is no reason to expect that mitigating climate change would necessarily have a negative effect on the trade balance. Indeed, the efforts to reduce greenhouse gas emissions would likely decrease oil exports to the United States, benefitting the trade balance. In short, we believe that the reason we need developing country participation is primarily because the problem is global and cost-effective solutions are essential, rather than to avoid adverse effects on competitiveness.

Source: President's Council of Economic Advisers. *The Kyoto Protocol and the President's Policies to Address Climate Change: Administration Economic Analysis.* Washington, D.C.: Government Printing Office, 1998.

—⁊⁊—

Document 4: The Undermining of American Prosperity, 1998

In July 1998, the Congressional Committee on Small Business held hearings on the science of climate change and potential economic impacts of the Kyoto Protocol. A representative from the Competitive Enterprise Institute, an influential think tank, argued that the more prudent option for an uncertain future was to increase resilience by promoting economic growth.

The fatal flaw in the precautionary case for Kyoto, as in environmental advocacy generally, is its complete one-sidedness. Environmentalists demand assurances of no harm only with respect to actions that government might regulate, never with respect to government regulation itself. But government intervention frequently boomerangs, creating the very risks that precautionists deem intolerable. . . . Regulatory schemes that divert attention, effort and money from major threats to minor risks can make us less safe. . . .

More importantly, for individuals as well as nations wealthier is healthier and richer is safer. There is an obvious connection between livelihoods, living standards, and lives. Wealth is the single most important factor affecting health and longevity. . . .

So here is a precautionary case against the Kyoto Protocol. Stabilizing greenhouse gases at levels low enough to cool the planet may require drastic reductions in energy use. An energy constrained world may be a poorer world. And a poorer world may have more starving people. . . .

Kyoto's partisans admonish us not to gamble with the only planet we have, yet they are perfectly willing to gamble with the only economy we have. They cannot logically have it both ways. . . . The administration claims that Kyoto is an insurance policy, and insurance by definition is supposed to make us safer. . . . This last point leads to a question that should be at the heart of the global warming debate: Which type of social insurance policy is likely to deliver the most protection? Should we try to prevent global change by rationing energy and further politicizing economic and technological development, or should we try to increase mankind's ability to adapt to change by reducing political barriers to enterprise, innovation and invention? . . . Wealthier, more technologically advanced societies, are better able to anticipate, withstand and recover from extreme weather events and other natural disasters.

A resiliency strategy is clearly the superior option, given the uncertainty surrounding the global warming hypothesis. Many possible catastrophes may befall us in the next century. . . . Making societies freer and wealthier is inherently desirable and would better prepare us to deal with whatever shocks and surprises the future may hold. In sharp contrast to Kyoto, this resiliency approach is all coverage and no premium.

The Kyoto Protocol would restrict our freedom, diminish and possibly crush our prosperity, and mobilize tremendous resources to fend off a threat that may prove to be nonexistent or trivial compared to the age old scourges of poverty, hunger and disease. America does not need and cannot afford that kind of insurance.

Source: Statement of Marlo Lewis, Jr., vice president of policy and coalitions of the Competitive Enterprise Institute. "The Kyoto Protocol: The Undermining of American Prosperity—The Science." Committee on Small Business, United States House of Representatives. Serial No. 105-62. Washington D.C.: Government Printing Office, 1998.

—∞—

Document 5: Senate Resolution Expressing Opposition to Binding Limits on Emissions under the UNFCCC, 1997

As preparations were underway to negotiate a new protocol to the United Nations Framework Convention on Climate Change (UNFCCC) in 1997, Senators Robert Byrd (D-W.V.) and Chuck Hagel (R-Neb.) sponsored a resolution expressing their opposition to binding limits that would hurt the U.S. economy or exempt developing countries. On July 25, 1997, the Senate unanimously supported the Byrd-Hagel Resolution (95-0).

Expressing the sense of the Senate regarding the conditions for the United States becoming a signatory to any international agreement on greenhouse gas emissions under the United Nations Framework Convention on Climate Change.

Whereas the United Nations Framework Convention on Climate Change (in this resolution referred to as the 'Convention'), adopted in May 1992, entered into force in 1994 and is not yet fully implemented; . . .

Whereas although the Convention, approved by the United States Senate, called on all signatory parties to adopt policies and programs aimed at limiting their greenhouse gas (GHG) emissions . . .

Whereas greenhouse gas emissions of Developing Country Parties are rapidly increasing and are expected to surpass emissions of the United States and other OECD countries as early as 2015; . . .

Whereas the exemption for Developing Country Parties is inconsistent with the need for global action on climate change and is environmentally flawed;

Whereas the Senate strongly believes that the proposals under negotiation, because of the disparity of treatment between Annex I Parties and Developing Countries and the level of required emission reductions, could result in serious harm to the United States economy, including significant job loss, trade disadvantages, increased energy and consumer costs, or any combination thereof. . . . Now, therefore, be it Resolved, That it is the sense of the Senate that—

(1) the United States should not be a signatory to any protocol to, or other agreement regarding, the United Nations Framework Convention on Climate Change of 1992, at negotiations in Kyoto in December 1997, or thereafter, which would—

(A) mandate new commitments to limit or reduce greenhouse gas emissions for the Annex I Parties, unless the protocol or other agreement also mandates new specific scheduled commitments to limit or reduce greenhouse gas emissions for Developing Country Parties within the same compliance period, or

(B) would result in serious harm to the economy of the United States; and

(2) any such protocol or other agreement which would require the advice and consent of the Senate to ratification should be accompanied by a detailed explanation of any legislation or regulatory actions that may be required to implement the protocol or other agreement and should also be accompanied by an analysis of the detailed financial costs and other impacts on the economy of the United States which would be incurred by the implementation of the protocol or other agreement.

Source: RESOLUTION Expressing the sense of the Senate regarding the conditions for the United States becoming a signatory to any international agreement on greenhouse gas emissions under the United Nations Framework Convention on Climate Change. S.R. 98. 105th Congress. 1st session. July 25, 1997.

—〰—

Document 6: Letter to Members of the Senate on the Kyoto Protocol on Climate Change, 2001

In March 2001, President George W. Bush sent a letter to Senators Jesse Helms (R-N.C.), Larry E. Craig (R-Idaho), Pat Roberts (R-Kan.), and Chuck Hagel (R-Neb.) in response to questions about his position on the Kyoto Protocol and policies to limit emissions of greenhouse gases. The president's letter was a reversal of his previous campaign position to limit carbon dioxide emissions from power plants. More important, it was also a clear rejection of the Kyoto Protocol. Below is the text of the letter.

March 13, 2001

Dear _____ :

Thank you for your letter of March 6, 2001, asking for the Administration's views on global climate change, in particular the Kyoto Protocol and efforts to regulate carbon dioxide under the Clean Air Act. My Administration takes the issue of global climate change very seriously. As you know, I oppose the Kyoto Protocol because it exempts 80 percent of the world, including major population centers such as China and India, from compliance, and would cause serious harm to the U.S. economy. The Senate's vote, 95-0, shows that there is a clear consensus that the Kyoto Protocol is an unfair and ineffective means of addressing global climate change concerns. As you also know, I support a comprehensive and balanced national energy policy that takes into account the importance of improving air quality. Consistent with this balanced approach, I intend to work with the Congress on a multipollutant strategy to require power plants to reduce emissions of sulfur dioxide, nitrogen oxides, and mercury. Any such strategy would include phasing in reductions over a reasonable period of time, providing regulatory certainty, and offering market-based incentives to help industry meet the targets. I do not believe, however, that the government should impose on power plants mandatory emissions reductions for carbon dioxide, which is not a "pollutant" under the Clean Air Act.

A recently released Department of Energy Report, "Analysis of Strategies for Reducing Multiple Emissions from Power Plants," concluded that including caps on carbon dioxide emissions as part of a multiple emissions strategy would lead to an even more dramatic shift from coal to natural gas for electric power generation and significantly higher electricity prices compared to scenarios in which only sulfur dioxide and nitrogen oxides were reduced.

This is important new information that warrants a reevaluation, especially at a time of rising energy prices and a serious energy shortage. Coal generates more than half of America's electricity supply. At a time when California has already experienced energy shortages, and other Western states are worried about price and availability of energy this summer, we must be very careful not to take actions that could harm consumers. This is especially true given the incomplete state of scientific knowledge of the causes of, and solutions to, global climate change and the lack of commercially available technologies for removing and storing carbon dioxide. Consistent with these concerns, we will continue to fully examine global climate change issues—including the science, technologies, market-based systems, and innovative options for addressing concentrations of greenhouse gases in the atmosphere. I am very optimistic that, with the proper focus and working with our friends and allies, we will be able to develop technologies, market incentives, and other creative ways to address global climate change.

I look forward to working with you and others to address global climate change issues in the context of a national energy policy that protects our environment, consumers, and economy.

Sincerely,
GEORGE W. BUSH

Source: "Letter to Members of the Senate on the Kyoto Protocol on Climate Change." John T. Woolley and Gerhard Peters. *The American Presidency Project.* Santa Barbara, Calif. (2001).

10

THE MAKAH WHALE HUNT:
Should the Makah Have Killed a Whale?

—⚇—

THE CONTROVERSY ──────────────────────────────

The Issue

In late spring 1999, a small group of Makah tribal members paddled a canoe into the cold waters off Washington's Pacific coast and harpooned and then shot a 33-foot gray whale. It was the first time the Makah had hunted a whale since the late 1920s, and the event was marked by a boisterous celebration of fellow tribe members and others who waited on shore to witness the historic event and participate in the ceremonies and feast that followed. The event was condemned by environmentalists, animal rights groups, and others. Since 1986, the international community had observed a global moratorium on whaling after centuries of hunting that had brought many species to the brink of extinction. The international treaty that protected whales made allowances for indigenous groups to continue traditional subsistence whaling. The Makah whale hunt, however, was deeply controversial, entangling the treaty rights of indigenous groups and the protection of whales.

♦ *Arguments for the Makah whale hunt:* Makah tribal members argued that whaling was an integral aspect of their sovereignty, cultural identity, traditions, and nutritional needs. The Makah, and other indigenous groups, had hunted whales sustainably for thousands of years. Their whaling had never been a threat to whale populations; it was industrial, commercial whalers that had caused so much damage. The Makah asserted a treaty-based right to resume whaling, a legal right that had been preserved in treaties with the United States since the 1850s and that was also recognized by the International Whaling Commission (IWC).

♦ *Arguments against the Makah whale hunt:* Opponents of the Makah whale hunt argued that the killing of whales was inhumane and unnecessary. They contested the Makah's legal or moral claims to the right to resume whaling. They argued that whaling was no longer necessary for Makah cultural or subsistence needs. Some critics argued that earlier

354

treaties were no longer relevant and that the Makah should not benefit from special exceptions. Whale protection advocates asserted that the killing of whales was simply wrong because whales are uniquely intelligent creatures. They were also concerned that a resumption of hunting would once again threaten the species.

—ᴧᴧ—

INTRODUCTION

On May 17, 1999, a seven-man crew of Makah tribal members set out on a canoe and harpooned and then killed a gray whale off the coast of Washington State. It was the first time the Makah had harvested a whale since the late 1920s. The event was celebrated by fellow tribal members and others who waited excitedly on shore to participate in this historic occasion. At the same time, opponents of the whale hunt heckled and condemned the whalers. The event was closely watched by the media, and it stirred deep controversy in the United States and abroad. Since the late 1980s, the IWC had instituted a global ban on commercial whaling in an effort to protect whale populations, many of which had been hunted to the brink of extinction. Indeed, the gray whale had been on the U.S. Endangered Species List since 1970. However, in the summer of 1994, the California gray whale was removed from the Endangered Species List after its population had recovered to numbers not seen in more than a century. It was then that the Makah sent a formal request to the federal government to petition the IWC on its behalf to receive permission to resume hunting whales.

The request put U.S. officials in an awkward position because the United States was one of the most ardent advocates of the global whaling moratorium and often at odds with nations that insisted on the right to continue whaling, such as Japan, Russia, Norway, and Iceland. In addition, the United States itself had implemented domestic laws to outlaw or severely restrict the hunting or trade in marine mammals since the early 1970s. Protection of the world's whales was one of the most iconic issues of the modern environmental movement.

Indigenous groups, such as the Makah tribe, occupied a unique social and legal position that was widely recognized by both the U.S. government and by the international community. The international moratorium on whaling applied to *commercial* whaling, and made specific exemption for *indigenous* whaling, for which the Makah petitioned. The Makah pointed to long-standing treaties with the U.S. government going back to the mid-19th century that specifically guaranteed the right of the Makah to continue whaling. As a trustee of tribal affairs, the United States was obligated to act on behalf of the Makah before the IWC. After intense negotiations, and with help from indigenous groups in other parts of the world, the IWC granted the Makah permission to harvest up to five whales a year. The U.S. government subsequently granted permission as well.

The Makah decision to carry out the hunt of a gray whale was controversial because it seemed to pit indigenous rights and cultural values against international environmental efforts at wildlife protection. For members of the Makah tribe, the resumption of whaling offered an important opportunity to revive a cultural practice that had defined their people for millennia. Like many of their customs, however, the Makah had been forced to abandon whaling because of overexploitation by commercial whalers and because of efforts by the United States to force the Makah to assimilate into Euro-American culture and abandon their traditions. However, the Makah had retained treaty rights to continue their traditional use of natural resources, including whaling, and these rights had been repeatedly upheld by U.S. courts. Moreover, the Makah tribe claimed the sovereign right to use its resources as it saw fit and the right to decide what was culturally important. Since contact with European and later American colonizers, the Makah had suffered greatly and seen their culture nearly destroyed. They argued that the Makah whale hunt did not represent a threat to whales; they had hunted whales sustainably for thousands of years. Reviving the whale hunt was an opportunity to reconnect with important traditions and to rehabilitate an endangered culture.

Opponents of the Makah whale hunt argued that whaling was unnecessary, dangerous, and inhumane. Critics argued that although the Makah had once hunted whales for subsistence, they had not done so in more than 70 years. In the meantime, their culture had adopted more modern ways of living, and whaling was simply no longer necessary for survival. More important, the rest of the world had changed as well and had begun to recognize whales as unique creatures warranting special protection.

Two Makah whalers stand triumphantly atop the carcass of a gray whale towed near shore in the harbor at Neah Bay, Washington, on May 17, 1999. This was the first successful whale hunt by the Makah since the 1920s and was celebrated as a milestone in their struggle for cultural survival. (Elaine Thompson/Associated Press)

As a result of shortsighted and wasteful economic thinking and brutal hunting methods, the world's whale species had been brought to the brink of extinction. It was only through a global ban on whaling that the survival of the species could be ensured. However, a number of nations, such as Japan and Norway, continued to hunt whales. Critics argued that allowing the Makah to hunt whales would only weaken global efforts to protect whales and might even set a dangerous precedent. The Makah, some argued, should be treated no differently than other Americans. For many whaling opponents, especially in the United States, the whale embodied the majesty and romance of nature—gentle, intelligent, and mysterious. Whales also represented the tragedy of human exploitation. As one environmentalist famously proclaimed, "If we can't save the whales, how can we save the environment?"

The controversy over the Makah whale hunt raised difficult questions about the relative priority of indigenous rights and wildlife protection. U.S. officials were presented with the unenviable task of determining if the Makah could be allowed to resume hunting of gray whales. However, the larger question for many was, should the Makah resume hunting of whales?

BACKGROUND

Early Whaling by the Makah and the United States

The Makah tribe is one of many indigenous groups that have occupied the northwest coast of present-day Washington State and southwestern British Columbia for thousands of years. Historically, the Makah were a maritime culture that depended on the coastal resources of Washington's Olympic Peninsula, a mountainous and heavily forested strip of land bounded by the Pacific Ocean to the west, the Strait of Juan de Fuca to the north, and Puget Sound to the east. The Makah drew their material and cultural sustenance from coastal forests, streams, rivers, and the ocean. They harvested wood and game from the forests, salmon and other fish from rivers and streams, and shellfish, halibut, and sea mammals from the ocean, including seals, sea lions, and whales. Whaling held special significance for the Makah, both economically and culturally. The Makah were acknowledged by surrounding groups as master whalers. During the cold early spring when other food sources were scarce, whales provided up to 80 percent of the Makah's diet. The whale bones and other parts of the animal were also used to create a vast array of utilitarian and ceremonial objects. Culturally, whaling was a sacred and privileged occupation, reserved for elites who were expected to observe rigorous spiritual preparation. However, the whale harvest was shared with everyone, and the Makah were renowned for their generosity.

While the Makah hunted many species of whale, they focused primarily on the gray whale. The Pacific gray whale is a baleen whale that feeds on tiny crustaceans by scooping up sediment from the seafloor and filtering it through its baleen, the comblike bone in its mouth. The gray whale migrates along the Pacific coast of North America twice a year on its journey between the Bering Sea near Alaska, where it feeds in spring and summer, and the warm lagoons off the coast of Baja California in Mexico, where females give birth in winter. This 5,000-mile trip is believed to be the longest annual migration of any mammal. Its only predators are orcas, or killer whales, and humans. The gray whale is a large creature, growing up to 50 feet long and more than 35 tons, but its relative slowness and coastal migration route made it particularly accessible to hunting by the Makah. However, the Makah were not the only ones interested in whales. With the spread of commercial whaling activities and territorial control by the United States, the Makah found themselves in a losing conflict over territory, whales, and other resources.

Since the late 1700s, European explorers had been attracted to the Pacific Northwest by its rich marine resources, especially fur-bearing mammals such as sea otters but also whales. By the 1840s, a growing influx of U.S. settlers resulted in increasing conflict with Native peoples over territory and resources. In the mid-1850s, the governor of Washington Territory negotiated a series of treaties with indigenous groups, including the Makah, in order to resolve these tensions. In the 1855 Treaty of Neah Bay (ratified in 1859) between the Makah and the governor's representatives, the Makah ceded all of their territory to the U.S. government but reserved the "right of taking fish and of whaling or sealing at usual and accustomed grounds and stations." (See "Treaty of Neah Bay, 1855," on page 385 in the Primary Sources sections.)

Makah representatives were adamant about preserving these particular subsistence rights, and their inclusion in the final treaty was significant. Many treaties with tribes in the Pacific Northwest included provisions for usufructory rights, which included off-reserve hunting, fishing, and gathering. Only the Makah had a reserved right to whale. Of the hundreds of treaties the United States negotiated with tribes throughout the continent, the Treaty of Neah Bay was the only one that secured a tribe's right to whale. However, the Makah found it difficult to exercise these rights in the face of a concerted campaign by U.S. officials to assimilate native groups and aggressive competition for resources—including whales.

By the 1830s, the United States had become the preeminent whaling nation of the world, boasting more whaling boats and people employed in the industry than any other country. Indeed, whaling had become a quintessential Yankee occupation, celebrated and romanticized for its rugged adventure and inherent danger. Unlike the Makah, for whom the whales were food, commercial whalers were interested primarily in whale oil, which was used as a fuel for lamps and a lubricant for industry. As the lucrative market for whale oil grew, American and European whalers rapidly depleted whale populations in the Atlantic and Caribbean coastal waters, especially right whales and humpback whales. As a result, American whalers, mostly concentrated in the northeastern United States, began to venture farther out in pursuit of whales. By the 1840s, commercial whalers had discovered the Pacific gray whale population and were aggressively harvesting them. Whalers pursued the gray whale down to the shallow lagoons along the Baja California coast in Mexico where they were more easily captured. By the late 19th century, gray whale populations were severely depleted.

The American whaling industry was also on a rapid decline as whale oil was replaced by petroleum and as whaling became less profitable. Nevertheless, the Pacific gray whale population continued to be affected by commercial whaling, and the Makah found it increasingly difficult to harvest whales. The Makah faced other barriers to traditional resource use as well. Since the signing of the 1855 treaty and the confinement of the Makah to a reservation, U.S. officials had embarked on aggressive efforts to assimilate Native peoples into Euro-American culture. Officials charged with overseeing Native reservations actively discouraged or even banned many traditional cultural practices or celebrations, arguing that these were counterproductive to assimilation. In addition, authorities who oversaw tribal affairs pushed the Makah to abandon traditional subsistence practices in favor of farming, forestry, or other preferred occupations. With the combined pressures of assimilation and depleted whale populations, the Makah hunted their last whale in 1926.

Rise of Modern Whaling and International Whale Conservation

While American whaling was winding down by the end of the 19th century, the global, modern whaling industry was just getting started. New technology, such as more powerful harpoons and diesel-powered ships, enabled commercial whalers to pursue larger and faster whales farther out to sea. (The pursuit of whales out at sea is known as pelagic whaling, in contrast with the traditional hunting of whales near the coast.) Great Britain and Norway emerged as leading whaling nations. In the early 1900s, Norwegian whalers discovered that the Antarctic Ocean was a rich and unexploited feeding ground for the world's pelagic whales, setting off a frenzy of whaling activity by numerous countries. In the late 1920s, the development of large factory ships with slip sterns—open entries at the rear of the ship with ramps to allow captured whales to be dragged aboard—allowed whalers to bring harpooned whales aboard where they could be processed while still out at sea, which saved considerable time from having to drag a whale carcass to shore for processing as had been done for centuries.

Tens of thousands of whales were harvested annually from the Antarctic waters, and it was increasingly apparent to those in the industry that such a pace of harvesting could not be sustained forever. As early as 1925, the League of Nations voiced concerns over the need for some sort of international agreement to regulate whaling, both to stabilize the price of whale oil and to ensure enough whales survived to perpetuate the industry. In 1931, Norway and Great Britain led the way on the first Convention for the Regulation of Whaling, which 22 nations signed in Geneva, Switzerland. This early agreement established basic conservation measures for whale species (such as not hunting pregnant or nursing females), although it lacked force. Moreover, it was not accepted by newly active whaling nations such as Japan, the Soviet Union, Chile, Argentina, and Germany, which now represented nearly one-third of global whaling activity. Indeed, the market for whales only expanded as new uses were found and more countries entered the industry. By the 1930s, whale oil had become a cheap and vital component of basic products, such as soap and margarine which were in high demand, particularly in Europe.

A more lasting international framework for regulation of whaling emerged after World War II. In 1946, the United States hosted an international conference in Washington, D.C., to revise previous international whaling agreements and establish new guidelines for future regulation of whaling. Although the United States was no longer a significant whaling nation, it nevertheless took the lead on the issue of whaling. The conference was attended by delegations from 18 whaling countries and resulted in the International Convention for the

Regulation of Whaling, a global agreement to "provide for the proper conservation of whale stocks and thus make possible the orderly development of the whaling industry." The agreement created the IWC to oversee and administer the convention. In principle, the international agreement gave the IWC broad powers over the determination of which whale species were to be protected, when and how whales could be hunted, as well as catch limits and approval for equipment and data collection. (See "International Convention for the Regulation of Whaling, 1946," on page 388 in the Primary Sources section.)

Despite its ambitious scope, the convention was limited in its authority, since it applied only to countries that voluntarily ratified the treaty. In addition, it was up to the individual countries themselves to monitor and enforce compliance. Finally, the convention's primary purpose was the conservation of the whaling industry and thus the early regulations were weighted toward the interests of whalers. As a result, whaling activity continued unabated and peaked in the late 1950s and early 1960s, with more than 38,000 whales caught in Antarctic waters in 1961 alone. Thereafter, catches only declined as whales became scarcer.

Emergence of the Movement to Save the Whales

Since the early 20th century, scientists had worried about the long-term viability of whale species, but it was not until the 1960s that a significant segment of the general public joined in this concern. The 1960s saw the emergence of a new environmental consciousness that was focused on environmental degradation of all forms, both at home and around the planet. Domestically, this widely shared concern motivated government officials to respond with an unprecedented number of new environmental laws and regulations dealing with everything from air and water quality to municipal waste and wildlife protection. In the realm of wildlife protection, it was the threat of extinction of unique species that motivated new and stricter laws. There were a number of beautiful and charismatic animals that captured public concern, but few like the whale. The whale became a cause célèbre—a symbol of magnificent nature threatened by human brutality and excess.

Whales and other marine mammals, especially dolphins, were embraced by popular culture as examples of intelligent life. Their popularity increased with exposure through the medium of television and the opening of marine water parks where the public could see these creatures up close. It was also in the 1960s that the dire situation of whale populations became most apparent, as increased scientific research revealed just how far whale populations had dropped. At a conference in 1967, scientists announced research showing that the blue whale population had declined from an estimated population of 100,000 in the 1930s to just over 1,000. However, concern for the plight of whales went beyond simple conservation. It also aligned with changing ideas about the importance of nature, wildlife, and animal welfare. Saving the whales became a deeply emotional issue that was as much about preventing extinction as it was about preserving beauty and preventing cruelty.

The late 1960s and early 1970s were watershed years for environmental policy and law. The United States created increased protections for species of wildlife that were deemed to be endangered or at risk of extinction. These laws provided federal officials with the power to create and enforce protections around specific species as concerns arose. In 1969 and again in 1973, the U.S. federal government passed laws to strengthen protections around any species that was threatened or endangered by the possibility of extinction. Public concern about marine mammals, including dolphins, seals, and whales, created particular pressure on government officials. In November 1970, Secretary of the Interior Walter Hickel placed eight species of whale on the Endangered Species List—fin, sei, sperm, bowhead, blue, humpback, right, and gray whales—and banned importation of virtually all whale products. This was a significant move. While the United States had only a handful of whaling boats left, it still accounted for nearly 30 percent of world consumption of whale-based products, largely for cosmetics, industrial lubricants, and pet food. A few months later in spring 1971, Secretary of Commerce Maurice Stans announced that all commercial whaling by the United States was now formally prohibited.

The concern over whales and other marine mammals was such that Congress began to explore ways to deter or even punish other countries and their fishing boats for harvesting species that were protected under U.S. law or international agreement, or else feared to be at risk. In 1972, the United States took the case for whales before the international community at the United Nations Conference on the Human Environment. Although the United States found itself at odds with many other countries over global priorities, the U.S. proposal for a 10-year global moratorium on whaling gained unexpected and near unanimous support, especially by key Western allies—former whaling powers that had since developed opposition to whaling, such as Great Britain. The positive reception of a blanket moratorium on whaling at the UN conference put pressure on members at the upcoming meeting of the IWC, especially on countries that supported whaling, such as Japan, the Soviet Union, Iceland, and Norway.

The United States continued to increase the political pressure by taking aggressive action at home. In October 1972, President Richard Nixon signed into law the landmark Marine Mammal Protection Act (MMPA), which established a general moratorium on the capturing or killing of all marine mammals in U.S. waters and on the importation of marine mammals and marine mammal products into the United States. (See "Marine Mammal Protection Act, 1972," on page 391 in the Primary Sources section, and the sidebar "Saving Flipper" on page 366.)

With the protection of whales and other marine mammals firmly established at home, the United States continued to lead international efforts for a global moratorium on whaling. Throughout the 1970s, the United States and a growing number of antiwhaling allies repeatedly proposed a global, 10-year whaling moratorium before the membership of the IWC. The rationale for the moratorium was ostensibly to allow whale populations the opportunity to recover and to allow scientists time to determine what level of harvesting the species could tolerate without being permanently harmed—a scientifically determined program of conservation. As research accumulated on the status of whales, both by the IWC's own scientific commission and by independent scientists around the world, quotas on catches and other restrictions were placed on individual species of whales.

In 1979, whale sanctuaries were created—areas of the world's oceans in which hunting of whales was prohibited—in the Indian Ocean and in the waters around Antarctica. During the annual IWC conference in Brighton, Great Britain, in 1982, three-quarters of the IWC member countries voted to approve a 10-year moratorium on commercial whaling to take effect in 1985. The blanket moratorium was opposed by the IWC's own scientific commission, which argued that only some species of whales required such protection. Seven countries also voted against it: the Soviet Union, Japan, Peru, Iceland,

Norway, Brazil, and South Korea. Nevertheless, a majority of members approved the momentous move. Although the moratorium was not observed by all countries, the IWC decision would define international agreements and expectations around whales for the next two decades. Indeed, the IWC had transformed from an institution concerned about the conservation of the whaling industry to one concerned about the protection of whales. However, one area that remained only partially resolved and that would be the source of ongoing tension was the issue of indigenous rights to whale.

Native Cultural Survival and Debate over Access to Natural Resources

Throughout their experience with the United States, the Makah had struggled to survive and to protect their cultural identity and their sovereignty. Although they had successfully negotiated a treaty with the U.S. government as a sovereign nation, the reality on the ground was much less clear. Despite guarantees of access to traditional hunting and fishing areas, Makah and other Native groups found themselves in increasing conflict with non-Native residents of Washington and with state officials. Until the 1960s, state governments were almost entirely responsible for the management of their wildlife and other natural resources, including those found in coastal waters. Moreover, the state's primary goal was to manage these finite resources in such a way as to maximize their utility by commercial interests (e.g., fishing and logging) as well as by fee-paying sports hunters and fishers.

In Washington, Native treaty-based claims to equal and unfettered access to commercially valuable resources, such as salmon, put them in direct competition and conflict with non-Natives and the state. This conflict reached a crisis in the 1950s and 1960s as Native groups deliberately resisted state authority and took the state to federal court over access to fish and other resources. To the surprise of many, the federal courts supported Native treaty claims. Although the courts acknowledged that state governments had a legitimate right to control access to natural resources for purposes of conservation, the courts ruled that states had the burden of proof to show that such restrictions were absolutely necessary, especially with regard to Native groups with whom the

(continues on page 368)

SAVING FLIPPER

When the Marine Mammal Protection Act (MMPA) was passed in 1972, it was aimed at addressing threats not just to whales, but also to other marine mammals, especially dolphins. Unlike whales, however, dolphins were not threatened because they were being hunted directly. Rather, the threat came from their association with tuna.

In the eastern tropical Pacific Ocean, off the coasts of Central America and northern South America, are found large schools of both yellowfin tuna and dolphins. For reasons still not completely clear to scientists, these creatures are often found traveling together. Schools of large yellowfin tuna regularly swim directly beneath the surface-swimming schools of dolphins. Tuna fishermen often looked for the telltale signs of leaping dolphins in order to find the highly prized tuna.

In the late 1950s, fishing boats began to use purse seine nets to catch more of the tuna. Purse seine nets are nylon nets that stretch more than half a mile long. Once the schools of dolphins and tuna were spotted, speedboats raced out to encircle them with the purse seine nets, which were then slowly pulled shut, ensnaring both tuna and dolphins. This method was very efficient at increasing the catch of tuna, but it took a heavy toll on dolphins. Fishermen had little interest in dolphins, but these air-breathing mammals often drowned in the nets. In the early years of purse seine netting, hundreds of thousands of dolphins were killed each year. By 1972, an estimated 5 million had been killed this way.

The impact of tuna fishing on dolphins was revealed in the late 1960s as the result of observations made by a National Marine Fisheries Service biologist who was stationed aboard tuna fishing boats for scientific observation. The issue gained public attention in July 1971 during congressional hearings over the proposed global moratorium on whaling (since the original language did not distinguish between dolphins and whales). The revelation caused an outcry from a public that had become increasingly sensitized to the plight of marine mammals, and especially the dolphin. Indeed, since the mid-1960s, one of the most popular shows on television was a program about a family and their companion dolphin, "Flipper," who together protected a Florida marine preserve and foiled mischief makers. Dolphins and their boisterous antics were also popular at the growing number of marine parks around the country. Congress and the tuna industry were besieged by critical letters and newspaper editorials. Thus, when Congress completed work on the landmark MMPA in 1972, members were well acquainted with the dolphin issue. The MMPA placed an indefinite moratorium on the taking of all marine mammals. However, the law made exceptions for scientific research, animals to be put on public display (such as in marine parks), Alaskan natives, and those engaged in commercial fishing. Congress made it clear that it wanted the killing of dolphins by tuna fishermen to stop, but it gave the commercial fishing industry time to develop new fishing methods that would spare the dolphin.

The American tuna fishing industry made dramatic strides in its efforts to reduce the number of dolphins killed—nearly 90 percent reductions between 1975 and 1980—but this still meant that tens of thousands were lost each year. Despite its progress, the industry was vilified by environmental organizations and a broad swath of the public. In 1976, Friends of Animals, an animal welfare organization, ran an advertisement campaign asking, "Would You Kill Flipper for a Tuna Sandwich?" Lawsuits by environmental organizations against the federal government for not adequately enforcing the MMPA put added pressure on tuna fishermen. The federal government responded by imposing stricter quotas on the number of dolphins that could be killed, as well as hefty fines. The final blow came in 1990 when the three major American tuna canners—StarKist, BumbleBee, and Chicken of the Sea—responded to a nationwide boycott of tuna by agreeing to purchase only tuna certified as dolphin safe. This meant that the canners would no longer purchase tuna caught with purse seine nets, regardless of whether dolphins had been killed or not.

Dolphin kill rates have continued to decline over time as a result of international agreements on dolphin conservation and as result of the successful dolphin safe labeling campaign for canned tuna. By 1994, only dolphin-safe tuna could be sold in the United States. This rule was important because the United States is the largest market for canned tuna. By the late 1990s, dolphin mortality dropped from more than 100,000 per year to approximately 3,000 reported dolphin kills per year. Scientists have speculated that the kill rates are sufficiently low for dolphin populations to recover, but the actual recovery has been much slower than expected. Dolphin populations remain at about one-third the size they were prior to the era of exploitation.

(continued from page 365)
United States had negotiated treaties. The most far-reaching decision followed the case of *United States v. Washington* in 1974, in which federal district court judge George Hugo Boldt ruled that "treaty Indians" had an unrestricted and reserved treaty right to fish on the reservation, a right to fish off the reservation for ceremonial and subsistence purposes, and a right to half of the allowable harvest of all fish. This momentous ruling put Native groups on an almost equal footing with state governments, and it was met by considerable shock and resentment by non-Natives, especially commercial fishermen. Nevertheless, the Boldt decision, as it came to be called, laid an important foundation for Native treaty rights.

The relationship between Native groups and the United States began to change in the 1960s. This change was due to a resurgence of activism on the part of Native groups seeking to reassert their sovereignty and cultural identity, the changing attitude of the federal government, and changes in governmental management of the environment. The Makah's pursuit of cultural recognition coincided with the 1960s Civil Rights movement. Like other racial and ethnic minorities, Native groups fought for cultural respect, an end to discrimination, and access to opportunities that were closed due to racial or ethnic bias. Unlike other groups, however, Native people's claims for cultural respect and recognition were tightly intertwined with their relationship to the land and its resources. Thus, they struggled both with racist ideologies and with hostile state wildlife regulations.

As the federal government began to intervene through the courts in the 1960s and 1970s, it also began to assume jurisdiction over wildlife regulation. The new federal wildlife laws were considerably stricter than many state laws had been, but they also made unique exceptions for cultural, religious, and subsistence claims of indigenous groups. Indeed, in 1962, Congress amended the long-standing Bald Eagle Act to allow permitted taking of eagles "for the religious purposes of Indian tribes" because of the importance of eagle feathers to many Native ceremonies. More significant still, the 1972 Marine Mammal Protection Act, which imposed a blanket moratorium on all taking of and commerce in marine mammals and marine mammal products, made specific exemption for takings by "any Indian, Aleut, or Eskimo who dwells on the coast of the North Pacific Ocean or the Arctic Ocean" so long as the taking is for subsistence or for "authentic" native handicrafts. A similar exemption was included in the 1973 Endangered Species Act, subject to federal permit. Although these exemptions were quite specific, they nevertheless reaffirmed the idea that indigenous resource claims, especially for subsistence or authentic cultural purposes, were to be respected and treated differently.

While the Makah began to make gains in their efforts at cultural recognition and respect, one significant area that still eluded them was their tradition of whaling. The Makah had not practiced whaling since the 1920s, but the idea of it gained new attention as part of the larger struggle for cultural survival. In the winter of 1969–70, an unusually strong rainstorm exposed the preserved remains of a Makah log house that had been buried by a catastrophic mudslide 500 years previously. Although the mudslide was remembered in Makah oral history, the discovery of the material remains strengthened the sense of historical legitimacy and continuity for many Makah members. Over the next 10 years, archaeological investigation revealed thousands of important cultural artifacts, which enabled a fuller accounting of Makah history, especially the unique importance of whaling. By 1979, the Makah Cultural and Research Center was erected on the site to house and display the artifacts and to support and perpetuate Makah culture. While understanding of Makah whaling culture increased, it was not until the 1990s that the opportunity to actually revive this tradition presented itself.

In June 1994, the Pacific gray whale was officially removed from the Endangered Species List as a result of population estimates that showed that the species had made a substantial recovery since its listing some 20 years previously. Shortly thereafter, the Makah held a referendum on whether or not they should resume whaling. Three-quarters voted in favor of resuming whaling. In May 1995, the Makah Tribal Council submitted a formal petition to federal officials to resume hunting of gray whales. Although the Makah believed that they did not really need permission to resume hunting, they nevertheless decided to operate within the international legal framework around whaling. They requested that the U.S. government petition on their behalf before the IWC.

The IWC had maintained a global moratorium on whaling since 1985, but the moratorium made specific exemption for whaling done for scientific purposes or for "aboriginal subsistence whaling," defined as "for purposes of local aboriginal consumption carried out by or on behalf of aboriginal, indigenous or native peoples who share strong community, familial, social, and cultural ties related to a continuing traditional dependence on whaling and on the use of whales." In order to obtain a whaling quota, the country representing its Native whaling community had to demonstrate the Native group's continuing tradition of both hunting and eating whales. This presented a problem for the Makah, since it had been more than 70 years since they last hunted a whale.

The United States submitted a proposal on behalf of the Makah at the annual IWC meeting in 1996 but was not able to overcome the fact that the Makah did not have a continuing tradition of whaling. The United States was forced to withdraw the proposal. The following year, however, the United States resubmitted the proposal, and the IWC amended the rules to establish a broader definition of indigenous whaling for "aborigines whose traditional aboriginal subsistence and cultural needs have been recognized." (See "Representative Jack Metcalf's Speech Opposing the Makah Whale Hunt, 1997," on page 392 in the Primary Sources section.)

The IWC was still reluctant to increase the allowed quota of whales that could be harvested. As a compromise, Russia and the United States submitted a joint proposal. The Russian Chukotki people were entitled to a quota of 124 gray whales out of an estimated gray whale population of 26,000. Members of the Alaska Eskimo Whaling Commission agreed to share part of their bowhead whale quota with the Chukotki and, in return, the Chukotki gave part of their gray whale quota to the Makah (four per year). In this way, no more gray whales would be harvested than had already been allotted to the Chukotki. The IWC permitted the Makah to harvest up to 20 gray whales over a five-year period, from 1998 through 2002.

THE DEBATE

Even with official permission in hand, the Makah faced significant challenges to conducting a successful whale hunt. The prospect of reviving a whaling tradition in which no living member had ever participated was a daunting task. How was the hunt to be conducted? How should the Makah prepare? Equally daunting, however, was the popular reaction to the Makah's decision. The tiny Makah village of Neah Bay on the remote outer tip of the Olympic Peninsula was inundated with media from around the world, intent on capturing not just the event itself but the spectacle of controversy. The Makah's decision had in fact attracted vehement condemnation from individuals and organizations opposed to whaling, and specifically to the Makah's declared right to resume the practice of whaling. These antiwhaling forces also descended on the Makah reservation in a desperate effort to either change the minds of the Makah or to stop them from killing a whale.

Makah tribal members gather around the remains of a harvested gray whale on the beach at Neah Bay, Washington, in the early 1900s. For centuries, gray whales were an important part of Makah heritage. (Associated Press)

The Case for Makah Whaling

Makah tribal members saw the revival of whaling as an important aspect of their cultural identity and a part of their cultural survival. They saw the 1855 Treaty of Neah Bay as an important and living document that established their sovereign status and relationship with the United States. The Makah had an unbroken, legal agreement with the United States that specifically reserved the Makah's right to whale. They had never relinquished this right and exercising this treaty right was an important way by which they reasserted their sovereignty. This treaty had been agreed upon in exchange for the vast territory of the Olympic Peninsula that the Makah had relinquished to the U.S. government. Many Makah argued that a resumption of the traditional whaling practice would have a positive impact on the Makah community, especially the youth. Like many rural communities, the Makah suffered from numerous modern-day social ailments: entrenched poverty, delinquency, and substance abuse, nutritional diseases such as obesity and diabetes, and depression. Reintroducing whaling would generate pride and purpose and provide the youth with a cultural practice that required discipline and focus. In addition, they argued that many nutritional ailments might be alleviated or at least lessened by a return to the traditional diet that had sustained the Makah for millennia. More than anything, the Makah defended their prerogative to practice their culture and to define what was culturally relevant and important for them.

However, the Makah were not acting in complete defiance of modern expectations or sensibilities. They attempted to answer their critics through the media. (See "'An Open Letter to the Public from the President of the Makah Whaling Commission,' 1998," on page 394 in the Primary Sources section.) They sought to work through the international legal framework of the IWC, as well as with U.S. federal authorities, to obtain quotas and a permit. The tribe formed a Makah Whaling Commission, consisting of representatives from traditional whaling families, to oversee and manage the hunt so that it was done in a way that respected both tradition and the law. The men chosen to conduct the hunt would undergo rigorous preparation so that they were physically, mentally, and spiritually ready. With the assistance of other indigenous groups who had much more experience whaling, particularly through the Alaskan Eskimo Whaling Commission, the whaling crew learned how to conduct a hunt efficiently and safely.

Consistent with Makah tradition, a seven-man crew would pursue the whale in a cedar dugout canoe and use a hand-thrown harpoon. However, in a concession to safety, the canoe would be accompanied by a support crew in a motorized boat. In addition, a Makah crew member would shoot the whale with a high-powered rifle immediately after it was harpooned in order to conduct the hunt more humanely. Otherwise, the whale's death would be prolonged for hours if not days as it slowly bled to death from the harpoon. The Makah argued that their revived hunt would be conducted in the safest and most humane way, consistent with traditional needs, and did not present a threat to the species. They pointed out repeatedly that the Pacific gray whale had been removed from the Endangered Species List because of its spectacular recovery. It was not to be forgotten, they argued, that it was the whaling activities of non-Natives that had nearly brought the gray whale to extinction. Indigenous whaling had always been conducted in a sustainable manner, and its continuance would pose no more threat. If anything, it was the Makah culture and sovereignty that faced an existential threat.

The Case Against Makah Whaling

Opponents of the Makah whale hunt ranged from individuals and organizations who opposed any killing of whales to those who resented the Makah's claims to treaty rights. At the forefront of opposition were several animal rights groups who opposed the hunting of whales. These groups, notably the Sea Shepherd Conservation Society and the Progressive Animal Welfare Society, led the charge against Makah whaling. They argued first and foremost that the hunting of whales was inhumane and unnecessary. Whales, they argued, were unique creatures of high intelligence, and it was immoral to kill them for any reason. Anti-whaling activists were vehement in their crusade. The Sea Shepherd Conservation Society boasted an aggressive reputation for its efforts to interfere with whaling on the high seas. In the 1980s, it was responsible for sinking two Icelandic whaling ships.

The Sea Shepherd Conservation Society was not alone in its convictions. It had strong financial support from numerous donors around the world who felt just as strongly about the need to protect whales from harm and from cruelty. Antiwhaling activists argued that allowing the Makah to resume whaling would threaten the species because it would set a precedent, opening the door for a resumption of whaling by other indigenous groups and, more important, a resumption of commercial whaling. Indeed, many critics suspected that the Makah tribe was seeking to hunt whales in order to sell them to whaling countries, rather than for personal consumption. Some argued that the Makah tribe was just a pawn in a larger game by whaling countries such as Japan, Russia, and Iceland to dismantle the IWC moratorium and resume commercial whaling.

Critics argued that the Makah's claims of a cultural need to resume whaling were disingenuous and unsupportable. They pointed out that the Makah had long since abandoned their whaling tradition and proven entirely capable of living without the practice. Also, their decision to employ motorized boats and a rifle showed that they were not in fact following tradition. More important, antiwhaling activists argued that tradition alone was not sufficient reason to revive an archaic practice that critics described as barbaric. "There isn't anyone alive today on that reservation who can go out there and kill a whale in a traditional manner," Sea Shepherd leader Paul Watson told the *New York Times*. "They used to keep slaves, as well. Do we go back to that? I don't see the point in making a distinction between natives having more of a right to kill whales than nonnative people."

Opposition to the Makah whale hunt sparked a unique alliance between antiwhaling activists and those who opposed Native treaty rights claims more generally. Among the latter were Washington senator Slade Gorton and Washington representative Jack Metcalf, longtime critics of Native claims to treaty rights and veterans of the infamous "Fish Wars" in the Pacific Northwest between Natives and non-Natives. (See the sidebar "The Northwest 'Fish Wars'" on page 376.) Gorton argued that treaty rights made Native people "supercitizens" and undermined the rights of others. Metcalf had a long antienvironmental history but nevertheless emerged as a leading critic of the Makah whale hunt. In 1996, he introduced a resolution in Congress condemning the

Makah hunt that passed unanimously in the House of Representatives Committee on Resources. In April 1998, when the federal government granted the Makah permission to whale on cultural and subsistence grounds, Metcalf led the group that filed a lawsuit against the decision. Opponents of the Makah whale hunt thus took their arguments to the public and to the courts.

OUTCOME AND IMPACT

Though the Makah had official sanction to harvest a whale by the spring of 1998, they did not do so for more than a year. In the meantime, the media and numerous antiwhaling activists, as well as other curious onlookers, came to witness and perhaps interfere with the event. The Makah announced no firm date on which they planned to actually kill a whale as they did not really know themselves. As everyone waited, tensions ran high, resulting in a number of minor skirmishes between tribal members and antiwhaling activists. The activists, positioned offshore, made repeated attempts to scare off the migrating whales and closely followed the Makah whenever they went out on the water. The Makah whalers made several unsuccessful attempts to harpoon a whale, but were thwarted by antiwhaling protesters. In fact, several antiwhaling boats were confiscated by the coast guard, ironically for harassing the whales and violating the Marine Mammal Protection Act.

In the early morning of May 17, 1999, seven Makah whale hunters in a 32-foot cedar canoe finally harpooned and then shot a 33-foot gray whale. The event was witnessed by news helicopters hovering overhead and coast guard vessels that accompanied the whalers in order to make sure that the hunt was conducted appropriately and to prevent interference by protesters. The whale carcass was towed to shore by a motorized boat, while two of the hunters stood triumphantly atop the whale. Hundreds of jubilant supporters lined the shore to celebrate the event. That evening, the whale was butchered and the meat distributed among tribal members.

Meanwhile, protesters just outside the Makah reservation and five hours south in Seattle held vigils and mourned the whale's slaughter.

The Makah's celebration was short-lived. In June 2000, the United States Court of Appeals for the Ninth Circuit suspended federal approval of the Makah whale hunt and ordered a new environmental study of its impacts. The court order was based on the lawsuit originally filed by

THE NORTHWEST "FISH WARS"

In the mid-1800s, the governor of Washington Territory signed a series of treaties with tribes throughout the Northwest, giving the U.S. government control over most of western Washington. Although the tribes ceded most of their territory and were relegated to small reservations, nearly all of the treaties used similar language to guarantee Native peoples continued access to fish and other resources. After Washington achieved statehood in 1889, however, state officials began to close important salmon and steelhead trout rivers to fishing in the name of conservation. The restrictions were a particular hardship for Native peoples reliant on these fish for food and trade.

However, the restrictions were not applied uniformly. Over the next 50 years, dramatic increases in non-Native commercial and sport fishing put intense pressure on salmon and other important species, which began to decline. Native Americans, already regarded with disdain and suspicion, were blamed for the decline, although their role was minor compared to that of the commercial and sports fishers. Indeed, the state's own records showed that Native catches were less than 5 percent of the harvestable fish in the region. Nevertheless, Washington State responded by stepping up enforcement against Native fishers, which culminated in aggressive raids and stings in the 1950s and 1960s. Native peoples, who continued to invoke their treaty rights, began to openly defy the state, precipitating what came to be known as the Northwest "Fish Wars." The Fish Wars came to a head in the late 1960s as Native protesters, particularly from the Nisqually and Puyallup tribes, adopted a civil disobedience–style opposition with fish-ins during which they fished in open defiance of state law. The protests attracted numerous sympathetic celebrities, such as Jane Fonda and Marlon Brando. However, this opposition also provoked more aggressive responses by state officials and non-Native vigilantes. The confrontations turned violent as state officials resorted to military-style enforcement, in some cases using tear gas and billy clubs. Native protesters continued to fish and fought back with stones

Congressman Metcalf in April 1998. The plaintiffs argued that the federal government inappropriately completed an environmental impact assessment of the whale hunt *after* it had already given the Makah

and their bare hands. Live broadcasts of these clashes attracted national attention. One of the most dramatic confrontations occurred in September 1970 when Tacoma police used tear gas and clubs to arrest 59 protesters at a fish-in camp along the Puyallup River. In the heat of the melee, gunshots were fired and protesters severely beaten. A month later, the federal government intervened on behalf of Native groups and sued Washington State in federal district court for violation of the tribes' treaty rights.

On February 23, 1974, federal district court judge George Hugo Boldt handed down a 203-page decision in the case of *United States v. Washington* affirming the right of tribes in Washington to continue to fish. Boldt argued that when the tribes ceded millions of acres of land in Washington Territory to the federal government, they did so with the explicit understanding that they were reserving the right to continue fishing. In fact, it was the tribes that had granted non-Native settlers the right to fish and not the other way around. He argued that Washington State had virtually no authority over tribal fishing. Of particular interest was a sentence included in most of the treaties negotiated with Washington tribes in 1854 and 1855: "The right of taking fish, at all usual and accustomed grounds and stations, is further secured to said Indians in common with all citizens of the Territory." Judge Boldt interpreted the phrase "in common with all citizens of the Territory" to mean that the tribes were entitled to *half* of the state's fishing resources. Although Native people represented only 1 percent of Washington's population, they were now entitled to 50 percent of its fish. The ruling shocked both Natives and non-Natives alike. Despite numerous legal appeals and widespread condemnation from non-Native residents, the ruling was eventually upheld by the U.S. Supreme Court and became a legal cornerstone for Native treaty rights. The Boldt decision engendered deep resentment among non-Natives, but it ended the Fish Wars, and it redefined the relationship between Native tribes and state governments, especially on issues relating to natural resource management.

permission. The court concluded that the review should have been completed before any agreement was signed with the tribe.

In January 2001, the National Marine Fisheries Service (NMFS) released a new environmental assessment of the Makah request. The report was opened for public comment, and forums were held in Seattle, leading to heated exchanges on both sides. In July, the NMFS released its final environmental assessment that concluded that the Makah whale hunt posed no threat to the eastern North Pacific gray whale population, with an estimated population of 26,000 animals. However, in December 2002, a three-judge panel of the United States Court of Appeals for the Ninth Circuit rejected the federal environmental assessment and ordered the NMFS to conduct a new and more stringent environmental impact statement. In addition, the court found that the federal government had also violated the MMPA by not issuing a waiver. In the meantime, the Makah were barred from conducting any more whale hunts.

The Makah argued that their treaty rights exempted them from the MMPA, as it did for the Inupiat and Siberian Yupik Eskimos living in northern and western Alaska, but the court was not moved. The federal government and the Makah petitioned the court to reconsider its decision, but the court disagreed. Thus, the federal government once again began the process to analyze the environmental impacts of a whale hunt and to solicit comments from the public. In February 2005, the Makah followed the court's direction and requested a waiver of the MMPA to hunt whales for ceremonial and subsistence purposes.

As the issue of the Makah whale hunt dragged on through the courts, and as the federal government worked its way through the environmental impact statement process, a group of frustrated Makah members took matters into their own hands. On the morning of September 9, 2007, five male Makah (including the captain of the previous crew) headed out into the open ocean in two motor boats. They harpooned and shot a 40-foot gray whale and then attached buoys to it as they prepared to bring it back to shore. Coast Guard officials heard the shots and rushed to the scene where they arrested the Makah whalers and confiscated their gear. The whale, mortally wounded but not yet dead, was cut loose and died some hours later. When Makah members heard of the incident, some went out to see the whale and to perform

A gray whale *(Eschrichtius robustus)* viewed beneath the water surface. Gray whales may reach a length of up to 52 feet and weigh more than 35 tons. Although they were once common to both the Atlantic and Pacific Oceans, centuries of hunting by commercial whalers left only a remnant population off the Pacific coast of North America. (Ken Drori/Shutterstock)

sacred songs over the dying animal. Tribal members were torn over the incident. Many sympathized with the frustration expressed by the men, but they were also upset at the way it had been done. The following day, the Makah Tribal Council issued a public condemnation of the unauthorized killing, calling it counterproductive and asking the public not to hold the Makah tribe at fault for the actions of the few. In October 2007, the five men were indicted by a federal grand jury on charges of conspiracy, violations of the International Convention for the Regulation of Whaling, and violation of the MMPA. In March 2008, three of the men accepted a plea deal and admitted guilt to one misdemeanor charge of taking a whale in violation of the MMPA. They were ordered to serve two years' probation and perform community service. The remaining two refused to plead guilty and were sentenced to five months and 90 days in jail, respectively, as well as one year's probation and community service.

In May 2008, the NMFS completed a 900-page draft of the court-ordered environmental impact statement and released it for public comment. Once again, the NMFS recommended that a Makah hunt be permitted, although with restrictions on time and place. In early 2012, the Makah's proposal to resume whale hunting was still under review by the NMFS. Meanwhile, new studies of the gray whale population since 2006 lowered the estimated size of the population, raising concerns among some people about the status of the species. At least one group, the California Gray Whale Coalition, has petitioned the NMFS to list the Pacific gray whale as depleted, which would require the federal government to devise a new conservation plan and possibly lead to a declaration that the species be returned to the Endangered Species List.

WHAT IF?

What if U.S. officials had declined to seek permission from the IWC on behalf of the Makah?

When Makah representatives approached federal officials with the petition to resume whaling, the United States was placed in an awkward position. As trustee of tribal affairs, the United States was expected to act in the tribe's interests. However, whaling was deeply unpopular with the American public, as well as with allied nations in the IWC. Moreover, the language of the existing moratorium was very strict in making exceptions for indigenous groups with a continuing tradition of whaling.

It took considerable negotiation by the United States to convince other countries to amend the IWC rules to allow the Makah to resume hunting. The United States could have declined to pursue the Makah petition or accepted the IWC's initial rejection. Without the United States seeking IWC approval on behalf of the Makah, the Makah would not have been granted a quota by the IWC, nor would they have been given permission by the U.S. government. Although the Makah believed that they had a sovereign and treaty-defined right to resume whaling, rejection by the international community and the United States would have put them in a much less defensible position, both politically and legally. If the Makah request had been rejected, it is likely that they would have continued to campaign for their right before the public and the international community. It is less certain whether the Makah would have hunted a whale in defiance, as happened later on. To some extent, the illegal hunting that Makah members did do may have been influenced by the sense of betrayal and frustration that followed the initial approval. Had permission never been granted, the Makah's expectations would have been lessened. At the same time, rejection by the United States would have invited criticism for cultural insensitivity. Indeed, the United States has already been censured by the international community for its refusal to adopt or ratify international treaties on human rights that acknowledge the right of indigenous groups and others to determine their cultural needs, especially with respect to food and lifestyle.

CHRONOLOGY

1832	U.S. Supreme Court observes that American Indian tribes are sovereign nations and declares that treaties with Indian tribes are to be respected.
1846–1852	U.S. commercial whaling activities hit their peak.
1855	*January 31:* Makah tribe signs Treaty of Neah Bay with the governor of Washington Territory.
1925	Factory whaling begins with the development of slip sterns.
1926	Makah conduct their last whale hunt until the late 20th century.
1946	*December:* International Convention for the Regulation of Whaling is signed in Washington, D.C.
1950s	Makah and other tribes repeatedly come into conflict with Washington State over treaty rights and access to fishing and other natural resources.
1969	U.S. Congress passes the Endangered Species Conservation Act.
1970	An ancient Makah log house and whaling station is uncovered, sparking excitement in the Makah community over a rekindling of lost traditions.
	November 24: Secretary of the Interior Walter Hickel places eight species of whale on the Endangered Species List and bans importation of virtually all whale products.
1971	*March:* Secretary of Commerce Maurice Stans announces that all commercial whaling by the United States will be prohibited.

July: The U.S. Senate unanimously passes a joint resolution instructing the State Department to negotiate a 10-year global moratorium on the killing of whales.

1972   *June:* At the United Nations Conference on the Human Environment in Stockholm, the United States proposes a 10-year moratorium on all whaling.

October: President Richard Nixon signs the Marine Mammal Protection Act (MMPA).

1973   U.S. Congress passes the amended Endangered Species Act.

1974   *February 23:* U.S. district court judge George Boldt in *United States v. Washington* affirms tribal treaty rights regarding access to fishing.

1979   Makah Cultural Resource Center opens to display artifacts discovered at ancient Ozette village site, including numerous whaling artifacts.

1980   The International Whaling Commission (IWC) bans factory whaling ships (except for minke whales).

1982   The IWC imposes a 10-year blanket moratorium on commercial whaling but allows subsistence whaling. The moratorium is scheduled to go into effect in 1985.

1983   Great whales are placed on Convention on International Trade in Endangered Species (CITES), Appendix I, marking them as a threatened species requiring higher levels of global protection.

1985   The International Whaling Commission (IWC) moratorium on commercial whaling goes into force.

1994   *June:* The Pacific gray whale is removed from the Endangered Species List.

1995   *May:* Makah tribe announces intention to revive whaling practices and petitions the federal government to seek a whaling quota from the IWC.

1996   The United States submits a proposal to the IWC for a Makah whaling quota but withdraws it after extended debate over continuing tradition or dependence.

June: Washington representative Jack Metcalf sponsors a resolution expressing opposition to the Makah whale hunt, which passes unanimously in the House Committee on Resources.

1997   The Sea Shepherd Conservation Society launches campaign to oppose Makah whale hunt.

IWC amends rules to recognize traditional aboriginal subsistence and cultural needs and issues the Makah a whaling quota: up to 20 whales over a five-year period.

1998   *April:* National Oceanic and Atmospheric Administration (NOAA) issues a federal notice stating that the Makah subsistence and cultural needs are recognized by the United States and IWC, allowing the tribe to take a whale.

April: Antiwhaling coalition led by Representative Metcalf files suit in federal district court accusing the federal government of violating the National Environmental Policy Act based on an inadequate assessment of the environmental consequences of granting the Makah a permit to resume whaling.

1999   *May 17:* A crew of Makah tribal members harpoons and harvests a gray whale.

2000   *June 9:* United States Court of Appeals for the Ninth Circuit suspends federal approval of the Makah whale hunt. The court orders a new environmental assessment.

2001   *July 12:* The National Marine Fisheries Service (NMFS) completes a new environmental assessment, concluding that the Makah hunt poses no threat to the eastern North Pacific gray whale population.

2002   *December 20:* United States Court of Appeals for the Ninth Circuit overturns and rejects the environmental assessment.

2005   *February:* The Makah tribe submits a letter to NOAA requesting a waiver of the MMPA to hunt whale for ceremonial purposes and subsistence.

2007   *September 9:* Makah tribal members illegally harpoon and shoot a 40-foot gray whale.

September 10: Makah Tribal Council issues a statement condemning the unapproved hunt.

	October: Federal grand jury indicts Makah tribal members of conspiracy, violations of the International Convention for the Regulation of Whaling, and violation of MMPA.
2008	*May 9:* NMFS completes 900-page draft environmental impact statement on the Makah whale hunt.
	June 30: Makah tribal members are sentenced to prison and community service for the unauthorized killing of a gray whale.

DISCUSSION QUESTIONS

1. Did the Makah have a right to resume whaling? Should they have resumed whaling? Why or why not?
2. Why was the resumption of whaling so important to the Makah?
3. Are gray whales, or other whale species, threatened by the Makah's resumption of whaling? Why or why not?
4. Some opponents of the Makah whale hunt question the cultural authenticity or legitimacy of the hunt. Was this a valid argument? If cultural claims are important, how should their legitimacy be decided?
5. How should the government balance the rights of indigenous groups with the larger society's norms or expectations on issues like animal rights or conservation?

WEB SITES

Greenpeace International. Whaling. Available online. URL: http://www.greenpeace.org/international/campaigns/oceans/whaling/. Accessed April 1, 2011.

The International Whaling Commission. Home Page. Available online. URL: http://www.iwcoffice.org/. Accessed April 1, 2011.

Makah Cultural and Research Center. Home Page. Available online. URL: http://www.makah.com/mcrchome.html. Accessed April 1, 2011.

National Council for Science and the Environment (NCSE). Native Americans and the Environment. The Makah Whale Hunt. Available online. URL: http://ncseonline.org/NAE/cases/makah/index.html. Accessed April 1, 2011.

NOAA Fisheries. Office of Protected Resources. Cetaceans: Whales, Dolphins, and Porpoises. Available online. URL: http://www.nmfs. noaa.gov/pr/species/mammals/cetaceans/. Accessed April 1, 2011.

Sea Shepherd Conservation Society. Home Page. Available online. URL: http://www.seashepherd.org/. Accessed April 1, 2011.

World Council of Whalers. Available online. URL: http://www. worldwhalers.com/. Accessed April 1, 2011.

BIBLIOGRAPHY

Coté, Charlotte. *Spirits of Our Whaling Ancestors: Revitalizing Makah & Nuu-chah-nulth Traditions.* Seattle: University of Washington Press, 2010.

Epstein, Charlotte. *The Power of Words in International Relations: Birth of an Anti-Whaling Discourse.* Cambridge: Massachusetts Institute of Technology, 2008.

Nagtzaam, Gerry J. "The International Whaling Commission and the Elusive Great White Whale of Preservationism." 2008. Available online. URL: http://works.bepress.com/gerry_nagtzaam/2.

Schoell, Mark. "The Marine Mammal Protection Act and Its Role in the Decline of San Diego's Tuna Fishing Industry." *Journal of San Diego History* 45, no. 1 (Winter 1999). Available online. URL: http://www. sandiegohistory.org/journal/99winter/tuna.htm.

Sullivan, Robert. *A Whale Hunt: Two Years on the Olympic Peninsula with the Makah and their Canoe.* New York: Scribner, 2000.

Tizon, Alex. "25 years after the Boldt Decision: The Fish Tale That Changed History." *Seattle Times* (7 February 1999). Available online. URL: http://kohary.com/env/bill_020799.html.

Tønnessen, J. N., and A. O. Johnsen. *The History of Modern Whaling.* Berkeley: University of California Press, 1982.

PRIMARY SOURCES

Document 1: Treaty of Neah Bay, 1855

In 1854 and 1855, representatives of the governor of Washington Territory met with tribal representatives throughout the region to sign agreements settling claims to territory and to resolve tensions between Natives and settlers over access to land and resources. The Makah made substantial concessions of territory to the U.S. government, but they were adamant about the need to retain access to fish and other marine resources, which were codified in the final treaty. Below are excerpts from the 1855 Treaty of Neah Bay signed by the U.S. government and the Makah. Note particularly Article 4, which focuses on fishing and whaling.

TREATY OF NEAH BAY, 1855

Articles of agreement and convention, made and concluded at Neah Bay, in the Territory of Washington, this thirty-first day of January, in the year eighteen hundred and fifty-five, by Isaac I. Stevens, governor and superintendent of Indian affairs for the said Territory, on the part of the United States, and the undersigned chiefs, head-men, and delegates of the several villages of the Makah tribe of Indians, viz: Neah Waatch, Tsoo-Yess, and Osett, occupying the country around Cape Classett or Flattery, on behalf of the said tribe and duly authorized by the same.

ARTICLE 1.

The said tribe hereby cedes, relinquishes, and conveys to the United States all their right, title, and interest in and to the lands and country occupied by it. . . .

ARTICLE 2.

There is, however, reserved for the present use and occupation of the said tribe the following tract of land, . . . which said tract shall be set apart, and so far as necessary surveyed and marked out for their exclusive use; nor shall any white man be permitted to reside upon the same without permission of the said tribe and of the superintendent or agent; but if necessary for the public convenience, roads may be run through the said reservation, the Indians being compensated for any damage thereby done them. It is, however, understood that should the President of the United States hereafter see fit to place upon the said reservation any other friendly tribe or band to occupy the same in common with those above mentioned, he shall be at liberty to do so.

ARTICLE 3.

The said tribe agrees to remove to and settle upon the said reservation, if required so to do, within one year after the ratification of this treaty, or sooner, if the means are furnished them. . . .

ARTICLE 4.

The right of taking fish and of whaling or sealing at usual and accustomed grounds and stations is further secured to said Indians in common with all citizens of the United States, and of erecting temporary houses for the purpose of curing, together with the privilege of hunting and gathering roots and berries on open and unclaimed lands: Provided, however, That they shall not take shell-fish from any beds staked or cultivated by citizens.

ARTICLE 5.

In consideration of the above cession the United States agree to pay to the said tribe the sum of thirty thousand dollars. . . .

ARTICLE 6.

To enable the said Indians to remove to and settle upon their aforesaid reservation, and to clear, fence, and break up a sufficient quantity of land for cultivation, the United States further agree to pay the sum of three thousand dollars. . . .

ARTICLE 7.

The President may hereafter . . . remove them from said reservation to such suitable place or places within said Territory as he may deem fit, on remunerating them for their improvements and the expenses of their removal, or may consolidate them with other friendly tribes or bands. . . .

ARTICLE 8.

The annuities of the aforesaid tribe shall not be taken to pay the debts of individuals.

ARTICLE 9.

The said Indians acknowledge their dependence on the Government of the United States, and promise to be friendly with all citizens thereof, and they pledge themselves to commit no depredations on the property of such citizens. . . .

ARTICLE 10.

The above tribe is desirous to exclude from its reservation the use of ardent spirits, and to prevent its people from drinking the same, and therefore it is provided that any Indian belonging thereto who shall be guilty of bringing liquor into said reservation, or who drinks liquor, may have his or her proportion of the annuities withheld from him or her for such time as the President may determine.

ARTICLE 11.

The United States further agree to establish . . . an agricultural and industrial school, to be free to children of the said tribe in common with those of the other tribes of said district and to provide a smithy and carpenter's shop, and furnish them with the necessary tools and employ a blacksmith, carpenter and farmer for the like term to instruct the Indians in their respective occupations. . . . And the United States further agree to employ a physician to reside at the said central agency . . . who shall furnish medicine and advice to the sick, and shall vaccinate them. . . .

ARTICLE 12.

The said tribe agrees to free all slaves now held by its people, and not to purchase or acquire others hereafter.

ARTICLE 13.

The said tribe finally agrees not to trade at Vancouver's Island or elsewhere out of the dominions of the United States, nor shall foreign Indians be permitted to reside in its reservation without consent of the superintendent or agent.

ARTICLE 14.

This treaty shall be obligatory on the contracting parties as soon as the same shall be ratified by the President of the United States. In testimony whereof, the said Isaac I. Stevens, governor and superintendent of Indian affairs, and the undersigned, chiefs, headmen and delegates of the tribe aforesaid have hereunto set their hands and seals at the place and on the day and year hereinbefore written.

Source: Treaty of Neah Bay, January 31, 1855. Ratified March 8, 1859.

—⚐—

Document 2: International Convention for the Regulation of Whaling, 1946

In 1946, 15 countries signed the International Convention for the Regulation of Whaling, which established the International Whaling Commission, the premier international body regulating the global whaling industry. The convention was based on the concept of conservation of whales, which meant managing them as a resource to be harvested at rates that could be sustained over the long term and without driving the species to extinction. Although the language of the convention provided for sweeping authority, it also gave the signatory sole power over enforcement. Moreover, the provisions clearly favored the whaling industry over the whales themselves. Below are excerpts from the convention.

INTERNATIONAL CONVENTION FOR THE REGULATION OF WHALING

The Governments whose duly authorised representatives have subscribed hereto, Recognizing the interest of the nations of the world in safeguarding for future generations the great natural resources represented by the whale stocks;

Considering that the history of whaling has seen overfishing of one area after another and of one species of whale after another to such a degree that it is essential to protect all species of whales from further over-fishing;

Recognizing that the whale stocks are susceptible of natural increases if whaling is properly regulated, and that increases in the size of whale stocks will permit increases in the number of whales which may be captured without endangering these natural resources;

Recognizing that it is in the common interest to achieve the optimum level of whale stocks as rapidly as possible without causing widespread economic and nutritional distress;

Recognizing that in the course of achieving these objectives, whaling operations should be confined to those species best able to sustain exploitation in order to give an interval for recovery to certain species of whales now depleted in numbers;

Desiring to establish a system of international regulation for the whale fisheries to ensure proper and effective conservation and development of whale stocks on the basis of the principles embodied in the provisions of the International Agreement for the Regulation of Whaling, signed in London on 8th June, 1937, and the protocols to that Agreement signed in London on 24th June, 1938, and 26th November, 1945; and Having decided to conclude a convention to provide for the proper conservation of whale stocks and thus make possible the orderly development of the whaling industry;

Have agreed as follows: . . .

Article III

The Contracting Governments agree to establish an International Whaling Commission, hereinafter referred to as the Commission, to be composed of one member from each Contracting Government. Each member shall have one vote and may be accompanied by one or more experts and advisers. . . .

Article IV

The Commission may either in collaboration with or through independent agencies of the Contracting Governments or other public or private agencies, establishments, or organizations, or independently

> encourage, recommend, or if necessary, organize studies and investigations relating to whales and whaling;
> collect and analyze statistical information concerning the current condition and trend of the whale stocks and the effects of whaling activities thereon;
> study, appraise, and disseminate information concerning methods of maintaining and increasing the populations of whale stocks.

The Commission shall arrange for the publication of reports of its activities. . . .

Article V

The Commission may amend from time to time the provisions of the Schedule by adopting regulations with respect to the conservation and utilization of whale resources, fixing *(a)* protected and unprotected species; *(b)* open and closed seasons; *(c)* open and closed waters, including the designation of sanctuary areas; *(d)* size limits for each species; *(e)* time, methods, and intensity of whaling (including the maximum catch of whales to be taken in any one season); *(f)* types and specifications of gear and apparatus and appliances which may be used; *(g)* methods of measurement; and *(h)* catch returns and other statistical and biological records.

These amendments of the Schedule *(a)* shall be such as are necessary to carry out the objectives and purposes of this Convention and to provide for the conservation, development, and optimum utilization of the whale resources; *(b)* shall be based on scientific findings; *(c)* shall not involve restrictions on the number or nationality of factory ships or land stations, nor allocate specific quotas to any factory ship or land station or to any group of factory ships or land stations; and *(d)* shall take into consideration the interests of the consumers of whale products and the whaling industry.

Source: International Convention for the Regulation of Whaling. Washington, D.C. December 2, 1946.

—∿—

Document 3: Marine Mammal Protection Act, 1972

During the most prolific period of national environmental legislation, President Richard M. Nixon signed the Marine Mammal Protection Act (MMPA) in 1972. The MMPA reflected the American public's concern over threats to wildlife, issues of animal welfare, and an improved understanding of the complex, and often unforeseen, ecological implications of human activity. The MMPA prohibited, with certain exceptions, the "taking" of marine mammals in U.S. waters and by U.S. citizens on the high seas, and the importation of marine mammals and marine mammal products into the United States. The legislation directly addressed concerns about the possibility of extinction, the need to manage and encourage the success of marine mammals, and the inadequate knowledge of the ecology of these creatures. Below is the preamble to the historic legislation.

FINDINGS AND DECLARATION OF POLICY

Sec. 2. The Congress finds that—certain species and population stocks of marine mammals are, or may be, in danger of extinction or depletion as a result of man's activities; such species and population stocks should not be permitted to diminish beyond the point at which they cease to be a significant functioning element in the ecosystem of which they are a part, and, consistent with this major objective, they should not be permitted to diminish below their optimum sustainable population. Further measures should be immediately taken to replenish any species or population stock which has already diminished below that population. In particular, efforts should be made to protect essential habitats, including the rookeries, mating grounds, and areas of similar significance for each species of marine mammal from the adverse effect of man's actions; there is inadequate knowledge of the ecology and population dynamics of such marine mammals and of the factors which bear upon their ability to reproduce themselves successfully; negotiations should be undertaken immediately to encourage the development of international arrangements for research on, and conservation of, all marine mammals; marine mammals and marine mammal products either—move in interstate commerce, or affect the balance of marine ecosystems in a manner which is important to other animals and animal products which move in interstate commerce, and that the protection and conservation of marine mammals and their habitats is therefore necessary to insure the continuing availability of those products which move in interstate commerce; and marine mammals have proven themselves to be resources of great international significance, esthetic and recreational as well as economic, and it is the sense of the Congress that they should be protected and encouraged to develop to the greatest extent feasible commensurate with sound policies of resource management and that the primary objective of their management should be to maintain the health and stability of the marine ecosystem. Whenever consistent with this primary objective, it should be the goal to obtain an optimum sustainable population keeping in mind the carrying capacity of the habitat.

Source: Marine Mammal Protection Act of 1972. Enacted October 21, 1972.

—⚐—

Document 4: Representative Jack Metcalf's Speech Opposing the Makah Whale Hunt, 1997

U.S. representative Jack Metcalf (R-Wash.) emerged as one of the most ardent opponents to the revival of Makah whale hunt. Shortly after the Makah announced their intention to resume whaling, Congressman Metcalf mobilized with other allies to oppose U.S. efforts to seek a quota from the International Whaling Commission (IWC). In 1996, he sponsored a resolution in the House Resources Subcommittee opposing the hunt and took this resolution to the IWC meeting in order to undermine the U.S. delegation's efforts to amend IWC rules in order to recognize the Makah's claim to indigenous whaling rights. Below is a speech he gave in the House of Representatives on October 22, 1997, the night before the IWC vote.

CONGRESS SHOULD OPPOSE INCREASES IN WHALING

Mr. METCALF. Mr. Speaker, for the last 3 days I have been in Monaco at my own expense to try to prevent the renewal of whaling in the continental United States.

From the beginning of this debate over whether the Makah Indian Tribe in Washington State should be allowed to resume the practice of hunting whales after a 70-year cessation, I have maintained what is being described as "aboriginal subsistence whaling" is not that at all. It will in fact lead to a tragic resumption of commercial whaling and a geometric increase in the number of whales killed worldwide.

Without now addressing whether the Makah Tribe itself is motivated by the $1 million value of a gray whale in Japan, other powerful evidence exists that indicates that we are on the threshold of a dramatic increase in whaling. The official U.S. delegation to the IWC has been asking for a change in the definition of aboriginal subsistence whaling, the only type of whaling now legal under the International Whaling Commission, which the United States has ratified.

In their shortsighted attempt to legalize the intentions of the Makah Tribe, the United States is asking the other nations at the IWC to expand the definition of subsistence whaling to permit cultural issues to be addressed. Why? Currently aboriginal whaling is solely for the physical nutrition of the tribe in question. In other words, they need the food. It is obvious the Makah do not need to eat whales to survive.

What is the problem with expanding the definition into the cultural realm? There are villages and people all over the world who have a cultural history of whaling but who do not now qualify under the current definition of subsistence.

Saturday at the IWC hearings, the Japanese repeatedly asked the United States delegation: What is the difference between the Makah request and the desire of our villages on the Taiji Peninsula to resume whaling? It is obvious the Japanese are going to use this loophole that our own delegation is attempting to create to increase their commercial harvest of the whales. Other nations will undoubtedly follow suit if the Makah are successful.

Mr. Speaker, we cannot allow this to happen. The killing of whales around the world is on the increase. For this fraudulent cultural subsistence to become a legal authorization for further killing would be a tragedy. In addition, staff members of other IWC delegations have indicated resentment at the tremendous pressure the U.S. delegation is putting on other nations to support this fraud. . . .

Mr. Speaker, they are not representing the best interests of our Nation or the sentiments of the vast majority of our people. It is now time for Congress to speak in a large, loud, bipartisan voice in condemnation of this blatant attempt at the expansion of commercial whaling. The vote [by the IWC] will be tomorrow, and this is a critical issue.

Source: U.S. House of Representatives. *Congressional Record,* p. 22,556. October 22, 1997.

—⁓—

Document 5: "An Open Letter to the Public from the President of the Makah Whaling Commission," 1998

Since their initial announcement that they planned to hunt a whale, the Makah tribe came under withering attack from animal rights groups and others opposed to the killing of whales. With the approval of a quota by the International Whaling Commission in April 1998, the argument only intensified. The Makah were not immune to the public pressure and attempted to answer their critics. Below is a open letter from the Makah Whaling Commission explaining the Makah's motivations and rebutting their critics' arguments.

My name is Keith Johnson. I am a Makah Indian and President of the Makah Whaling Commission, made up of representatives from 23 traditional whaling families of our Tribe. For the past three years we have been reading the attacks made on us by animal rights organizations, aimed at stopping our whale hunt. These attacks contain distortions, exaggerations and outright falsehoods. Reading these things has sickened and angered me and I feel I must speak out. . . .

Why Does the Tribe Want to Do This?

Whaling has been part of our tradition for over 2,000 years. Although we had to stop in the 1920s because of the scarcity of gray whales, their abundance now makes it possible to resume our ancient practice of whale hunting. Many of our Tribal members feel that our health problems result from the loss of our traditional sea food and sea mammal diet. We would like to restore the meat of the whale to that diet. We also believe that the problems which are troubling our young people stem from lack of discipline and pride and we hope that the restoration of whaling will help to restore that discipline and pride. But we also want to fulfill the legacy of our forefathers and restore a part of our culture which was taken from us. . . .

Will the Makahs Sell Any of the Whale Meat?

Absolutely not! Yet animal rights groups like Sea Shepherd continue to insist that we secretly plan to sell whale meat to Japan. That claim has been repeated endlessly by other animal rights groups. It is utterly false.

Although our Treaty guaranteed a commercial right, we have agreed to limit ourselves to noncommercial whaling. We are bound by Federal Law and our own Tribal Law not to sell any whale meat. We have no plan to sell whale meat in the future. We also believe that Sea Shepherd is well aware of this but chooses to continue to accuse us of planning to sell whale meat in order to generate continued financial contributions.

Though it may be difficult for some people to accept, we are acting out of purely cultural motives. In fact, it is costing our Tribe an enormous amount of money to carry on the whale hunting program. It is conducted solely because that is our Treaty right and because it fulfills a deep cultural need in our members. It is, if you please, part of our religion, because for us, culture means religion.

Is There Any Conservation Issue If We Take Whales?

Absolutely not. The Eastern Pacific or California gray whale has been studied by scientists around the world and it is established that the gray whale population is currently at an all-time high of around 22,000. The population continues to increase at 2½% per year, despite an annual harvest which has gone as high as 165 by Russian aborigines, called Chukotki. . . .

The fact that no one can legitimately argue that this is a conservation threat is one of the main reasons why two of America's leading conservation organizations have refused to join in the attack on our whaling: The Sierra Club and Greenpeace. There are animal rights activists within those organizations who are trying to get them to come out against our whaling, but they have steadfastly refused because they do not see this as a conservation issue, they refuse to be drawn into the animal rights issue and they will not oppose indigenous people's rights.

The Wishes of the Tribe

Our attackers continue to claim that we are disregarding the views of the majority of our members. They repeatedly publicize in the media and elsewhere the views of two women who are members of the Tribe and are outspoken opponents of whaling. While we respect the right of all of our members to hold and to express their views on any subject, I must respectfully point out that these two women do not speak for anywhere near the majority of the Tribe and there are other Elders who strongly support whaling. . . .

We were the premier whalers on the American continent and were able to enjoy a prosperous life because of our whaling trade. Our forefathers bequeathed our right to whale to us in our Treaty and we feel that a treaty right which cannot be exercised is no right. I can tell you that our Tribe is not prepared to abandon our treaty right. . . .

What Is Our Cultural Need for Whaling?

It is hard for us to explain to outsiders our "cultural" attitudes about whaling. Some of us find it repugnant to even have to explain this to anyone else. But let me tell you about my own case. I have a Bachelors Degree in Education from Central Washington University. I was the first Makah teacher in the Neah Bay School System from 1972 through 1976. I received my principal's credentials from Western Washington University in 1975 and served as Vice Principal of the Neah Bay Schools in 1976 and between 1990 and 1997.

Have I lost my culture? No. I come from a whaling family. My great grandfather, Andrew Johnson, was a whaler. He landed his last whale in 1907. My grandfather, Sam Johnson, was present when the whale was landed and told me he played on the whales tail. I lived with my grandfather for 16 years and heard his stories about our whaling tradition and the stories of family whaling told by my father Percy and my uncle Clifford. When I was a teenager I was initiated into Makah whaling rituals by my uncle Clifford. While I cannot divulge the details of these rituals, which are sacred, they involve isolation, bathing in icy waters and other forms of ritual cleansing. These rituals are still practiced today and I have been undergoing rituals to prepare me for the whaling which is to come this year. Other families are using their own rituals. When the idea of resuming whaling first spread through our village, I was intensely excited, and so was my whole family. In fact, I can say I was ecstatic about the idea of resuming the hunt; something my grandfather was never able to do. I am proud to carry on my family legacy and my father is overjoyed because he is going to see this in his lifetime.

I can tell you that all of the Makah whalers are deeply stirred by the prospect of whaling. We are undergoing a process of mental and physical toughening now. I feel the cultural connection to whaling in my blood. I feel it is honoring my blood to go whaling. We are committed to this because it is our connection to our Tribal culture and because it is a treaty right—not because we see the prospect of money. We are willing to risk our lives for no money at all. The only reward we will receive will be the spiritual satisfaction of hunting and dispatching the whale and bringing it back to our people to be distributed as food and exercising our treaty right. Recently the Progressive Animal Welfare Society (PAWS) distributed a brochure in which they implied we have lost our cultural need for whaling because we have adapted to modern life. They cite our ". . . lighted tennis courts . . . Federal Express . . . and other amenities. . . ." Well, excuse me! I want to tell PAWS that the two tennis courts on our high school grounds have no lights. How about the fact that Federal Express makes deliveries to our reservation? Does that mean that we have lost our culture?

These attacks on our culture and our status are foolish. No one can seriously question who we are; we are a small Native American Tribe who were the whalers of the American continent. We retain our whaling traditions today. It resonates through all of our people from the youngest to the oldest, and we don't take kindly to other people trying to tell us what our culture is or should be. . . .

The Ethical Issue

The arguments and claims put out by Sea Shepherd and the other anti-whaling groups are designed to inflame the public against us and to attack the honesty of our motives. They mask the real aim of these groups: to prevent the killing of a single whale.

Some people honestly believe that it is wrong to kill one of these animals. Maybe their minds are made up, but I want to say to them that we Makahs know the whales, probably better than most people. We are out on the waters of the ocean constantly and we have lived with and among whales for over 2,000 years. We are not a cruel people. Some of us have even gone into the water to free whales who became entangled in nets—a dangerous undertaking. But we have an understanding of the relationship between people and the mammals of the sea and land. We are a part of each other's life. We are all part of the natural world and predation is also part of life on this planet. So orca whales attack and eat whales and whale calves as well as seals and fish. Those who regard the orcas simply as cute may prefer to ignore this side of their nature. But there is a reason they are called "killer whales." In fact, they were originally called "whale killers."

I want to deal with the claims of those who would romanticize the whale and ascribe almost human characteristics to it. To attribute to gray whales near human intelligence is romantic nonsense—as any professional whale biologist can tell you. The photographs of gray whales surfacing to be petted by people are all taken in the calving lagoons of Baja, California and Mexico. This behavior is not exhibited by gray whales anywhere else, particularly by migrating whales passing through our waters.

The whales we will hunt are migrating whales and we will not hunt any mother whale with a calf.

Whales have captured the public's fascination. Whales are definitely "in." Does that mean that Indians are "out"? The world has had a similar fascination with us and our cultures, but whenever we had something you wanted or did something you didn't like, you tried to impose your values on us. The Federal government even tried to stamp out our potlatch tradition because they thought it was backward and impoverishing. Too often white society has demonstrated this kind of cultural arrogance. We don't take well to Sea Shepherd or PAWS telling us we should rise to a "higher" level of culture by not whaling. To us the implication that our culture is inferior if we believe in whaling is demeaning and racist.

We feel that the whaling issue has been exploited by extremists who have taken liberties with the facts in order to advance their agenda. We understand that there are many people who legitimately believe that it is wrong to kill a whale. But we feel that the zealousness and self-righteousness which emanates from the animal rights community has led to dishonesty and extremism. To them I would say that we may have deeper feelings for the whale than you or your forebears. We ask that you show some respect for Indian culture and that you stop the lies and distortions. The Makah people have been hurt by these attacks, but nevertheless we are committed to continuing in what we feel is the right path.

We Makahs hope that the general public will try to understand and respect our culture and ignore the attacks of extremists.

Sincerely,

Keith Johnson

President, Makah Whaling Commission

Source: "An Open Letter to the Public from the President of the Makah Whaling Commission." Keith Johnson, president of the Makah Whaling Commission. August 6, 1998. An edited version of this letter was published on the *Seattle Times* op-ed page on August 23, 1998.

ENVIRONMENTAL RACISM:
Was the Siting of a Cement Plant in a Poor, Nonwhite Neighborhood Environmental Discrimination?

—◊◊◊—

THE CONTROVERSY

The Issue

In 2001, a group of residents from a poor, nonwhite neighborhood in Camden, New Jersey, sued their state department of environmental protection for issuing permits to allow the establishment of a cement-processing plant in their community. The Camden residents joined a larger movement for environmental justice around the country, which had drawn increasing attention to evidence of unequal concentration of environmental burdens in poor and nonwhite communities. However, the Camden case was especially significant because it was the first to successfully invoke the charge of illegal discrimination on the basis of unequal environmental impact. It placed a question with far-reaching implications before the courts and society at large: Does unequal environmental impact constitute discrimination?

- ♦ **Arguments that siting cement plant was discriminatory:** Camden residents argued that their neighborhood was already host to a disproportionate concentration of environmental burdens, and this inequity was due to the fact that theirs was a largely poor and nonwhite community. Opponents of the cement plant argued that the state had failed to consider the cumulative impact of so many environmental burdens. They argued that decisions that have a racially disparate impact violate civil rights laws.

- ♦ **Arguments that siting of cement plant was not discriminatory:** State officials and cement plant owners argued that racial discrimination had nothing to do with their decisions. They asserted that the plant met all relevant environmental laws and regulations and therefore did not pose a threat. Plant owners argued that they were motivated by sound economic principles. Moreover, their proposed plant was not a burden because it would bring needed economic opportunities to the city.

—∞—

INTRODUCTION

In 2001, a group of South Camden residents sued the state of New Jersey for allowing a cement-processing facility to locate in their neighborhood. The basis of their lawsuit was environmental racism. The residents complained that their community—a poor and largely nonwhite neighborhood of Camden, New Jersey—bore more than its fair share of environmental burdens. Their one-square-mile neighborhood was already home to the county sewage waste facility, the county waste incinerator, and numerous other polluting facilities and contaminated properties. Why, they asked, were so many noxious industries concentrated in their neighborhood? Why weren't officials worried about their health or their quality of life? Why weren't these burdens shared more equally throughout the county or state? To residents and other critics, it was no coincidence that officials and companies repeatedly placed noxious industries in this poor, nonwhite community. Numerous other communities throughout the country had asked similar questions about the unequal distribution of environmental burdens. In fact, an entire movement for environmental justice had emerged on just this issue. However, the lawsuit by Camden residents was the first one to successfully argue that the racially unequal distribution of environmental burdens was discriminatory and illegal.

When the St. Lawrence Cement Company (SLC) chose to locate its cement facility in the South Camden neighborhood, the site it chose was zoned for industrial use. The Waterfront South community was by most accounts a blighted neighborhood full of vacant or abandoned lots, exceedingly poor, and suffering from high unemployment. Moreover, the area already had a high concentration of public facilities and other industry that had been there for decades. City and state officials welcomed the prospect of new business because Camden was desperate for economic activity and investment. The Waterfront South community had long been industrial, but it had also always been residential.

Opponents of the cement facility argued that their community already bore far more than its fair share of environmental burdens, while deriving virtually no benefits. Their tiny community was already home to dozens of noxious and polluting facilities, as well as contaminated sites and some of the worst air quality in the country. Moreover, the community already suffered from above average rates of asthma, cancer, and other ailments. Many residents believed these problems were directly attributable to the high levels of local pollution. Residents argued that the New Jersey Department of Environmental Protection (NJDEP) failed to consider the cumulative impact of so many polluting industries on their community. More important, however, they asserted that the NJDEP violated their civil rights by increasing the disproportionate concentration of polluting facilities in their nonwhite neighborhood and creating a racially disparate impact.

Supporters of the cement plant argued that racial discrimination had nothing to do with the siting of the cement facility. The NJDEP asserted that it had acted lawfully and only considered the relevant environmental standards. Moreover, they disputed that the plant represented a health threat to the community because it did not violate existing environmental regulations that were intended to be protective of public health. SLC and its supporters argued that the facility was a benefit to the community, not a burden. Camden and the Waterfront South community in particular were in desperate need of economic activity and investment. Supporters asserted that the company had made every effort to work with the community. Finally, supporters argued that the unequal distribution of industrial facilities was neither proof nor adequate grounds for the charge of discrimination.

Government officials and the courts were presented with difficult questions: Was the siting and permitting of a cement-processing facility in the Waterfront South community discriminatory? More broadly, did unequal environmental impact for nonwhite communities constitute illegal discrimination?

BACKGROUND

Until the mid-19th century, Camden was a bucolic suburb for people working in Philadelphia wanting to escape the gritty urban center. After the Civil War, Camden itself grew into a prosperous industrial center. By 1880, Camden was the leading city in New Jersey, boasting 13 schools and 32 churches, as well as being the home of the poet Walt Whitman. Camden's prosperity as an industrial center continued to grow into the early 20th century, but its industrial growth came at a cost to its residential qualities. Camden had no land use zoning and allowed industry to develop side by side with residential areas. As the city became more industrial, wealthier people began to move out of the congested inner urban core and into surrounding suburbs. Until World War II, the option to leave the city and take up residence in the suburbs was only possible for the privileged few. After World War II, the suburban ideal opened up for many middle- and working-class Americans. These changes would contribute to the economic decline of old industrial cities like Camden and their increasing racial and economic segregation.

Suburbanization, Segregation, and Decline

Camden had always been racially segregated, but it became more so after World War II. New federal policies administered by the U.S. Federal Housing Administration (FHA) encouraged middle-class families to move out of the city and purchase homes in the suburbs. The policies were intended to stimulate the economy and alleviate a housing crisis for returning veterans, but the result was a mass exodus out of the cities and into the suburbs. Older cities, like Camden, lost population and business.

While owning a home was a welcome opportunity for many families, the federal policies specifically denied these opportunities to nonwhite households and urban communities. According to FHA guidelines, multifamily homes, apartments, mixed-use (residential and commercial) and older housing stock could not qualify for the same level of financial support as newly built, detached, single-family houses. More important, the new federal housing policies specifically discouraged investment in neighborhoods that were nonwhite or racially mixed. The rationale of federal officials and the real estate industry was that such areas were a threat to home values, although this only served to justify racist practices in housing, especially by home owners who wanted to keep nonwhites out of their neighborhoods.

In fact, in many suburbs throughout the country, it was a long-standing practice of white homeowners to develop covenants, or contracts, in which white homeowners promised not to sell their homes to nonwhites if they moved. However, it was the practice of redlining that had the greatest impact. Federal officials in cooperation with lending institutions classified neighborhoods based on their desirability and value, which determined the degree of financial support they could receive from the federal government. Areas that housed nonwhites, or areas that looked like they might become nonwhite or racially mixed, were redlined as undesirable and financially unfavorable and thus excluded from receiving FHA support. Without FHA support, banks were reluctant to lend money to these areas, making it very difficult for people to either buy or sell homes. These redlined areas became, by definition, less valuable. As a result, the suburban opportunity was largely restricted to whites who took the advantages and moved out of the cities in droves to the clean, new, and racially homogenous suburbs. This led to a massive disinvestment in older urban cores and an exacerbation of residential racial segregation.

As middle-class white residents fled for the suburbs, urban neighborhoods became progressively poorer and nonwhite. As did many older cities in the East, the loss of population and business sent Camden on a downward economic spiral. In the 1950s and 1960s, municipal officials tried to revive inner urban areas by clearing out the slums and razing dilapidated areas of the city, but they only succeeded in displacing residents and further contributing to the blight when investment did not return. Racist housing laws began to be dismantled after the late 1960s, but their legacy continues as a result of accumulated inequalities in wealth and opportunity. The impact of this history is still visible in the segregated geography of neighborhoods and economic activity.

In Camden, the combination of concentrated poverty, government neglect, and ongoing racial tensions led to riots in the late 1960s and early 1970s, which only served to reinforce the perception of urban decline. Many suburban communities maintained their economic and racial homogeneity through locally restrictive land use zoning rules that dictated minimum lot sizes and limited the types of development that could occur in the community. These exclusionary zoning rules had the effect of keeping property prices high, which kept out poorer people and also prohibited undesirable types of land use, such as low-income housing or noxious industry. As a result, these types of land uses were relegated to the few places that would still allow them, such as Camden.

From the 1970s onward, South Camden and the Waterfront South neighborhood increasingly served as a site for Camden County's more noxious facilities. In 1975, the city adopted a zoning ordinance that split South Camden into two zones: industrial and industrial-residential. The zoning designation formalized what had already become practice. In 1977, the Camden County Municipal Utilities Authority (CCMUA) opened a sewage treatment facility in South Camden, which treated most of the county's waste in an open-air facility. The noxious odors from the facility permeated the neighborhood. Residents complained to no avail. In the early 1980s, despite opposition by residents and local community leaders, city officials agreed to expand the waste facility and approved the construction of a new waste incinerator in the neighborhood as well. In response to statewide concerns about air pollution, New Jersey governor James Florio imposed a moratorium on further

A heavy truck rumbles past the corner of Fourth and Ferry in Camden's Waterfront South neighborhood in New Jersey. Residents complained about excessive noise and air pollution from truck traffic and local industry and worried about an increase in traffic from new industry, such as the St. Lawrence Cement plant. (Michael Bryant/MCT/Newscom)

development of incinerators within the state. However, the incinerator in South Camden was grandfathered in and allowed to continue in operation.

The influx of industry into South Camden led to a continuing loss of residents and an increase in its gritty, industrial character. By the 1990s, two neighborhoods remained in the Waterfront South area: a four-block area known as the Terraces containing approximately 41 families and, a few blocks north, another area with 400 families. At one time the Terraces had been an area of attractive row houses that housed shipbuilders who worked at the nearby New York Shipyards. When the shipyards closed in the late 1960s, the white residents moved to the suburbs and sold their homes to black residents. During the period of urban renewal, the city began to demolish these homes but ran out of money. As a result, a few row houses still dotted the area, separated by weed-covered vacant lots where their neighbors once stood. Vacant houses fell into disrepair, were vandalized, or became occupied by drug dealers and other undesirable squatters.

Waterfront South Begins to Protest

In the late 1990s, Camden mayor Milton Milan proposed the creation of a 90-acre industrial park stretching from Interstate 676 to the Delaware River—a move that would close in the fourth side of the neighborhood. The mayor and others argued that the area was already largely industrial. Indeed, the approximately one square mile of Waterfront South was already hemmed in by high traffic corridors—Atlantic Avenue to the north, Interstate 676 to the east, and the Walt Whitman Bridge to the south. The neighborhood was also home to a variety of industry and abandoned, contaminated sites from its long history as an industrial area—scrap metal yards, food-processing companies, and car-wrecking facilities, as well as the sewage-treatment facility and the waste incinerator.

In 1997, 10 Waterfront South residents formed South Camden Citizens in Action (SCCIA) and countered the mayor's proposal with a plan of their own to upgrade and maintain the remaining homes. Their plan gained the endorsement of the Camden City Council. They also brought complaints about the sewage-treatment facility to the attention of city and state officials. They launched a campaign to get residents to make formal complaints to the NJDEP whenever the facility violated odor rules. In April 1998, SCCIA sued CCMUA in state superior court for violation of the state air pollution control act. CCMUA settled with SCCIA in November 1999, agreeing to take active steps to correct the odor problems and to pay $110,000 in penalties. While SCCIA battled one noxious local industry, it also engaged with the city to devise plans to deal with the multitude of abandoned industrial properties in the community that were suspected or known to be contaminated—areas known as brownfields. Brownfields worried residents because of the potential toxins they might harbor, but they were equally problematic as a social and economic blight. (See the sidebar "Brownfields and Hopes of Economic and Environmental Revitalization" on page 420.) It was at this time that SCCIA was attempting to reclaim control over the community that it was confronted by a new challenge—the siting of a cement-processing facility.

A New Business Comes to Town

In the late 1990s, St. Lawrence Cement (SLC), a cement company based in Ontario, Canada, selected a site for a new cement-processing facility in South Camden, New Jersey. The property was one block away from the Terraces community. In March 1999, SLC signed a 45-year lease for 12 acres of land in the Waterfront South area from the South Jersey Port Corporation, a state agency. Soon after, SLC began preliminary negotiations with the NJDEP to construct and operate a granulated blast furnace slag-grinding plant. The sandlike slag, a by-product of the steel-making industry, would be processed into GranCem, an alternative additive to strengthen Portland cement. In order to establish the plant, SLC had to obtain permits from the NJDEP for the projected air emissions from its plant. Under the federal Clean Air Act Amendments of 1990, facilities that emit significant amounts of particulate matter or other regulated substances into the air must first be reviewed by state environmental agencies in order to ensure that the emissions do not worsen the air quality of the region. The NJDEP required SLC to model its emissions of PM_{10}, or fine particulate matter, in order to ensure that it would comply with the National Ambient Air Quality Standards (NAAQS). SLC estimated that it would emit about 60 tons of particulate matter into the air per year, which did not violate the NAAQS.

While it was preparing its air permit application in 1999, SLC launched an aggressive public relations campaign that summer to generate city and community support for the proposed plant. It hired a former Camden city solicitor to gather input from residents and to offer relocation assistance to nearby residents of the Terraces community, a number of whom were excited by the prospect of getting financial assistance to move out of the blighted neighborhood. In addition, SLC offered to train and hire Camden residents. These overtures garnered the support of Reverend Al Stewart, a local religious leader and head of the Waterfront South Neighborhood Partnership. However, members of SCCIA were more skeptical. In August 1999, SLC representatives met with residents at the home of SCCIA president, Rose Townsend, in hopes of getting a letter of support. At the meeting, attendees discussed the operation of the facility, the potential for employment of Waterfront South residents, and environmental issues relating to the operation of the facility. In the end, SLC representatives left without any assurance of support. That same month, the company submitted a formal application to the NJDEP for air emissions permits. In September, SCCIA convened a community meeting at the Camden Fellowship House to discuss the impact of the facility and decided that it would oppose the facility.

In November 1999, the NJDEP notified SLC that its permit applications were "administratively complete"—it had submitted all of the information that the NJDEP needed to review and evaluate the proposal and to decide whether or not to approve air emissions permits for the facility as planned. Under state law, SLC was at that point legally entitled to begin construction of the facility, although it did so at its own risk and with no assurance that it would actually receive the necessary permits. SLC nevertheless began construction of the facility. It also continued to cultivate relationships with sympathetic community members.

In January 2000, it convened a community advisory panel and provided funding for the panel to hire independent technical experts to evaluate the environmental impacts of the facility's operations. That same month, NJDEP commissioner Robert C. Shinn appointed Reverend Stewart to head the state's Environmental Equity Advisory Council, providing another sympathetic ear for the company. When the NJDEP issued its first call for public comment on the draft air emissions permits for the facility in July 2000, the facility was already 50 percent complete.

Public hearings a month later—the first on the proposed facility—generated mixed but largely negative reactions from residents. In response, the NJDEP issued a 33-page "Hearing Officer's Report Responses to Public Comments on Draft Air Permit" in which the state agency responded to the concerns raised by community members, including environmental questions or concerns about environmental justice, preexisting local environmental issues, SLC's emission limits, the results of SLC's air quality impact analysis, truck emission standards and carbon monoxide air quality evaluation results, and the protection of the health and safety of Waterfront South residents.

It was clear by this point that the NJDEP intended to approve air emissions permits for the cement plant. On October 4, 2000, SCCIA and its supporters led a procession of chanting and sign-waving protestors to an NJDEP field office. The group hoped to deliver an administrative complaint in person, but NJDEP officials refused to open the door, claiming that the office did not handle complaints. Nevertheless, with the help of public interest lawyers from Camden, Philadelphia, and Rutgers-Camden School of Law, the group filed an administrative complaint with the NJDEP and with the U.S. Environmental Protection Agency (EPA) requesting a grievance proceeding. In its complaint, SCCIA alleged that the NJDEP permit review procedure violated the residents' civil rights because the NJDEP did not consider the racially disparate impact of the facility, something required under the EPA's own office of civil rights.

Neither the EPA nor the NJDEP responded to the requests for a grievance proceeding and on October 31, 2000, the NJDEP issued the final permits for the SLC slag cement-processing plant. On February 13, 2001, SCCIA filed its suit against the NJDEP in district court, alleging that the NJDEP violated Title VI of the federal Civil Rights Act by issuing permits for a cement plant without considering its impact on the largely minority residents of the Waterfront South neighborhood. SCCIA requested that the court impose an injunction against operation of the plant.

THE DEBATE

A lawsuit by a local community organization alleging environmental racism was not entirely new. Indeed, environmental justice groups around the country had attempted to take legal action to prevent the siting of noxious industries in poor and minority communities with only minor success over the previous 10 years. Since the early 1980s, a growing concern over environmental inequalities had spawned numerous community and advocacy organizations, as well as governmental initiatives, to deal with evidence of systematic environmental inequality. (See the sidebar "Environmental Justice" on page 412.) Most efforts for environmental equity focused on the *procedures* by which environmental decisions were made. However, an ambitious few sought to deal directly with inequitable *outcomes.* SCCIA was one of these. Although many observers did not expect SCCIA to be successful in its lawsuit, everyone recognized that the stakes were high. A victory for SCCIA would provide a powerful new legal standard for discrimination and environmental inequality. Moreover, such a victory would present a formidable obstacle to controversial development in other communities.

Argument That Siting of SLC Plant Was Discriminatory

SCCIA and its lawyers argued that the NJDEP violated their civil rights when it approved the air emissions permits for the cement plant because it failed to consider the disparate impact on a minority community that was already overburdened with environmentally polluting facilities. The impact from the new facility, they argued, was unfair, and it would further diminish residents' quality of life and likely have an adverse impact on their health. Opponents of the cement plant argued that the Waterfront South neighborhood already bore far more than its fair share of polluting facilities. Indeed, this one square mile of South Camden already hosted two Superfund sites (one contaminated with radioactive thorium), 15 brownfield sites, four sites known or suspected by the EPA to be releasing hazardous substances, seven scrap metal recyclers and junk yards, a petroleum coke transfer station, several auto body shops, a paint and varnish company, a chemical company, three food-processing plants, a county-run sewage treatment plant, a county-run trash-to-steam incinerator, and a cogeneration gas-fired power plant.

In addition, the community's water supply was contaminated. Though only one of 23 Camden neighborhoods, Waterfront South hosted 20 percent of the city's contaminated sites. Studies showed that the South Camden community had more than twice the average number of facilities with permits to emit air pollution than the typical New Jersey neighborhood. By its own admission, SLC would add another 60 tons of fine-scale particulate matter into the air, substances known to contribute to respiratory and cardiovascular health problems, as well as another 40 tons of mercury, lead, manganese, nitrogen oxides, carbon monoxide, sulphur oxides, and volatile organic compounds. In addition, opponents complained that the NJDEP had only considered emissions of PM_{10} in its air permits but not the impact of $PM_{2.5}$, ultrafine particulate matter.

The EPA's own research had determined that $PM_{2.5}$ was especially damaging to health because it penetrated deeper into the lungs. Equally significant, SLC estimated that its business would generate 77,000 truck trips per year to and from the plant. SCCIA argued that this massive increase in truck traffic would worsen the area's already bad air quality, especially ground-level ozone and smog, and be a severe nuisance to residents because of noise and traffic.

SCCIA and its lawyers argued that the NJDEP had failed to take into account the existing environmental burdens or the cumulative impact of the cement facility's presence in the neighborhood. Residents complained that their health was already affected by the concentration of pollution-emitting facilities. Surveys of the neighborhood revealed that residents of Waterfront South experienced elevated rates of asthma, cardiovascular diseases, and cancer in comparison to the rest of the city, the state, and even the country. More than 40 percent of Waterfront South residents were children, making this community especially vulnerable to pollutant exposure. SCCIA and its allies asserted that every person is entitled to a healthful environment where children can grow up without exposure to harmful pollutants. They asserted that residents' need for clean air and water and a decent quality of life is paramount and at least equal to business' right to survive. SCCIA argued that the unfairness was compounded by the fact that Waterfront South residents would bear all of the costs while receiving virtually none of the benefits. Although the plant would be located in Camden, the city would receive no revenue because the plant sat on state land and was exempt from city taxes. Only 15 jobs would be created at the plant, of

(continues on page 414)

ENVIRONMENTAL JUSTICE

Environmental justice refers to efforts to improve the living environment of communities that have been economically and politically marginalized or neglected. The ideas behind this are rooted in the unequal environmental experiences of lower income and racial minority communities and are often described as a product of the Civil Rights movement of the 1960s and the environmental movement of the 1970s. The environmental justice movement traces its origins to 1982 when residents of Warren County, North Carolina, organized to oppose the siting of a PCB (polychlorinated biphenyl) landfill in their community. The protesters argued that their community had been chosen because it was largely black (65 percent), and they mounted a civil rights protest, lying down in the road to block waste trucks, chaining themselves to equipment, and committing other acts of nonviolent civil disobedience. More than 500 people were arrested during the protests, including one member of Congress. Residents were unable to block the landfill, but their actions drew national attention.

Numerous studies in the wake of the Warren County environmental justice protest seemed to support claims that environmental burdens were inequitably distributed. In 1983, the U.S. Government Accounting Office, the investigative arm of Congress, found that three out of the four off-site hazardous waste landfills in the Southeast were located in predominantly poor black communities. A national study by the United Church of Christ Commission on Racial Justice in 1987 found that a community's racial composition was the most significant factor in explaining the location of hazardous waste treatment, storage, and disposal facilities. It also documented the large concentrations of abandoned hazardous sites in communities of color, particularly in metropolitan areas.

The growing awareness and concern about these environmental inequalities motivated communities throughout the country to take a more critical look at their own environments and the ways in which decisions were made. The landmark event for the environmental justice movement was the First National People of Color Environmental Leadership Summit in Washington, D.C., in 1991, which brought together thousands of activists and scholars from across the country from a wide variety of causes. This summit created a sense of solidarity among a wide variety of social and environmental issues, from residents of inner cities contending with abandoned industrial sites, to migrant farm workers dealing with pesticide exposure, to indigenous claims over access to natural resources, all under the banner of environmental justice. Summit delegates adopted 17 principles of environmental justice, which include: 1) demands that "public policy be based on mutual respect and justice for all peoples, free from any form of discrimination or bias"; 2) affirmation of the "fundamental right to political, economic, cultural and environmental self-determination of all peoples"; and 3) demands for "the right [of all people] to participate as equal partners at every level of decision making, including needs assessment, planning, implementation, enforcement and evaluation."

The environmental justice movement had an important impact on public policy. By the early 1990s, a number of federal agencies were beginning to look more closely at the concerns expressed by otherwise marginalized communities. Officials gave new attention to two issues in particular: 1) the cumulative impact of exposure from multiple sources of pollution and stress; and 2) the procedural fairness and inclusiveness of environmental decision making and enforcement. In 1994, President Bill Clinton issued Executive Order 12898, "Federal Actions to Ensure Environmental Justice in Minority and Low Income Populations." The Executive Order directed federal agencies to improve methods for assessing and mitigating impacts and health effects on communities, to collect data on low income and minority populations that may be disproportionately at risk, and to encourage participation of the affected communities in these processes.

Most state environmental agencies eventually followed the federal lead. In 1998, New Jersey was one of five states awarded a grant from the Environmental Protection Agency to start a pilot program on environmental racism, defined as "any policy, practice or regulation that is an intentional or unintentional disproportionate imposition of environmental hazards on minority communities." Shortly thereafter, New Jersey Department of Environmental Protection commissioner Robert C. Shinn formed an advisory council of environmental equity to review the agency's permit procedures. Like most states, and even the federal government, New Jersey's approach to environmental justice focused on procedural fairness. None attempted to prohibit unequal impacts or outcomes. This would have to be resolved by the courts.

(continued from page 411)
which a dozen might be made available to Camden residents. Products made by SLC would go to suburban-based construction firms and other cities and states in the Mid-Atlantic region. This absence of local benefit had convinced the Camden City Council to pass a resolution to oppose the facility as well. However, because the proposed site was on state-owned land, the City Council had little control over the approval process. (See "Resolution Supporting Citizen Efforts to Prevent Operation of the St. Lawrence Cement Slag Grinding Facility, 2001," on page 427 in the Primary Sources section.)

Opponents of the cement plant argued that it was no surprise that SLC had chosen South Camden or that the NJDEP had approved the permits. While Camden County as a whole was 80 percent white, Waterfront South was 91 percent nonwhite, with a median per capita income of $15,000 compared to $67,000 for the rest of the state. Opponents asserted that the NJDEP and industry had chosen the most vulnerable neighborhood to site a noxious facility, while amenities mainly benefited wealthier, more powerful, and generally whiter groups in the suburbs. They alleged that the neighborhood had been targeted by companies and the government because their poverty and racial and ethnic composition was associated with a lack of political power that made them less likely to oppose, or be able to stop, a pollution permit.

The legal crux of SCCIA's argument was that the NJDEP violated the EPA's disparate impact regulations under Title VI of the Civil Rights Act of 1964. The Civil Rights Act of 1964 outlawed discrimination based on race, color, or national origin. Title VI of the Civil Rights Act directed federal agencies to create specific regulations, or rules, to implement the antidiscrimination law. Following passage of the Civil Rights Act, most federal agencies adopted regulations that prohibited funding of programs that have a discriminatory impact. Shortly after its creation in 1970, the EPA issued regulations that prohibited recipients of federal funding (which meant all state governments) from engaging in activities that create discriminatory effects. In fact, EPA regulations specifically mentioned the siting of facilities in its Title VI regulations:

> A recipient shall not choose a site or a location of a facility that has the purpose or effect of excluding individuals from, denying them the benefits of, or subjecting them to discrimination under

any program to which this Part applies on the grounds of race, color, or national origin or sex; or with the purpose or effect of defeating or substantially impairing the accomplishment of the objectives of this subpart.

SCCIA argued that the NJDEP had indeed taken actions which created discriminatory effects. They argued that the already existing disparate distribution of industrial facilities throughout the state and in Camden County was part of a pattern of policies and decision making by government officials that led to a racially disparate distribution of environmental burdens. (See "Evidence of Disparate Distribution, 2001," on page 429 in the Primary Sources section.) Moreover, residents complained that the way in which the NJDEP made its decisions denied them the opportunity to be meaningfully involved in decisions that affect their lives.

Argument That Siting of SLC Plant Was Not Discriminatory

The NJDEP argued that it did not target Waterfront South for racial reasons, nor did it violate any laws. Officials argued that the state agency had met its civil rights obligations by basing its permitting decision solely on environmental standards. Under the federal Clean Air Act and regulations issued by the EPA, the NJDEP's legal duty was to review the emissions potential of the proposed facility and to determine whether or not its emissions would violate the NAAQS or otherwise pose an unacceptable threat to human health. Based on air modeling, the NJDEP found that PM_{10} emissions from the facility would not violate the NAAQS. Modeling also indicated that emissions of lead, manganese, and radioactive materials would not violate state and federal requirements. Finally, because the NAAQS are health-based laws, lawyers argued that the NJDEP's decision meant that there would be no adverse health impact from the operation of the facility.

In response to the complaint that the agency had not considered the impact of truck traffic or other issues, the NJDEP argued that it only has legal jurisdiction over emissions from stationary sources. Air emissions from trucks and other vehicles are regulated by the New Jersey Department of Motor Vehicles through annual, individual tailpipe inspections and random roadside inspections. The defendants argued that the NJDEP does not have to consider the impact of truck traffic in its permitting decision. On the issue of the EPA's proposed rule to regulate $PM_{2.5}$, the NJDEP responded that these rules were not final and thus did not have the force of law. The NJDEP could not deny a permit to SLC based on standards that were not codified in law; to do so would simply expose the agency to a lawsuit from the company. Finally, the NJDEP argued that it was not obligated to perform a disparate impact analysis. The agency had followed the law to the letter.

Based on existing environmental standards, there was no evidence that the facility would pose a health hazard to anyone, and therefore there was no reason to conduct a disparate impact analysis. While the NJDEP made its most important arguments inside the courts, it also took its case directly to the public in order to counter wider criticism. (See "New Jersey Department of Environmental Protection Statement on St. Lawrence Case, 2001," on page 430 in the Primary Sources section.)

Although the lawsuit was directed at the NJDEP, SLC joined the NJDEP as defendants in order to argue against the allegations of discrimination and to defend its business. Representatives for SLC argued that their company had selected the site in South Camden based solely on business principles and that it had made every effort to work fairly with the community. SLC representatives explained that they had chosen the site because Camden is a port city and SLC needed a deepwater port to accommodate the large cargo ships bearing its raw material from Europe. In addition, the company wanted to expand its business into the Philadelphia-New Jersey-Delaware market, and this port was the best location for the company's base of operation. Finally, the South Jersey Port Corporation already had trained workers and equipment for unloading shipments, providing the necessary infrastructure and expertise.

More generally, supporters pointed out that Waterfront South had been zoned for industrial activity for years and had in fact been a highly industrialized area for decades. There was nothing unusual about siting an industrial facility in an industrial area. Supporters argued that SLC went out of its way to reach out to nearby residents.

After selecting the site and initiating negotiations with state and local officials, SLC asserted that it made good-faith efforts to contact local community members in order to make them aware of what was going on and to hear their concerns. SLC helped to form a community advisory panel (CAP), which in turn created a technical advisory group to provide CAP members and other interested parties with an "independent assessment of the environmental issues implicated by the Facility's operations." Members of the CAP nominated and selected technical experts to evaluate the impact of the proposed facility on traffic, air quality, storm water management, and health, all at SLC's expense. SLC also made offers and attempts to solicit support from other industries in the area to develop a fund to help pay for relocation of residents who wanted to move out of the area. However, SLC maintained that the presence of its facility in Camden was not a burden but a benefit to the community. SLC and its supporters argued that Camden, and especially South Camden, was in dire need of investment and economic activity.

SLC would be the largest private investment in the Waterfront area in 30 years. The company projected revenue of $25 million in the first five years of operation, which would be good for the area. The facility itself would train and hire local residents, but more important, it would contribute to the generation of hundreds of related jobs and services. SLC had already completed the facility, investing millions of dollars. An injunction against operation of the facility would result in losses of $200,000 per week and would be unwarranted and unfair. SLC disputed that there was a maldistribution of industrial facilities. However, even if there was, it argued that companies have a right to operate even in poor and minority communities and should only be required to comply with applicable laws. The company had acted legally and followed the rules and regulations as dictated by the NJDEP. If the NJDEP had somehow violated Title VI regulations, SLC should not be penalized for the mistakes of the agency. Business groups across the country issued their own statements in support of SLC because they saw that the case could have far-reaching implications. (See "Chamber of Commerce Southern New Jersey Position Statement on St. Lawrence Cement Camden Facility, 2001," on page 431 in the Primary Sources section.)

Supporters of the cement plant argued that SCCIA had no legal basis for its allegations or even the lawsuit. They argued that SCCIA had failed to show that the NJDEP or SLC intended to discriminate against the community. They argued that plaintiffs had also failed to prove that the disparate distribution of industrial facilities was caused by the state agency's decision-making policies for air permit applications. Finally, they asserted that civil rights laws were never intended to ensure equal outcomes. Civil rights are about ensuring equal opportunity, not equal outcome.

OUTCOME AND IMPACT

In April 2001, Judge Stephen Orlofsky of the district court of New Jersey ruled in favor of SCCIA, revoking the air permits issued by the NJDEP and imposing an injunction against operation of the SLC facility. (See *"South Camden Citizens in Action v. New Jersey Department of Environmental Protection,* 2001," on page 432 in the Primary Sources section.) The district court justice concluded that SCCIA had made a convincing case of disparate impact discrimination on the basis of race, despite the fact that the facility would be in compliance with applicable air pollution laws. Judge Orlofsky argued that the NJDEP had interpreted EPA Title VI civil rights regulations too narrowly; it should not have relied on the NAAQS as "the sole and determinative measure of adversity impact." He argued that complying with the NAAQS did not automatically mean that there could be no adverse impact. The NJDEP should have taken a more comprehensive look at the larger context in determining whether there might be an adverse impact. In particular, the judge found that the NJDEP should have considered the health consequences of the cumulative environmental burden faced by the community, that Waterfront South already suffered high rates of disease, the fact that the area was already in severe noncompliance for ground-level ozone (due to vehicle traffic), and that the SLC facility would emit levels of $PM_{2.5}$ exceeding what the EPA's research indicated was safe, even though these rules had not yet been finalized. According to the judge, the plaintiff's analysis revealed "a statistically significant association between the permitting and placement of environmentally regulated facilities in New Jersey and the percentage of minority residents in those communities." This finding established that the NJDEP's permitting practices were partly responsible for the unequal distribution of environmental burdens and the disparate racial impact alleged by plaintiffs. Finally, the judge ordered the NJDEP to conduct a cumulative impact analysis in order to better understand the total burden experienced by the Waterfront South neighborhood as a result of permitting new facilities that would add to the burden.

Judge Orlofsky's decision was groundbreaking because it was the first court ruling in the United States to support an accusation of illegal discrimination based on disparate environmental impact or outcome. Some legal and business scholars predicted economic ruin for industries attempting to locate new businesses. The ruling was hailed by many in the civil rights and environmental justice communities as a significant breakthrough. However, the celebration was short-lived.

Five days after the district court ruling, the U.S. Supreme Court issued a ruling in a completely different case, *Alexander v. Sandoval,* which undid the basis of the Camden ruling. The *Sandoval* case involved a lawsuit against Alabama over its English-only driver's license test. The plaintiffs argued in that case that the Alabama law had the effect of discriminating against individuals who do not speak English very well and thus had a discriminatory effect against individuals based on national origin. This discriminatory effect violated civil rights regulations of the federal Department of Transportation, which had rules prohibiting discriminatory effects similar to those of the EPA. Although the United States Court of Appeals for the Eleventh Circuit in Atlanta ruled in favor of the *Sandoval* plaintiffs, the Supreme Court ruled that individuals do not have a right to sue government agencies under Title VI of the Civil Rights Act of 1964, the section of the Civil Rights Act that gives federal agencies authority to create their civil rights regulations. Notably, the ruling did not address the question of whether the discriminatory effect was illegal, only that an individual does not have a right to sue (i.e., private right of action) on that basis. For the Camden case, the Supreme Court ruling meant that SCCIA had no right to sue the NJDEP. SCCIA and its lawyers went back to Judge Orlofsky to amend their argument to base it on another broader law that gives individuals the right to sue whenever a law or their constitutional rights are violated. Judge Orlofsky accepted this argument and maintained the injunction against the cement plant.

SLC and the NJDEP appealed the amended ruling to the third circuit court of appeals. On June 15, 2001, the appeals court suspended the injunction pending a full hearing in September. Three days later, SLC began operating the plant. Although it had been placed on the defensive with the appeals court's suspension of the injunction, SCCIA and its allies continued to apply public pressure against the NJDEP.

(continues on page 422)

BROWNFIELDS AND HOPES OF ECONOMIC AND ENVIRONMENTAL REVITALIZATION

The proposed cement-processing facility in Waterfront South was only one of the many environmental worries faced by residents and city officials. An oft-repeated concern was that of abandoned and contaminated industrial properties. These sites represented not only a potential source of exposure to toxins or other pollution but also a form of blight and lost economic opportunity.

Similar to other old industrial cities throughout the East, Camden, New Jersey, suffered a debilitating loss of population and business after World War II through a combination of federal housing and transportation policies, racial tension, and deindustrialization in the 1970s that shuttered old manufacturing facilities as a result of global competition. When industries left the city, they left behind abandoned buildings and properties, as well as the residue of their activities. With little tax revenue, cities such as Camden were unable to do much about the abandoned properties. Moreover, city officials were usually more concerned about how to attract businesses and residents back to the city than addressing contamination. However, concern about buried toxins surged in the late 1970s and early 1980s after a series of scandals in which communities—places like Love Canal in Niagara Falls, New York, and Times Beach, Missouri—discovered massive contamination as a result of improper disposal of toxic industrial wastes in the past.

Congress responded by passing the Comprehensive Environmental Response, Compensation, and Liability Act of 1980—otherwise known as the Superfund. The Superfund legislation created a program to help identify and clean up the nation's most contaminated sites. In addition, the Superfund program also established new standards of liability to hold industries accountable for the costs of proper disposal and cleanup. Superfund was not responsible for the cleanup of all contaminated or hazardous waste sites across the country, only the most severely contaminated. The Environmental Protection Agency (EPA) created a system for ranking hazardous waste sites, so that only the most serious were added to a national priority list (NPL). The states were responsible for cleaning up sites that did not make it onto the NPL. In fact, most states created their own hazardous waste programs, often modeled after Superfund. Together, the federal Superfund and state programs identified thousands of contaminated or potentially contaminated sites across the country. While these programs were successful in identifying and bringing under control numerous sites of toxic contamination, they had an unintended economic impact.

Cities such as Camden had numerous abandoned industrial sites and no resources to do much about them. While these sites caused quite a bit of concern for residents, they also became unattractive to new industries. The new laws concerning liability meant that potential property owners of old sites would have to ensure that the sites were safely cleaned up before any new activity could take place there. The costs for such cleanup were frequently unknown until initiated, and they could be quite high. Companies were thus reluctant to take on unknown and possibly ruinous risks of contaminated sites. As a result, inner city areas with abandoned industrial properties, such as Camden's Waterfront South neighborhood, were now stuck with potentially toxic sites, no way to clean them up, and legal liability obstacles to economic revitalization. In response to these concerns, federal and state officials created new programs to reduce liabilities for companies and to entice them back into older industrialized areas, enabling both cleanup and economic revitalization. In 1995, the EPA announced its brownfields initiative to provide small grants to help states and cities identify brownfields and create redevelopment plans. The EPA defines a brownfield as "a property, the expansion, redevelopment, or reuse of which may be complicated by the presence or potential presence of a hazardous substance, pollutant, or contaminant." The EPA's initiative was followed by significant amendments to Superfund and other laws that specifically encouraged businesses to invest in brownfields—lower taxes, assistance with the cost of remediation, and more flexible rules around liability. In 1996, the EPA selected Camden as an early recipient of brownfields grants to assist in identification and cleanup. New Jersey created its own brownfields program in 1998, offering to reimburse developers up to 75 percent of the remediation costs. Thus, the term *brownfields* came to mean both (potentially) contaminated sites and (potential) economic opportunity.

(continued from page 419)

In late October, the Sierra Club and the National Association for the Advancement of Colored People (NAACP) joined SCCIA in a theatrical protest march in front of NJDEP offices. (See "A Letter of Invitation to Environmental Commissioner Robert C. Shinn, 2001," on page 434 in the Primary Sources section.)

However, on December 17, 2001, the court of appeals overturned Orlofsky's ruling against the NJDEP for disparate racial impact. Working from the Supreme Court's *Sandoval* case, the court of appeals ruled that plaintiffs do not have a right to sue based on the EPA rules prohibiting discriminatory impact because the Civil Rights Act only prohibits *intentional* discrimination, not a discriminatory *outcome*. Therefore, the EPA's regulations prohibiting disparate impact were not enforceable by litigation because the agency regulations went beyond what Congress had intended with the original law. According to the court of appeals, SCCIA had no right to sue for disparate racial impact under Title VI of the Civil Rights Act of 1964. In order to sue for illegal discrimination, the plaintiffs would have to show that the NJDEP and SLC *intended* to discriminate against the residents of Waterfront South when they selected the community for the cement facility and issued air-pollution permits. The fact that the cement facility would only further add to the very unequal concentration of polluting facilities in a nonwhite community was unfortunate but not a sufficient basis for showing illegal discrimination. As many other litigants had learned, proving intentional discrimination is nearly impossible, but SCCIA nevertheless brought their case back to the federal district court, arguing intentional discrimination. In 2006, the district court found that the defendants were not guilty of intentional discrimination and SCCIA's legal case of discrimination against the NJDEP and SLC was finally concluded.

While the legal case for environmental discrimination was essentially ended in 2001, concern over the high environmental burden of South Camden residents continued. In September 2002, New Jersey launched a study of air toxins in the Waterfront South neighborhood with a $100,000 grant from the EPA. Announcement of this new program followed on the heels of an earlier EPA study that found that two census tracts in Camden had the highest cancer risk from airborne toxic substances in the nation. In 2004, New Jersey governor John Corzine signed an executive order creating an interdepartmental task force to receive complaints from neighborhoods about pollution and to hold public meetings or even withhold permits. The governor also reconstituted the state Environmental Justice Advisory Council to assist the task force. Complaints and concerns about the impact of so much industry in Waterfront South continued. In March 2004, the mayor of Camden and the City Council asked the NJDEP to determine if the area was too contaminated for residents to live there. Once again, city officials raised the idea of moving residents out of the neighborhood, although this option was hotly contested by remaining residents and local community organizations.

WHAT IF?

What if the ruling of discriminatory impact had not been overturned?

If the ruling against the NJDEP had been upheld, the decision would have had far-reaching impacts on federal and state environmental policies across the country. Many regulatory agencies, especially those dealing with similar air emissions permitting, would have had to reassess their policies and regulations in order to determine the current geographic distribution of environmental burdens and to prevent decisions that contribute to existing concentrations of industrial activity or noxious land use. For many poorer and more industrialized urban areas dominated by nonwhite residents, such as Waterfront South, the decision would have put an almost immediate halt to permitting of any new industries that attracted opposition. It is likely that the ruling would have been followed by numerous private lawsuits across the country as communities sued state and federal agencies to stop unwanted industry or land use. In South Camden, there is no doubt that SLC and similar industries would have been barred. While such an outcome would have solved the immediate problem of new sources of pollution, it would have done little for existing economic problems or past pollution. In fact, it is possible that economic problems for the community might have been exacerbated as industry actively avoided the community. Less clear is whether the enforced prohibition against disparate environmental impact would have created a more equitable distribution of environmental burdens across the country, since this would generate significant opposition from wealthier and more politically influential communities. The resulting crisis would likely have drawn Congress into the debate and a reconsideration of EPA civil rights regulations.

CHRONOLOGY

1940s–1950s Middle class white residents leave Camden for suburbs in response to federal housing policies.

1950s–1960s Repeated attempts at urban renewal to attract investments results in demolition of significant housing stock and largely displace and isolate black residents, especially in South Camden.

1964 *July 2:* President Lyndon B. Johnson signs the Civil Rights Act of 1964.

1973 Environmental Protection Agency institutes regulations under the Civil Rights Act that prohibit intentional discrimination as well as the use of "criteria or methods having the effect of discrimination."

1977 Camden County Municipal Utilities Authority (CCMUA) commences operation of an open-air waste treatment facility.

1999 *March 8:* St. Lawrence Cement (SLC) signs a 45-year lease for 12 acres of land in the Waterfront South area from the South Jersey Port Corporation, a state agency.

November 30: South Camden Citizens in Action (SCCIA) settles its case against the CCMUA sewage treatment plant.

2000 *October 31:* New Jersey Department of Environmental Protection (NJDEP) issues the final permits for the SLC slag plant.

2001 *February 13:* SCCIA files suit against the NJDEP in U.S. district court.

April 19: Federal district court judge Stephen Orlofsky grants SCCIA's request for an injunction against the cement plant's operation.

April 24: U.S. Supreme Court rules 5-4 in *Alexander v. Sandoval* that Title VI does not create a private right of action, which undermines SCCIA's standing to sue the NJDEP for discriminatory impact.

June 18: SLC facility in Waterfront South begins operating.

	December 17: U.S. Court of Appeals for the Third Circuit overturns the ruling against the NJDEP for disparate racial impact.
2002	*September:* New Jersey launches a study of air toxins in Waterfront South neighborhood.
2004	*February:* New Jersey governor signs an executive order creating an interdepartmental task force to receive complaints about pollution.
	March: City officials ask NJDEP to analyze whether the Waterfront South community is too polluted for residents to stay there.
2006	*March 31:* U.S. district court judge Freda Wolfson dismisses all discrimination claims against the NJDEP and SLC.

DISCUSSION QUESTIONS

1. Was the siting of a cement facility in Waterfront South discriminatory? Why or why not?

2. In its defense, NJDEP argued that it was only legally responsible for air pollution from the SLC plant itself. Judge Orlofsky argued that NJDEP should have considered other sources of environmental disruption, such as air pollution and noise from truck traffic. Do you think NJDEP had an obligation to consider other sources of environmental stress in the neighborhood, even if these were outside of its legal control? Why or why not?

3. EPA's antidiscrimination regulations prohibited intentional discrimination and actions that lead to a discriminatory outcome. Should the guarantee of equal treatment under the law mean protection from unequal outcomes?

4. Should residents of a community have a right to make decisions over the businesses and other activity in their neighborhood? Why or why not?

5. If intentional discrimination on the part of the NJDEP and SLC was not the cause of unequal environmental burdens for non-white residents in Camden, then what was?

6. Not all Waterfront South residents were opposed to the cement plant. A group of residents led by Reverend Martin lauded SLC for its outreach efforts and opportunities. Who represents the community? How could government officials or a company determine who to listen to or who best represents a community?

WEB SITES

Environmental Justice/Environmental Racism. Available online. URL: http://ejnet.org/ej. Accessed April 4, 2011.

NJDEP. Environmental Justice Program. Camden Waterfront South Air Toxics Pilot Program. Available online. URL: http://wwwanjdep/ej/camden. Accessed April 4, 2011.

Scorecard. The Pollution Information Site. Pollution Locator/Superfund. Available online. URL: http://www.scorecard.org/env-releases/land/. Accessed April 4, 2011.

South Jersey Environmental Justice Alliance. Environmental Issues in Camden. Available online. URL: http://www.sjenvironmentaljustice.org/index.htm. Accessed April 4, 2011.

U.S. EPA. Brownfields and Land Revitalization. About Brownfields. Available online. URL: http://www.epa.gov/brownfields/about.htm. Accessed April 4, 2011.

———. Civil Rights. Major Milestones of EPA's Title VI Policy Development. Available online. URL: http://www.epa.gov/civilrights/milestones.htm. Accessed April 4, 2011.

———. Environmental Justice. Available online. URL: http://www.epa.gov/environmentaljustice/. Accessed April 4, 2011.

BIBLIOGRAPHY

Cody, Brendan. "South Camden Citizens in Action: Siting Decisions, Disparate Impact Discrimination, and Section 1983." *Ecology Law Quarterly* 29 (2002): 231–262.

Cole, Luke, and Sheila Foster. *From the Ground Up: Environmental Racism and the Rise of the Environmental Justice Movement.* New York: New York University Press, 2000.

Cooper, Mary H. "Environmental Justice: Does the Movement Help Poor Communities?" *CQ Researcher* 8, no. 23 (1998).

Godsil, Rachel D. "Viewing the Cathedral from Behind the Color Line: Property Rules, Liability Rules, and Environmental Racism." *Emory Law Journal* 53, no. 4 (2004): 1,807–1,885.

Jackson, Kenneth T. *Crabgrass Frontier: The Suburbanization of the United States.* New York: Oxford University Press, 1985.

Massey, Douglas S., and Nancy A. Denton. *American Apartheid: Segregation and the Making of the Underclass.* Cambridge, Mass.: Harvard University Press, 1993.

United Church of Christ. Toxic Wastes and Race at Twenty 1987–2007: A Report Prepared for the United Church of Christ & Witness Ministries. March 2007. Available online. URL: http://www.ucc.org/environmental-ministries/environment/toxic-waste-20.html.

PRIMARY SOURCES

Document 1: Resolution Supporting Citizen Efforts to Prevent Operation of the St. Lawrence Cement Slag Grinding Facility, 2001

The Camden City Council initially supported the proposal by St. Lawrence Cement (SLC) to build a cement plant in Camden, New Jersey, but changed position after complaints by South Camden Citizens in Action and others, and because SLC was exempt from city taxes or control. Below is a resolution passed by the City Council in opposition to the facility on April 12, 2001, only days before the district court issued its injunction.

Resolution Supporting Citizen Efforts to Prevent Operation of the St. Lawrence Cement Slag Grinding Facility Located on South Jersey Port Corporation Land in South Camden

WHEREAS, St. Lawrence Cement (SLC) has constructed a slag grinding facility on South Jersey Port Corporation land adjacent to the residential neighborhood known as Waterfront South; and

WHEREAS, thanks to the efforts of citizens and elected officials, the City Council of Camden has learned that the cement plant will emit almost 60 tons of very small particulate matter into the air each year, and will generate 77,000 diesel truck trips between the Beckett St. terminal and the SLC facility; and

WHEREAS, technical experts from Johns Hopkins University, the Center for Disease Control, and the NJ [New Jersey] School of Medicine and Dentistry have demonstrated that this level of pollution will increase hospitalization and mortality rates in Camden; and

WHEREAS, because the facility is constructed on South Jersey Port Corporation land, no local authority, including the Planning Board, the Environmental Commission, and City Council, had any authority to review or evaluate this proposed development to determine whether it would be beneficial for the City of Camden; and

WHEREAS, the SLC facility will pay no taxes to the City of Camden and is expected to employ only 15 people; and

WHEREAS, the NJDEP [New Jersey Department of Environmental Protection] had the sole authority to regulate this facility, and in so doing, apparently did not consider the well-being of the residents in Waterfront South, conditions in the neighborhood, the existence of eleven other major polluters in the neighborhood, nor the fact that previous studies show an unusually high rate of asthma and respiratory disease among neighborhood residents; and

WHEREAS, we do not know what controls will be placed on the material which is ground at this facility, and various press reports have established the possibility that materials other than slag, such as hazardous waste materials, could be ground at this facility; now, therefore

BE IT RESOLVED that the City Council, adding its voice to many others, believes that the St. Lawrence Cement facility poses a serious threat to the people of Camden, offers very few benefits, and therefore should not be allowed to operate.

BE IT FURTHER RESOLVED that letters of support, which members of this body offered for this project before full disclosure of information regarding its operation and the impact on the people of Camden, are rescinded and are null and void; and

BE IT FURTHER RESOLVED that the Camden City Council endorses the efforts of our State legislative delegation to review NJDEP procedures and see that a strong policy is in place to prevent environmental discrimination, and the efforts of South Camden Citizens in Action to litigate this issue to prevent St. Lawrence from operating; and finally

BE IT RESOLVED that this body will not support any development in or around Waterfront South that will contribute additional air pollution to an area which is already overburdened, harmed and suffering because of what already exists.

Source: Resolution Supporting Citizen Efforts to Prevent Operation of the St. Lawrence Cement Slag Grinding Facility Located on South Jersey Port Corporation Land in South Camden. City Council of Camden. Resolution MC-01:233 I. April 12, 2001.

—∞—

Document 2: Evidence of Disparate Distribution, 2001

In their lawsuit, South Camden Citizens in Action relied heavily on a study done in 2001 by Michel Gelobter, a researcher at Rutgers University in Newark, which presented systematic evidence of inequitable distribution of environmental burdens throughout the state of New Jersey and in Camden. Below is a description of the study's findings as presented to the third circuit court.

Using U.S. Census Bureau figures and the EPA's [Environmental Protection Agency's] most comprehensive, publicly-available database, Envirofacts, plaintiffs' expert Dr. Michel Gelobter analyzed the distribution of EPA-regulated facilities across New Jersey, to determine if there was a pattern which could be discerned in the distribution of such facilities. . . . Dr. Gelobter found a pattern of racially disparate impact in the distribution of polluting facilities in New Jersey. . . . Dr. Gelobter determined that in New Jersey Zip Codes with . . . higher than average population of non-whites have almost twice as many . . . facilities per Zip Code than those with below average non-whites. Looking at New Jersey Zip Codes in predominately white communities (70% or more white) and predominately non-white communities (70% or more non-white), Dr. Gelobter found the pattern held true: Zip Codes that are 70% and greater non-white have an average of 14.6 . . . facilities, while Zip Codes that are 70% and greater white have an average of 8.2 . . . facilities. There are therefore 78% more . . . facilities in Zip Codes of 70% or more non-white population.

Focusing this analysis on the Camden area yields even more disparate results: Zip Code 08104, which includes the Waterfront South community of Camden, NJ and several adjoining census tracts, has 21 . . . facilities. This number of facilities is 270% of the average in Zip Codes where the population of non-whites is proportionally at or below the state average percentage of non-whites. Since the average Zip Code in the state has 7.6 . . . facilities, Zip Code 08104's count represents 277%

of the statewide average calculated independent of racial composition. These stark statistics demonstrate that polluting facilities are not equally distributed in New Jersey, and that something in the way New Jersey permits such facilities has allowed such a disparate impact to occur, in violation of [EPA's Title VI regulations] 40 CFR §7.35(b). Indeed, Dr. Gelobter found the statistical significance of the disparity so strong, that "for every 10% increase in the percentage of non-white residents, a Zip Code area would experience an approximately 20% increase in number of facilities over the statewide average for EPA-regulated facilities. . . ."

Plaintiffs have not yet identified which particular aspect of DEP's permitting program has caused, or allowed, this disparity to occur across New Jersey, and to bloom with such ferocity in Camden. However, plaintiffs have demonstrated here that DEP's permitting actions have a discriminatory impact on the basis of race, both in Camden and statewide, in violation of the EPA's Title VI regulations.

Source: Pomar, Olga D. Camden Regional Legal Services, Inc. Statement for plaintiffs in *South Camden Citizens in Action v. New Jersey Department of Environmental Protection.*

―⚏―

Document 3: New Jersey Department of Environmental Protection Statement on St. Lawrence Case, 2001

As the main defendant in the lawsuit, the New Jersey Department of Environmental Protection (NJDEP) found itself the subject of withering criticism. On September 25, 2001, the day of the scheduled hearing before the appeals court, the NJDEP issued a public statement defending its actions, both to the court and the general public.

NJ DEPT. OF ENVIRONMENTAL PROTECTION NEWS RELEASE
DEP STATEMENT ON ST. LAWRENCE CASE

We hope the court will recognize that our department was very responsive to the needs of the community when developing the terms for the St. Lawrence permit. We limited the hours of delivery and the number of truckloads, and specified the trucks must be kept covered and clean. Moreover, we did air monitoring and made sure that federal air quality standards would not be violated as a result of any air emissions either from the facility or the trucks.

The public also needs to know that New Jersey is a leader in environmental equity and is committed to incorporating environmental equity concerns into our decision making. We've called upon several equity advocates to help us institutionalize equity concerns in our permitting process, and as a result we're leading the nation in this field. The court can dissect this case and hopefully will find we've been very proactive, but if you look at DEP's body of actions on this entire subject, there's no question that New Jersey is ahead of the curve on this issue. Furthermore, our commitment to the City of Camden is clear. We've advanced the city's quality of life through our Green Acres program and our Brownfields program, assisting with waterfront developments and site clean-ups, infrastructure improvements, Clean Communities funding and other initiatives, and we intend to continue these supportive efforts, and we're working with the DRPA and the Administration on this issue.

Source: NJDEP News Release. September 25, 2001.

—⚭—

Document 4: Chamber of Commerce Southern New Jersey Position Statement on St. Lawrence Cement Camden Facility, 2001

National and regional business groups warned that a ruling in support of South Camden Citizens in Action would set a dangerous precedent for industry. Below is a position statement supporting St. Lawrence Cement issued by the Chamber of Commerce Southern New Jersey in July 2001.

CHAMBER OF COMMERCE SOUTHERN NEW JERSEY POSITION STATEMENT ON ST. LAWRENCE CEMENT CAMDEN FACILITY

The Chamber of Commerce Southern New Jersey supports the efforts of the St. Lawrence Cement Company facility to continue to operate in Camden City. The Chamber has long been committed to the economic revitalization of Camden City. . . .

This litigation threatens to undermine urban revitalization and brownfields development efforts in Camden City, Southern New Jersey, and in urban areas throughout the State. St. Lawrence Cement's direct investment in Camden City and the employment opportunities provide the city with an opportunity to revitalize blighted areas and redevelop the city as a whole. . . .

If the district court ruling is allowed to stand, it will have chilling effects on the efforts to rebuild our State's urban areas by opening up any permit ever issued to a new review under the terms of the court's ruling. Therefore, every industrial facility that has been built, under construction, or proposed for development or expansion in an urban industrial zone, would be subject to such review. Allowing for this review to be conducted after a permit is issued, will impact retroactively every air and water permit issued. Therefore, a facility which has already satisfied all requirements to receive its permits, could have its operations halted while this review is conducted, potentially resulting in millions of dollars in lost revenue to the company. The St. Lawrence project has already suffered significant negative economic impacts as a result of the District Court decision. In two months, the company lost $4 million and was forced to lay-off the majority of its Camden employees. The Chamber is hopeful that the Appellate Court will consider the chilling impacts of the District Court decision, and overturn that decision.

Source: Chamber of Commerce Southern New Jersey Position Statement on St. Lawrence Cement Camden Facility. July 2001.

—〰—

Document 5: *South Camden Citizens in Action v. New Jersey Department of Environmental Protection,* 2001

On April 19, 2001, federal district court judge Stephen Orlofsky issued a landmark ruling, imposing an injunction against the St. Lawrence Cement facility and finding that the New Jersey Department of Environmental Protection (NJDEP) violated antidiscrimination regulations by permitting a facility that contributed to a racially disparate environmental impact. In this excerpt, Judge Orlofsky argues that the NJDEP was obligated to consider factors outside of its strict legal requirements.

. . . much of what this case is about is what the NJDEP failed to consider. It did not consider the level of ozone generated by the truck traffic to and from the SLC facility, notwithstanding the fact that the Waterfront South community is not currently in compliance with the National Ambient Air Quality Standard ("NAAQS") established by the EPA for ozone levels, nor did it consider the presence of many other pollutants in Waterfront South. It did not consider the preexisting poor health of the residents of Waterfront South, nor did it consider the cumulative environmental burden already borne by this impoverished community. Finally, and perhaps most importantly, the NJDEP failed to consider the racial and ethnic composition of the population of Waterfront South.

At this stage of these proceedings, this Court must resolve the following complex questions: (1) Whether the criteria and methods used by the NJDEP to evaluate air permit applications, namely, its exclusive reliance on EPA emissions maximums, especially the NAAQS for particulate matter ("PM-10"), without consideration of the totality of the health and environmental circumstances of the community in which the proposed facility will be located, violates the regulations promulgated by EPA to implement Title VI of the Civil Rights Act of 1964, which prohibits discrimination based on race and national origin; and (2) Whether the NJDEP's decision to issue the necessary air permits to SLC to operate its proposed facility in the Waterfront South Community constitutes disparate impact discrimination based on race and national origin in violation of EPA regulations. . . .

With respect to whether the EPA will consider compliance with environmental laws as equivalent to compliance with Title VI, the Draft Revised Investigation Guidance specifically states:

Compliance with environmental laws does not constitute per se compliance with Title VI. Frequently, discrimination results from policies and practices that are neutral on their face, but have the effect of discriminating . . . There may be instances in which environmental laws do not regulate certain concentrations of sources, or take into account impacts on some subpopulations which may be disproportionately present in an affected population. For example, there may be evidence of adverse impacts on some subpopulations (e.g., asthmatics) and that subpopulation may be disproportionately composed of persons of a particular race, color, or national origin. Title VI is concerned with how the effects of the programs and activities of a recipient are distributed based on race, color, or national origin. A recipient's Title VI obligation exists in addition to the Federal or state environmental laws governing its environmental permitting program.

Source: South Camden Citizens in Action v. New Jersey Department of Environmental Protection, Defendant, and St. Lawrence Cement Co., LLC., Defendant-Intervenor. Civil Action No. 01-702. United States District Court for the District of New Jersey. 145 F. Supp. 2d 446; 2001 U.S. Dist. April 19, 2001.

—∞—

Document 6: A Letter of Invitation to Environmental Commissioner Robert C. Shinn, 2001

On October 30, 2001, South Camden Citizens in Action, the Sierra Club, the National Association for the Advancement of Colored People, and other opponents of the cement plant led a protest march to New Jersey Department of Environmental Protection (NJDEP) headquarters carrying mock coffins, representing the impending deaths of residents as a result of the added pollution from the new facility. The protesters released a public letter asking NJDEP commissioner Robert Shinn to share their undesirable experience.

South Camden Citizens in Action/
Camden Environmental Justice Coalition
P.O. Box 2940, Camden, New Jersey

October 30, 2001

Robert C. Shinn, Commissioner
NJ Department of Environmental Protection
401 East State Street
Trenton, NJ 08625-0402

Dear Commissioner Shinn:
The members of South Camden Citizens in Action and the Camden Environmental Justice Coalition cordially invite you to spend a night in the Waterfront South community of Camden. If there is no "disparate (health) impact" on the residents of Waterfront South from the St. Lawrence Cement Company, and the many other polluting facilities in our community, as the NJDEP's impact analysis claims, then you should feel free to accept our invitation. Perhaps those who prepared the impact analysis ought to join you as well.

If you and your staff accept our invitation, we hope that you won't have to sit up in bed until exhaustion forces you to go to sleep, as our children have to do because they can't breathe well at night and are kept awake coughing. We hope that when you awaken, you won't have coughing and gagging fits, fighting to catch your breath, as we do each morning because of the cement dust and other pollution. And we hope you won't be awakened by the sound of numerous trucks spouting diesel fumes and thundering through our neighborhood with granulated blast furnace slag for delivery to the cement plant.

We advise you not to exert yourself too much physically because you'll probably have to use an inhaler, as do the students at Sacred Heart School after recess. You should wear old clothes and drive an older model car so the cement dust and pollutants from the incinerator and other facilities won't ruin them. If you find the odor of garbage offensive, then please wear something to prevent you from smelling the foul odors from the sewage treatment plant. Look both ways before crossing the streets so the St. Lawrence trucks won't run you down!

Bring bottled water because our city water is often filtered sludge. And please remember not to walk near the Superfund site that's contaminated with radioactive thorium. Also don't sit in the park in our neighborhood; the nearby pollution is bad for your health.

We can arrange for your visit at your convenience. Please accept our invitation, and have a pleasant stay.

Sincerely yours,
South Camden Citizens in Action/
Camden Environmental Justice Coalition

Source: Letter from South Camden Citizens in Action to the New Jersey Department of Environmental Protection (NJDEP) inviting the NJDEP Commissioner to spend the night in Waterfront South. October 30, 2001.

HURRICANE KATRINA:
What Was Responsible for the Devastating Flooding of New Orleans?

—✺—

THE CONTROVERSY

The Issue

In late August 2005, New Orleans, Louisiana, was devastated by flooding that followed Hurricane Katrina. At least 80 percent of the city was inundated, hundreds of thousands were left homeless, and almost 1,500 people were killed in Louisiana and another 300 in neighboring Gulf states. Estimates of damage exceeded $100 billion. It was the costliest disaster to ever strike the United States and one of the deadliest. The flooding was traced to breaches and failures in the city's hurricane protection system, but disputes erupted over the cause of these failures and blame for the devastation. Was this a natural disaster or a consequence of development decisions and environmental degradation? Who or what was responsible for the devastating flooding of New Orleans?

♦ **Arguments that flooding was a natural disaster:** The U.S. Army Corps of Engineers (Corps) argued that Hurricane Katrina was an unusually powerful storm that exceeded the design capacity of the city's hurricane protection system. The Corps asserted that its efforts to improve the protection system were hampered by inadequate funding and opposition to projects that could have lessened the impacts of the storm surge and resulting flooding.

♦ **Arguments that flooding was due to faults in engineering:** Critics of the Corps argued that the failure of the flood protection system was due primarily to poor design and engineering. In addition, they claimed that the Corps had undermined its own system by constructing and improperly maintaining navigation channels that exposed the city to greater hurricane storm surge and degraded existing barriers, including those provided by coastal wetlands.

♦ **Arguments that flooding was due to inappropriate development and environmental degradation:** Other investigators argued that the

436

devastation in New Orleans was due to a long history of inappropriate and excessive development in naturally flood-prone areas that put
people directly in harm's way and exacerbated the risks. They argued
that environmental degradation increased vulnerability and removed
natural buffers to hurricane storm surge and flooding.

—⚏—

INTRODUCTION

On Monday, August 29, 2005, Hurricane Katrina made landfall just east
of New Orleans, Louisiana. It was the fourth major hurricane to strike
the Gulf Coast that summer, but it was by far the most destructive.
Winds in excess of 90 miles an hour battered the coast, creating a tide
nearly 20 feet above its normal height, inundating the low-lying delta
plain that is the Gulf Coast. New Orleans was surrounded by hundreds
of miles of levees and flood walls, but as the hurricane made its closest approach, these defenses were breached by the surging waters. The
city's neighborhoods, many lying below sea level, were quickly filled
with water nearly 10 feet deep in some places. More than 80 percent of
the city found itself underwater when the hurricane finally passed hours
later. The disaster was compounded by the slow and inadequate emergency assistance for the tens of thousands still stranded on rooftops
or in makeshift public shelters. The widespread flooding left hundreds
of thousands of people homeless and more than 1,800 dead across the
Gulf Coast, most of them in New Orleans. Estimates of the damage
exceeded $100 billion, making it the costliest disaster to ever strike the
United States, as well as one of the deadliest.

The scope of the disaster shocked the country, and it had widespread economic and social impacts. Although the catastrophe was
precipitated by a hurricane—a natural and somewhat predictable phenomenon—the disaster sparked heated controversy over the cause of
the flooding of New Orleans and who or what was to blame. Was the
failure of the city's flood protection system simply due to natural forces
beyond human control, or was it instead a consequence of human
development and bad decision making? Who or what was responsible
for the devastating flooding of New Orleans? The answers to these
questions carried the potential for heavy financial liabilities and were

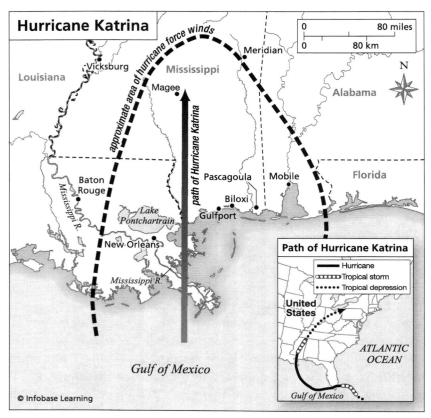

Hurricane Katrina began as a tropical depression on August 23, 2005, forming southeast of the Bahamas. It reached hurricane status the next day, crossing over the southern tip of Florida and leaving behind $1 billion in damage and several dead. In the warm waters of the Gulf of Mexico, Hurricane Katrina intensified, eventually making landfall just east of New Orleans, Louisiana, on the morning of August 29. Storm surge more than 20 feet high battered and flooded the coast, while hurricane-force winds reached out more than 100 miles from its center. The storm left behind nearly 1,500 dead and more than $100 billion in damages.

central to future development decisions and priorities along America's Gulf Coast.

Since its founding in 1718, New Orleans has been subject to flooding from the Mississippi River and hurricanes. The greater New Orleans metropolitan area is situated between the tidal lowlands of Lake Pontchartrain to the north and the Mississippi River on its southern side. The oldest parts of the city sit on naturally higher ground, but over the last two centuries engineers drained and reclaimed lower lying areas once occupied by swamps and coastal wetlands, allowing the metropolitan area to expand. In order to protect the low-lying metro area, engineers erected an extensive system of levees and flood walls intended to hold the Mississippi within its banks and keep out the surge of ocean water that accompanied hurricanes roaring in from the Gulf. After 1965, Congress charged the Corps with the responsibility of designing and constructing a hurricane protection system with the ability to better withstand these storms. Despite the significant investments in hurricane protection, researchers and journalists warned that the city was uniquely vulnerable to flooding from a strong hurricane and that it was only a matter of time before disaster would strike. When that time came, the disaster seemed to fulfill these dire predictions, even as it shocked the nation.

In the immediate aftermath of the flooding, investigations were launched by government officials and others to understand what had gone wrong. The Corps, the principal government agency in charge of design and construction of the city's hurricane protection system, found that the system had suffered engineering failures, but argued that most of the failures were due to the extreme power of the hurricane. The storm had simply exceeded the design capacity of the city's hurricane protection system. Without greater investment in the system, there was little that could have been done.

Critics of the Corps disputed this explanation. They argued that the hurricane protection system was inadequately constructed and failed well before it had reached its design capacity. In addition, they asserted that the system had been undermined by the Mississippi River-Gulf Outlet (MRGO), a shipping channel constructed by the Corps to provide more direct access from the city to the Gulf of Mexico that increased the city's exposure to storm surge and degraded surrounding wetlands that acted as natural buffers. Other investigators into the flooding of New Orleans painted a broader picture that highlighted historical decisions to expand development into flood-prone areas and the environmental modification that increased the city's vulnerability. They emphasized that efforts to control flooding and enable the metropolitan area to grow had caused environmental degradation and undermined the natural protections of coastal wetlands. These people argued that much more attention was needed to restore the local environment.

Why did New Orleans suffer such devastating flooding during Hurricane Katrina? Was it a natural or man-made disaster? The debate carried big and costly implications for residents and the government, and the answers would have significant influence on the future of development along Louisiana's southeast coast.

BACKGROUND

The land that makes up southeast Louisiana is part of the Mississippi River delta and was built up over the last 6,000 years from sediment deposited by the Mississippi River. The Mississippi River carries enormous quantities of soil and silt that are suspended in the moving water and deposited at the mouth of the great river, which empties into the Gulf of Mexico. As silt accumulated at the mouth of the river over the millennia, it built up land extending into the Gulf, creating the ground under modern-day Baton Rouge and areas to the south now occupied by New Orleans, St. Bernard Parish, and Plaquemines Parish. This fragile toehold of land has always been threatened by the encroaching waters of the Gulf of Mexico, held back only by the replenishment of soil from the Mississippi River and the unique wetland vegetation that managed to anchor itself in the soft soils at the interface of fresh and salt water.

When French colonists arrived in the Mississippi River delta in the late 17th and early 18th centuries, they encountered a vast and wild land of fresh and saltwater marshes, massive estuaries, cypress swamps, and a maze of bayous, all teeming with an enormous variety of fish, birds, and other wildlife. They also encountered the native Chitimacha people who had been there for millennia. On the advice of native inhabitants, Jean-Baptiste Le Moyne de Bienville established the settlement of New Orleans in 1718 on a crescent of higher ground along a bend of the Mississippi River. Over the last few centuries, the Mississippi River had built up its banks into natural levees as a result of silt deposited during periodic flooding. Land along the banks of the river was somewhat elevated relative to the surrounding lowland swamps and marshes and thus provided a site that was somewhat less prone to flooding.

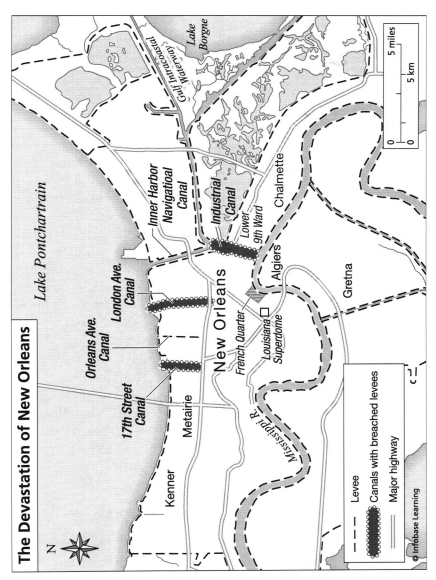

The Devastation of New Orleans

Lake Borgne

Gulf Intracoastal Waterway

Lake Pontchartrain

Inner Harbor Navigational Canal

Industrial Canal

Lower 9th Ward

Chalmette

London Ave. Canal

Orleans Ave. Canal

New Orleans

Algiers

Gretna

17th Street Canal

French Quarter

Louisiana Superdome

Metairie

Mississippi R.

Kenner

N

Levee

Canals with breached levees

Major highway

© Infobase Learning

5 miles

5 km

New Orleans sits within the Mississippi River delta of southeastern Louisiana, on the east and west banks of the Mississippi River and along the banks of Lake Pontchartrain. Prior to Hurricane Katrina in 2005, the greater New Orleans area was home to more than 1 million people and protected by hundreds of miles of levees, flood walls, and nearly 100 pumping stations. (Map by Dale Williams)

Equally important, the location of New Orleans provided the shortest overland route between the Mississippi River and Lake Pontchartrain. Lake Pontchartrain is not a true lake, but a shallow estuary that is connected to Lake Borgne, a lagoon that opens up into the Gulf of Mexico. Indeed, the purpose of New Orleans was to guard the trading route and portage between the Mississippi River and Bayou St. John, a smaller waterway which led to Lake Pontchartrain and ultimately the Gulf of Mexico. From its start, New Orleans was advantageously situated at the nexus between the main water route into the interior of the continent and the Gulf that provided access to the open ocean. New Orleans was approximately 50 miles upriver on the main stem of the Mississippi River, which added some distance for ships arriving in the Gulf, but those miles of intervening coastal wetlands provided valued shelter from the threat of periodic hurricanes.

New Orleans was perpetually plagued by flooding. In the spring, the Mississippi River regularly left its banks, flooding the surrounding lowland areas. In the late summer, the warm waters of the Gulf of Mexico brought forth powerful hurricanes, whose winds and waves and rain easily crossed the 50 miles of coastal wetlands that separated the city from the open ocean waters. In 1722, the settlement was almost wiped out by a hurricane whose winds blew down nearly every structure. However, the settlers were determined to stay. They recognized that in order for the city to thrive, it had to deal with the related problems of drainage and flooding. Early efforts focused on containing the Mississippi River within its banks and providing for more rapid drainage of water out of the city, whether from rain or swollen rivers.

Early Development, Flood Control, and Drainage

During its first two centuries, New Orleans devoted considerable effort to protecting itself from the threat of flooding and to improving drainage. Extensive levees, usually in the form of raised earthen berms, were erected along the banks of the Mississippi River and later the southern shore of Lake Pontchartrain. Within the city itself, engineers dug a network of drainage canals to carry water out of developed areas and into surrounding water bodies, such as Lake Pontchartrain.

Although flooding was greatly reduced by these early works, the city's drainage problems were a continual problem, especially as the population grew. With the advent of steam-powered boats after 1810, trade on the Mississippi River increased dramatically, and New Orleans emerged as a major transshipment center for river-borne and sea-borne commerce and as a major port of immigration. The population of the city doubled in the 1830s with the influx of settlers. By 1840, the city's population had grown to more than 100,000, making it the fourth most populous city in the United States. Population growth was threatened in the 1850s and again in the 1870s by a series of disastrous yellow fever outbreaks. Medical professionals of the time were still unclear about the etiology of disease, but they strongly suspected that standing or stagnant water and poor drainage were important factors in its transmission. As a result, municipal and state officials redoubled their efforts to improve drainage for this economically vital city, instituting a system of tax assessments to pay for expansion and maintenance of drainage canals, as well as steam-powered water lift systems to carry water out more quickly via the drainage canals.

By the early 20th century, technological advances enabled New Orleans to take more control of drainage and development. After 1915, the city began to install new pumps developed by a local engineer that dramatically increased the amount of water that could be pumped out of the city. Indeed, this pumping infrastructure would remain an integral part of the city's drainage system for the next century. The ability to quickly remove more water diminished the perennial problem of stagnant water and street flooding from the region's heavy rainfall, but it also opened up the opportunity to physically expand the city. With new pumping technology and improved engineering ability, the city embarked on an ambitious plan to permanently reclaim the lowland areas from the higher ground of New Orleans all the way to the shores of Lake Pontchartrain. The frequently flooded lowland areas formerly occupied by wetlands and cypress swamps were drained and opened to development, increasing the city's urban acreage by 700 percent. In the early 1930s, the city filled in portions of Lake Pontchartrain along its southern shore, increasing developable area by another 1,800 acres. The reclaimed areas around New Orleans and near (and on) Lake Pontchartrain became prime real estate.

Land reclamation was not the only environmental transformation. While water posed a perennial threat, it was also the economic lifeblood of New Orleans. City leaders were eager to expand the city's capacity to accommodate shipping and water-based industry. In 1923, New Orleans celebrated the opening of the Inner Harbor Navigation Canal (known locally as the Industrial Canal), a shipping canal more than five miles long, 1,600 feet wide, and 30 feet deep that directly connected the Mississippi River to Lake Pontchartrain. The Industrial Canal was an engineering feat of the time, because it connected two water bodies of differing heights (the Mississippi River is at a higher elevation than Lake Pontchartrain) using lock technology that had been pioneered by engineers of the Panama Canal. The completion of the Industrial Canal was only the beginning of efforts to reengineer the drainage and geography of the city to enhance the region's economic and growth prospects.

New Orleans was not the only place undergoing a radical transformation of its environment. Throughout the Mississippi River Valley, communities were engaged in efforts to control drainage, prevent flooding, reclaim land, and improve navigation as a matter of survival and to spur economic growth. A major turning point in the valley's development followed the Great Mississippi Flood of 1927. The deluge was preceded by record rainfall beginning in the summer of 1926 and extending through the spring of 1927. Levees all along the Mississippi River broke, inundating 27,000 square miles of rich farmland, displacing 700,000 people, killing 1,000 (including 246 in New Orleans), and damaging or destroying 137,000 structures. The following year, Congress passed the Flood Control Act of 1928 that authorized the Corps to design and construct projects for the control of floods on the Mississippi River and its tributaries.

The Corps is a federal agency charged with public works, dating back to the founding of the country. In 1931, the Corps began the Mississippi River and Tributaries Project, the largest flood control project in the world. The plan sought to provide protection to 36,000 square miles of the lower Mississippi Valley and all along the river from Cape Girardeau, Missouri, to Head-of-Passes, Louisiana. The project sought to control the flow of the Mississippi River through an extensive system of improved levees, bypass floodways, channel improvements, and dams. These changes greatly reduced the incidence of flooding and enhanced navigation on the river. Congress continued to assign a high national priority to flood control with regular amendments to the Flood Control Act and gave the Corps expanded responsibility for the design and construction of flood control structures across the country. (See the sidebar "Saving Louisiana's Wetlands" on page 446.)

In addition to flood control, the Corps was responsible for improving navigation channels along the Gulf Coast. In 1939, the Corps began dredging the Gulf Intracoastal Waterway (GIWW), a navigable waterway that would run more than 1,000 miles from the panhandle of Florida to Brownsville, Texas, on the Mexican border. The GIWW provided a navigation route that allowed ships to move inside the coast of the Gulf of Mexico, protected from the Gulf's open waters by the intervening marshlands and barrier islands. When the project was completed in 1949, it connected with numerous other navigable rivers and waterways all along the Gulf Coast, including New Orleans's Industrial Canal. After passing behind barrier islands off the Alabama and Mississippi coasts, ships entered Lake Borgne and then entered Lake Pontchartrain. From Lake Pontchartrain, ships could pass through the Industrial Canal to enter the Mississippi River. With the completion of the GIWW, New Orleans now sat at an enhanced shipping crossroads between the Mississippi River, the Gulf of Mexico, and an extensive network of intra-coastal waterways. The expanded economic potential only whet the appetite of New Orleans leaders for new navigation possibilities. Shipping traffic through these waterways never rose to the volumes promised, but this fact did not deter calls for expansion.

Local boosters had lobbied the Corps and Congress since the 1930s for construction of another, more direct deepwater outlet from New Orleans to the Gulf of Mexico. The idea was initially opposed by the Corps because, as they argued, it lacked economic justification. By 1951, however, the Corps reversed its position and issued a report to Congress endorsing the proposal, adopting the argument of local supporters that an alternative route would be in the interests of national security (in case of attack on the Mississippi River or the Port of New Orleans), and would offer a shorter and safer route between the Port of New Orleans and the Gulf of Mexico.

Congress approved construction of MRGO in the River and Harbors Act of 1956. MRGO would extend from the Industrial Canal, through the GIWW, and to the Gulf of Mexico via a new channel that would be much straighter and shorter than the Mississippi River route from New Orleans to the Gulf—75 miles instead of 120. To do this, the Corps would dredge a 36-foot-deep, 500-foot-wide channel straight through the shallow bays, coastal marshes, and cypress swamps of St. Bernard Parish. There were few environmental laws at the time to

SAVING LOUISIANA'S WETLANDS

Over the past 75 years, more than 2,300 square miles of coastal Louisiana have been converted to open water by human activity—an area of wetlands equivalent in size to the state of Delaware. Human alteration of this landscape accelerated much of Louisiana's coastal land loss. Levees built to facilitate and maintain navigation and flood protection along the Mississippi River have choked off the rich sediment that once built and replenished wetlands. Additionally, thousands of miles of oil and gas pipelines and canals that provide energy to the nation slice through Louisiana's wetlands, hastening the erosion of this sediment-starved landscape. Projections indicate that another 900 square miles could be lost by 2050 if present trends continue, causing the Louisiana shoreline to move inland as much as 33 miles in some areas.

Coastal Louisiana's 2.5 million acres of fresh, brackish, and saltwater marshes account for more than half of the tidal marshes in the lower 48 states. These ecosystems provide numerous important environmental services. Louisiana's coastal landscape provides a habitat for millions of migratory birds and 17 threatened or endangered species and supports the largest shrimp, oyster, and blue crab production in the United States, providing more than a quarter of the seafood consumed in the lower 48 states. Its coastal wetlands also protect coastal regions and critical infrastructure, such

impede the ambitious project, but wildlife managers did raise concerns about the channel's impact on the coastal ecosystem. Before construction began, the Louisiana Wildlife and Fisheries Commission issued a statement of concern, warning of potential negative impacts on fish and wildlife resources, including the valuable shrimp, oyster, and wetland areas, worth more than $24 million annually to the local economy. The U.S. Department of the Interior offered a similar assessment, cautioning that environmental modification could seriously degrade marshes and have widespread ecological consequences. These warnings carried little weight at the time, however, and construction of MRGO began in 1958. MRGO was officially completed in 1968. Even before it was completed, it became embroiled in controversy over the city's hurricane vulnerability, a concern that would persist for decades.

as oil and gas platforms and pipelines, from the storm surges that accompany tropical storms and hurricanes. Wetlands act as a storm buffer against hurricanes and storms. They serve as flood control devices by holding excess floodwaters during high rainfall (much like a sponge). Wetlands replenish aquifers, and they purify water by filtering out pollutants and absorbing nutrients. Wetlands also provide habitat for a variety of wildlife. Coastal Louisiana lands are the breeding grounds and nurseries for thousands of species of aquatic life, land animals, and birds of all kinds. While wetland loss has been a common problem throughout the country, 80 percent of coastal marsh loss in the lower 48 states occurs in Louisiana.

In the late 1980s and early 1990s, Louisianans recognized that coastal land loss was becoming a severe problem. In 1990, Louisiana senators J. Bennett Johnston and John Breaux proposed a program to save the vanishing wetlands and persuaded Congress to enact the Coastal Wetlands Planning, Protection and Restoration Act (CWPPRA). The CWPPRA was designed to identify, prepare, and fund construction of coastal wetlands restoration projects. The CWPPRA was the first federally mandated restoration effort to take place along Louisiana's coast and the first program to provide a stable source of federal funds dedicated specifically to coastal restoration. Since its inception, 144 coastal restoration or protection projects have been built, benefiting more than 110,000 acres in Louisiana.

Until the mid-1960s, hurricane protection was largely the responsibility of states and municipalities. This arrangement changed after a particularly devastating hurricane in 1965. On September 9, 1965, Hurricane Betsy made landfall at Grand Isle, Louisiana, just to the southwest of New Orleans with gusts up to 160 miles per hour and a storm surge of more than 15 feet that completely overwhelmed the island. In New Orleans, winds were recorded at 125 miles per hour and a storm surge on Lake Pontchartrain raised the water level in the Industrial Canal by more than nine feet, flooding the Ninth Ward, Gentilly, Lake Forest, and St. Bernard Parish communities. Some parts of the Lower Ninth Ward and neighborhoods west of the Industrial Canal were flooded to depths of eight feet. Nearly all of Plaquemines Parish was flooded. Eighty-one people were killed and damage in southeast Louisiana exceeded

$1 billion. Hurricane Betsy was the first natural disaster in the United States to exceed the billion-dollar mark. The hurricane revealed numerous inadequacies in the levee protection system surrounding the city. A month later, Congress passed the Flood Control Act of 1965, which authorized $85 million for the Lake Pontchartrain and Vicinity, Louisiana Hurricane Protection Project. The program directed the Corps to design an enhanced system of levees and barriers around New Orleans with the goal of protecting the city against the "most severe combination of meteorological conditions reasonably expected."

Working with the U.S. Weather Bureau (now the National Weather Service), the Corps interpreted its congressional mandate to design a system that would protect the city from the equivalent of what is now described as a fast-moving Category 3 hurricane (with winds more than 110 miles per hour). This was not the strongest possible hurricane, but it was considered the most likely or reasonably expected threat to the city. Although federally authorized, the project was structured as a joint federal, state, and local effort, with 70 percent of the cost assumed by the federal government, primarily for design and construction, while state and local governments would assume the cost and responsibility of maintenance and operation.

Residents of New Orleans surely welcomed the national investment in their protection from hurricanes, but the Corps faced both skepticism and resistance. Indeed, shortly after Hurricane Betsy, several residents of Orleans and St. Bernard Parishes whose homes had flooded sued the Corps. They argued that their homes had been flooded as a result of hurricane-driven waters overflowing MRGO, something that had never happened before the channel was constructed. They contended that the Corps should have taken appropriate steps to prevent such exposure to storm surge before constructing the channel. In fact, many residents began to refer to MRGO as a hurricane highway, arguing that the channel funneled hurricane storm surge from Lake Borgne into the heart of the city. The Corps vehemently denied this accusation but felt compelled to commission a study of the channel's potential effect on storm surge conveyance. The study, conducted by National Engineering Science Company and released in September 1966, concluded that the effect of MRGO on storm surge was negligible. Nevertheless, the description of MRGO as a hurricane highway persisted. The lawsuit was dismissed in 1971, but the judge noted in that case (*Graci v. United States*, 456 F.2d 20

(5th Cir. 1971)) that the Corps could be sued for negligence in construction of the canal, although plaintiffs faced a high standard of proof.

The Corps encountered many obstacles in its efforts to fortify New Orleans against hurricane storm surge. It faced numerous project delays and cost increases as a result of technical difficulties, environmental concerns, legal challenges, and local opposition to more expensive proposals. Corps engineers encountered foundation problems during construction of levees and flood walls (due in part to the exceptionally soft underlying swamp and marsh soils), as well as opposition to the acquisition of rights-of-way. After 1970, environmentalists, newly empowered by the National Environmental Policy Act, challenged Corps plans to control the flow of water between Lake Pontchartrain and Lake Borgne. The Corps planned to prevent storm surge from entering Lake Pontchartrain through the installation of floodgates, but opponents argued that such changes to tidewater movement could cause unacceptable environmental damage. This opposition was supported by the courts in December 1977. In response, the Corps chose instead to heighten the levees along Lake Pontchartrain. When the hurricane protection project was first authorized in 1965, it was supposed to have been completed within 13 years at an estimated cost of $85 million. By 1982, however, the project was only 50 percent complete and project costs had ballooned to $757 million, with a revised completion date pushed back to 2008. Corps plans were further revised in the mid-1980s as a result of complaints by the local Orleans Levee District that floodgates at the mouths of the city's drainage canals would be too expensive to maintain. By 2005, the project was estimated to be between 60 and 90 percent complete, depending on the area, with a revised completion date of 2015. In May 2005, however, the Corps warned that the president's budget request for fiscal years 2005 and 2006 was insufficient to fund planned construction projects, leaving a number of areas exposed.

A Disaster Long Foretold

Despite increasing investments in engineered hurricane protection, concerns about New Orleans's vulnerability to a devastating hurricane actually grew in the two decades leading up to Hurricane Katrina. A growing number of scholars, journalists, and government officials drew attention to the precarious situation of New Orleans, some arguing that it was only a matter of time before the celebrated city would succumb to a catastrophic hurricane. Many of these concerns began with observations about existing vulnerabilities (such as the fact that a significant proportion of the city was at or below sea level) and the rapidly changing environment within and around greater New Orleans. (See the sidebar "Dead Zone in the Gulf" below.)

For years, scientists and conservation organizations noted with alarm the loss of coastal wetlands across the Gulf Coast, but especially

DEAD ZONE IN THE GULF

Coastal wetland degradation from development and changing hydrology is only part of larger impacts on the Gulf Coast ecosystems. Ironically, while coastal wetlands have been starved of necessary nutrients because of reduced and redirected silt loads from the Mississippi River, deeper waters in the Gulf of Mexico have been overloaded by excessive nutrients. Since the early 1970s, researchers have observed a growing problem in the Gulf of Mexico—large areas of hypoxic, or low oxygen, conditions where marine life is absent or dead. Hypoxic conditions typically occur in deeper levels of the ocean when dissolved oxygen levels in the water fall below the threshold necessary to sustain animal life.

Initially, researchers noted patches of hypoxic areas near the mouth of the Mississippi River and occurring in the spring and summer every two to three years. By the mid-1980s, however, these hypoxic conditions were occurring annually. By the 1990s, the area of hypoxic conditions more than doubled in size. In 1999, this hypoxic region encompassed an area of more than 7,700 square miles—the size of the state of Massachusetts—stretching from the mouth of the Mississippi River to beyond the Texas border. The phenomenon was labeled the Gulf of Mexico Dead Zone. Researchers have traced the cause of the Dead Zone to excess nutrients, specifically nitrogen and phosphorus, washing into the Gulf from the Mississippi River. Much of these excess nutrients come from runoff laden with fertilizers from agricultural areas which eventually end up in the Mississippi River.

The Mississippi River basin covers 41 percent of the continental United States and contains 52 percent of U.S. farms. The runoff from this entire area in southeast Louisiana. This loss was traced to overdevelopment of navigation canals, increasing pollution from land and shipping, the growing presence of the petroleum industry in coastal areas since the 1950s, and deprivation of silt and other nutrients as a result of damming and artificial channeling of the Mississippi River. Although it was not appreciated at the time, control of the Mississippi River since the 1930s had decreased the amount of silt that sustained the land of southeast Louisiana, which also threatened the integrity of the shoreline. The loss of

---

drains into the Gulf of Mexico through the Mississippi River. Over the past century, use of nitrogen and phosphorus fertilizers has increased dramatically. In addition to increased concentrations of nitrate and phosphate in the lower Mississippi, there is also a growing amount of inadequately treated or untreated sewage and other urban pollution. When these excess nutrients enter the Gulf, they stimulate explosive blooms of algae, far beyond what the ecosystem can normally handle. As these large populations of algae die off, they sink to the bottom and are decomposed by bacteria. The process of decomposition requires large quantities of dissolved oxygen, which rapidly depletes the dissolved oxygen available in those lower depths to other organisms. Creatures that can swim or move away will evacuate the area, while those that cannot, will suffocate and die. Hypoxic waters appear normal on the surface, but on the bottom, they are covered with dead and sickened creatures, and, in extreme cases, layers of blackened and putrid sediment. These hypoxic conditions displace or kill many aquatic species, altering the food chain and decreasing biodiversity.

The Dead Zone in the Gulf of Mexico has created significant concern among conservationists and the fishing industry. This area is the single largest source of many types of fish in the country and represents more than $2 billion in annual income for the region. Efforts to combat the Dead Zone have focused on reducing the amount of nutrient loading into the Mississippi River, which is a large task given the area and number of people and industry involved. While understanding of the phenomenon has increased, control has not. The five largest Gulf Dead Zones on record have occurred since 2001. The biggest of these oxygen-starved regions developed in 2002 and measured 8,484 square miles.

coastal wetlands was particularly alarming, not only for the loss of habitat for valuable species, but also for the loss of protection from hurricanes and encroaching ocean waters. Scientists estimated that every mile of wetland had the potential to decrease storm surge by one foot, and that without this natural buffer, coastal communities would face ever worse flooding and the loss of land. These warnings garnered some attention. In 1990, President George H. W. Bush signed the Coastal Wetlands Planning, Protection and Restoration Act. The law provided modest resources to identify, prepare, and fund construction of coastal wetlands restoration projects, but the resources were miniscule relative to the size of the problem.

In the early 1990s, the *Times-Picayune,* a New Orleans–based newspaper, began to take particular interest in local community complaints about the rapidly eroding wetlands around the MRGO channel. Studies by the Corps and other researchers since the canal's completion had revealed that the canal was allowing salt water to intrude further into formerly freshwater marshes, increasing the water's salinity and killing off cypress trees and other plants intolerant of saltier conditions. As this vegetation died off, it exposed the fragile marsh soil underneath, which easily washed away under the onslaught of natural tide and wave action, as well as the wake created by passing ships. By the 1990s, the impacts were abundantly evident to residents of St. Bernard Parish, some of whom watched their own coastal properties diminish in size.

What was clear was that the MRGO Reach 2 was rapidly widening far beyond its original design specifications, exposing more and more open water in the wetlands between Lake Borgne and St. Bernard Parish. Ironically, the widening of the channel actually complicated its maintenance because the eroding soils along its banks tended to slump into the center of channel, making it shallower and hindering ship traffic. Although the channel served relatively few ships, the wake and waves created by their passage were more than enough to accelerate wetland loss and erosion of the channel borders. As a result, the Corps was forced to repeatedly dredge the channel to maintain its depth, but the disruptive process of dredging actually accelerated the loss of surrounding wetlands, releasing more soil, requiring more dredging, and reinforcing a vicious cycle.

By the early 2000s, the wider environmental context of New Orleans's situational vulnerability was coming to the attention of the wider public. Articles in major newspapers and magazines such as *Popular Mechanics, National Geographic,* and *Scientific American* pointed out that New Orleans was in worse shape than originally thought because the city was sinking. Although a significant portion of the greater New Orleans area had always been plagued by its low elevation relative to surrounding water bodies, new research showed that much of the city had actually sunk well below sea level over the past century and was continuing to sink at a rate of three feet per century. According to some reports, the city as a whole now averaged six feet below sea level, and up to 11 feet in some parts of the Lower Ninth Ward and Lakeville neighborhoods.

The possible reasons were many, but one theory was that this subsidence (i.e., sinking) was actually a consequence of the greatly improved pumping technology and drainage. As water was removed from former marsh and swamplands, the underlying soils, high in spongy, organic content, simply compressed and sank. A significant portion of greater New Orleans thus sat below the water level of the Mississippi River to the south and Lake Pontchartrain to the north. If the levees ever breached, these low-lying areas would quickly fill with water. When combined with the rapid loss of protective coastal wetlands and shoreline, there seemed to be no doubt among an increasing number of scientists and journalists that New Orleans's defenses would eventually be breached by a powerful hurricane, leading to catastrophic flooding.

Government officials were not ignorant of these predictions. In 2001, a report by the Federal Emergency Management Agency (FEMA) concluded that catastrophic flooding of New Orleans was among the three likeliest disasters facing the country; the other likely disasters included a terrorist attack in New York City and a major earthquake in San Francisco. In 2004, FEMA gathered together more than 200 local, state, and federal officials for a weeklong simulation of the effects of a catastrophic hurricane hitting New Orleans. Based on computer modeling by researchers at Louisiana State University, officials operated under a scenario in which greater New Orleans was inundated by 10 feet of water as a result of a Category 3 or higher storm, leaving up to 500,000 people stranded and surrounded by floodwaters filled with debris, rotting corpses, and an unknown quantity of hazardous chemicals from the numerous chemical and petroleum facilities in the area. While the exercise provided a valuable opportunity for officials to become acquainted with each other and to consider emergency planning, it seemed to make little difference when the catastrophe actually happened a year later.

Disaster Finally Strikes

Hurricane Katrina began its existence as "tropical depression 12" of the 2005 hurricane season, forming to the south and east of the Bahamas on August 23. Unusually warm waters gave rise to a collection of thunderstorms that had begun to coalesce and spiral around an area of low pressure created by the rising warm and humid air. By the morning of August 24, the rapidly organizing system was upgraded to a tropical storm and officially named Katrina. Weather forecasters were now watching the storm carefully. With unusual rapidity, Tropical Storm Katrina reached hurricane status a day later, with winds that exceeded 74 miles per hour. Two hours after reaching hurricane status, it crossed the southern tip of Florida as a Category 1 hurricane, leaving in its wake a billion dollars of damage and several dead. As it crossed the peninsula, the hurricane weakened in intensity, cut off from the warm ocean waters that supplied its energy. However, Katrina regained its strength with a vengeance once it entered the even warmer waters of the Gulf of Mexico, rising to a Category 3 on Friday, August 26. By Saturday, August 27, the National Hurricane Center was issuing increasingly stern hurricane warnings for coastal areas from Morgan City, Louisiana, to the Alabama-Florida border. On Sunday, August 28, Hurricane Katrina intensified to the rarely seen Category 5 storm, with sustained winds of 175 miles per hour.

The giant, spiraling mass of clouds and wind and rain reached out with tropical storm force winds for more than 200 miles in every direction from its center. The National Weather Service's New Orleans/Baton Rouge office issued a bulletin predicting that areas in the path of the monstrous storm would suffer devastating damage and might be uninhabitable for weeks. That morning, the mayor of New Orleans issued the city's first-ever mandatory evacuation order. Most people heeded the warnings, with nearly 80 percent of the city's population successfully evacuating—the largest and quickest evacuation of an American city.

Hurricane Katrina finally approached Louisiana's coast near Buras, east of New Orleans, at sunrise on Monday, August 29. Just before the hurricane made landfall, a National Data Center buoy less than 100 miles south of Dauphin Island, Alabama, recorded an ocean wave height of 55 feet—the largest wave height ever measured. Katrina's strongest force was exerted on its northeast quadrant, where spiraling winds combined with the storm's forward momentum to push ashore a surge of ocean water 30 feet high in the vicinity of Waveland and Pass Christian, Mississippi, nearly removing all evidence of human habitation in some coastal neighborhoods. Closer to New Orleans, Plaquemines Parish was inundated by a 20-foot storm surge.

In the city, rising waters had begun to leak through the levee system in numerous places even before the storm had made landfall.

A neighborhood near Interstate 10 in New Orleans on September 7, 2005, still surrounded by floodwaters more than a week after Hurricane Katrina made landfall on August 29. Approximately 80 percent of the city was flooded. (David J. Phillip/ AFP/Getty Images/Newscom)

By 7:30 A.M., the Industrial Canal experienced catastrophic failures, releasing a wall of water into the Lower Ninth Ward, carrying off cars and floating houses off their foundations to be used like battering rams as they plowed into neighboring homes. Stranded residents had little time to escape, and many drowned. Sometime after 8:00 A.M., a surge of water from Lake Borgne filled the intervening wetlands and flooded St. Bernard Parish communities from Poydras to Chalmette. New Orleans East suffered similar flooding as waters filled and then over-topped levees around B. Sauvage National Wildlife Refuge. Massive failures followed along the 17th Street and London Avenue canals, violently flooding adjacent neighborhoods. As Hurricane Katrina passed to the north, it made landfall near Slidell on the north shore of Lake Pontchartrain. Storm surge along the lake's northern shoreline rose 15 feet and reached more than five miles inland at some points. St. Tammany Parish neighborhoods from the Rigolets all the way to Madisonville were flooded. By early afternoon, the storm's fury had passed to the north and residents emerged to find at least 80 percent of their city underwater.

DEBATE

In the immediate aftermath of Hurricane Katrina, emergency response and recovery were the top priorities. Rapid repair to the levee system was also important in order to forestall further damage from other storms. Indeed, only a month after Hurricane Katrina, the Gulf Coast was struck again by Hurricane Rita, which reactivated breaches in the levee system and set back efforts to drain the city. However, there were also demands by affected residents and others across the nation for answers about why the disaster had been as bad it was. Numerous damage claims would be filed for insurance, for government relief, and for compensation from those who might be liable. Finally, government officials had to understand what had gone wrong in order to plan for the future and to prevent a similar disaster from recurring, if possible. Investigations of the disaster were challenged by the chaos that followed the disaster, but they were also under the pressure of time to recover evidence before it was inadvertently lost by the process of cleanup and emergency repairs. Finally, there were competing explanations about what had gone wrong, each of which assigned blame differently and prescribed different remedies.

The Argument that Flooding Was a Natural Disaster

In the immediate aftermath of the hurricane, officials for the Corps described the storm as a Category 4 hurricane when it made landfall, an unusually powerful storm that exceeded the design capacity of the city's hurricane protection system as mandated by Congress. As the principal agency in charge of the city's hurricane protection system, however, the Corps came under critical scrutiny. In order to provide more authoritative answers, Lieutenant General Carl Strock, commander for the U.S. Army Corps of Engineers, established the Interagency Performance Evaluation Task Force (IPET) to determine the facts concerning the performance of the hurricane protection system. The subsequent IPET report acknowledged that a significant proportion of failures in the overall levee system were due to design flaws but argued that nearly half of the failures were due to overtopping by excessive storm surge, particularly on the southern shore of Lake Pontchartrain and on the western shore of Lake Borgne. (See "Interagency Performance Evaluation Task Force, 2006," on page 467 in the Primary Sources section.)

The explanation of excessive storm surge from Lake Pontchartrain, which led to overtopping along the drainage canals, also supported arguments by Corps officials that efforts to improve the protection system were compromised by opposition from environmentalists to install floodgates around the lake that could have lessened the impacts of storm surge and flooding. The Corps report also argued that MRGO had virtually nothing to do with the heightened storm surge. Rather, the Corps argued that some of the levees had sunk by as much as two feet as a result of subsidence. Defenders of the Corps also pointed out that the construction of the hurricane protection system had been hampered by inadequate funding. A month after the release of the IPET report, the American Society of Civil Engineers (ASCE) released its own report, which declared its support for the Corps report. Notably, the chair of the ASCE study committee made a point of publicly dismissing theories that MRGO had anything to do with the storm surge or flooding.

The Argument that Flooding Was Due to Faults in Engineering

Critics of the Corps identified a number of inconsistencies in the Corps's account of the flooding, not the least of which was the National Hurricane Center's downgrading of Hurricane Katrina to a Category 3 storm—ostensibly within the design specification of the hurricane protection system. They argued that the failure of the flood protection system was due primarily to poor design and engineering. In addition, these critics argued that MRGO was implicated in some of these failures.

These critiques were supported principally by two independent studies, one led by researchers from the University of California at Berkeley and funded in part by the National Science Foundation—the Independent Levee Investigation Team (ILIT), and another sponsored by Louisiana and researchers at Louisiana State University—Team Louisiana (TL). (See "Independent Levee Investigation Team, 2006," on page 468, and "Team Louisiana, 2006," on page 469 in the Primary Sources section.) Investigations by these independent groups concluded that the disastrous flooding that followed Hurricane Katrina was largely a man-made disaster and due in large part to flaws and failures in the design, construction, and organization of the hurricane protection system that surrounded greater New Orleans. In particular, these investigators concluded that the vast majority of catastrophic failures in the levee system occurred long before the waters had an opportunity to reach sufficient heights to overtop them, and most of the failures could not be blamed on excessive storm surge. The investigators also concluded that catastrophic flooding of St. Bernard Parish and New Orleans East was due to improper use of unstable dredge spoils to construct levees, especially along the MRGO canal. As a result, these levees failed quickly, exposing adjacent communities to direct attack by hurricane storm surge. While the ILIT acknowledged large, systemwide failures, some of which the Corps had little control over, TL laid blame squarely at the feet of the Corps. Moreover, TL investigators argued that MRGO had acted as a funnel, exacerbating storm surge into the heart of the city, especially around the Industrial Canal.

The Argument that Flooding Was Due to Inappropriate Development and Environmental Degradation

Another group of critics argued that New Orleans was the victim of its own shortsighted economic development priorities and population growth, which undermined the functioning and protection of natural coastal environments and placed a greater number of people in harm's way. While not necessarily denying the engineering failures of the hurricane protection system, these critics emphasized the role of environmental modification and degradation in exacerbating the city's vulnerability to the ravages of the hurricane and subsequent flooding. (See "'Hurricane Katrina: A Nation Still Unprepared,' 2006," on page 471 in the Primary Sources section.)

The elimination of cypress swamps and coastal wetlands figured prominently in their critiques, which, they argued, removed much of the coast's natural protection from hurricane storm surge. This coastal degradation was closely related to the loss of shoreline. These changes could be traced to three major factors: 1) alteration of the natural flow of water and silt from the Mississippi River and other drainage systems, which deprived the coastal areas of necessary nutrients to sustain vegetation and the shoreline; 2) coastal oil and gas exploration since the 1950s, which had led not only to extensive pollution but also to physical fragmentation of wetlands from ship traffic, drilling, and the laying of numerous pipelines; and 3) the construction of MRGO. (See "'Can We Save New Orleans?' 2006," on page 472 in the Primary Sources section.)

In the last case, critics pointed out that few developments along the coast had a larger impact on the destruction of coastal wetlands. The impact came initially from dredging itself and the wake of passing ships, but the largest impact came from the intrusion of salt water, which killed off many freshwater plants, especially cypress trees, and left behind degraded environments or even open water. By the time Hurricane Katrina arrived in August 2005, coastal wetlands were in tatters, and there was little to buffer against the storm's impact. Indeed, critics argued that this change in the coastal wetland environment was one of the few significant differences between the experiences of hurricanes in the 1960s, when the city's protection system was much less developed and yet resulted in much less catastrophic flooding, and the arrival of Hurricane Katrina 40 years later, when the protection system was arguably better developed (albeit incomplete).

OUTCOME AND IMPACT

Hurricane Katrina and the levee failures resulted in the deaths of at least 1,464 Louisiana residents, nearly half of which were the result of drowning, followed by trauma and injury. The storm displaced more than a million people in the Gulf Coast region, creating one of the largest internal migration events in U.S. history. Katrina damaged more than a million housing units in the Gulf Coast region, half of which were in Louisiana. In New Orleans alone, 134,000 housing units—70 percent of all occupied units—suffered damage from flooding. The total damages from Hurricane Katrina were $135 billion, with another $15 billion as a result of Hurricane Rita.

Thousands of lawsuits were filed against the Corps by private residents, businesses, and the city of New Orleans itself. Most of the lawsuits filed by private residents were consolidated into a single class action suit, which sought to hold the Corps liable for failure of the hurricane and flood protection system. A few residents sought to sue the Corps for degradation of levees caused by MRGO. While these cases wound their way through the courts, Congress and the Corps were already engaged in major changes to New Orleans's hurricane protection system. In June 2006, Congress authorized the construction of an Inner Harbor Navigation Canal surge barrier to reduce the risk of storm surge coming in from the Gulf of Mexico and Lake Borgne. In addition, Congress also requested a plan for deauthorization of MRGO. In July 2007, the Corps released a 128-page report outlining closure of MRGO. Notably, Corps officials asserted that the closure decision was based largely on environmental and economic factors. Greg Miller, a Corps project manager, told reporters, "This is not a hurricane protection project. We're talking about a dam that will rise 5 feet above the surface of the water. It's not designed to stop storm surge." The Corps report also cited a study concluding that MRGO had minimal impact on

Hurricane Katrina's storm surge. In a follow-up public announcement about its recommendation, Corps officials explained that their decision was based largely on cost benefit analyses which showed that maintenance costs for the canal outweighed the benefits for the few ships that used the canal. In the final MRGO closure report issued to Congress in January 2008, the Corps also outlined a program to begin restoration of surrounding wetlands degraded by MRGO. That same month, the U.S. District Court for the Eastern District of Louisiana dismissed the class action suit against the Corps for failure of the levee system because the Flood Control Act of 1928 declared the federal government to be immune for damage arising from flood control projects. However, the district court judge did allow a separate case alleging damage from MRGO to go forward.

In May 2009, construction began on the Inner Harbor Navigation Canal surge barrier, a two-mile-long barrier, up to 26 feet high, running north-south across the waterway where MRGO and the GIWW meet. This complex and massive structure would act as a floodgate to block storm surge, while still allowing ships to pass through between the Industrial Canal and the GIWW. Corps officials described the $695 million project as the largest civil works project in the agency's history. Two months later, in July 2009, the construction company contracted to close off the MRGO channel declared the project complete—a rock structure consisting of 352,000 tons of stone material, rising eight feet above the water, now blocked the deauthorized channel.

In November 2009, Judge Stanwood R. Duval of the U.S. district court found the Corps responsible for the flooding of St. Bernard Parish by not properly maintaining MRGO Reach 2. While the Corps could not be held liable for damage resulting from flood control projects, Judge Duval ruled that MRGO was not a flood project but a navigation project, and the Corps was thus not protected by the immunity granted by the Flood Control Act of 1928. Duval accepted the argument that residents in St. Bernard's parish were exposed to the damaging effects of storm surge by the uncontrolled expansion of MRGO as a result of wetland destruction and improper use of soft dredge spoils to construct the abutting levee. When waves generated by the hurricane moved across Lake Borgne and the now-open water of the widened channel and began to batter the improperly constructed levee, it quickly collapsed, allowing water to flood the intervening wetlands

Hurricane Katrina on August 28, 2005, one day before striking New Orleans. The Category 5 hurricane, with sustained winds more than 150 miles per hour, covered much of the Gulf of Mexico and was one of the strongest storms to ever strike the United States. The storm dropped in intensity to Category 3 when it made landfall on August 29. (NASA/Goddard Space Flight Center Scientific Visualization Studio)

that separated St. Bernard Parish from Lake Borgne and leading to catastrophic flooding. (See *"In Re Katrina Canal Breaches Consolidated Litigation*, 2009," on page 474 in the Primary Source section.) The judge awarded a total of $719,000 to only five plaintiffs, but the ruling opened up the possibility of additional lawsuits against the federal government.

WHAT IF?

What if MRGO had never been built?

If MRGO had not been built, there would have been substantially less damage done to the wetlands along Lake Borgne's western edge. Based on the findings of the district court and other investigators, this would have meant that a significant part of the flooding that affected St. Bernard Parish would have been avoided. Until the 1950s, before dredging of MRGO had begun, the area occupied by St. Bernard Parish had long been separated from Lake Borgne by a massive freshwater swamp of tall cypress trees. Dredging of the canal allowed saltwater intrusion, which poisoned the freshwater marshes and swamps, killing the trees and leaving behind expanses of dead tree stumps, a few remaining clumps of healthy trees, and open water.

According to studies by the Corps and the Congressional Research Service, MRGO destroyed nearly 23,000 acres of Louisiana's coastal wetlands and raised salinity levels significantly in another 30,000—a total impacted area of more than 78 square miles. Had those healthy cypress swamps still been standing, Hurricane Katrina's storm surge would have been lessened, reducing it by several feet. However, MRGO was not the only cause of coastal wetland destruction. Destruction was effected by the existing channel of the GIWW, ship traffic, pollution, stress from oil and gas development, and the reduction in nutrients from the reduced silt load from controlled flow from the Mississippi River. These wetlands were under assault from many directions. Less clear is whether the absence of MRGO would have had a significant impact on other areas of New Orleans that flooded, particularly those around the Industrial Canal. Many critics argued that MRGO was a hurricane highway that funneled damaging storm surge into the city, increasing the damage potential, and putting added stress on levees and flood walls, resulting in failure. This idea remains highly contested. Most of the levee and flood wall failures that occurred during Hurricane Katrina happened long before storm surge had reached their tops or exceeded their design potential. While it is possible that MRGO could contribute to exacerbated storm surge, this does not appear to have been the only cause of levee and flood wall failure during Hurricane Katrina.

CHRONOLOGY

1718   New Orleans is founded by Jean-Baptiste Le Moyne de Bienville, a representative of France, on a crescent of high ground along a bend in the Mississippi.

1810   With the steamboat era, New Orleans emerges as the major transshipment center and a major port of immigration.

1875   New Orleans becomes the ninth largest American port.

1893	Following a record hurricane, New Orleans constructs a shoreline levee six feet above the normal surface of Lake Pontchartrain.
1900–1914	Lowland cypress swampland between Mid-Town and Lake Pontchartrain is drained and subdivided for development.
1915	New Orleans contracts for 13 patented Wood screw pumps, which greatly increases the ability of New Orleans to drain water and thus expand.
	September 29: Grand Isle Hurricane with 140 mile per hour winds is the most damaging hurricane to strike New Orleans.
1919	Congress authorizes construction of the Gulf Intracoastal Waterway (GIWW).
1923	*May 5:* Dedication ceremonies are held for completion of Inner Harbor Navigation Canal, also known as the Industrial Canal.
1926–1934	Lakeshore Improvement Project reclaims over 1,800 acres of land from the Lake Pontchartrain south shore with fill.
1927	The Great Mississippi Flood is the largest ever recorded in the lower Mississippi Valley.
1928	*May 15:* Congress authorizes the Mississippi River and Tributaries (MR&T) project under the Flood Control Act of 1928.
1936	Flood Control Act of 1936 establishes a national flood control policy to be administered by the Corps.
1949	*June:* GIWW is enlarged to 12-feet-deep by 125-feet-wide channel and officially completed.
1956	*March:* Congress authorizes Mississippi River-Gulf Outlet (MRGO) project.
1965	*September 9:* Hurricane Betsy makes landfall at Grand Isle and tracks just southwest of the city, the first natural disaster costing more than $1 billion.
	October 27: Flood Control Act of 1965 authorizes the Corps to design and construct the Lake Pontchartrain and Vicinity, Louisiana Hurricane Protection Project.
1968	MRGO project is officially completed.
1969	*August 17:* Hurricane Camille, the second Category 5 hurricane to ever make landfall on U.S. soil (since 1851),

strikes Mississippi coast at Pass Christian, about 52 miles east-northeast of New Orleans.

1985   *October:* Hurricane Juan causes many supposedly safe homes in New Orleans to flood, primarily on the west bank.

1990   President George H. W. Bush signs Coastal Wetlands Planning, Protection and Restoration Act into law.

2004   *August:* Federal Emergency Management Agency conducts simulations of a catastrophic hurricane in New Orleans.

2005   *August 29:* Hurricane Katrina makes landfall at Buras, Louisiana, east of New Orleans as a Category 3 hurricane shortly after 6 A.M.

September 24: Hurricane Rita hits Gulf Coast, causing a second flooding of New Orleans.

October 11: The Corps finally succeeds in removing floodwaters from eastern New Orleans.

2006   *June 15:* Congress requests a plan for deauthorization of MRGO and authorizes the Inner Harbor Navigation Canal (IHNC) surge barrier to reduce the risk of storm damage.

2007   *February:* U.S. district court judge Stanwood R. Duval rules that the corps may be sued over defects in MRGO.

2009   *May:* Construction begins on IHNC surge barrier.

July 9: MRGO is closed off by a rock barrier.

November 19: District court finds the Corps responsible for the flooding of St. Bernard Parish by not properly maintaining MRGO.

DISCUSSION QUESTIONS

1. Was the devastating flooding of New Orleans a natural disaster? Why or why not?
2. To what extent was the Corps responsible for the flooding? Explain.
3. How was the vulnerability of New Orleans increased by human activity?
4. What were the causes of environmental degradation along the southeast Louisiana coastline?

5. How did this environmental degradation affect the city's vulnerability to hurricanes?
6. By the late 20th century, many people were well aware of New Orleans's vulnerability to hurricanes. Could anything have been done at that time to prevent the catastrophic flooding that occurred with Hurricane Katrina? Why or why not?
7. How should the nation invest in protecting New Orleans from future hurricanes?

WEB SITES

Greater New Orleans Community Data Center. Available online. URL: http://www.gnocdc.org/. Accessed April 4, 2011.

National Hurricane Center. Hurricane Preparedness. Hurricane History. Available online. URL: http://www.nhc.noaa.gov/HAW2/english/history.shtml#katrina. Accessed April 4, 2011.

New York Times Topics: Hurricane Katrina. Available online. URL: http://topics.nytimes.com/top/reference/timestopics/subjects/h/hurricane_katrina/index.html. Accessed April 4, 2011.

NOLA Environmental. New Orleans, Louisiana, Environmental Compliance Data Bank. Available online. URL: http://www.nolaenvironmental.gov/. Accessed April 4, 2011.

NOLA.com. Hurricane Katrina. Latest news, photos, videos and complete archives of storm, struggle and recovery. Available online. URL: http://www.nola.com/katrina/. Accessed April 4, 2011.

BIBLIOGRAPHY

Brinkley, Douglas. *The Great Deluge: Hurricane Katrina, New Orleans, and the Mississippi Gulf Coast.* New York: HarperCollins, 2006.

Dyson, Michael Eric. *Come Hell or High Water: Hurricane Katrina and the Color of Disaster.* New York: Basic Civitas Books, 2005.

Freudenberg, William R., Robert Gramling, Shirley Laska, and Kai T. Erikson. *Catastrophe in the Making: The Engineering of Katrina and the Disasters of Tomorrow.* Washington, D.C.: Island Press, 2009.

Independent Levee Investigation Team. Investigation of the Performance of the New Orleans Flood Protection Systems in Hurricane

Katrina on August 29, 2005. July 31, 2006. Available online. URL: http://www.ce.berkeley.edu/projects/neworleans/.

Team Louisiana. The Failure of the New Orleans Levee System during Hurricane Katrina: A Report Prepared for Secretary Johnny Bradberry, Louisiana Department of Transportation and Development, Baton Rouge, Louisiana. State Project No. 704-92-0022, 20. December 18, 2006. Available online. URL: http://www.dotd.louisiana.gov/administration/teamlouisiana/.

U.S. Army Corps of Engineers. Interagency Performance Evaluation Task Force. Performance Evaluation of the New Orleans and Southeast Louisiana Hurricane Protection System. Draft Final Report of the Interagency Performance Evaluation Task Force. June 1, 2006. Available online. URL: https://ipet.wes.army.mil/.

PRIMARY SOURCES

Document 1: Interagency Performance Evaluation Task Force, 2006

The U.S. Army Corps of Engineers established the Interagency Performance Evaluation Task Force in 2005 to determine the facts concerning the performance of the Hurricane Protection System in southeast Louisiana during Hurricane Katrina. Below is an excerpt from the executive summary.

The system did not perform as a system: the hurricane protection in New Orleans and Southeast Louisiana was a system in name only. . . . The system's performance was compromised by the incompleteness of the system, the inconsistency in levels of protection, and the lack of redundancy. Incomplete sections of the system resulted in sections with lower protective elevations or transitions between types and levels of protection that were weak spots. Inconsistent levels of protection were caused by differences in the quality of materials used in levees, differences in the conservativeness of floodwall designs, and variations in structure protective elevations due to subsidence and construction below the design intent due to error in interpretation of datums. . . .

The storm exceeded design criteria, but the performance was less than the design intent: sections of the hurricane protection system were in many ways overwhelmed by the conditions created by Hurricane

Katrina. This is particularly true for the sections of the Gulf Intracoastal Waterway (GIWW) along New Orleans East, and the levees in St. Bernard and Plaquemine Parishes where the combination of record high surge and long period waves exceeded the design conditions and devastated the levees. This devastation, however, was aided by the presence of incomplete protection, lower than authorized structures, and levee sections with erodible materials. While overtopping and extensive flooding from Katrina were inevitable, a complete system at authorized elevations would have reduced the losses incurred. The designs were developed to deal with a specific hazard level, the Standard Project Hurricane as defined in 1965; however, little consideration was given to the performance of the system if the design event or system requirements were exceeded.

Source: U.S. Army Corps of Engineers. Interagency Performance Evaluation Task Force. Performance Evaluation of the New Orleans and Southeast Louisiana Hurricane Protection System. Draft Final Report of the Interagency Performance Evaluation Task Force. June 1, 2006.

—⚇—

Document 2: Independent Levee Investigation Team, 2006

In 2005 and 2006, researchers from the University of California at Berkeley led a National Science Foundation–funded project to investigate the causes of the catastrophic flooding during Hurricane Katrina. Below is an excerpt from the final report's executive summary.

In the end, it is concluded that many things went wrong with the New Orleans flood protection system during Hurricane Katrina, and that the resulting catastrophe had its roots in three main causes: (1) a major natural disaster (the Hurricane itself), (2) the poor performance of the flood protection system, due to localized engineering failures, questionable judgments, errors, etc. involved in the detailed design, construction, operation and maintenance of the system, and (3) more global "organizational" and institutional problems associated with the governmental and local organizations responsible for the design, construction, operation, maintenance and funding of the overall flood protection system. . . .

Our findings to date indicate that no one group or organization had a monopoly on responsibility for the catastrophic failure of this regional flood protection system. Many groups, organizations and even individuals had a hand in the numerous failures and shortcomings that proved so catastrophic on August 29th. It is a complex situation, without simple answers. . . .

Simply updating engineering procedures and design manuals will not provide the needed level of assurance of safety of the population and properties of this major metropolitan region. Design procedures and standards employed for many elements of the flood protection system can be traced back to initial development and use for design and construction of levees intended for protection of largely unpopulated agrarian land, not a major urban region. . . .

There is also a need to resolve dysfunctional relationships between federal and more local government, and the federal and local agencies responsible for the actual design, construction and maintenance of such flood protection systems. . . .

And there is some urgency to all of this. The greater New Orleans regional flood protection system was significantly upgraded in response to flooding produced by Hurricane Betsy in 1965. The improved flood protection system was intended to be completed in 2017, fully 52 years after Betsy's calamitous passage. The system was incomplete when Katrina arrived. As a nation, we must manage to dedicate the resources necessary to complete projects with such clear and obvious ramifications for public safety in a more timely manner.

New Orleans has now been flooded by hurricanes six times over the past century; in 1915, 1940, 1947, 1965, 1969 and 2005. It should not be allowed to happen again.

Source: Independent Levee Investigation Team. Investigation of the Performance of the New Orleans Flood Protection Systems in Hurricane Katrina on August 29, 2005. July 31, 2006.

—ɯ—

Document 3: Team Louisiana, 2006

In response to apparent discrepancies between observations and early U.S. Army Corps of Engineers statements about the causes of levee and flood wall failures during Hurricane Katrina, researchers from Louisiana State University conducted their own state-sponsored investigation in 2005 and 2006. Below are excerpts from their report.

Question 1. Was the GNO [Greater New Orleans] HPS [Hurricane Protection System] properly conceived to accomplish the 1965 Congressional mandate to protect against the "most severe combination of meteorological conditions reasonably expected?"

Answer 1. No. The . . . 1959 U.S. Weather Bureau 1 in 100 year Standard Project Hurricane (SPH) was known to be obsolete by 1972, just as construction of initial parts of the GNO HPS was getting underway. . . . The New Orleans District USACE [U.S. Army Corps of Engineers] was aware of this deficiency in the original analysis . . . but never revised the original SPH-based analysis to reflect the new understanding of the threats. . . .

Question 2. Were the levees and floodwalls at or above the crown elevations specified in designs for HPS elements necessary to resist overtopping by surge and waves associated with the Standard Project Hurricane?

Answer 2. No. Floodwall and levee crown elevations were built 1 to 2 ft low because of an erroneous assumption . . . no provision was made to account for the 3 to 4 ft/century subsidence rates characteristic of the GNO area even though this rate was known at the time of authorization. . . .

Question 3. Did the USACE follow existing engineering practice and USACE guidance for construction of levees and floodwalls?

Answer 3. . . . The New Orleans District USACE failed to conduct appropriate analyses of the potential for seepage to compromise levee and floodwall stability. . . . The New Orleans District USACE did not follow standard engineering practice or Corps guidance when evaluating whether to protect (armor) earthen sea dikes from erosion caused by waves in the funnel area east of the city. . . .

Question 4. Did the free-flowing, deep-draft navigation canal that pierces the HPS on its eastern side compromise system performance?

Answer 4. Yes. The MRGO [Mississippi River-Gulf Outlet] and GIWW [Gulf Intracoastal Waterway] channels provide efficient conduits to funnel surge into the heart of New Orleans. As a result, surge elevations peaked in Lake Borgne and the IHNC almost simultaneously at higher levels relative to levee and floodwall crowns, and earlier, than would have been true if the MRGO had not been built, and if the wetland loss it caused had not occurred. . . .

Question 5. Was the system maintained and operated to assure the required level of protection through time?

Answer 5. No. The GNO HPS was managed like a circa 1965 flood control museum. Design assumptions and policy made in 1965 continue to diminish the HPS today. Local sea level has risen 0.4 ft since the 1960s and much of New Orleans has sunk over 1.5 ft in the same period for a combined change of nearly 2 ft relative to sea level. . . .

Prudent engineers operating in coastal Louisiana have made allowances for subsidence for a century. . . . It is inexcusable that this was not done for what was the most critical urban coastal protection project in the country.

Source: Team Louisiana. The Failure of the New Orleans Levee System during Hurricane Katrina: A Report Prepared for Secretary Johnny Bradberry, Louisiana Department of Transportation and Development, Baton Rouge, Louisiana. State Project No. 704-92-0022, 20. December 18, 2006.

—៷៷—

Document 4: "Hurricane Katrina: A Nation Still Unprepared," 2006

Within two weeks of Hurricane Katrina, the U.S. Senate Committee on Homeland Security and Governmental Affairs conducted hearings on what went wrong. The focus was on emergency planning and response, but the committee's report provided official recognition of the significance of environmental integrity to the area's vulnerability and its future sustainability.

A vital part of the Hurricane Katrina story lies in nearly two centuries of natural and man-made changes to the Louisiana coastline. When New Orleans was settled in 1718, the primary flood threat was from the Mississippi River, not the Gulf of Mexico. An expansive coastal landscape separated the city from the Gulf and served as a buffer from any storms moving ashore. That protective landscape no longer exists. The ever-changing and disappearing coastline has left New Orleans more susceptible to hurricanes and contributed to the damage inflicted by Katrina. Should this trend continue, New Orleans and the rest of coastal Louisiana will become even more vulnerable to damage from future storms, and efforts to protect the city with levees and floodwalls will be undermined. . . .

The changes to Louisiana's coastline have serious implications for the long-term sustainability of the region. Land subsidence and predicted global sea-level rise during the next 100 years mean that areas of New Orleans and vicinity now 5 to 10 feet below mean sea level will likely be 8 to 13 feet or more below mean sea level by 2100. At the same time, the loss of wetlands, barrier islands, and other natural features could eliminate protection from waves and allow for higher and faster moving storm surges. According to the National Academy of Sciences, these trends will make much of Louisiana's southern delta uninhabitable without substantial new engineering projects.

In the long term, New Orleans and other regions of the Louisiana deltaic plane cannot be protected without taking proper account of the tremendous change that is continuing to occur to Louisiana's coastal landscape.

Source: U.S. Senate Committee on Homeland Security and Governmental Affairs. "Hurricane Katrina: A Nation Still Unprepared." S. Rept. 109-322. Washington, D.C.: Government Printing Office, 2006.

—∞—

Document 5: "Can We Save New Orleans?" 2006

Noted environmental law professor Oliver Houck provided critical and widely quoted explanations of the relationship between the disastrous flooding during Hurricane Katrina and environmental degradation. Houck argued that shortsighted thinking had made southeast Louisiana vulnerable by sacrificing its environment for economic gain.

. . . everything about the run-up to the Katrina disaster had fantasy written all over it: on slab development, on fill development, subdivisions in wetlands (protected by wooden fences), condos on beaches (protected by nothing), canals as senseless as the Mississippi River Gulf Outlet (MRGO), oil and gas channels by the thousands, coastal mitigation programs that failed to work (failed even to materialize), disappearing levee money, tinker-toy levee plans, what-the-hell levee construction, drive-by-and-when's-lunch levee inspections—and we haven't even gotten to FEMA [Federal Emergency Management Agency] yet. Detailed reporting in local papers, science colloquiums, National Geographic, NOVA, and government planning sessions predicting this very storm in this very way with these very results were tossed away like so many Mardi Gras beads. So there is plenty of fantasy to go around. . . .

The sad fact is, [flood control for developed urban areas] doesn't make money for anyone. But leveeing off wetlands for new development makes lots of money in real estate. . . . Floating boats also produces identifiable payouts. . . . Even converting cypress swamps to soybeans has a market price. By contrast, lives saved by levees don't receive economic benefits in the decisions that justify Corps projects and determine their funding priorities. Nor do they attract powerful lobbyists. . . .

A final and most perverse effect of the water resources game is that it produces projects that not only conflict with flood control for money and fame, but that cause floods as well. Big ones. The role of the MRGO in the Katrina and Rita flooding is by now undeniable. . . .

What we have here, then, is a game that is not focused on flood control, and never has been. It has been focused on making money first for people with boats and then for as many people as possible, even when that has meant increasing hurricane risks and putting other people right into harm's way. It has been in denial about its impacts, and remains largely in denial. And it has been accompanied by a similar series of body blows to the coastal zone from another source which is even more powerful and more difficult to turn around: the oil and gas industry. . . .

The impact of oil and gas extraction on the natural systems of the Louisiana coast is hard to exaggerate. The initial space of the access canals is relatively minor. It's what happens next that matters. The canals erode, exacerbated by wave wash from passing boats. In 10 years the widths have doubled; then they double again. While intact, the spoil banks cut off the natural drainage for hundreds of yards around, impounding half of the marsh and drowning the other half. Up the canal comes saltwater from the Gulf. The grasses go belly up, the root masses die, the soils are released, the whole thing falls apart. . . .

The sum is daunting. Apart from the major navigation systems across the coastal zone, we have another 8000 miles of canals and pipelines and they are all eroding. . . . Every scientific study available places the cumulative impacts of oil and gas activities ahead of even the Mississippi levees as a leading cause of land loss in Louisiana, with responsibility above 50% overall, and up to 90% in heavily exploited fields.

And here is the mystery: nobody talks about it. It's like this big secret. Daddy's got a drinking problem. We walk quietly around him. After all, Daddy is very big. And he is also paying the bills.

Source: Oliver Houck. "Can We Save New Orleans?" *Tulane Environmental Law Journal* 19, no. 1 (2006): 1–68. Reprinted with the permission of the *Tulane Environmental Law Journal*, which holds the copyright.

—◊◊◊—

Document 6: *In Re Katrina Canal Breaches Consolidated Litigation,* 2009

On November 18, 2009, the United States District Court for the Eastern District of Louisiana found the U.S. Army Corps of Engineers liable for the flooding of St. Bernard Parish during Hurricane Katrina. The court accepted the arguments that improper construction and maintenance of levees along the Mississippi River-Gulf Outlet (MRGO), as well as loss of protective wetlands, was the cause of catastrophic flooding. Below are excerpts from the Judge Stanwood R. Duval's ruling.

Plaintiffs have proven that the Corps knew the dangers that the MRGO was creating by virtue of its own engineering mistakes. The most glaring issue the Court sees is in the context of the state negligence claim itself—its failure to implement foreshore protection when it recognized or should have recognized the extreme degradation that failure caused to the Reach 2 Levee. In addition, the Corps' failure to warn Congress officially and specifically and to provide a mechanism to rectify the problem by properly prioritizing the requested funding to alleviate life threatening harm which the MRGO posed is the key. . . .

The failure of the Corps to recognize the destruction that the MRGO had caused and the potential hazard that it created is clearly negligent on the part of the Corps. Furthermore, the Corps not only knew, but admitted by 1988, that the MRGO threatened human life . . . and yet it did not act in time to prevent the catastrophic disaster that ensued with the onslaught of Hurricane Katrina. . . .

Clearly, in this instance the Corps shortchanged the inhabitants of New Orleans and the environs by its myopic approach to the maintenance and operation of the MRGO. It simply chose to ignore the effects of the channel; it only examined the requirements to keep the channel open regardless of its effects on the environment and the surrounding communities. Indeed, prior to Hurricane Katrina, it grounded its engineering position that the MRGO had no adverse effects with respect to storm surge on the Bretschneider and Collins report done in 1966. The findings of that study were based on the "as designed" parameters of the channel—that is 500 feet wide by 36 feet deep. By 1972, any layperson, much less an engineer, could see that the dimensions of the channel had already grown excessively. . . .

It is the Court's opinion that the negligence of the Corps, in this instance by failing to maintain the MRGO properly, was not policy, but insouciance, myopia and shortsightedness. For over forty years, the Corps was aware that the Reach II levee protecting Chalmette and the Lower Ninth Ward was going to be compromised by the continued deterioration of the MRGO, as has been exhaustively discussed in this opinion. The Corps had an opportunity to take a myriad of actions to alleviate this deterioration or rehabilitate this deterioration and failed to do so. Clearly the expression "talk is cheap" applies here. . . . The failure to maintain the MRGO properly compromised the Reach 2 Levee and created a substantial risk of catastrophic loss of human life and private property due to this malfeasance. Nothing the Corps has introduced into evidence tips the balance in its favor.

Source: United States District Court, E. D. Louisiana. *In re Katrina Canal Breaches Consolidated Litigation.* Civil Action No. 05-4182. Nov. 18, 2009.

◊◊◊◊◊◊◊◊◊◊◊◊◊◊◊◊◊◊◊◊ INDEX ◊◊◊◊◊◊◊◊◊◊◊◊◊◊◊◊◊◊◊◊◊◊

Italic page numbers indicate illustrations; page numbers followed by *c* indicate chronology entries; page numbers followed by *m* indicate maps; page numbers followed by *t* indicate tables.